SPEAKING YIDDISH TO CHICKENS

Holocaust Survivors on South Jersey Poultry Farms

SETH STERN

RUTGERS UNIVERSITY PRESS
New Brunswick, Camden, and Newark, New Jersey
London and Oxford, UK

Rutgers University Press is a department of Rutgers, The State University of New Jersey, one of the leading public research universities in the nation. By publishing worldwide, it furthers the University's mission of dedication to excellence in teaching, scholarship, research, and clinical care.

Library of Congress Cataloging-in-Publication Data

Names: Stern, Seth, author.
Title: Speaking Yiddish to chickens : Holocaust survivors on
    South Jersey poultry farms / Seth Stern.
Other titles: Holocaust survivors on South Jersey poultry farms
Description: New Brunswick : Rutgers University Press, [2023] |
    Includes bibliographical references and index.
Identifiers: LCCN 2022021366 | ISBN 9781978831612 (paperback) |
    ISBN 9781978831629 (hardcover) | ISBN 9781978831636 (epub) |
    ISBN 9781978831643 (pdf)
Subjects: LCSH: Jews—New Jersey—Vineland—History—20th century. |
    Vineland (N.J.)—Social life and customs—20th century. | Poultry
    farms—New Jersey—Vineland—History—20th century. | Jewish farmers—
    New Jersey—Vineland—History—20th century. | Immigrants—New
    Jersey—Vineland—Social conditions. | Holocaust survivors—New Jersey—
    Vineland—Social conditions.
Classification: LCC F144.V7 S74 2023 | DDC 974.9/004924—dc23/eng/20220706
LC record available at https://lccn.loc.gov/2022021366

A British Cataloging-in-Publication record for this book is available from the British Library.

References to internet websites (URLs) were accurate at the time of writing. Neither the author nor Rutgers University Press is responsible for URLs that may have expired or changed since the manuscript was prepared.

♾ The paper used in this publication meets the requirements of the American National Standard for Information Sciences—Permanence of Paper for Printed Library Materials, ANSI Z39.48-1992.

www.rutgersuniversitypress.org

Manufactured in the United States of America

For my mother, Ruth Stern

CONTENTS

AUTHOR'S NOTE

This book began as a series of conversations that I had with my grandmother, Bronia Green, in the fall of 1998. We spoke about a different part of her life each day over lunch while I was home on Long Island studying for finals during my first semester of law school. I conducted more formal interviews with her over the course of the next eight years. I subsequently began speaking with my mother, Ruth Stern, about growing up on poultry farms in Vineland in a series of interviews that extended from 2006 to 2021. Unless otherwise noted, all quotes from both of them come from those interviews. An oral history Ruth conducted with her parents around 1980 also provided quotes from my grandfather, Nuchim, who died before I started work on this project.

I did additional research that included visits to my grandparents' hometown of Lublin, Poland, and the site of the displaced persons camp in Bensheim, Germany, where my family stayed after the war. A number of early interviews cited in the book relate to my grandparents' experiences during the war through their time in New York. But I ultimately decided to focus on their experiences as poultry farmers and broadened out my research to include other survivors who settled on farms in Vineland and the surrounding area. I use the terms "Grine" and "survivor" interchangeably to refer to Eastern European Jews who survived the war in captivity, by hiding passing as non-Jews, or by escaping to the Soviet Union. Smaller numbers of Jewish survivors from Western European countries also settled on south Jersey farms. I have relied on the YIVO system for transliteration of Yiddish words except when quoting other sources.

I relied on oral histories conducted by or in the collection of the U.S. Holocaust Museum, the USC Shoah Foundation's Visual History Archive, the Jewish Federation of Cumberland County, the Rutgers Oral History Archive, the University of Florida, and the University of South Florida, as well as by sociologist William Helmreich. I also conducted in-person and phone interviews with eighty-six people, including survivors and others involved in the south Jersey poultry industry, their children and contemporaries, as well as academic experts.

Given the limitations of oral history, I have attempted to verify recollections using contemporaneous records and noted instances where they diverge. The full list of archives and other institutions that provided records is referenced in the acknowledgments. I obtained records specific to my family maintained by the Jewish Agricultural Society and the United Service for New Americans, which are both housed at the Center for Jewish History in New York. I obtained other records specific to my family from the German reparation authority and Social Security Administration, which made it possible to determine my grandmother's work history. I relied on records of ship passages maintained by the National Archives and Records Administration and more recently made available on ancestry.com. The Cumberland County clerk's office provided property records. My mother shared a small collection of correspondence and paperwork my grandparents saved from their voyage to the United States and early years in the country. Eva Neisser shared records of the German-Jewish Poultrymen's Club of Vineland, an organization led by her father Martin Berwin.

I also read press accounts from the Jewish Agricultural Society's *Jewish Farmer*, the *Poultryman* trade publication, and the *Vineland Times Journal* in chronological order for the period from 1947 through 1964 in paper or microfilm form at the Vineland Public Library, Rutgers University, and the Center for Jewish History. I relied on keyword searches once the *Jewish Farmer* and *Times Journal* were digitized and made available online by the National Library of Israel and newspapers.com, respectively.

SPEAKING YIDDISH TO CHICKENS

PROLOGUE

HALFWAY BETWEEN PHILADELPHIA and oceanfront Atlantic City, a lesser-known city named Vineland sits adjacent to southern New Jersey's wooded Pine Barrens. In 1950, this community of thirty thousand largely retained its rural, small-town character nearly a century after its founding.[1] Farms and factories still mingled on its perfectly straight street grid. The descendants of Vineland's original Italian immigrant settlers worked in garment, glassmaking, and food processing plants or grew vegetables and fruits on family-owned farms.

Grain silos towering over all the other buildings in town hinted at how another branch of agriculture—poultry farming—had come to dominate the city's topography and the community's identity. Vineland High School even nicknamed its sports teams the "Poultry Clan." Many of the local hatcheries and chicken feed mills were owned by Jewish businessmen, who catered to the community's numerous Jewish farmers.

Visitors might have noticed other signs of an outsized Jewish presence for a rural community Vineland's size. By 1950, Vineland had three synagogues and just as many Zionist groups plus a half-hour-long local radio show every Sunday morning called the *Voice of Israel*. Here, kosher butchers and delis, which had disappeared from much of rural America, shared the main commercial district with midcentury mainstays like an F. W. Woolworth five-and-dime store and a Pontiac car dealership. On weekends, you could smell the bagels, pumpernickel rye, and onion rolls for sale at Freedman's Bakery on Plum Street half a block away.

Southern New Jersey had long been a magnet for Jewish immigrants from Europe seeking a better life. Idealistic young Russians arrived first in the 1880s. They built collective farming colonies amid the nearby wilderness of scrub oak and stunted pines.[2] In the late 1930s and early 1940s came some of the few escapees from Nazi Germany. These middle-aged lawyers and doctors were reduced to repurposing cotton feed bags as curtains, skirts, and bedspreads.[3]

Another group of refugees started to arrive in large numbers after World War II ended in 1945 as part of a broader settlement of Jewish displaced persons on American farms. Thousands of Jewish refugees who came to the United States in the first decade after the war wound up on farms at a time when most American Jews had begun moving from city to suburb.[4] More displaced persons settled on farms in and around Vineland than anywhere else. These survivors of what later became known as the Holocaust found an unlikely refuge and gateway to new lives in America on local poultry farms.

The new immigrants, mostly from Eastern Europe, were known as *Grine* (pronounced Grin-eh), a play on the Yiddish word for greenhorn. Rumors of easy money or the promise of a quieter, more independent life lured the sons and daughters of shopkeepers and entrepreneurs. The chickens didn't care if they spoke Yiddish, and the Jewish charities helping them didn't care that few had ever farmed before. Grine here could take comfort in all the familiar Jewish cultural and religious institutions more typical in New York City while enjoying an idyllic rural life. Perhaps only in 1950s Vineland could a Jewish day school share the same stretch of rural road as a horse show. The survivors' children grew up on ten-acre farms rather than walk-up apartments, exploring neighborhood sand washes and streams rather than playing stickball in alleys.

These refugee farmers are part of a larger nearly century-long global story of Jewish agricultural settlement. From the late nineteenth century through the mid-twentieth, hundreds of thousands of Eastern European Jews settled on farms on four continents.[5] A small but steady trickle of Jews had farmed in all forty-eight then-existing states and every conceivable branch of agriculture. But agriculture never captured the imagination of the average immigrant to the United States, and the era of Jewish farming is largely forgotten by their descendants.

The story of the Grines—who proved to be the final mass wave of American Jewish agriculture—has particular relevance today as public opinion has again turned against admitting refugees. These farmers show how refugees struggle to assimilate while preserving their identities. They found ways to commemorate what they lost while trying to move beyond past trauma. They embraced their new American identities and enriched the communities where they settled, working hard in unfamiliar jobs for often meager returns. These novice farmers helped make New Jersey a poultry powerhouse that ranked in the top ten nationally in total egg production in the 1950s and supplied nearly one in five eggs to the New York City market.[6] The survivors' role in boosting the poultry industry remained largely unknown beyond south Jersey.

———◆———

Feeling unwelcomed by the established Jewish community in south Jersey, the Grine kept largely to themselves at first. It was easier that way. Fellow survivors didn't stare at the numbers tattooed on their arms or wonder why so few children had grandparents. German refugees had felt no more welcome when they arrived in Vineland a decade earlier. Now, most established American-born Jews and the more recent German refugees, not yet feeling fully accepted themselves, kept their distance from the unassimilated Grine.

In time, the more observant Grine established small synagogues called *shtiblekh*, often built with their own hands, within walking distance of their farms. They hosted concerts featuring famous Yiddish performers. They claimed their own patch of sand along the nearby Maurice River for sunbathing and card playing. They organized a summer camp and Purim parties for their kids, while also making sure the children joined Scout troops and Little League baseball teams.

Not that it was all a paradise. No matter how hard or how long they worked, Grine remained at the mercy of the market and chickens' fragile health. Within a decade, falling egg prices and the rise of industrial-scale agriculture in the South would drive almost all of these novice poultry farmers out of business, many into bankruptcy. Some would remember their time on south Jersey farms as their best years in America; others hated every minute here. These farmers, like all Holocaust survivors, varied widely in how well they coped with traumatic pasts and in how much success they would enjoy in their new country. Some made fortunes in other business. Others never quite found their footing.

Nothing better symbolized the diverging trajectories than my grandfather Nuchim Green and another Polish Jew, Miles Lerman, who both survived the war fighting as forest partisans and met for the first time after liberation. These two men started life in America on the exact same day after walking off the same former troop transport named the *Marine Perch*. On this day, they began an improbable journey that would take them to chicken farms in this obscure town in southern New Jersey.

1 ▸ PASSAGE

O N A COLD, gray Tuesday afternoon in January 1947, Bronia and Nuchim Green carried their nine-month-old daughter Ruth up the gangplank of the *Marine Perch*, a former U.S. military transport ship docked at Bremerhaven, Germany. All their worldly possessions fit in eight pieces of luggage as they set off for a new life in America.

Eight months had passed since a sister ship, the *Marine Flasher*, carried the first contingent of displaced persons traveling to America, an occasion momentous enough that a U.S. Army band played "Sentimental Journey" as the passengers boarded in Bremerhaven.[1] In the months since, such transatlantic refugee crossings had become somewhat routine. But another year would elapse before Congress finally began easing discriminatory quotas limiting immigration from Eastern European countries. So the 310 Jewish refugees, who accounted for a third of the passengers on this voyage, all might have considered themselves fortunate.[2]

Once aboard, Nuchim split off from Bronia and Ruth. Even married couples couldn't room together on this voyage. Nuchim made his way three decks below where passengers were stacked three high in swinging hammocks.[3] The ship felt less crowded than on its transpacific voyage after the

Japanese surrender in 1945, when it raced to get more than two thousand U.S. service members aboard home in time for Christmas.[4] Now refurbished to carry nine hundred civilian passengers, the ship remained cramped enough that women slept six to a room in bunk beds in hot windowless cabins. The toilets had no doors or partitions.

Despite the rough conditions, Nuchim felt hopeful as they prepared to leave for America. The war had not dimmed his innate optimism. Nuchim was encouraged when his two uncles, who had emigrated from Poland before the war, immediately agreed to sponsor him and Bronia, signing an affidavit promising they wouldn't let their niece and nephew "become public charges."

Surely, Nuchim thought, these uncles would welcome him into their tannery business and help restore his prewar prosperity. He'd grown up in Lublin, a city of 122,000 people in southeastern Poland where his family had operated a recycling business for half a century on the outskirts of town. Horse-drawn carriages brought rags, scrap metal, bottles, and animal bones from the countryside to be sorted for export abroad. The junk trade afforded his family a single-family home outside the Jewish ghetto and allowed both of his older sisters to attend college. His estranged older brother had moved away and Nuchim grew up expecting to inherit the family business, which he lost during the war along with his entire family.

---·---

Bronia and Nuchim had no flowers, photographer, or *chuppah*, the traditional canopy under which the bride and groom say their vows, on their wedding day in February 1942. Only a few close family members joined them in the apartment of her grandfather's rabbi inside Lublin's ghetto. There wasn't enough food for a reception, and no one had any valuables to spare for a proper gift. Bronia wore a plain dress rather than a wedding gown. The only accoutrement of a Jewish wedding available, given Nuchim's family business, was a glass for the groom to break with his foot at the conclusion of the ceremony. This particular tradition, designed to temper the joy of the wedding day with some sadness, wasn't necessary under the circumstances.

Marrying Nuchim provided Bronia access to perhaps the most valuable commodity left inside the ghetto: a work permit. The Germans had recently divided the ghetto into two sections, separating the employed from the unemployed. Everyone feared what might happen next. Bronia and Nuchim knew something was coming and wanted to be together. A month later, Nuchim and Bronia were living in his parents' recycling plant along with other Jewish workers with work permits when SS soldiers and Ukrainian guards surrounded the ghetto and set up floodlights in the main square. Starting at the ghetto's western edge, shouting soldiers barged into apartments and ordered sleeping inhabitants into the street. A few hours later, the local Gestapo chief gathered the Nazi-imposed Jewish administrative council for the ghetto known as the *Judenrat* for a meeting where he announced that everyone without a work permit would be deported from the city.[5]

Few Lublin Jews understood what was happening. Lublin was the first large ghetto liquidated in this part of Poland, and the Germans spread misinformation about resettling deportees in newly occupied Soviet territory, according to Polish historian Robert Kuwalek.[6] The Judenrat's chief had little doubt about what was to come. He showed up for the deportation wearing a traditional mourner's garment and carrying no luggage.

What little Bronia and Nuchim knew about the fate of Lublin's Jews came from peasants who brought scrap metal and glass to the recycling plant. They mentioned mysterious trains traveling through the countryside. The truth spread slowly via word of mouth among Poles who whispered to one another about what they saw and heard. Railway workers described arriving at a site about eighty miles from Lublin near the village of Belzec with boxcars full of prisoners and returning in empty trains. Passengers on the train between Lublin and Lvov recounted shutting the windows to keep out the acrid stench of burning flesh.[7] Lublin's few remaining Jews had no illusions about their fate. "We are in terrible danger," wrote thirty-year-old Hirsh Melekh Talmud, the sole rabbi inside Lublin to survive the liquidation. "There is not even the [smallest] spark of hope that we will be saved."[8]

Bronia could barely eat or sleep, and when she did, she dreamed of the family she assumed had been murdered, including her twenty-one-year-old sister Etka and ten-year-old brother Monik. She lost everybody at once.

Nuchim and Bronia had survived the liquidation of Lublin's ghetto, thanks to the sympathetic German manager of Nuchim's family recycling business. After the manager warned that the Germans planned to empty the ghetto, Nuchim organized a group of seven men he trusted at the recycling plant and began plotting an escape. He collected whatever money they had and sent a couple of men to the countryside in search of guns. He realized that the only thing that could help a Jew die as a Jew was a gun.[9] He also managed to buy forged identity papers for himself and Bronia but had no intention of using them or of ever being taken to any camp alive. He knew they would be separated in a camp. The group escaped the city and found a hiding spot on the edge of the woods where a peasant family hid them in a barn's hay-filled loft in exchange for whatever money or jewelry they had left. The host family kicked them out after a close call with a German patrol.

Cast out of their last refuge, Nuchim had no choice but to lead Bronia beyond civilization into the forests. Nuchim and his companion had guns they could use to intimidate Poles into giving them food or supplies—and not turn them into the Germans. For shelter, they dug an underground building—the sort of bunker dotting Eastern European forests known as *zemlyankas* in Russian where Jews hid like animals underground. In this patch of forest between the towns of Głusk and Piaski, seventy or eighty people lived scattered in bunkers, cooperating as necessary in "actions" to obtain food and supplies. Nuchim divided their bunker, hidden by tree trunks and dirt, into three sections: a room to sleep on a bed of leaves and straw with barely enough room to stretch their legs; a rudimentary kitchen; and a sitting area, with only a tiny slit for daylight. "It was like a grave," according to a fellow survivor who hid in the same forest.[10]

By the fall of 1943, Bronia and Nuchim had been living for six months in the underground dugout in a Polish forest with a ragtag detachment of Jewish partisans. They cooked and ventured above ground only at night for fear of being discovered. Even going to the bathroom brought risks. They had to bury their waste so the smell didn't give them away. Bronia worried when Nuchim left their hiding place in search of food, supplies, or news of German positions. She had no privacy but plenty of time to brood about her family, half mourning, half hoping that perhaps someone survived. Nuchim protected and sheltered Bronia, but equally important was the way he kept her spirits up with his undying optimism, never doubting—at least in front of Bronia—that they would get through this.

———•———

As a mother and a young infant, Bronia and Ruth were assigned more comfortable quarters—a private cabin where naval officers once slept. While most passengers had to eat standing up, traveling with an infant entitled Bronia to dine in a tablecloth-covered former officers dining room, luxuries also reserved for the elderly. Bronia's closest childhood friend, Dina, and her infant daughter, Dorothy, settled into a private cabin nearby.

Dina and Bronia were born two weeks apart in March 1918 and, after meeting in grade school, remained inseparable, until the German invasion in 1939. They reunited back in Lublin after Bronia and Nuchim returned from the woods in the summer of 1944 and had stayed together ever since. Dina talked little about how she hid with her younger sister Sheina after their parents and two older brothers were murdered. Dina and Sheina stayed together in the home of a Polish family in Lublin long after the ghetto's liquidation. But when she returned one day after searching for food, Dina discovered her fifteen-year-old sister had vanished. Someone had disclosed their hiding place to the Germans. She survived the rest of the war after bleaching her hair blonde and passing as a Pole.

In liberated Lublin, Dina met another survivor named Jack Liverant, who grew up around the corner from Bronia and had served together with Nuchim in the Polish Army. Jack first hid openly as a Pole during the war. Then after being captured, he was imprisoned at the Majdanek concentration camp on the outskirts of Lublin, classified as a non-Jewish political prisoner. He escaped a Lublin work camp and fled to the woods where his fair hair, light eyes, and familiarity with Catholic prayers allowed him to pass as Pole in a partisan unit. Dina and Jack married three months after Lublin's liberation in an accelerated courtship common among lonely survivors desperate to restart their lives.

The two couples traveled first to Lodz, where Bronia and Dina both gave birth to baby girls within two weeks of each other in the spring of 1946. Then, after a brief stop in Prague, they moved together to a displaced persons camp in Bensheim, a small picturesque German town in the American occupation zone. They lived for five months in a converted school classroom before their visas cleared and they traveled one last time as displaced persons to Bremerhaven to board the *Marine Perch*.

These modest shipboard accommodations cost Bronia and Nuchim three hundred fifty dollars, a considerable sum at a time when New York's Gimbels department store sold diamond rings for three hundred dollars. The United Service for New Americans (USNA), an aid organization that helped Jewish refugees, provided a loan to cover the cost of the ticket, plus thirty dollars in visa fees and twenty dollars for shipboard expenses, payment due in a year.[11]

————•————

By the time Bronia woke up on their first morning aboard, the *Marine Perch* had cleared the ice-encrusted Weser River and entered the North Sea. The 12,410-ton ship was big enough that many passengers got lost on their first full day aboard but still felt so confining that most had to go above deck for any time alone.[12] The few deck chairs quickly filled up as passengers gathered to gaze at the ocean in a rare moment of shipboard solitude.

Bronia, soon to turn twenty-nine, must have felt relief once the ship passed the white cliffs of Dover in the English Channel the next day and she saw nothing but ocean for the first time in her life. She was happy to lose sight of Europe and all that she'd lost, as if the pain would ease the farther she got from Poland.

Bronia possessed only a few pieces of jewelry and some family photos from before the war that Nuchim managed to hide in his family recycling plant before they'd fled to the forest. She couldn't bear to look at the handful of pictures that chronicled how, in the course of three generations, her family had abandoned traditional shtetl ways for a more modern lifestyle. She must have found it hardest to look at the last photo of her father. Noech, who provided his family a comfortable prewar life as a manager of a gas depot, has a shaved head in this photo taken during the German occupation, perhaps after he barely survived a ghetto typhus infestation. He is so gaunt that his buttoned-up shirt hangs loosely on his shrunken neck. He is nearly fifty and looks decades older in this picture taken not long before Bronia saw him for the last time.

————•————

The *Marine Perch*—and most passengers' stomachs—rolled as huge waves crashed over the ship's bow and tossed it around like a "nutshell," as one young woman aboard wrote in a letter.[13] Winter storms buffeted the ship as soon as it cleared the coast of England, and the weather only worsened as the voyage progressed. The ship's engines filled with water and the mess halls emptied as the ranks of the seasick grew. Somehow, Bronia's stomach stayed steady even as most other young mothers in nearby cabins, including Dina, fell violently ill.

Passengers below deck fared worse. The cabins reeked of a mix of stale air, vomit, and diesel fuel. The toilets overflowed. Many passengers couldn't even make it to the latrine, getting sick in the passageways. Among those suffering down below with seasickness was a twenty-one-year-old Polish Jewish survivor named Chris Lerman, whom Bronia and Dina had first met in Lodz.[14] Chris had endured much worse alongside her older sister Anna, who was about to turn fifteen, and her younger sister Regina, not quite ten, when the war began in September 1939. Together, they had survived several forced labor and concentration camps, including Auschwitz and Ravensbrück.

At the beginning of the occupation, Chris, then thirteen, was walking with her father in her hometown of Starachowice when they encountered a German angry about having to share the sidewalk with Jews.[15] He pushed Chris's father, elegantly dressed in a suit as always, into the gutter. The German then kicked her father over and over again, leaving him dirty, bruised, and humiliated. She later learned how much worse was to come when a filthy, frightened Jewish teenage boy with a wild look on his face suddenly emerged from the bushes in her backyard. The teen explained how he had been taken by train and immediately separated from his parents at a place called Treblinka. He somehow managed to escape by holding on to the undercarriage of a train car.

Chris watched helplessly from the window of the brick factory where she worked as the Germans liquidated Starachowice's ghetto. Chris could see the railroad siding where those selected were led away to cattle cars.[16] Among them, she later learned, was her mother, who promised not to leave a distraught widowed friend alone. Her mother and the friend left for Treblinka together. Separated for a time from her sisters, Chris worked at a slave-labor camp and slept in a barracks where bed bugs fell from the ceiling at night and lice covered her skin and clothes. She declined a fellow inmate's offer of a cyanide vial. "I wanted to live in the worst possible way," Chris recalled.[17] In 1944, Chris and her sisters traveled in a packed cattle car for two days without food, water, or a bathroom and only a tiny window covered by an iron bar for air.[18] Their father was in another car of the train, and they waved goodbye to him from a distance upon arriving at Auschwitz.

Chris and her sisters had their hair cut short and numbers tattooed on their arms upon arrival. They received consecutive numbers: A14176 for Anna, A14177 for Chris, and A14178 for Regina.[19] Their routine included marching naked to shower without soap and barely any water and learning to use the bathroom in less than three minutes or risk getting clubbed. "We were humiliated every step of the way," she later recalled.[20] On the worst of days, Chris and her sisters returned soaking wet and covered in mud after cutting back marshland along a river to clear the sightlines for the camp watchtowers. The guards sicced dogs on them for marching out of step. They'd almost made it back to the barracks when Anna collapsed from exhaustion. Chris fell to her knees, pleading, "Please don't die."[21] Chris and Regina propped Anna up between them and managed to keep her upright during inspection, when prisoners had to stand perfectly still. Chris and Anna later carried Regina, who was delirious and hallucinating, upright during a death march to Ravensbrück during winter when they licked snow for water and rubbed it on their faces to stay awake.[22] Chris was the practical one, who always managed to find them a little extra food. At Ravensbrück, she gave up her birth name of Rosalie and assumed a Christian name, Krystina, that her sisters shortened to Krysia and was later Americanized to Chris.[23]

After liberation, the sisters wound up in Lodz, which is where Chris met an intrepid nightclub owner named Miles Lerman, who had survived the war hiding in a forest in a Jewish partisan unit. Miles and a handful of other prisoners hacked two Ukrainian guards to death with picks and shovels. He then escaped into a Polish forest with only a single working rifle.[24] Miles survived almost two years in the forest as a partisan, conducting guerrilla raids, blowing up depots, and burning food supplies to sow fear among Germans.[25] Miles and his fellow partisans always saved the last bullet for themselves. They preferred suicide to capture.[26]

American Jews might have recoiled at the story of what happened when Miles heard a Ukrainian had delivered a Jewish mother and her eight- or nine-year-old daughter to the Gestapo in exchange for a bottle of vodka or five kilograms of sugar.[27] Miles went to the village that night with some other partisans and knocked on the door of the offender. They dragged him outside and strung up him in a tree as a warning that this is the fate that awaited anyone who turns over Jews.[28]

Miles remembered falling in love at first sight when he spotted this dark-haired, almond-eyed Auschwitz survivor in the nightclub he named "Little Hell."[29] In Lodz, Chris and Miles first met Jack Liverant, who introduced them to Dina, Nuchim, and Bronia. Chris later remembered the Liverants taking over the Lermans' Lodz apartment when she and Miles left for Germany. Chris's older sister Anna got engaged first before moving to Warsaw to study diplomacy.[30] So Miles and Chris took responsibility for her younger sister Regina, and she joined them as they first moved to a Berlin displaced persons camp and then boarded the *Marine Perch*. Regina, who still qualified as a child on this passage, slept in a cabin with three other girls on a higher deck and felt no ill effects of sea sickness.[31] She and the other healthy teenagers had the run of the ship.

————•————

Eventually, the storms cleared and Bronia and Dina reunited with their husbands above deck. They bundled up in heavy winter coats while cradling Ruth and Dorothy, who wore matching scarves, blankets, white hats, and mittens. Bronia and Dina, who both lost their entire immediate families, treated each other more like sisters than friends since reuniting—and they raised their daughters like twins. The adults took turns snapping pictures of each other, squinting in the sun at the ship's edge with the vast Atlantic as a backdrop. They were joined in some photos by Miles and Chris and her sister Regina, who posed alongside the ship's railings with Nuchim. Miles posed alone for a picture as the *Marine Perch* arrived in New York four days late due to the storms. Winter winds swept both his straight dark hair and overcoat collar to the side on a day that the temperature topped out at thirty-seven degrees in New York.

Miles had inherited his parents' entrepreneurial instincts.[32] His father owned several flour mills, and his mother imported coffee, tea, and spices. His family also operated a wholesale liquor business. Miles had already proven to be a scrappy businessman at every stop since liberation. He'd opened a leather business in Lublin and the nightclub in Lodz where he met Chris. In his most lucrative pursuit, Miles obtained permission to supply the Polish government food he purchased on the black market, which he exchanged for textiles he then sold on the open market.[33] He had just as much confidence in his ability to make it on his own in America, too.

As the *Marine Perch* entered New York Harbor on February 11, 1947, the Liverants, Lermans, and Greens joined all the other passengers gathered on one side of the ship.[34] A hush came over passengers as they passed by the

Statue of Liberty in what one recalled as "a moment of awe."[35] Lady Liberty left less of an impression on Bronia, who had no idea what the giant copper statue symbolized. At least one landmark looked familiar to Bronia.[36] Just to the right, halfway across Manhattan, stood the tallest building in the world. The 1933 film *King Kong*, in which a giant prehistoric ape climbs atop the Empire State Building, had played in movie theaters back home in Lublin.

2 ▸ NEW YORK

Bronia and Nuchim disembarked from the *Marine Perch* at a chaotic Pier 84. Western Union messengers delivered telegrams; Red Cross volunteers offered coffee, milk, and donuts; dock workers dumped trunks, duffle bags, and suitcases on the ground.[1] As news photographers from four of the city's daily newspapers snapped photos, Bronia and Nuchim slipped away unnoticed. They were guided through customs and medical exams by representatives wearing silk armbands from the National Council of Jewish Women and the United Service for New Americans (USNA), the aid organization that had loaned them the money for passage.

Inside the cavernous pier, family members waited several rows deep behind a neck-high white picket fence, holding handwritten signs or relying on loudspeaker announcements to identify relatives they may never have met before.[2] More than a decade had passed since Noah Freedman, forty-one, last saw his nephew Nuchim, who was only eight years younger and more like a cousin. Standing beside Noah at the pier was his older brother Morris, forty-seven, who had emigrated from Poland when Nuchim was just a boy, and Morris's wife, Bella, who had lived in the United States for three decades. Much had changed in the years since they last saw each other—so much, in fact, that they had very different recollections of how Noah wound up in the United States.

Nuchim remembered his family making Noah's emigration possible. In need of someone to help their recycling business deal with customers in the United States, they had asked Noah to move on their behalf. Noah recounted arriving with nothing except vague plans to go into business with his brother. Noah and Morris spent years building up their wholesale leather business, and their hard work eventually paid off. As Nuchim's family lost everything during the war, Noah and Morris prospered. Nothing better symbolized Morris's success in his adopted country than his address on the Grand Concourse in the Bronx, the go-to destination for upwardly mobile, first-generation Jewish immigrants who made it out of the Lower East Side. They had mostly lost their foreign accents and adapted the mannerisms, clothes, and tastes of fully acculturated New Yorkers.

Nevertheless, Noah and Morris worried about family trapped inside Poland. After the war, Morris's teenage daughter regularly delivered letters to the Manhattan offices of the Hebrew Immigrant Aid Society to support relatives' visa applications.[3] Now, finally, Noah and Morris were greeting their first relatives to arrive in person, a prospect that might have made them uneasy. Survivors were still a rarity in New York, and media accounts portrayed them as broken in body and spirit. Magazine articles and newsreels showed emaciated concentration camp survivors and corpses piled like cordwood. Even a series of USNA-sponsored radio broadcasts aired later in 1947, designed to provide New Yorkers some sense of the "tragedy and hope" of these newcomers portrayed them as psychologically tormented. In one episode, a female survivor just off the boat in New York Harbor arrives with a "strange look in her eyes, as if she were peering far beyond what the ordinary eyes see."[4]

The sun had already begun to set by the time the Freedmans greeted Bronia and Nuchim in a mix of Polish and Yiddish and emerged together from the pier. Noah drove Nuchim, Bronia, and Ruth to a Manhattan hotel for the night. The Liverants and Lermans left the pier with their uncles and aunts. The next morning, Bronia and Nuchim got their first glimpse of American prosperity when they arrived at the three-bedroom, sixth-floor penthouse apartment where Bella and Morris lived on the Grand Concourse. Nuchim marveled at the dark green and burgundy wallpaper, the Chinese lamps, and the hand-carved richly detailed Victorian wooden furniture. Seeing the fruits of his uncles' success must only have heightened his already inflated expectations of what they might do to help him.

———•———

Bronia, Nuchim, and Ruth didn't stay long on the Grand Concourse. After two weeks, they moved across the East River to Brooklyn. A postwar housing shortage made finding their own place difficult, so they had taken a spare bedroom in the Canarsie apartment of an older, childless couple who came from the same hometown in Poland as Nuchim's uncles. The Liverants were staying nearby with Jack's uncle and aunt. Bronia and Dina met up regularly to push their daughters' carriages along the same stretch of Brooklyn's shore where they passed just a few weeks earlier aboard the *Marine Perch*. Even without knowing any English, Bronia could talk to neighborhood shopkeepers who spoke Yiddish or Polish.

Nuchim left early in the morning to work at his uncles' business in Manhattan and attended late English classes three nights a week at a neighborhood public school. Going back to school at Evening Elementary School 167 could not have been easy for Nuchim, who even as a child much preferred the soccer field or family business to a classroom. Now at the age of thirty-three he sat in night school, struggling to learn English.

Harder still was going to work at the modest offices that housed Noah and Morris's hide business in midtown Manhattan. Their business didn't require much space or more than a couple of employees, since most of the work occurred at a tannery in Upstate New York. They may have asked Nuchim to wrap finished hides, the kind of low-skill work most refugees found. But Nuchim was deeply disappointed. "He thought we would come to the United States and Noah would welcome him with open arms, set him up," Bronia said. "But he took him in as a worker."

Such disappointment seemed almost inevitable for survivors like Nuchim, who arrived in America with such impossibly high expectations. They harbored fantasies that distant relatives would fill the void left by the parents and siblings they'd lost. "The newcomers needed to feel that finally they were not alone in the world; that someone, especially *mishpaca* (family) cared," historian Beth Cohen wrote in her account of survivors' experiences upon arriving in the United States.[5] American relatives often had very different expectations, never intending to extend themselves beyond providing the affidavits that made the refugees' immigration possible.

Nuchim's uncles treated him better than some refugees' relatives who didn't show up at the pier or reneged on promises before the ship even docked. But Nuchim had hoped for more and couldn't bear to continue working at a business as his uncles' subordinate.

He quit and decided to set out on his own, harboring a deep disappointment that lasted the rest of his life. Not that he talked to Bronia about any of it. Nuchim still saw himself as her protector and wasn't going to burden her with his hurt feelings. So Nuchim probably didn't tell Bronia about his destination on April 9, 1947: USNA's office in Lower Manhattan. He so desperately wanted to free himself from dependency on his uncles that he'd come to ask for a loan to buy clothes for his wife and a piece of furniture to store them. Nuchim explained in Yiddish to the caseworker that although his family had provided substantial assistance, he no longer wanted to be dependent on them and would prefer taking out a loan to asking his relatives for more help. But when the caseworker said she would first have to investigate whether his family could provide additional help, Nuchim opted to withdraw his aid application.

Three months later, Nuchim returned to the USNA office in even more desperate straits, this time accompanied by Bronia and Ruth. They met with a different case worker, who described Ruth as looking "pale and poorly dressed." Nuchim had had little success finding a job, and without support from his uncles, they were now "financially destitute," the case worker wrote in her notes. Bronia had to sell her gold watch for forty-five dollars so they had money to eat and pay rent.[6]

To make matters worse, Bronia had developed a thyroid condition possibly caused, or at least exacerbated, by a lack of iodine in their wartime diet. Bronia's thyroid condition left her feeling increasingly nervous and tired. The caseworker described Bronia as "an attractive young woman" who "was obviously under physical and emotional strain largely due to her thyroid disease and the family's difficulties in making a beginning in this country." She was "constantly at the verge of tears," as Nuchim explained their situation. A doctor whom Nuchim's uncle had referred them to said Bronia needed surgery, but they couldn't afford to pay for it, the caseworker wrote. She noted, "Mr. G. also seemed extremely upset about his wife's illness and their helplessness in relation to it."

Nuchim grew agitated when the caseworker said she'd first need to check how much assistance his uncles could provide before making a hospital

referral. "They found it very difficult to accept the fact that I did not immediately and unconditionally promise help," the caseworker wrote. After all
the years of staying composed, particularly in Bronia's presence, Nuchim
finally lost his cool. Months of pent-up frustration and simmering helplessness about being unable to provide for his wife and daughter came out all at
once. "Our uncle is good to us and helped us as long as he could but other
people whose relatives assumed no responsibility whatsoever are helped by
you!," he shouted. Bronia, unaccustomed to Nuchim displaying this kind of
emotion, burst into tears.

Still, when the caseworker made clear it was the only way to proceed,
Nuchim swallowed his pride and agreed to ask his uncle to contact her.
After Freedman indicated they were unable to assist, the USNA agreed to
provide fifteen dollars for a baby carriage and nine dollars and thirty-four
cents for Ruth's clothes. USNA also took care of the bill when Bronia was
admitted to the Jewish Hospital of Brooklyn on August 23, 1947, for surgery
to remove her thyroid. (She would be discharged ten days later "in apparent
good health.")

On the day before Bronia's hospital admission, a change had taken hold
over her and Nuchim, who were suddenly "more optimistic about the
future," their caseworker noted.[7] The source of their optimism: an article or
ad Nuchim had seen in a Yiddish newspaper, offering to help Jewish people
settle on poultry farms.

3 ▸ FINDING A FARM

Nuchim grew up in a city, and his only previous farm experience consisted of hiding in a peasant's hayloft. But between the housing and health problems, job and family disappointments, Nuchim had all but given up on New York after half a year there. Here was a way to escape the city, to be free of distant relatives and meddling caseworkers. Dina's husband, Jack, found the idea equally appealing. He had drifted through a variety of jobs in New York, including fixing window screens and a single day selling hot dogs at Yankee Stadium.

Bronia was more hesitant, at least at first. She had hoped their hardships were over when they came to the United States and had started to grow accustomed to life in New York. It wasn't that she recoiled at the thought of country life. Unlike some survivors who grew up in big cities, she had fond memories of summers in a cottage in the woods, where she collected strawberries and mushrooms and bathed in pine water. But the only experience Bronia had with chickens was with the ones at Lublin's outdoor market, where she accompanied her mother Cyrla as a young girl every Thursday to prepare for the Jewish Sabbath. Bronia had looked with wonder at the brown chickens farmers brought from the countryside. Raising thousands of them was another matter entirely. "We didn't know nothing about a farm," she said.

Nevertheless, she put her doubts aside and deferred to Nuchim, just as she'd done throughout the war. They felt as if they didn't have any other good options. "Without the language, with small children, what could we do?," she asked. "We couldn't make a living in New York, it was hard with children, it was hard to find an apartment after the war. This was the one way." Given their limited resources, Nuchim, Bronia, Jack, and Dina decided to try to find a single farm where they could all live together. "We were in the same situation," Bronia said.

———•———

Perhaps Nuchim and Jack would have been more wary, like their wives, if they knew about the experience of another group of Eastern European Jews who settled on American farms in the 1880s. Strict limits in Tzarist Russia on where Jews could live and how they could earn a living combined with waves of anti-Jewish violence prompted mass immigration to New York and other big American cities. A few idealistic Russian Jews instead seized on the idea of establishing egalitarian farm colonies in places like Sicily Island, Louisiana, and New Odessa, Oregon. Many backed out as soon as they disembarked in New York. Most of these colonies "conceived in haste and planned under stress" quickly failed due to hostile climates, ideological infighting, and the colonists' inexperience.[1] Malaria, yellow fever, and Mississippi River flooding destroyed the crops and doomed the Louisiana colony within a year.[2] New Odessa lasted less than six years.[3]

Only a cluster of colonies in southern New Jersey remained viable for long. It certainly wasn't anything about the land that explained the survival of these colonies with names like Alliance and Carmel. Southern New Jersey's loamy, sandy soil couldn't support grains.[4] But the twelve hundred acres of scrub oak and pine woods on the western bank of the Maurice River where Alliance was established could support grapes, cranberries, and strawberries.[5] The scouts who originally came to New Jersey also had the good sense to pick a site near a railway line connecting Philadelphia and New York.[6] The colonists lived close enough to important markets where they could sell their wares—and far enough away to avoid the "temptations of the city."[7]

Alliance, the first Jewish colony in New Jersey, nicknamed "New Jerusalem" by neighbors, hardly felt like the Promised Land to colonists.[8] Life here proved neither easy nor lucrative.[9] Alliance's first residents lived in surplus U.S. Army tents and then communal barracks before ultimately moving into two-room houses.[10] Come harvest time in the spring, they woke up at five in the morning and covered their hands with worn-out stockings to protect against thorns while picking berries.[11] Colonists supplemented meager farm incomes by working in factories.[12] Even so, life remained hard. A reporter visiting Alliance in 1891 observed "many a long, low, rambling shed, infested with at least twenty families, the men and women to be seen making cheap cigars within, the children running wild about the premises."[13] As time went by, more colonists and their children fled to New York or Philadelphia, or to the much smaller city less than five miles away: Vineland.

The New Jersey colonies probably would not have survived at all without the support of philanthropists like Baron Maurice de Hirsch, a wealthy German-born Jewish financier.[14] He funneled much of his vast fortune into helping settle Jews on farms from New Jersey to Brazil through several charities, including one that eventually became the Jewish Agricultural Society (JAS). "I shall try to make for them a new home in different lands where, as free farmers on their own soil, they can make themselves useful to the country," de Hirsch wrote in 1891.[15] Elite philanthropists such as de Hirsch believed that agriculture might blunt anti-Semitism by dispersing Jewish immigrants and proving Jews could lead productive lives outside of cities. Returning Jews to the soil came to be seen as "a sweeping cure for many Jewish ills—unemployment, poverty, slum living, disease, crime, prejudice, and discrimination," writes one historian.[16] In reality, farm life was no panacea, as hundreds of Russian Jewish immigrants discovered after settling as homesteaders in North Dakota.[17] Hailstorms there could wipe out a whole season's crops in minutes.[18] "It was next to impossible to eke out a living on the farm, no matter how hard the entire family worked," recalled one homesteader's daughter.[19]

Farming never took hold among Jewish immigrants in the United States as a primary pathway to assimilation. The typical first-generation Jewish immigrant was far more likely to start out in a New York garment factory or, if they ventured into rural America, as a peddler, selling door-to-door whatever they could carry.[20] But a small number of American Jews continued to farm well into the twentieth century. In the mid-1930s, an estimated eighty thousand Jews lived on farms, roughly 2 percent of the more than four million Jews in the United States.[21] Jews operated farms in all forty-eight states then in existence, and in every branch of agriculture. They grew potatoes in Maine, bluegrass seeds in Kentucky, and wheat in Kansas and raised cattle in Colorado.[22]

The JAS had given up on supporting far-flung collective settlements in the "distant hinterland," preferring to help settle individual families on farms close to existing Jewish communities.[23] Most clustered in small colonies in the Northeast, stretching from the Berkshires in western Massachusetts, down through Connecticut and New York's Catskill Mountains and into central and southern New Jersey. They tended to operate small dairy or poultry farms and organized cooperatives to help jointly purchase feed for their animals and market their milk and eggs.[24]

Historian Joseph Brandes probably exaggerated when he credited the chicken with saving Jewish agrarianism.[25] But poultry did prove particularly attractive to prospective Jewish farmers throughout the Northeast and as far away as California. Farmers raising chickens for their eggs or meat didn't need as much capital or training as in other branches of agriculture. Nor did poultry require as much land, which made farming feasible in the well-settled, more expensive areas that fellow Jews preferred to live. Chickens began generating income faster than crops, and poultry operations were less vulnerable to natural hazards such as droughts and storms.

For all these reasons, the JAS embraced poultry farms as the perfect place to settle Jewish refugees escaping Nazi Germany in the late 1930s with little money. Raising chickens was also less physically demanding than other forms of farming, an important consideration for highly educated urban refugees who were often in their fifties and sixties.[26] It was the perfect Depression-era solution: every refugee placed on a farm was one less Jew who could be accused of taking an American's job. "In the city, where competition is already keen and where jobs are scarce, every new storekeeper, every new professional, every new worker adds to the pressure and tends to create feeling against refugees and in a measure against Jews in general," Gabriel Davidson, the JAS general manager, noted in September 1939. "No such conditions exist on the farm."[27]

The JAS had helped settle 324 refugee families by the time the United States entered World War II in late 1941 and started up again after the fighting stopped.[28] At a board meeting on February 11, 1947—the very day the Greens and Liverants arrived on the *Marine Perch*—JAS officials explained how they'd convinced the Baron de Hirsch Fund to provide additional resources to aid refugees. As a first step, the JAS and the fund decided "loans to refugees should be liberalized," with less thought given to capital requirements "than to personal factors."[29] As the year progressed, the number of refugees contacting the JAS almost tripled to 310.[30]

The JAS insisted that it "studiously avoided all extravagant back-to-the-land propaganda" and encouraged farm settlement only for pragmatic reasons.[31] The original nineteenth-century colonists' idealism had largely given way to a focus at the JAS on what was most practical. And yet the organization couldn't help but talk about its work in more high-minded terms. One JAS annual report posed the question of "what is the virtue of a Jewish farm movement?" "Is it to add to the country's food supply? Is it to scotch the myth that Jews have neither the desire nor the aptitude for farming? Is it to demonstrate that Jews can till and toil and derive joy therefrom? Is it to relieve city congestion, even if only in a small way? Is it to diversify Jewish occupational composition? Is it to mitigate, even in small measure, anti-Jewish prejudice? It is all this. It is more. The Jewish farmer is the exemplar of a new way of life."[32] The assistance of the JAS was vital for refugees with little savings or access to credit. The JAS offered low-interest loans repaid over long periods rather than extending outright charity. It effectively served as a guarantor of loans by offering second mortgages to applicants.[33] In private, the JAS board remained ambivalent about whether to underwrite additional farm settlement. At a meeting in the fall of 1947, one board member asked if "we are serving our prospective farmers wisely by encouraging them to settle on farms at a time when farm real estate is high and general economic conditions uncertain."[34] The discussion that followed included "prophets of boom and prophets of bust." The consensus: "to adopt a general policy of dissuasion would not be right and that all that the Society can do is to acquaint prospective applicants with the situation as it appears to the Society's experts, to weigh each case individually, and to proceed with the utmost caution."

That fall, most JAS loans still went to refugees, mostly from Germany, who had arrived before the United States entered the war or to American-born Jews, including veterans seeking "a quiet pastoral life."[35] Postwar displaced persons had just started to apply. The JAS rejected an application that October from a fifty-five-year-old refugee "with practically no farm experience," who the JAS concluded had sought too "large a sum to set up a childless couple."[36] The JAS would continue to reject a handful of refugee applications, while giving aid to many more in the months ahead. Still, the misgivings didn't go away. At one 1948 meeting, JAS board members asked, "Are we justified in encouraging people to go on farms at a time of high costs? Does that fact that a man has been in a concentration camp, or is a DP, qualify him for farming? Is there not too much concentration upon poultry?" The board members agreed that applicants "should be scrutinized and screened even more carefully than at present."[37]

———•———

When Nuchim arrived at the offices of the United Service for New Americans (USNA) for an appointment on October 7, 1947, he was worried about convincing the agency's representative that they knew how to farm. That's why he embellished his prior agricultural work experience. Nuchim claimed that he and Bronia had worked on a farm in Poland during the war and then he and Jack had worked together on a poultry farm for a year in Germany after liberation, neither of which was true.

The officials reviewing the application from Jack and Nuchim probably were more concerned about them sharing a single plot of land than their lack of farming experience. The JAS understood the appeal of partnerships among refugees. "People who survived Hitler's concentration camps, guerilla warfare in swamps and forests or life in the labor camps of Siberia were afraid to start a new life alone on a 'far off farm,'—a term which they associated with a feeling of loneliness and insecurity," two top JAS officials later wrote.[38] But long experience had shown that the advantages of communal living were outweighed by the problems when "all members of the families are thrown into close contact."[39] Still, the JAS "against its own best judgment, had to adopt a policy of letting settlers bent on partnership learn from their own mistakes."[40]

Nuchim and Bronia had already tried to assure their caseworker that a partnership with their friends could last. They "strongly emphasized that this friendship means a great deal to them and is a stable one," the caseworker noted.[41] Now, Nuchim tried to convince the USNA agent, who recounted their argument in a letter to the JAS. Nuchim and Jack noted they had gone to school together, their wives had known each other since childhood, and their friendship had already survived a war, so how much of a strain could life together on a farm be? "It is for these reasons that they are anxious to work together, for they feel that they have been able to go along through difficult periods, and are confident that they will manage together now that they are embarking on a farm project in a new environment."[42] The USNA agent seemed convinced, telling the JAS, "we shall be glad to go along with you in your recommendation for a loan."

Bronia and Nuchim's income dwindled further as searching for a farm became a full-time job. Nuchim had to borrow forty dollars from their butcher so he could travel to look at farms in New Jersey. At the JAS's suggestion, Nuchim and Jack focused on Vineland, the same community where residents of Alliance and other nearby colonies migrated earlier. In all, they made five trips to Vineland as well as two nearby towns, meeting with two real estate agents and a lawyer.[43]

Bronia stayed behind in their latest apartment on Manhattan's Upper West Side, pleading with yet another caseworker for help buying winter clothes and paying for Nuchim's travel expenses. Two weeks later, Bronia called the caseworker again with word they had found a farm. For twenty-three thousand dollars including a fifteen-hundred-dollar down payment, Jack and Nuchim jointly purchased a ten-acre farm, thirty-three hundred hens, and all the farm's equipment.[44] The sellers, a fifty-seven-year-old Russian immigrant and his wife, had raised two children during two decades on the farm. To fund the purchase, Nuchim and Jack borrowed from their uncles and the JAS and USNA each loaned them thirty-five hundred dollars on top of an eight-thousand-dollar first mortgage.

Their lives as a single household began in early December when Jack and Nuchim met with their caseworkers to plan their purchases. The Grins' caseworker offered to subsidize the furniture and household provisions, while the Liverants' caseworker would pay to ship it all to New Jersey. Both also wrote out a separate worksheet detailing their bedroom furniture and clothing needs. When Nuchim met his caseworker one last time in December before departing, he assured the social worker that he and Jack "would make a go of it" on the farm together.[45] "His face brightened up as he began to describe the town of Vineland and its resources," she wrote. There was one other change: mail to Nuchim Grin was now addressed to the Americanized "Nathan Green," and Bronia had become Betty.

4 ▸ SETTLING IN

IN HER PROPER hat and gloves, Betty looks as out of place beside her equally overdressed husband, who wears a suit, tie, and fedora as they drive along country roads in a dilapidated pickup truck toward their new farmhouse. A cage full of chickens is perched on the roof, while a cow, a goat, and a sheep share the truck bed. Ropes hold down trunks full of their belongings above the wheels. A burst of wind blows Betty's hat off her head and onto the truck bed, where, much to Betty's alarm, the goat promptly eats it. "It seems so far away," Betty says forlornly before drifting off to sleep on her husband's shoulder.[1]

Betty's husband wakes her up as they near their new home. "Close your eyes, I want to surprise you," he says. Betty certainly looks surprised as she opens her eyes and sees their rundown and weather-worn farmhouse for the first time. Things only look worse out back, where a broken wagon sits between a pig pen and the chicken coop.

"Isn't this the life, Betty?" he says with contentment.

"I guess so, once you get used to it," she replies dejectedly.

That was Hollywood's version of another young wife named Betty's trip to a chicken farm in the 1947 movie, *The Egg and I*. In a 1945 best-selling

eponymous book Betty MacDonald first chronicled her experiences settling on a Pacific Northwest egg farm. The movie version premiered in the
spring of 1947, six months before Bronia set out for her farm in New Jersey.
Betty's embellished account is full of comic pratfalls from the minute her
husband, Bob, tells her—on their wedding night in the movie version—
that he's bought a chicken farm. Both the movie and the book leave out the
real-life unhappy ending: Betty abandoned the egg farm after three years
and filed for divorce.[2]

Even without a goat eating her hat, Bronia's transition was no less jarring.
One day in late December 1947, she woke up in a Manhattan apartment
building and went to bed that same night on a chicken farm seven miles
outside downtown Vineland, a community of thirty thousand people.
Bronia made that leap one morning between Hanukkah and Christmas
as she set out on her second new beginning in America in less than a year.
Unlike Betty MacDonald, Bronia didn't have her husband along for support.
He stayed on the farm while Jack went back to New York to bring down their
wives and daughters.[3]

The most accurate sense of what Bronia's trip was like comes from a
May 1948 newspaper account of an Austrian Jewish refugee family's move
from a Bronx tenement to a Vineland poultry farm.[4] The story, headlined
"New Seed on American Soil," offers a vivid portrait of the Blau family,
which had survived the Theresienstadt ghetto and labor camp and arrived
in Vineland a few months after the Greens and Liverants: "It was late when
the station wagon entered Landis Avenue, the leading thoroughfare of Vineland, but the town was wide awake, except for the darkened shop windows.
Lights flashed outside the three movie theaters and the numerous diners
and grills. There were two hotels and a sign announcing that a third would be
erected soon. There was a newspaper office, a fresh-looking bank building and
many smart apparel shops. Along both sides of the street, automobiles were
closely parked at angles, with no room to spare." Beyond the business district,
spacious houses mixed with modest dwellings and the occasional factory producing clothing and glass or canning foods. A few miles out of town, Mr. Blau
came outside to meet his family as they arrived at the farm, just as Nuchim
had done a few months earlier as Bronia, Jack, Dina, and their daughters
pulled up to their brick farmhouse on Tuckahoe Road.

The yard and fir trees surrounding the front porch undoubtedly made a
better first impression on Bronia than what Betty MacDonald described in

The Egg and I. No matter how ambivalent Bronia might have felt about becoming a chicken farmer, at this moment at least, she must have felt relief. After eight nomadic years of war and life as a refugee, she finally had a home of her own, albeit one shared with another family and three thousand or so chickens. More importantly, she and Nuchim could finally put down roots for Ruth, who as she neared her second birthday had already lived in six cities in four countries and three New York City boroughs. Ruth, who was just learning to walk, would have a farmhouse and ten acres of land to explore rather than a crowded urban apartment.

The house may have felt cramped to the four adults sharing a space designed for a single family. But it was certainly better than a room in the apartment of strangers in Brooklyn. Each couple had their own bedroom, and Dorothy and Ruth would share a room, just like Bronia did with her sister Etka growing up. The United Service for New Americans (USNA) helped equip the kitchen with appliances, table linens, dishes, and matching high chairs.[5] However, they had little time to relax and enjoy their new surroundings. The USNA would cut off their assistance on New Year's Day, and the hens out back weren't going to buy their own feed.

————·————

Maybe it was the thick stench of feces. Or the feathers floating in the air and scattered on the straw-covered floor. Or maybe it was the cacophonous chorus of hundreds of hens clucking at once, loud enough to keep city visitors up at night. Whatever fantasy of an idyllic country life Bronia harbored must have faded as soon as she stepped out the farmhouse's backdoor and down the concrete steps, walked across the dirt range, and entered one of the two wooden chicken coops for the first time.

What Bronia later remembered best from this first visit to the coops was that these chickens looked nothing like the brown hens she saw during childhood visits to Lublin's outdoor market with her mother. Nuchim and Jack inherited a flock of leghorns, a breed originally from Italy. The variety they purchased with the farm was all white, except for the red combs and the fleshy lobes of skin that hung from the side of their head called wattles that helped keep them cool. These leghorns laid the white eggs that New York consumers preferred at the time.

Their hens looked like shorter, thinner, female versions of Foghorn Leghorn, the cartoon rooster with the southern accent and overbearing manner who debuted in the Warner Bros. *Looney Tunes* cartoons in 1946. But as Nuchim and Jack had already discovered, these chickens lived a barnyard version of *Lord of the Flies* or *The Hunger Games*. The hens attacked each other if they spotted blood, a common sight on their backsides after they laid eggs. The term "pecking order" came from the tendency of the strongest chickens to establish by force the power to peck at all the others and get fed first. At the first sign of weakness, the strong chickens would pounce viciously on the vulnerable. As one 1947 egg-farming guide warned, "Cannibalism is a vice that soon becomes a habit."[6]

Nuchim and Jack would learn these foul-tempered fowl were also quite fragile. The sound of Vineland's Saturday afternoon air raid siren drill whipped the easily startled chickens into such a panic they smothered each other to death while crowding into a corner of the coops. Farmers whistled or talked loudly to themselves before opening the door so a sudden entrance didn't induce panic. When sunlight faded in the fall and the chickens molted and lost their feathers, they might stop laying eggs for weeks. And they retired early, ceasing laying eggs altogether, after just a few years.[7]

Buying a farm stocked with chickens meant Nuchim and Jack avoided, at least at the outset, the challenges associated with raising baby chicks. Newly hatched chicks remained vulnerable to all sorts of poultry diseases and needed help staying warm until they grew feathers. Chicks had to be taught "survival behaviors," including how to eat and sleep properly near the brooding stoves.[8] Unattended chicks might wander too far from the warming stoves and freeze to death. A few months would pass until vaccination crews could arrive to corral the chicks in the coop, grab them with a leg hook, and jab needles in the web of their wings.

Adolph Blau, his family's patriarch, who was born in 1894 and worked as a textile salesman in Vienna before the war, wouldn't let anyone else in the coops once his family's fourteen hundred baby chicks had arrived.[9] Blau set up brooding stoves and fed them a special mash mixed with fish oils. Still, he expected to lose nearly a third of the chicks within a few days, which wasn't all that unusual. Sometimes, an entire flock might get sick and die. Blau knew he had little margin for error. He estimated his flock would earn about fifty to sixty dollars a week after all his expenses. More than 60 percent of his income would go to paying the feed bill. He expected no profit the first year: everything earned would go back into the business for more chicks and equipment.

—————•—————

Around the same time that the Greens and Liverants arrived in Vineland, the USNA cosponsored a radio play about a fictional new refugee poultry farmer in New Jersey that aired in New York.[10] The program, titled *This Is New Jersey*, tells how neighbors in an unidentified town helped the farmer rebuild his chicken coop that lost its roof in a storm.

"My farm is up the road a piece, I heard you had a little accident this morning," one neighbor says. Another adds, "We can fix up that roof as good as new in a couple hours."

"You mean, all of you came to help me?" the startled refugee asks in thickly accented English.

"When a man needs help, his neighbors are there to give it to him," a neighbor replies.

In reality, new arrivals like the Greens and Liverants could expect little assistance. Jewish Agricultural Society (JAS) records suggest they were among the first half dozen or so Eastern European refugee families to settle on a Vineland-area poultry farm. The JAS had switched to instructing high school students at its training farm in northern New Jersey once the U.S. entry into World War II had cut off the flow of additional refugees.[11] Several years would pass before the agency opened a branch office in Vineland with an agent who could help new arrivals with farming and conversational English classes. Nuchim and Jack certainly could have used some guidance. Fibs to the JAS aside, they didn't know the first thing about the poultry business and largely had to figure it all out on their own. The farm's prior owner provided some help to Nuchim and Jack, and a middle-aged, non-Jewish Polish neighbor across the road taught Bronia how to grow potatoes, carrots, and grapes for wine.

The best Nuchim and Jack could do was subscribe to the *Jewish Farmer*, a monthly bilingual magazine, which the JAS claimed was the world's first Yiddish agricultural paper when it debuted in 1908.[12] In their early months on the farm, the *Jewish Farmer*'s "Poultry Pointers" column chronicled all the pitfalls from cannibalism to frozen water pans and the many illnesses chickens could contract. The publication warned in January 1948 that Newcastle disease, a highly contagious and virulent virus, "is hitting" Vineland "much harder" than elsewhere.[13]

As their English improved, Nuchim and Jack also started reading a two-page section published once a month in the *Times Journal* by the Vineland and South Jersey Cooperative Egg Auction and Poultry Association, the local co-op where many farmers sold their eggs.[14] "The South Jersey Poultryman" was full of ads from feed mills, hatcheries, poultry equipment sellers, and vaccine makers in the area, many of them owned by Jewish entrepreneurs. In the January 1948 edition, the Jacob Rubinoff Company promised "better feeds for all needs," while Vineland Poultry Laboratories, under the direction of Dr. Arthur Goldhaft, assured readers "our products are noted for their purity and effectiveness."[15]

———•———

Living seven miles from downtown Vineland meant Bronia and Dina had little contact with the world beyond their farm at first, except for traveling salesmen. Lacking their own vehicle made the isolation worse. Bronia and Dina hitchhiked into town for the occasional escape, at least until the day a man picked them up in his pickup truck—and started driving in the wrong direction. The incident gave Bronia her biggest fright since the war. The driver—a police detective—eventually identified himself and explained he wanted to teach them a lesson about the dangers of hitchhiking. From then on, Bronia and Dina relied on rides from people they knew.

Bronia remembered little about her first trip to Vineland's central commercial strip, Landis Avenue. Vineland's main street was as wide as any boulevard in Lublin, although the community had just a quarter of her hometown's prewar population. This small town was quite a culture shock for many refugees raised in European cities, who still clung to their prewar sophistication. "When I came in, I almost fainted," recalled Goldie Finkelstein, who grew up in Sosnowiec, a Polish city roughly the same size as Lublin.[16] "Did anyone live here all year round?" It wasn't just the reality of small-town life but what farming symbolized to refugees still trying to accept their new, lower station in life. Survivors could more easily convince themselves their fall in status was temporary while on the move as displaced people. Now, these Grine—many of whom grew up in Polish cities thinking that only peasants raised chickens—had no better option than poultry farming.

Bronia had not considered herself a big-city sophisticate growing up in Lublin. The familiar-sounding names on Landis Avenue façades might have even been comforting reminders of storefronts back in Jewish Lublin's pre-war shopping district. Silverman's, a clothing store for men and boys, and Kotok Hardware shared Landis Avenue with shops catering specifically to Jewish residents, including Goldstein's, which billed itself as "Vineland's Original Kosher Delicatessen." Russian-born Isadore Goldstein had sold pastrami and corned beef cured in-house here since 1932.[17] Another deli recently opened two blocks away, featuring a complete line of Hebrew National products plus whitefish for ninety cents a pound.[18] Nearby Plum Street had two kosher butcher shops, Woldar & Sons and Rosen's, in addition to Freedman's Bakery, which promised the "best in Jewish Rye" alongside bagels and onion rolls on weekends.[19]

More unusual for someone accustomed to the narrow warren of cobblestone streets in Lublin's Old Town was Vineland's wide and perfectly straight street grid, home to both farms and factories. This unique planned community was the vision of Charles K. Landis. At the age of twenty-eight, Landis, a Philadelphia attorney turned utopian land speculator, built this city from scratch in the mid-nineteenth century.[20] Instead of fields of grain, Landis envisioned residents growing more profitable vines and fruit trees.

No detail was too minor to Landis as he laid out his town in one of the earliest instances of what later became known as suburban planning.[21] Foreshadowing Levittown, he dictated the width of the streets and how far homes had to be set back from the road.[22] He demanded homebuyers build a house as well as clear and cultivate two and a half acres of land within a year of purchase. Landis discouraged fences so animals would fertilize the fruit trees and vineyards while grazing. In the center, he laid out a one-hundred-foot-wide main commercial strip that transected the town like the equator and was later named in his honor.

Unfortunately for Landis, few buyers in the 1860s wanted a piece of this planned utopia in the wilderness. With the Civil War under way, he coaxed some settlers by buying them exemptions from service in the Union Army. He advertised in America's first newspapers aimed at Italian immigrants and sent agents to Italy to recruit settlers.[23] The outreach worked: by 1911, south Jersey's 956 Italian farm families, drawn first from northern Italy and later from Sicily and the south, was the largest such cluster in the United States.[24] Many of the families settled on a tract east of town known as "New Italy" with two Italian Catholic churches and street names like Piacenzia, Genoa, Venezia, and Italia.[25] These Italian truck farmers found the soil best suited for cultivating vegetables such as peppers and sweet potatoes or strawberries.

Along with Italian immigrants fleeing big cities came devotees of an odd mix of fringe movements: free lovers, teetotalers, and bloomers, the latter a group of women who rejected social norms of the time and insisted on wearing pants in public.[26] Many of the newcomers must have felt duped. For years, the town's promoters mailed brochures to potential settlers more likely to conjure images of California's Napa Valley than south Jersey. "There is probably no section of the United States, east of California, that bears a closer resemblance to the land of the Pacific slope," declared one from 1893 that promised a "healthful climate, a productive soil abounding in luscious fruits in a beautiful improved country."[27]

Despite the town's name and its founder's wishes, grapes never took hold as Vineland's signature product. The exception was a local teetotaler dentist who prepared a batch of grape juice in Vineland as an alternative to alcoholic wine for Communion at his Methodist church. Thomas Bramwell Welch's concoction became America's most famous grape juice, but only after he moved to Upstate New York.[28] Instead, farmers discovered they could earn a year-round income by raising a few chickens and selling the eggs along with seasonal crops. By 1890, a thousand farmers around Vineland had at least a few chickens in their yards laying eggs destined for breakfast tables in Philadelphia or New York. Business boomed during World War I as scarce eggs sold for as much as a dollar a dozen. Vineland billed itself as the "poultry center of the Eastern United States."[29]

By the time the Greens and Liverants arrived, poultry farming was just one part of a diversified economy that also included truck farms growing fruits and vegetables, as well as glass and garment factories and food processing plants. Befitting Landis's outreach to Italians, Vineland's food makers included Uddo & Taormina, two families that opened a plant in an old factory when World War II made importing from Italy impossible.[30] After the war, the company introduced a minestrone based on an old family recipe, what it later claimed was the first canned, ready-to-serve soup in America, under the brand name of Progresso.[31] The recipe included a bucket of olive oil and a shovel of potatoes, and was painted on the plant's wall.[32]

But poultry inordinately defined Vineland's identity. It wasn't just that Vineland High School's sports teams called themselves the "Poultry Clan" or that grain silos towered over every other building in town. For a time, a huge bright red neon chicken also topped the Vineland Electric Utility plant.[33] Seventeen poultry feed mills and twenty-five hatcheries and poultry dealers operated in the area while Vineland's daily paper tracked poultry prices as closely every day as the New York tabloids covered the Yankees.[34] The *Poultryman*, a weekly newspaper published in Vineland dedicated to covering the industry, offered only good news as Nuchim and Jack took up farming. The week they arrived, the *Poultryman*'s front-page headline declared, "Egg prices reach highest December figure since 1920."[35]

5 ▸ SMALL-TOWN JEWS

$\bigwedge$ SMALL JEWISH presence wasn't at all unusual in a place like Vineland in the decades leading up to World War II. While most Jews had always settled in big cities, "a significant minority" had opted for rural communities.[1] Jews had migrated west with the shifting frontier, settling in nearly every corner of rural America from Appalachian coal country to California Gold Rush boomtowns. Some had just arrived from Europe; others had tried living in big cities first. Many set out first as peddlers before opening dry goods and grocery stores.[2] They became fixtures on small-town main streets like Washington Avenue in Greenville, Mississippi, where two-thirds of the merchants were Jewish in 1880.[3]

As in other rural towns, Vineland's earliest Jewish settlers were merchants who opened small shops downtown. Vineland proved an alluring destination among struggling farmers in the nearby colonies seeking more secure work and better education for their children. Residents tended to ignore the early Jewish presence. A pamphlet published in 1911 to celebrate Vineland's fiftieth anniversary included pictures of six churches but referenced neither of its two synagogues at the time: Ahavas Achim and Sons of Jacob.[4] Vineland's local newspaper treated Jews like curiosities with exotic rituals. When a local *mohel* performed Vineland's first circumcision in 1898, the *Vineland Evening Journal* called it "a grand christening event."[5] A decade later, when the Ahavas Achim congregation prepared to add a *mikveh*, or ritual bath, to its Plum Street synagogue, the paper praised the "orthodox Hebrews" for creating "quite a commodious looking church" by adding "a Turkish bath house or swimming pool."[6]

Less forgivable than misunderstandings about religious customs were the ugly stereotypes directed at Jewish shopkeepers. Merchants lobbying in 1879 in favor of posting retail prices condemned "the miserable jew system of overcharging with the expectation of being 'beat down.'"[7] A local Jewish clothing shop owner would plead at a April 1920 Chamber of Commerce meeting that he wasn't "the money grabber some made him out to be."[8] Another Jewish merchant dropped out of a local board of education race in 1924 after finding a cross burning in front of his house.[9] Jews—along with local Italians and Blacks—felt uneasy as the Ku Klux Klan marched Saturday nights in Vineland in the 1920s.[10]

Nevertheless, many of the original Jewish settlers' children prospered in Vineland, establishing lucrative businesses tied to the local poultry industry. Jacob Rubinoff, for example, a Jewish immigrant born in Russia, had settled as a child on a Vineland truck farm with his family.[11] He and a partner later established a grain, seed, and horse supply business, which evolved into the Jacob Rubinoff Company. By the time he died in 1948 at the age of sixty-five, his chicken feed company operated the largest mill of its kind on the Eastern Seaboard and four area retail stores. He had become a member of Vineland's Jewish elite, helping found one of its two leading synagogues, Beth Israel. His family leaped from immigrant to Ivy League in a single generation. Rubinoff's son graduated from the University of Pennsylvania's Wharton business school, while one of his four daughters attended Cornell.

The most successful son of the original generation of farmers had an even steeper climb. Arthur Goldhaft's Russian-immigrant parents twice failed at farming in Alliance.[12] He grew up largely in Philadelphia, where his father found work as a seasonal matzoh baker while his mother traveled back to Alliance as a midwife. Goldhaft's rise from poverty began at the Baron de Hirsch agricultural training school in Woodbine, New Jersey, located about twenty-five miles south of Vineland. Then, after working as a farmhand, he enrolled at the University of Pennsylvania for college. Penn didn't have an agricultural school, so he instead trained to be a veterinarian. Goldhaft started out caring for livery horses in Philadelphia until the arrival of Model T Fords convinced him he needed a new specialty.[13] He found his calling in caring for chickens. He branched out into vaccinations and founded Vineland Poultry Laboratories. His company's vaccine for Newcastle disease sold out of all fifteen million doses within forty-eight hours in 1948.[14] His son Tevis, daughter Helen, and son-in-law Nathan Wernicoff all graduated Cornell's veterinary school and eventually joined the family business.

Goldhaft put his knowledge about poultry science to good use when refugees fleeing Nazi Germany in the 1930s began settling in south Jersey. He delivered lectures and offered informal advice to these new farmers, whom the Jewish Agricultural Society (JAS) had directed to "the Vineland-area where poultry farms were considerably less expensive."[15] That explains why more than 40 percent of the 324 refugee families settled with help from the JAS by the end of 1941 ended up living in Vineland or nearby towns.[16] These doctors, lawyers, and businessmen had to leave their homes with little more than a suitcase and a violin in one case. Many refugees first lived in New York, where, with the Depression still under way, they couldn't find even the sort of menial jobs they once relegated to servants. Professionals educated in Germany's best schools, who could speak Latin or Greek fluently, "harbored vague and fantastic notions" about what farming involved.[17] They shortened dresses previously worn to the theater or opera as work clothes for the chicken coops. When those old clothes wore out, some repurposed the cotton bags they used to store chicken feed as skirts, as well as curtains, aprons, and bedspreads.[18]

The roughly 140 German and Austrian refugee farm families didn't feel welcome by the existing Jewish community in Vineland.[19] Established American-born Jews called them *Yekkes*, a derogatory reference to their reputation for fastidiousness. German refugees sensed that they embarrassed more established descendants of Vineland's original Russian Jewish settlers. "We were poor, they were well off," recalled one German Jewish refugee.[20] "It was language, it was background. Then they thought we were stuck up because we discussed . . . literature and classical music." A son of German refugees who moved to a Vineland poultry farm at the age of thirteen recalled, "We were always the poor refugees in the eyes of the Russian Jews."[21] German Jewish refugees similarly felt treated like inferiors in other communities where they settled, an inverse of the dynamic that played out a half century earlier in New York and elsewhere. Then, more established German Jews looked down on newer Eastern European arrivals as an embarrassment and a burden.[22]

Jewish American schoolchildren in Vineland's public schools shunned the Yekkes' school-age children, put off by their unusual accents and foreign clothing styles. Nearly eighty years later, American-born Renee Kreisworth still felt guilty about how she behaved when her parents encouraged her to befriend the refugee children who enrolled in her elementary school. "They weren't like we were," said Kreisworth, who was born in 1932. "Looking back, it was a terrible thing to do."[23] Sadly, after the United States entered World War II, many non-Jews in Vineland lumped the German refugees together with the Nazi regime they fled. One German Jewish refugee, who settled on a Vineland farm in 1941 at the age of twelve, recalled her family had to turn in their cameras and shortwave radio after the Japanese bombed Pearl Harbor due to fears they might be spies. She recalled her geography teacher confronting her one day and saying, "It's because of you that my son has to go to war."[24]

In the face of their neighbors' indifference or hostility, refugees in Vineland retreated inward. "They kept to themselves and we kept to ourselves," recalled Eva Neisser, who came to the United States in 1938 from Germany at age eighteen before settling with her family on a Vineland farm three years later.[25] Her father, Martin Berwin, helped found the Poultrymen's Club, a self-help and social organization that allowed them to recapture their formerly cultured lives every Saturday night. In a rented social hall above a photography studio on Landis Avenue, the refugees listened to chamber music, opera, and lectures in German by visiting philosophers over coffee and cake or würstel and potato salad.[26] German Jewish refugees tended to keep to themselves no matter where they settled, including Washington Heights, the Upper Manhattan neighborhood home to the largest enclave of refugees from Nazi Germany in the United States.[27] German Jewish refugee women similarly founded their own social clubs in farming communities in Binghamton, New York, and Farmingdale, New Jersey.[28]

Nothing prevented newcomers like Nuchim and Jack from attending the Poultrymen's Club programs, including a viewing of educational films about poultry farming two weeks after they moved to Vineland.[29] But Jack and Nuchim would have had trouble getting back and forth to downtown

Vineland on a Saturday night with no vehicle of their own yet. Even if they could, neither Nuchim nor Jack understand English well enough yet to get much out of instructional films—or feel comfortable socializing with German Jews. Jack and Nuchim, like the German Jews before them, felt like double outsiders, uncomfortable not just in the larger community, but also among fellow Jews who had settled earlier.

——•——

In the spring of 1948, the Greens and Liverants had some of their first overnight farm guests from New York. Their first visitor was Miles Lerman, the fellow survivor whom Jack had first met in Lodz before they all shared passage to the United States together. The Lermans had experienced their own share of adjustment challenges since disembarking from the *Marine Perch*. Miles's elderly aunt and uncle, who arrived in the United States decades earlier, had outdated notions about Poland and the Jews who lived there. Miles's aunt seemed amazed that he, Chris, and her younger sister Regina wore modern clothes, could operate a camera, or could speak so many languages.[30] (Miles spoke half a dozen or so, none of which included English, when they came to the United States.) Upon arriving at their apartment, his aunt showed them how to put on the lights and flush the toilet.[31] Miles, Chris, and Regina, so appreciative for their help, didn't want to tell their elderly host that the Poland she left so long ago was not the country they fled.

After a few days, a Jewish relief agency helped the Lermans find a second-floor walk-up apartment in the Crown Heights section of Brooklyn. Regina attended Thomas Jefferson High School, and Chris and Miles enrolled in night school to learn English. Miles found a job in a Brooklyn grocery store, quickly getting promoted from clerk to store manager and then ultimately to supervisor of a warehouse for olive oil and other foods imported from Italy. The job was a good one, particularly in comparison to what many other refugees landed. But Miles, who came from a family of entrepreneurs, grew restless and was eager to set out on his own rather than work for someone else.[32]

That's why a letter, probably from Jack, piqued his interest about poultry farm life. Miles must have heard good things from Jack. If a letter Bronia saved from a friend is any guide, the Greens and Liverants tended to focus on the positive in letters to friends back in New York. "We are mighty glad to know you got a nice 7 room house a nice farm," friends in Brooklyn wrote

Bronia after receiving a postcard from her. "And the main thing, that you are doing good business."

Miles and Chris considered themselves city people, but they enjoyed living in New York less after the birth of their first child, a daughter they named Jeanette.[33] They could no longer explore the city as much, and farm life suddenly seemed like an attractive alternative. Miles, perhaps with Chris along, headed down to Vineland to see for himself on a visit to the Liverants and Greens.[34] "It was springtime, and it was green, and it was beautiful, and serene and I liked it," Miles later recalled.[35] Chris was won over, too. "They were happy and they had two little girls and I had a little baby," Chris said many years later.[36] Plus, the county seemed "so beautiful, away from the city, away from the heat."[37] The Lermans started looking for a Vineland farmhouse of their own.

A photo taken on the joint Green-Liverant farm in June 1948 captured the idyllic tableau Miles observed during his visit. Dina sat on the brick steps outside the farmhouse with Dorothy and Ruth, who were just over two years old at the time, on either side of her. The two girls are dressed identically in white dresses and white shoes, just as they're dressed alike in nearly every other photo of them as toddlers on the farm. Often, the girls even have the same hairdos, their hair twirled into a bouffant with the sides flowing over their ears.

Dina and Bronia, consciously or unconsciously, had decided to raise their daughters as twins—or at least siblings—long before they arrived on the farm. Without their mothers, aunts, or any other surviving relatives to guide them, all Dina and Bronia had was each other as they tried figuring out how to be mothers in Lodz, Poland, when the girls were born. By the time they reached the displaced persons camp in the summer of 1946 in Bensheim, Germany, with their four-month-old daughters, Bronia and Dina had already started dressing Ruth and Dorothy in identical clothing.

Here on the farm, Ruth and Dorothy contracted German measles together and played with identical dolls, their only toys. Jack's aunt had given the girls the dolls with pale faces, white dresses, and bonnets. Just like their matching dolls, Ruth and Dorothy dressed the same and spent nearly all their time together. "It was nice thinking of us as siblings," Ruth said. "That meant family."

Jack and Nuchim worked side by side. Bronia and Dina jointly raised their daughters and cooked together, with a menu, not surprisingly, heavy on chicken. They baked, roasted, or fried chickens or boiled them in soup. They ate dinner together while talking about their days in Yiddish or Polish. They soon bought their first television and a pickup truck painted "G + L Poultry Farm" with the first letter of their last names. "We shared everything," Bronia said. Chris Lerman later marveled how "they existed beautifully together, they worked well together."[38]

That's not to say it was always easy. Neither couple had any private space beyond their own bedroom. But after living in an underground forest bunker, as Nuchim and Bronia had done, or surviving a concentration camp, as Jack did, a three-bedroom farmhouse didn't feel quite so cramped. More challenging were the interpersonal dynamics within and between two couples, which each had one domineering and one more passive member. Ever since they first met as schoolgirls in Lublin, Dina always talked more than Bronia and tended to seize the spotlight, as is evident in a photo taken at their elementary school. The occasion was Purim, a festive holiday that marked the Jewish people's victory over an ancient Persian villain named Haman. The two girls and all of their classmates came dressed up for the occasion as is customary, posing for a photo as clowns, kings, jesters, and one solitary Polish cowboy. An expressionless Bronia stood off to the side dressed like a dancer with a simple scarf over her head. Dina kneeled front and center in a light-colored shirt and feathers on her head. Just like in the photo, Dina tended to overshadow Bronia, a dynamic that continued on the farm. Bronia chafed silently about how Dina bossed her around, sharing some of her frustrations only much later in life when Ruth was an adult.

There was one topic about which the usually voluble Dina stayed uncharacteristically quiet. In all the time Dina and Bronia spent together in their shared household, she never once talked about the guilt she harbored about the death of her younger sister. Sheina was captured in their Lublin hiding place while Dina went out looking for food. "She never talked about her," Bronia said. "She just said she lost her." Even later, long after they'd left Vineland and talked nearly every day, the subject still never came up. Not that Bronia was particularly eager to talk about the war, either. "It was too hard," Bronia said. "Maybe I didn't want to know." Dina didn't discuss it with Dorothy, either. What little Dorothy learned about Sheina came from her father. "That was the great pain of her life," Dorothy said. "She wouldn't talk about it."[39] Only much later did Dorothy learn that Dina allegedly hired someone in postwar Lublin to kill the man she suspected of telling the

Germans about their hiding spot.[40] She felt a little better after the vigilante execution, but that didn't quell her guilt.

Bronia had to learn to live under the same roof simultaneously with both her domineering best friend and her dominant husband. Nuchim loved Bronia dearly. Still, as with Dina, it was hard at times for Bronia to get a word in edgewise. That's evident in an oral history Ruth taped with her parents a few years before Nuchim's death. On the tape, Nuchim has no qualms about cutting off Bronia, whom he refers to as "mummy," when he thought she was saying something unimportant. Quiet by nature, she deferred to Nuchim throughout the oral history interview just as she did throughout their marriage.

Jack's experience paralleled Bronia's. He was largely overshadowed in his marriage by Dina, who did most of the talking. Nuchim likewise took the lead in the coops. They had exaggerated the extent of their prior relationship in their loan application. The truth was they didn't really know each other all that well. What they had was a lot of shared experiences: growing up blocks apart in Lublin, concurrent military service, daughters born within weeks of each other, and then the journey as displaced persons to America and onto the farm. They worked well enough together, even if Jack silently brooded about being treated at times like the junior partner in the business relationship.

The tensions that result when two families live under a single roof is one of the reasons the JAS discouraged joint living. "A partnership in a farm puts not only the head but the entire family into the partnership," JAS managing director Gabriel Davidson observed in 1943.[41] "A clash of temperament is almost inevitable. Many promising farm undertakings have been wrecked because of the imponderable human elements."

No matter the difficulties, their partnership surely worked out far better than most that followed them. Some partners had no prior ties and little to bind them beyond a common desire for a farm and not enough savings for a down payment. Cultural differences could further complicate awkward living arrangements. Two Jewish families from Ukraine and Lithuania who settled together in one south Jersey farm had trouble understanding each other's Yiddish accents—or appreciating each other's recipes.[42] The ranks of Vineland's shared refugee farms produced mostly angry recriminations and hurt feelings and the occasional lawsuit, even among prewar friends or relatives. Israel Goldman, a Polish survivor, started out on a shared farm with a friend he knew before the war. "It worked out terrible," Goldman said decades later, describing his friend turned business partner as "a bad man." "What he wanted I didn't want and what I wanted he didn't want."[43]

As was usually the case, the JAS had warned Goldman not to go in with a partner, advice that he, like many other survivors, ignored. The society later lamented how these partnerships "seldom exceeded a year."[44] "Then an S.O.S. call would reach the Society's offices asking for a representative to mediate the dispute between partners," two JAS officials later wrote. "It often meant endless discussions into the wee hours of the morning, and emotional outbursts on the part of all members of the families involved before the Society's agent would finally succeed in bringing the partners to their senses and they would agree to accept a reasonable settlement."

Bernard Kolb, a German Jewish refugee who had moved to a Vineland farm in 1947 soon after arriving in the United States, shared a farmhouse with an uncle who treated him like an unpaid helper. It got so bad that, in the middle of winter, Kolb suggested to his wife and twenty-five-year-old son that they move into a neighbor's unheated chicken coop. Having survived two years in the overcrowded Theresienstadt ghetto and labor camp, "there was no way we would go along with his idea," Kolb's son later recalled.[45] The Kolbs found a small farmhouse of their own after four or five months with Kolb's uncle.

———•———

Miles couldn't tell a chicken from a turkey when he impulsively bought a Vineland poultry farm after his visit to the Greens and Liverants.[46] At least that's the way Chris remembered it. In her telling, Miles liked what he saw so much that, when his hosts mentioned a nearby property was for sale, he decided to buy it on the spot. Only then did Miles call her back in New York to say he had purchased a farm.[47] In reality, Lerman probably didn't move quite that fast. Even with a loan from Miles's uncle, they couldn't afford to purchase a farm and the JAS didn't approve his loan application until early 1949.[48] The path taken by the Lermans from city to farm would soon become a familiar one among the Grine.

6 ▸ WORD-OF-MOUTH MIGRATION

SURVIVORS DISSATISFIED WITH life in New York—or whichever city they'd initially landed in—usually heard about poultry farming by word of mouth. Perhaps a distant relative had moved there first. More often, it was a *landsman* from their hometown they'd known before the war, or as in the case of the Lermans, someone they'd met afterward in Poland or a displaced persons' camp. This single chain of migration that started with Nuchim and Jack and extended first to the Lermans ultimately connected many more survivors to poultry farming in south Jersey.

Jewish immigrants had long followed family and friends who came before them to new cities and trades. The previous settlement of a relative or acquaintance was "perhaps the most important single factor in drawing Jewish migrants to a specific community," notes historian Lee Shai Weissbach. "Early arrivals served as very good sources of information about local employment opportunities."[1] The same kinds of kinship networks also shaped the settlement patterns of non-Jewish immigrants.[2] The survivors' pattern was notable in one respect: the war had disrupted or in many cases

destroyed their social networks. That explains why they often relied on distant relatives or new acquaintances.[3]

Five members of Miles's forest partisan group also settled in the area.[4] So
did survivors with more indirect connections to the Lermans. Irving Raab
survived the war by fleeing into the Soviet Union, only to be falsely accused
of espionage afterward in Soviet-occupied Germany.[5] He was imprisoned
for three years before arriving in the United States in December 1950. He
heard about Vineland through a friend of his wife Esther's parents who had
come to New York before the war. The friend's daughter had survived Auschwitz with Chris. Raab took a bus down to Vineland where Miles picked him
up, gave a farm tour, and provided a realistic sense of what owning a farm
involved. "It was not easy," Raab recalled Lerman telling him.[6] That warning
didn't dissuade Irving and Esther, who put a deposit on a farm on West Landis Avenue in early 1951, just before their first son's birth.

Chris only vaguely knew Sol Finkelstein, an Auschwitz survivor, before
the war in Radom, Poland, where he grew up the son of a chocolate company salesman. Their sisters went to school together. Finkelstein, who found
work in New York as a Fuller Brush salesman and shipping clerk, visited the
Lermans during a trip to Vineland.[7] Sol, who was not quite fourteen years
old when the war started, viewed poultry farming as an appealing option
given his limited education. He liked the fact that farmers didn't have anyone telling them what to do. Plus, rather than dragging a baby carriage down
from their walk-up apartment on the Lower East Side, Sol and his wife
Goldie would have their own house and a yard where their kids could play.
"It looked so ideal," Finkelstein recalled.[8] In 1951, Finkelstein and his brother
Joseph bought adjacent properties just north of Vineland in Newfield,
where they operated a joint farm. Their sister Ann and her husband Norbert
Berman followed, too.

Many newcomers expected farming would be easy. "You don't do nothing. Just collect the money," one survivor remembered hearing in Detroit
before he moved to Vineland, as if chickens laid ten-dollar bills instead of
eggs.[9] "They were buying them like hotcakes." Similar rumors spread
decades earlier about prospects in the Northern California poultry community of Petaluma, located about forty miles north of San Francisco. "You lie
on the couch and you make money," Los Angeles Jews would say in
Yiddish.[10] Nothing better captured the Grines' high hopes about farming
than a song performed decades later at the annual fundraising show of

Vineland's Hebrew Women's Benevolent Society, which helped area Jewish families in need. The song, written by the daughter of German Jewish refugees, to the tune of "When You're Smiling," mocked their long-ago naivete with lyrics that included:

When you're farming,
Chicken farming,
You know you're set for life.
Self-employment
What enjoyment!
You share work with your wife.
And you know it's Nature's guaranteed way
That a hen that's fed is programmed to lay
Yes it's true dear,
Me and you, dear,
At last we'll make some hay![11]

The impossibly high expectations fueled by the Grines' word-of-mouth network exasperated officials at the Jewish Agricultural Society (JAS). Its publication, the *Jewish Farmer*, cautioned against "the tendency of many would-be farmers to rely entirely on the advice of their recently settled friends, who tell them that they know of a good farm and who assured them that the Society will make them a loan."[12] The *Jewish Farmer* advised, "We are sorry to say it, but we must point out that a farmer with a year or two of experience is not the best judge of real estate, and a prospective farmer should rely on other advice than that of his friends who have had only little more experience than he."

———•———

The number of refugees settling on south Jersey chicken farms increased substantially in 1949. A new law enacted the previous year finally eased discriminatory 1920s-era quotas limiting immigration from Eastern Europe. The "blatantly anti-Semitic" Displaced Persons Act of 1948 still strictly limited how many Jewish refugees could qualify for the new visas.[13] Most slots were reserved for refugees with farming experience or from countries annexed by the Soviet Union. To qualify, displaced persons had to have reached Germany by the end of 1945, even though most Polish Jews didn't begin to arrive until the following year. But lifting the quotas did allow for at least a modest bump in Jewish immigration, which soon led to more inquiries to the JAS. The number of refugee families settled on farms with the help of the JAS nearly doubled from seventy-five in 1948 to one hundred forty-five in 1949.[14]

Grine farmers landed far from south Jersey in 1949 and the years that followed. Some headed to the Midwest or California. Petaluma, a city of ten thousand, billed itself as the "Egg Basket of the World" early in the twentieth century and had 175 Jewish poultry farming families by 1944.[15] But the community's heyday had largely passed by the late 1940s, and only about three or four dozen displaced person families settled there.[16] More than one hundred opted for Southern California, with the largest cluster in Fontana, a new Jewish farming community about fifty miles east of Los Angeles on the southern edge of the San Gabriel Mountains.[17] Roughly two hundred refugee families settled on farms in New England, with the biggest contingent of sixty to seventy choosing Connecticut, where they helped build a new Jewish community in Danielson.[18]

Relatively few survivors settled in the two regions in the Northeast with the largest existing concentration of Jewish farmers. Approximately twelve hundred Jewish farmers lived in the communities of Lakewood, Toms River, and Farmingdale, located seventy to ninety miles northeast of Vineland.[19] Most had arrived before the war and fewer survivors followed, in part because farms there had gotten too expensive. High farm prices also explain why only about one hundred fifty displaced person families settled on farms in small towns around the Catskill Mountains north of New York City.[20] As was the case with the earlier German refugees, "the Displaced Persons, most of whom possessed limited means, had to seek low-priced farms, in or near established Jewish farm settlements," the JAS noted. "South Jersey met their requirements and they settled there in large numbers."[21]

Cheap farms made south Jersey an attractive destination. But Vineland's unusually large population of Jewish residents explains why so many of them stayed rather than joining the majority of American Jews who lived in a handful of cities or suburbs. Of American Jews, 70 to 80 percent resided in just ten metropolitan areas, with 40 to 45 percent living in and around New York City, according to a 1958 Jewish demographic study.[22] Only a "small minority" of Jews lived in communities with a population of less than a hundred thousand and even fewer in cities of under fifty thousand people.[23]

Jews still lived in small towns throughout America in the mid-twentieth century, although it's not easy to determine the exact number.[24] In his definitive account of small-town Jewish life, Weissbach included Vineland among 490 "urban places" that had between a hundred and a thousand Jewish residents in 1927.[25] He focused on these "triple-digit" communities after concluding those with less than one hundred Jewish residents couldn't necessarily support "fundamental communal institutions" and those larger than one thousand were "on the verge of becoming a midsize Jewish center."[26] Vineland, which had roughly seven hundred Jewish residents in 1927 thanks to the influx of former farm colony residents, was on the cusp of being a midsize community in 1937. At the time, it had nine hundred fifty Jewish residents.

Vineland's Jewish community was notable for its size relative to the city's overall population. For perspective's sake, the average population of a city with a Jewish population of a thousand or more in 1930 was 210,711.[27] In two-thirds of small cities of fifty thousand or less, like Vineland, Jews accounted for less than 1 percent of the population.[28] Prior waves of immigrants combined with the displaced persons meant Jews would soon account for 7 percent or more of the local population in Vineland and its surroundings.[29] Vineland particularly stands out for how its Jewish community continued to expand after World War II. Of the 490 "triple-digit" communities Weissbach studied, only twenty-one grew to become communities of more than a thousand Jews after the war.[30] Vineland is one of only seven "triple-digit" communities that had Jewish populations of two thousand or more in 1950.[31] The other six are either towns subsumed into larger metropolitan areas like Englewood, New Jersey, and Port Chester, New York, or fast-growing sunbelt destinations like West Palm Beach, Phoenix, and Tucson.[32]

Compare Vineland's burgeoning Jewish presence with the trajectory of smaller rural Jewish communities. In 1949, a native of a seacoast village of nine thousand in Maine, where about thirty-five Jewish families lived, noted that "the Jews in town no longer have the lusty and perhaps misguided enthusiasm for Jewish affairs that once led to the founding of two synagogues and two cemeteries."[33] The synagogue was "virtually unused" and the B'nai B'rith lodge was "so inactive that the charter was revoked." "The cohesiveness of the Jewish community seems to have vanished completely," the author wrote. Three years later, Rabbi Lee Levinger, who was born in

Burke, Idaho, and led his first congregation in Paducah, Kentucky, lamented the "disappearing small-town Jew" in *Commentary* magazine.[34]

In such communities, one sociologist later observed, "Jewish norms and values and concern with other Jews' opinions are not of paramount importance to their way of life; they are concerned with their neighbors' opinions, because it is with their neighbors that they associate."[35] These Jews often felt self-conscious about being Jewish, particularly when called upon to be ambassadors or representatives who could provide the "Jewish point of view."[36] A sociologist's wife recounted the burdens of being the only Jewish family living in a small, unnamed Ohio college town in a 1959 *Commentary* article. She and her husband, both Chicago natives, got asked if they'd ever been west of New York before and became accustomed to ministers calling with questions about rainfall in Israel or local teachers and community groups extending well-meaning invitations to help celebrate Hanukkah.[37]

Even during the height of the Jewish influx, Vineland remained more an Italian than a Jewish town. For every small business, attorney, or doctor with a Jewish name in the Vineland phone directory in the late 1940s or early 1950s, even more had Italian ones. Italians also dominated city hall in this era when Frank Testa succeeded Mayor John Gittone and was himself replaced by Albert Giampietro. Italian Americans owned many of the biggest garment factories and food processors and went to work in large numbers at the giant Kimble Glass factory, where the culture did little to accommodate Jewish employees. One survivor working at a local glass factory won a canned pig in the annual Easter raffle. His wife refused to let him bring the nonkosher winnings into the house, so he gave them to a next-door neighbor.[38] The Italians and Jews coexisted in peace for the most part, largely living separate lives, including on their farms. Italian families mostly preferred truck farming, which involved growing vegetables, to raising poultry. As one daughter of survivors explained, "Italians didn't do chickens and the Jews didn't do vegetables."[39]

But the critical mass of Jews in the Vineland meant they could be their own "primary reference group" even while still a minority in the larger community.[40] The closest parallel may have been the three communities in central New Jersey where most of the Jewish poultry farmers had arrived before the war. Farmers in Lakewood, Farmingdale, and Toms River enjoyed a "rich and full community life" with evenings "busy with Zionist meetings, lectures, forums, occasional art exhibits and musical recitals."[41] Farmingdale's

Jewish Community Center housed a synagogue, social hall, and school and hosted dozens of groups, including a Jewish farmers chorus.[42]

Due to the survivor surge, south Jersey, with eleven hundred farmers, soon surpassed central New Jersey and New York's Catskills as the nation's most populous Jewish agricultural area.[43] Vineland's denser concentration of Jewish residents allowed for a richer cultural and religious life. At a time when many Jewish rural communities struggled to support a single synagogue, Vineland was more akin to the "little enclaves" in Manhattan, Brooklyn, and the Bronx where survivors congregated with easy access to synagogues, bakeries, and delis "reminiscent of their homelands."[44] Having so many familiar institutions in Vineland comforted refugees trying to find their footing in what most experienced as an alien environment. That ensured far less attrition than in larger cities with smaller Jewish communities, where sociologist William Helmreich noted survivors were often "lonely and lacking in enthusiasm for their new homes."[45] By 1952, only one of seven immigrants in Montgomery, Alabama, assisted by the United Service for New Americans remained; in Savannah, Georgia, only five of twenty-six families still lived there.

But in Vineland, the numbers kept growing.

7 ▸ MIXED RECEPTION

Aspiring grine farmers often found their way to the Vineland office of I. Harry Levin, a Yiddish-speaking, forty-something-year-old country lawyer and one-man welcome wagon. Levin, the Jewish Agricultural Society's (JAS) local attorney, accompanied families on farm tours. He prepared purchase documents and hosted the closings, often looking the other way when clients couldn't afford the fee. Levin, who later became a local judge and loved nothing more than officiating weddings, was generous by nature. As the grandson and son of farmers, he also felt a deep connection to Jewish agriculture. To the Grine, his quiet acts of kindness stood out all the more because of how unwelcome most American-born Jews made them feel at first.

If deep roots foster snobbery, then Levin had more grounds than anyone to look down on these newcomers. He was as close to royalty as the original colony of Jewish agricultural settlers in Alliance ever produced. His maternal grandfather, a Russian-born lawyer, was one of two scouts who searched the New Jersey countryside for a colony site. His grandfather later named the colony in honor of the Alliance Israélite Universelle, to recognize the organizations that had aided the newcomers.[1] His mother was one of the first children born at the colony. His father moved there at age nine, a member of another of Alliance's original forty-three settler families.[2]

Levin, who was born in 1905, remembered his childhood in Alliance as something out of *Fiddler on the Roof*.[3] On Fridays, everyone rushed to finish their work and get ready for Shabbat before services began at one of the colony's four synagogues. His grandfather served as Alliance's justice of the peace for forty years, relying as much on Talmudic as on civil law for his rulings. Levin thought he'd become a rabbi but instead attended the University of Pennsylvania's business and law schools.[4] He then returned to Vineland and opened a law office on Landis Avenue. "I don't think he ever would have left this area," his daughter Marsha said.[5] "He was a country boy." Levin eventually settled in the family farmhouse in Alliance, right next to the cemetery, joking that his neighbors were great: they kept to themselves and were never any trouble.[6]

Levin could speak a half dozen languages—including Yiddish, German, and French—and taught Hebrew School on the side to help pay the rent early in his legal career.[7] He built a generalist small-town solo practice, handling tax preparation, some trusts and estate work, the occasional divorce, plus real estate and a bit of immigration. "Fortunately, there was enough of it to keep me in business," Levin said. "I didn't want to be a rich lawyer, I just wanted to do my job."[8]

Levin, like Arthur Goldhaft the poultry vaccine maker and Jacob Rubinoff the feed mill owner before him, had made it in America well beyond their immigrant forefathers. Yet his generation of Ivy League–educated Jewish professionals never felt fully accepted as Americans. They still were subjected to subtle forms of anti-Semitism, if not the cross burnings of a generation earlier. When Levin called up a favorite seafood restaurant in Atlantic City for a weekend dinner reservation, the maître d' told him they were booked as soon as he heard Levin's Jewish-sounding name.[9] A friend with a non-Jewish-sounding name then called up and secured the reservation immediately. This insecurity explains, in part, why some of Levin's contemporaries may have resented the refugees. They reminded other Americans that Jews were different at a time when American Jews just wanted to fit in.

To his credit, though, Levin did everything he could to help refugees, starting with the German Jews. At times, he acted as both real estate lawyer and press agent. In a 1948 interview, he insisted that Jewish refugees "make excellent farmers, contrary to the popular belief that Jews are at home only in trade."[10] "Their land has prospered," Levin said. "They pay off their mortgages regularly and uninterruptedly, almost without a single exception." Levin acknowledged that there had been some antagonism in the town toward refugees—some who haggled over prices and others who had clung to their prewar standing and earned reputations as being overbearing. "Now they get along fine," Levin said. "The merchants in town have benefited by their business. They pay their bills promptly, and they are hard-working and ambitious. Everybody in the family works, either on the farm or in one of the many other factories there. They become naturalized immediately. Even the older ones try to talk English all the time. You will not find any clannishness among them."

Levin was equally helpful to the postwar arrivals. His children joked he wouldn't have made any of them pay if his wife Dorothy wasn't the one who sent out the bills. In all, Levin would formally help more than one hundred Jewish refugee families including the Greens and Liverants settle on farms— and, informally, many more.[11] Why was he so generous? He felt a genuine kinship with Jewish farmers. His father still operated his own egg farm, retiring only around 1954 when he was nearly eighty years old.[12] His brother Manny, who also lived in Alliance, was a chicken and egg dealer.[13] On the wall of his office, right in the middle of the framed diplomas and awards, Levin hung the certificate from Rutgers proving he'd completed a course in egg and poultry farming.[14]

Good deeds just came naturally to Levin, who volunteered for all sorts of local civic and religious causes, whether collecting toys for poor children or serving as president of his local B'nai B'rith chapter. (His wife Dorothy was equally civic minded, serving more than a decade on their local school board.) A few years later, Levin was appointed a part-time municipal judge in his local township, where his docket included mostly assault and thefts with the occasional homicide or attempted kidnapping.[15] His favorite part of the job was officiating weddings, something he did with such frequency and such joy in the decades ahead that he became known as "the Marrying Judge." This was purely a labor of love to Levin; municipal judges couldn't charge for their matrimonial services. He usually earned no more than a wedding invitation and a free dinner. "That's why I got this," Levin told a reporter, pointing to his potbelly.[16]

Whatever his motivation, the Grine would remain deeply appreciative of his help. Many years later, one of the farmers acknowledged all he had done for the postwar refugees, most of whom had lost their parents, in a tribute with the highest possible compliment: "He was always like a father to us and he deserves a real thank you for his devotion and his generous character."[17]

———•———

For decades, conventional wisdom held that American Jews largely ignored newly arrived survivors. More recent scholarship has upended that myth of indifference. "American Jewry articulated a deep bond between itself and the survivors," historian Hasia Diner wrote in 2009.[18] American Jews donated tens of millions of dollars to meet displaced persons' material needs and publicly commemorated those lost.[19] Vineland's Jewish community certainly did its part. Synagogue sisterhood members knit and sewed layettes for babies born "to destitute Jewish mothers in Europe," and local Hadassah and B'nai B'rith chapters collected food, medicine, books, and toys for a national "supplies for overseas survivors" campaign.[20] In 1949, the Vineland Allied Jewish Appeal set a goal of raising a hundred thousand dollars—over one million dollars in 2021.[21] "The transfer of homeless Jews must be carried out at once because it's 'now or never' for many tens of thousands of them," the chairman of the local appeal said in urging members of Vineland's Jewish community to attend a 1950 fundraising event at a local country club.[22]

Some displaced persons remembered feeling welcome by Vineland's Jewish community. A few soon developed close friendships with American-born Jews. But many Grine later recalled being treated like outcasts in Vineland by the same community that gave so generously to help displaced persons abroad. At the beginning, "they looked at us as third-class citizens" at best or, at worst, "like we were criminals," recalled one Polish-born survivor.[23] Louis Goldman, a Polish Jew who moved to Vineland with his parents in 1949, the year he turned twelve, recalled, "They were cool to us, like we were invading their turf" as the trickle of survivors "became like an avalanche."[24]

At times, Grine recalled American-born Jews could be downright cruel. Goldie Finkelstein was ten years old when the war began and was so sick with dysentery and typhoid fever that she weighed only eighty pounds upon liberation at Bergen-Belsen five and a half years later.[25] Finkelstein recalled American-born Jews in Vineland telling her she must have done something wrong to wind up in a concentration camp.[26] "Why would they put you in a prison?," she recalled being asked. Referring to her husband

Sol's concentration camp number, people would say, "Only prisoners have tattoos, you know."

How to reconcile Vineland Jews' undeniable generosity toward displaced persons abroad with survivors' memories of feeling ostracized when they arrived? Diner said she's frequently asked about the same sort of disconnect in other communities where displaced persons settled.[27] She cautioned against relying too heavily on recollections shared decades after the fact in order to measure acceptance. What survivors experienced as cruelty might have been fumbling attempts by American-born Jews unsure about what to say unintentionally saying the wrong thing. Even the most well-meaning American Jews found it difficult to relate to survivors face-to-face. They had no conception of what survivors had endured or how to talk to them about it. Relief agencies like the United Service for New Americans and United Jewish Appeal probably didn't make connection any easier, with their early portrayals of survivors as traumatized, "ragged and destitute."[28]

Some survivors may have avoided American-born Jews because they felt self-conscious around them. "These feelings may reflect the insecurity of the immigrant, the awareness of coming from and belonging to a different, and perhaps less 'advanced' place," Aaron Hass, a psychology professor and son of survivors, noted in his study of survivors' psychological well-being.[29] Jay Greenblatt was a teenager in Vineland when the Grine arrived and later came to believe that these insecurities rather than the existing Jewish community's attitudes explain why they felt so alienated. "They had an inferiority complex, they felt like they were second class, and I guess that they transferred that into feeling that they were looked down upon," said Greenblatt, who returned to Vineland as an attorney.[30] "And I think they were wrong, very wrong. It's sad, it's a shame. But there wasn't a great intermingling." The problem with blaming the divide on Grine insecurities is that German Jewish refugees recalled similar treatment, regardless of when they settled in south Jersey. "American Jews didn't mix with refugee Jews," recalled Ursula Bernstein, a German Jewish refugee who arrived in Vineland after the war ended.[31] "You would think that the Jews had all come off the Mayflower, the more established Jews."

In theory, Grine might have found common ground with the German Jews, who had experienced the same humbling transition to farming and also still grieved loved ones lost during the war. Both of these waves of refugees knew how it felt to be outsiders both in the broader community and among fellow Jews in Vineland. But German Jews and Grine largely stayed separate at first. In some respects, these two refugee communities replicated the dynamic common decades earlier elsewhere in the United States, in which more established German Jews looked down on newer Eastern European arrivals. "I am sorry to say that many of us German Jews considered themselves superior to Polish Jews," said Elsa Blau, an Austrian Jewish refugee whose family's move to Vineland was chronicled by a New York newspaper in 1948.[32] "But the gas chambers did not make any distinction. The Nazis threw everything into the pot and no one asked what kind of a Jew are you." More than seven decades later, one son of German Jewish refugees who settled on a Vineland farm in the 1940s remembered hearing the message that Eastern European survivors were more hardened and less ethical than his more sophisticated and well-educated parents and their friends. His parents made clear they'd much prefer he marry a non-Jew than an Eastern European Jew. "Those prejudices were there," he said. "It was drilled in."[33]

Some German Jews resented what they perceived as the friendly reception the postwar arrivals received from the same American-born Jews in Vineland who didn't want anything to do with them a few years earlier.[34] German Jewish farmers also resented how "easy" the displaced persons had it, settling on farms at a time when egg prices were high. Refugees who arrived before the war and struggled during the Depression "figured that when we came, we should have to do the same thing," said Irving Raab, a Polish survivor.[35] "They felt, 'You have to wait your turn,'" his wife Esther recalled.[36]

The most neutral explanation is that both blocs of refugees simply felt more comfortable among their own. German Jewish refugees tended to keep to themselves no matter where they settled. The same held true among postwar arrivals in Vineland.[37] Ron Schwarz, whose family moved to a south Jersey farm in 1950, recalled his parents socialized almost entirely with fellow German Jews. "If you didn't mix with the other tribe back in Europe, you didn't mix with that tribe in Vineland," said Schwarz, who was born in 1943.[38] To Schwarz, the Yekkes and Grine were two separate tribes, with different languages and their own ways of worship. Similarly, one survivor farm wife recalled, "We spoke the same language, all of us knew in life the same thing."[39] Even when German Jews reached out to Grine, as was the case in Pittsburgh, many survivors still recalled preferring to socialize with other displaced persons.[40]

At times, non-Jews seemed more empathetic than coreligionists. Richard Flaim, who was born in 1939, had a number of survivors on his newspaper delivery route growing up in Vineland, where his father was an Italian American truck farmer. He noticed the tattoos on some of the survivors' arms and that a few always had their curtains drawn or shades closed. He was put off when he knocked and customers pulled back the curtain for a quick peek before coming to the door, as if he was untrustworthy. Flaim mentioned it to his father, who had his own firsthand encounters with survivors when he bought chicken manure directly from poultry farmers to fertilize his crops. "Rich, you have to understand, these are Jewish refugees, many of whom were in concentration camps and some of them lost all or most members of their family," Flaim recalled his father telling him.[41] "If they seem suspicious of you, please be understanding." His father's words had a lasting impact. In the 1970s, Flaim helped create one of the earliest Holocaust education classes in the country at Vineland High School.[42]

8 ▸ GETTING NOTICED

By THE FALL of 1949, the *Times Journal* began to take notice in its pages of the refugees settling in the area. In a span of a week, Vineland's daily paper published three different stories on displaced persons. The first to appear in October 1949 profiled a non-Jewish Latvian family that had come from a displaced persons camp in Germany three weeks earlier.[1] A story two days later chronicled a Russian-born, non-Jewish teenager who was attending Vineland High School after arriving in the United States six months earlier.[2] Then followed what is likely the first story on a Jewish displaced person operating a Vineland-area poultry farm, although the article makes no reference to his religion.[3] Alvin Goodman is described as a Czech-born member of the underground in Slovakia during the German occupation. His history is largely an aside in a story focused on the enormous new chicken coop he built on Landis Avenue—jokingly dubbed a "veritable poultry hotel" by the reporter—that was twice as large as the typical coop.

These first tentative reports on Vineland's recent arrivals appeared in the *Times Journal* soon after the family-owned newspaper's leadership underwent a sudden, tragic transition. In May 1949, the paper's editor and publisher, Max Leuchter, died from injuries sustained in a car accident.[4] Max, whose Austrian

Jewish immigrant parents both died by the time he was five years old, lived in an orphanage until he was thirteen. He started out as a cub reporter in Camden at twenty-one and subsequently founded a weekly newspaper, the *Vineland Times*. The paper eventually became a daily in 1927, a year after his wife Cecelia gave birth to their son, Ben. Much of the credit for the enterprise's success belongs to Cecelia, who was only the second woman lawyer in Philadelphia by day and also worked as the paper's business manager by night.[5] They later bought out the rival *Vineland Journal* and merged the two into the *Vineland Times Journal*.

Their son Ben graduated from Vineland High School in 1942 and enlisted in the Merchant Marine on his seventeenth birthday in 1943, self-conscious that his friends were already in uniform.[6] After the war, Ben enrolled at Haverford College in Pennsylvania, where he edited the student newspaper. His college yearbook described him as the school's "chief journalistic mainstay." Then, three years after Ben graduated college, Max died at the age of fifty-three when a milk truck hit his car as he traveled to Princeton to visit his younger son, Joel. Ben, who turned twenty-three in 1949, soon succeeded his father as editor; Joel later joined the paper as assistant publisher. Losing his father so suddenly was a tremendous shock to Ben; so was taking over the small-town paper his father had built. Ben did his best to fill the shoes of a father he clearly idolized. There was one subject, at least, about which Ben second-guessed his father: how their family-owned newspaper had covered the Holocaust.

Toward the end of his life, Ben wrote a largely hagiographic book honoring his father in which he noted, "No aspect of the compilation of this anthology has been more difficult for me than attempting to evaluate my father's editorial comments, or lack of them, on Nazi persecution of the Jews."[7] He said he wished "with all my heart that I could write now that Max Leuchter was an exception, that he called out to President Roosevelt to take concrete steps to end the mass murder of the Jews." Max "excoriated Hitler frequently" and "assailed the barbarism of the Fuhrer and his legions." Yet Ben couldn't find a single instance after a 1933 column in which Max Leuchter "specifically mentioned the Jews as Hitler's victims" until 1945.

Max died before Ben had the chance to ask him about his silence. Decades later, Ben emphasized that his father, who helped found Vineland's Beth Israel congregation, had a strong Jewish identity.[8] But Max also understood that 1930s America was an isolationist nation and that a "vast segment of America was anti-Semitic," Ben wrote. He also observed that Max might not have wanted to alienate potential readers in Vineland, where Italian Americans were the largest ethnic group in the newspaper's circulation area, at a time when Italy was aligned with Germany. Most of all, Ben concluded his father didn't want the families of the soldiers and sailors and airman to "blame the Jews for all this bloodshed, all this tragedy, all this fear."

As Ben assumed more responsibility, the *Times Journal* began to shed its discomfort about writing about Jews as a unique category of Nazi victims. But this early in Ben's stewardship, the paper's staff remained reluctant to draw attention to the large numbers of Jewish survivors moving into the area. Perhaps that explains how delicately the *Times Journal* approached its first story about a survivor farmer in October 1949. Goodman might have been the first Grine to settle in the Vineland area. The Jewish Agricultural Society granted his loan in September 1947, two months before the Greens and Liverants. But the *Times Journal* leaves out the fact that he's Jewish and doesn't explain why he spent three and a half years hiding in makeshift bunkers alongside his wife and young daughter, with nothing to eat for a time but rose hips.[9]

When five hundred Jewish farmers gathered for the Jewish Agricultural Society's annual south Jersey field day in August 1949, the *Jewish Farmer* noted in its story that those assembled include "those from European D.P. camps who now found themselves making a new start in the same section of the New World" as previous settlers.[10] The *Times Journal*, in contrast, made no such reference to the new refugee farmers. Similarly, the paper noted in January 1950 the "wave of unprecedented construction of poultry houses" in the Vineland area, while ignoring that many of the buyers were survivors.[11] The article scolded new arrivals for assuming farming would be easy. "Many persons, who didn't know a rooster from a hen or a White Leghorn from a Rhode Island Red, paid huge sums for poultry farms on the Vineland tract, some selling as high as $50,000. All seemed to feel they could make a fortune—and with little work."

———·———

Vineland's newspaper was the medium through which local residents learned about the new refugees in their midst. But the Grine turned to a newer form of media just beginning to arrive in American homes to gain insights into their new homeland's culture: television.

That explains, in part, why every Tuesday night at eight, the Greens and Liverants, joined often by the Lermans, squeezed onto the couch on their finished porch waiting for Milton Berle to appear on their new black-and-white television. Philadelphia's was one of the first stations broadcasting NBC network television programs, and Vineland was close enough to pick up the signal. Television sets were just beginning to shift from a novelty to a more common sight but remained an expensive purchase.[12] In 1949, D'Ippolito's on Landis Avenue sold them for $189.95, equivalent to roughly $2,100 in 2021 dollars.[13] The Greens and Liverants, confined largely to the farm and with few friends except for the Lermans, splurged together on this rare indulgence. "We didn't have any other entertainment," Bronia said.

None of them understood much of what they saw on Berle's show at first, given their limited English. "We looked at the pictures," Bronia said. You didn't need fluent English to appreciate the kind of physical comedy Uncle Miltie, as everyone soon began calling him, mastered as one of television's earliest stars. He started out in television in 1948 after a comedy career spanning movies, vaudeville and Broadway. Berle would do anything for a laugh on his television show, *Texaco Star Theater*. He'd get whacked with sacks of flour after shouting "Makeup!" or dress up like singer Carmen Miranda, his head swathed in her signature turban piled high with fruit. "It was very funny," Bronia said, smiling at the memory. Berle's comic shtick attracted as much as 80 percent of the television audience in this era of limited options. Berle claimed toilet pressure suddenly dropped nationwide at nine o'clock, when viewers all rushed at once to the bathroom at the end of his show.[14]

The six adults gathered in the farmhouse found something particularly comforting about Berle, himself a Jewish kid from Harlem born Mendel Berlinger to a struggling house painter and a department store detective.[15] Berle served as their Jewish guide to American pop culture and a reliable source of laughs. They never knew what would happen with the weather, the price of eggs, or their chickens' health, but Berle guaranteed them at least one hour of fun each week. Each episode started with a jingle that began with four men dressed as gas station attendants singing, "Oh, we're the men of Texaco, We work from Maine to Mexico . . ." and ended with

Berle's signature signoff that began, "There's just one place for me, near you. / It's like heaven for me to be near you. . . ."

Nuchim preferred the other television genre they watched when the Lermans came over: Westerns. Nobody dared to speak when they watched Westerns with fascination, marveling at the new technology that brought the moving screen inside American homes. Tales from the frontier fascinated Nuchim, whatever the medium. Louis L'Amour's Western novels still filled his bedside table decades later. Nuchim never traveled in the United States farther west than Michigan. But substitute a Polish forest for the barren American prairie or sandstone mesas of Utah's Monument Valley, and Nuchim probably saw a lot of himself in those cowboys struggling to survive in unforgiving, hostile territory.

Nuchim's favorite Westerns starred John Wayne, the most famous symbol of American individualism and courage ever manufactured by Hollywood. Nuchim could have seen all of Wayne's latest movies or the re-releases that came back to Vineland's Landis Theatre, like *Stagecoach* in June 1949 or *The Fighting Kentuckian* that November. No message would have resonated more with Nuchim after the war than Wayne's affirmation as two of the actor's biographers put it "that there was a rough justice at work, and that if good was not always rewarded, evil was always punished."[16]

———•———

A few years later, another popular television show would provide many Americans with their first exposure to "an individual's story of surviving Nazi persecution."[17] In May 1953, NBC's *This Is Your Life* devoted a thirty-minute episode to Hanna Bloch Kohner, an Auschwitz survivor from Czechoslovakia who was now living in California. Kohner was the first non-celebrity featured on the show, which plucked its surprised subjects from the studio audience and brought figures from their past onstage to help chronicle their lives. Host Ralph Edwards said Kohner, an attractive thirty-three-year-old, seemed more like a "young American girl just out of college, not at all like a survivor of Hitler's cruel purge of German Jews," a mischaracterization of the scope of Nazi victims. The six guests include a fellow concentration camp prisoner, an American soldier who helped liberate Kohner, and her brother, a doctor in Israel whom she hadn't seen in ten years. Edwards notes her parents and first husband died at Auschwitz but focuses more on how she reunited with her teenage sweetheart, Walter, whom she married after the war.

Had they watched the show, Bronia, Nuchim, and their friends might have related to Kohner's wartime losses but not necessarily to her present circumstances. Her husband Walter was a Hollywood agent working for his brother's talent agency that managed film stars like Greta Garbo and Henry Fonda.[18] She lived in a world apart from south Jersey poultry farms.

9 ▸ VICISSITUDES

THE GRINE STOOD apart in many respects from other American Jews, described by sociologist Herbert Gans in 1951 as "by and large second generation, mostly business and professional in occupation, and overwhelmingly middle class."[1] One commonality was a preference for being their own boss. While many American Jews continued to be wage earners, particularly in urban centers like New York, as a whole they were self-employed at a far higher rate than the overall population.[2]

Being an independent businessman held obvious appeal to survivors. They didn't want to be beholden to anyone after years of captivity and confinement. But few refugees had the capital needed to start their own businesses or the education required to enter a profession. Most who lived in New York or other cities took whatever low-skill, low-wage work they could find.[3] With time, many would ultimately seek out jobs that allowed them to work for themselves, whether as craftsmen or as small business owners.[4] For refugees, lacking other avenues to immediate self-employment, chicken farming held the promise, in the words of the Jewish Agricultural Society, that they "could satisfy the urge to be their own masters on their own land."[5]

But Grine farmers quickly learned that being their own boss didn't mean they had much control over their fate—or even their schedules. The workday began around six o'clock, whether they liked it or not. Someone had to make sure the water fountains hadn't frozen overnight or clogged with feathers. The chickens never seemed to stop eating, which required manually refilling their troughs. Nuchim and Jack couldn't yet afford any automatic feeders, so by the end of the day each would haul about four hundred pounds of feed, nearly a ton and a half per week, into their respective coops. They could never take a day off since the chickens needed tending seven days a week. At most, farmers could go out for an hour or two between the midday egg collection and afternoon feeding.

Each day involved a never-ending series of repetitive tasks. Farmers had to vigilantly cull the old and the sick, looking for signs that a hen had stopped laying such as shriveled and rough flesh around the vent, which is the opening where the egg gets expelled.[6] Trucks from local chicken processors or the Campbell Soup Company, based in nearby Camden, picked up the chickens that had stopped producing eggs. The farmers and their wives also spent hours more getting eggs ready for sale, often in cold, damp cellars that served as their storage and packing plant. In a process called candling, they held up each egg to an electric lamp, checking for bloody spots, discolored yolks, or air pockets, any of which would make an egg unfit for sale. If the egg passed muster, they carefully cleaned the dirt and feces off the shell with a damp cloth with no soap that might strip off the protective coating. Finally, they weighed the egg on a small scale to determine if it was fancy, large, or medium-sized before packing it into cardboard boxes the egg dealer collected for sale.

Poultry farmers—like their peers in any other field of agriculture—could do everything right and yet their fate rested largely with forces beyond their control. Faraway commodities exchanges determined egg prices, which farmers listened for on the radio or checked six afternoons a week in the *Times Journal*. As in all branches of animal husbandry, so much depended on their hens' health. Even in good years, the Grine felt as if chickens conspired against them, getting sick and laying fewer eggs as soon as prices rose. One survivor farmer in Vineland later summed up the dilemma this way: "When you got the eggs, there's no [good] price and when you got the [good] price, there's no eggs."[7] Miles and Chris Lerman had learned that raising livestock was quite different from managing a business with merchandise on the shelves as he had back in Brooklyn. "You don't know what to expect," Chris later recalled.[8] "They're susceptible to so many diseases. You can be wiped out overnight."

Either winter storms or heat waves could kill whole flocks just as quickly as disease. The remaining hens laid fewer eggs. Chickens that survived diseases and bad weather could still fall victim to thieves, fires in the coops started by malfunctioning brooding heaters, or wild dogs. In one typical attack, a pair of dogs snuck onto the range of an East Chestnut Avenue farm and managed to kill 104 chickens in less than half an hour.[9] The owner estimated he'd lost a thousand birds in three years to marauding dogs.

Many newcomers, who had hoped for a stable, quiet life, recoiled at all the uncertainty and often paltry returns. Some dropped out of the poultry business as soon as they arrived. One survivor lasted only nine weeks raising chickens before he found a job making draperies and slipcovers for the Sears, Roebuck and Co. department store on Landis Avenue.[10]

Nuchim and Bronia didn't enjoy farming any more than those who fled. "Who liked it?," Bronia said. "We got used to it. We had to make a living." Equally important was Nuchim's resolve. If the Germans couldn't defeat him, neither could a bunch of chickens. They kept muddling along, just like they did as new parents, figuring things out without much in the way of guidance.

Miles and Chris also managed to adjust to farm life. Chris came from a town more or less the same size as Vineland, so she didn't experience the worst of the culture shock. They were close enough to Philadelphia and New York that the occasional escape seemed at least theoretically possible. She came to view taking care of chickens much like taking care of children. "If you know how to handle them, it's fine," Chris said. "Otherwise, it's very difficult."[11] The hardest part might have been not having either of her sisters nearby. Chris's younger sister Regina stayed behind in New York to study at Brooklyn College when they moved to south Jersey.

Poultry farming wasn't necessarily fulfilling work. But neither were the menial jobs most survivors found initially in New York.[12] In a 1979 book, journalist Helen Epstein described how her father, a Czech-born concentration camp survivor who worked as a Manhattan garment cutter, "came home tired from the scrap-strewn factories of Seventh Avenue, irritated by the filth and rudeness of the subways."[13] These novice farmers may have started out with unrealistic ideas about easy money and being their own boss, but they had no illusions about being part of some larger agricultural movement that would cure anti-Semitism. They just wanted to make a living. Working long hours at home meant they could at least be a presence in their children's lives in a way that was much harder in a big city. Long hours also had a "therapeutic quality" for survivors, as sociologist William Helmreich wrote.[14] In the context of farming, worrying about chickens left less time to dwell on what they'd lost and how they suffered.

Somehow, those who stayed, like the Lermans and Greens, mostly managed to avoid the embarrassing missteps that became the butt of jokes among veteran poultrymen and local veterinarians. They never washed their eggs with water so warm that the eggs wound up hardboiled inside the shell. They didn't repeat the mistake of one farmer who, told to give his chickens a teaspoon of vaccine, substituted an old family heirloom spoon three times too big and poisoned his whole flock.[15] They avoided con men selling roof coatings for the coops that only made leaks worse and fended off traveling salesmen hawking living room furniture and television sets on installment.[16] "You'd be surprised how fast you can learn if you're in a jam," recalled Shirley Gottesman, a Czech-born Auschwitz survivor.[17] "We had to make a living, and take care of the children, and you just did it. We were fast learners. We had to be."

———•———

In October 1949, the Grine experienced their first dip in egg prices, which reached a four-year low for the month in a slump that continued into the winter. The situation worsened at the start of 1950, when wartime price controls finally ended. A New Deal–era law had guaranteed that farmers who grew basic commodities like wheat, corn, and rice earned a price that ensured them the same purchasing power farmers enjoyed between roughly 1910 and 1914.[18] The federal government extended these "price parity" protections during World War II to include other agricultural products, such as eggs and chickens. But legislation signed into law by President Harry Truman in October 1949 rolled back some of the protections for eggs and other products that had received price support only since the war.

The U.S. Department of Agriculture said it would prop up egg prices as of January 1, 1950, only to a level that ensured farmers had 70 to 75 percent of the purchasing power during that magical period early in the century, rather than 90 percent as had been the case since wartime.[19] That created a potential double hit for egg farmers. They would earn less on every dozen eggs they sold while paying the same amount for their biggest expense—chicken feed—since the government continued to prop up the price of wheat and corn at the higher level. Vineland farmers viewed this policy change as a serious threat. "We may not be able to meet production costs and may be forced out of business," a local poultry industry group warned in a *Times Journal* ad.[20] At a December 1949 meeting, four hundred local poultrymen unanimously urged the USDA to keep parity support levels at 90 percent, the same as grains, but federal officials rejected this request and set it at 75 percent.[21]

Poultry farmers felt the impact of loosened price supports immediately. Between mid-December 1949 and mid-January 1950, the average price of eggs fell to a seven-year low. The *Times Journal* noted that "poultrymen in this area have seen better days than the present."[22] The Greens and Liverants needed to do something to cover the growing gap between their egg revenue and feed bill. The solution they came up with was for Bronia to go to work at a local garment factory while Dina watched their daughters. "I was handy and I knew what to do," said Bronia, who learned to stitch by hand from her mother, in explaining why she was the one to go to work off the farm.

Labor-intensive farms often required both spouses' involvement, as with shops or other small businesses operated by earlier Jewish immigrants.[23] Survivors discovered, just like so many Jewish small farmers before them, that agriculture alone often couldn't support a family. Earlier in the century, farmers in Upstate New York and New England had supplemented their income by hosting boarders seeking summertime escape from city life.[24] Summer farm boardinghouses had mostly faded by the late 1940s. Increasingly prosperous Jews had more travel options, and boarding was never an option anyway on south Jersey farms, which couldn't compete with more alluring nearby beach communities as vacation destinations. Instead, one spouse often had to seek a job outside the farm while the other tended to the chickens. The need for a second income further undercut aspirations for self-employment.

Grine wives gravitated to Vineland's many garment factories, which hired workers with little prior experience. But regardless of whether they worked on the farm or elsewhere, these women still bore the brunt of domestic responsibilities, including raising the children.[25] Sharing a farm meant the Greens and Liverants had more flexibility. One of the wives could work while the other picked up more of the domestic duties and watched both girls.

That's how Bronia wound up among the two hundred fifty employees at the Crown Clothing Company factory on Paul Street founded in 1940 by Sydney Levin, a Jewish immigrant from England. His family had operated garment factories in Vineland as early as 1918.[26] Crown was one of eighteen garment factories in Vineland at the time, many sustained by military contracts to produce uniforms. The mostly female workforce at Crown stitched designs on the collar and lapels of men's sports coats for roughly thirty dollar a week. The Greens and Liverants still shared a single pickup truck, so a Crown company employee picked her up every day and dropped her off at home. She talked throughout the day with other farm wives in Polish and also had her first up-close contact with Italian women, who composed the rest of the factory's workforce. The Jewish and Italian women, whose families had immigrated a generation or two earlier, got along well, talking about food and teaching each other a few words in their native tongues.[27]

Levin was a good boss, as far as garment factory owners go. As the number of Grine seeking work increased, he'd hire women who didn't know how to sew and brought them along slowly because he knew they needed the income. Unions represented all the garment workers, and a collective bargaining agreement governed their working conditions and wages. Still, the women employed here did often mind-numbingly repetitive work in uncomfortable conditions. It was exactly the kind of work more common among survivors in New York that Grine farmers had sought to avoid. Zosia Waiman, an Auschwitz survivor who later lived around the corner from Bronia, complained all the time to her daughter about the piece work quotas and oppressive heat. "She hated every minute of it," Waiman's daughter, Helen said.[28] Bronia, as was her way, mentioned nothing negative when asked about the job she held intermittently as egg prices fluctuated.

———•———

The Grine came no closer to the action in the Korean War that began in June 1950 than the newsreels they saw during movies at the Landis Theatre. "Korea somehow seems far away, almost on another planet," the *Jewish Farmer* noted in July 1950.[29] Its editors predicted that, as during World War II, farmers might have to pay more for supplies and have trouble finding equipment. But contrary to expectations, the Korean War proved to be a boon for Vineland's poultry farmers. Survivors who lost so much in the last war stood to gain this time. Mobilizing the U.S. military and the industrial base needed to supply it put more money into workers' pockets, drove up demand for eggs, and boosted farmers' profits. By the spring of 1951, the *Jewish Farmer* noted the "sudden and dramatic" turn in the egg market in the past year. Egg prices reached all-time highs for the month of April 1951—and again in June and August.[30]

The boom benefited Vineland poultry entrepreneurs. In 1951, Arthur Goldhaft's Vineland Poultry Laboratories, which began as a two-room clinic, added ten thousand square feet of new buildings to its thirty-five-acre headquarter campus.[31] Goldhaft's son Tevis and daughter-in-law Bryna could afford to hire a Philadelphia architect to build a custom four-bedroom house completed in 1951.[32] Tevis and his brother-in-law Nathan Wernicoff had assumed more responsibility at the company as his father stepped back and became a globe-trotting elder statesman. Goldhaft often traveled for three months in the summer to Europe and Israel. Rising egg prices also gave many Grine their first taste of prosperity since before World War II. They could suddenly afford a new car or TV, a second child, or their own home. Thanks to a war seven thousand miles away, the Grine embrace of self-employment seemed to finally be paying off.

10 ▸ COMFORT ZONES

THE SPIKE IN egg prices caused by the Korean War allowed
Bronia to stop working at the garment factory. And after three years of joint
living, she and Nuchim could finally start thinking about a home of their
own. They set out to buy a new farm in a hot market. The Displaced Persons
Act of 1950 had further loosened some of the restrictions that made it hard
for Jewish refugees to enter the United States, which in turn explains why
the number of refugees the Jewish Agricultural Society (JAS) helped settle
on farms more than doubled in 1951 from the year before to 159.[1] The
increased demand drove up prices for poultry farms. Noting the "continu-
ous increase in prices paid for poultry farms by new settlers," the *Jewish
Farmer* warned prospective farmers in October 1951 to "be careful of assuming large mortgages on difficult terms."[2]

Only a few years earlier, the JAS considered Vineland an affordable
alternative to central New Jersey destinations like Lakewood and Farmingdale. Vineland and adjoining communities continued to attract a dispro-
portionate share of survivors interested in farming. But rising farm prices
prompted some to settle farther afield in sections of Cumberland, Atlantic,
and Salem counties. Buying a farmhouse farther from Vineland was no

guarantee of finding a bargain. One refugee family bought an Estell Manor farm in 1950 without a bathroom, so the family had to use an outhouse twenty feet in back of the house.[3] The kitchen faucet produced so little water they had to use a pump outside to bathe, wash clothes, or cook. Two years would pass until the family could afford a farm with indoor plumbing closer to the outskirts of Vineland.

Even experienced farmers ran into trouble buying at the market's peak. One had already lived on a farm in Mays Landing for two years when he bought five and a half acres of land in 1953 on the site of a former peach orchard on Tuckahoe Road near the Liverant-Green farmhouse. The family used up what money they had building a three and a half room house and coop and had nothing left over to buy chickens. The father had to go to work as a tailor and get credit with a feed company in order to raise his first flock of chickens raised for meat, known as broilers.

To Nuchim, taking on more debt was the price to pay to regain a bit of his prewar status. Nuchim, who turned thirty-eight in 1952, had grown up in a large, single-family home and was no doubt eager to set off on his own for the first time as an adult. His partnership with Jack, which had lasted more than four years, had been a long and successful one compared to all those that ended in rancor or litigation. The joint farm had eased their adjustment to rural life and warded off the loneliness experienced by many Grine who found farm life so isolating at first. Living together provided a cushion when egg prices fell, allowing Bronia to work at a garment factory while Dina watched their daughters. Yet that did not mean it was easy cohabitating with another family for so long. Nuchim and Jack never replicated their wives' close relationship, and both men probably looked forward to operating independently untethered to a partner.

———•———

Nuchim and Bronia found a property on Orchard Road about ten miles away from the joint farm—and just three miles south of downtown Vineland. They took possession of the farm in June 1952 from a Norwegian immigrant family, which later relocated to a dairy farm in Upstate New York. Jack and Dina probably bought out the Greens' share of the farm or at least assumed the remaining mortgage. Buying the property was just the first step. With a ten-thousand-dollar mortgage and a three-thousand-dollar second mortgage from the JAS, Nuchim set out to build their own home with the help of a local contractor. The chicken coops went up first so they could start earning money as quickly as possible. When the farmhouse wasn't ready on time, Nuchim, Bronia, and Ruth moved into a motel on Delsea Drive. Ruth started classes at the Orchard Road School, a nearby public elementary school, that fall while living in a motel room.

They eventually moved into the new ranch house with a brick façade and shingles painted a grayish turquoise. A mimosa tree stood above the long driveway that wound its way up from Orchard Road and ended on the right-hand side of the house. The coops stood on the left side of the house. Bronia later grew her own grapes on the back fence. The coop featured labor-saving amenities such as a conveyor belt to carry feed and eggs. A separate living space could house a laborer. The coops also had enough room to clean, candle, and pack the eggs. Unlike on the joint farm, none of the chicken business would be done inside their new house.

This three-bedroom farmhouse situated on eleven acres of land provided Nuchim and Bronia an amount of private space that would have been unattainable had they stayed in New York. Grine families and other members of New York's Jewish working class often lived in crowded tenements and apartment buildings in densely packed neighborhoods, as journalist Joseph Berger describes in his 2001 account of growing up the child of displaced persons. Berger recalls his family started out in a gray tenement in a "scruffy, low-rent neighborhood" on Manhattan's West Side before moving to a Bronx apartment building among "its rabble of wage earners and storekeepers."[4] They visited fellow survivors in apartments "that looked out on grimy airshafts," including one family that shared a single room filled with a double bed, dining table, and "a tiny archaic kitchenette on one wall."[5]

The sounds of city life intruded into these small apartments. "We could hear men and women screaming at each other through open windows, and dogs barking in discomfort, and babies bawling, and the whole world seemed to feel a keen irritation at the strain of holding everything together," Berger wrote.[6] Outside, they lived under the watchful gaze of neighbors gathered on stoops or in aluminum folding chairs on the edge of the sidewalk. They exchanged awkward small talk on the High Holidays in their broken English with American-born Jewish neighbors who treated them as if they carried "musty Old World baggage."[7]

The promise of more living space proved irresistible to Bernard Becker, an Auschwitz survivor living in a two-bedroom Bronx walk-up apartment with his son and wife, as well as her parents and unmarried brother. The apartment grew even more crowded on Shabbat when two other sisters-in-law and their families joined them. In Vineland, Becker could enjoy "wide open spaces" away from the crowds while still living among "his own kind," said his son Ronald, who grew up on the family's Landis Avenue poultry farm.[8]

If not for the sound of the hens, Bronia and Nuchim's new house might have had more in common with the typical homestead that drew newly affluent American-born Jews to the suburbs beginning in the late 1940s. Five years had passed since the first residents moved into new mass-produced, four-room, Cape Cod–style homes twenty-five miles east of Manhattan in a hamlet dubbed Levittown.[9] The kind of ranch-style home Bronia and Nuchim built became a symbol of post–World War II suburban life suggesting "spacious living and an easy relationship with the outdoors."[10] Bronia and Nuchim actually had a lot more space—fifty to a hundred times more—than owners of the typical suburban home, which averaged between a fifth and a tenth of an acre.[11]

It's important not to overglamorize the Grines' farmhouses, particularly older ones that lacked modern amenities—or even indoor plumbing. The expense of building a new house left Bronia and Nuchim without much extra money for furniture. Their common rooms remained mostly bare—waiting to be furnished as the vicissitudes of farm income allowed. Even those farmers able to conduct all business in their coops had no real separation between work and home given the presence of thousands of hens on their property. But having private space on their farms was itself a luxury. This aspect of farm life that some Grine raised in cities found isolating was a balm to others. Refugees who had lost their homes and had little control over their surroundings during the war now had a physical and emotional buffer that allowed them to avoid uncomfortable interactions with nonsurvivors. "To a certain extent, rural settlements were a refuge within the larger refuge of the United States," historian Françoise S. Ouzan wrote.[12]

———•———

The comfort zone extended beyond their own property line to the surrounding neighborhood. Unlike when Bronia, Nuchim, and Ruth first arrived in Vineland as some of the first survivors in the area, their new street was full of Grine by the time they moved here. Refugees occupied all but one of the half dozen or so farmhouses on their stretch of Orchard Road.

Directly across the street lived two Polish Jews, Herz Lederman and his wife Rosa, who both survived several concentration camps. They met in Germany after the war and moved to this Vineland farmhouse in 1950, a year before their only child, Leah, was born.[13] Growing up directly across the street, Leah thought it was funny that the Green family lived in a green-colored house. The Ledermans' farmhouse hid its share of secrets, such as the fact that Herz lost his first family—including a daughter—during the war. Leah didn't learn of her deceased half sister until high school.[14]

A few houses down Orchard Road in the opposite direction lived David and Sylvia Liebel, two survivors who met after the war and flew to the United States with their six-month-old daughter in 1951. A cousin who bought a south Jersey farm invited David to visit. He liked what he saw and suggested Sylvia, who had survived the war passing as a Pole while working in a Berlin factory and then a small family farm, should see it for herself. Sylvia thought she knew something about chickens, having kept a brown hen as a pet when she was eleven years old. "Poultry farming," she'd already discovered, "was very different."

Nuchim, and particularly Bronia, grew closest to their next-door neighbors, Sally and Joseph Hyman. As time went on, Bronia and Sally discovered they had much more in common than just their fair skin. Sala Putter grew up in Tarnogród, a small town seventy-five miles south of Lublin where her family operated a lumber business.[15] Only later did they learn of their shared roots in Biłgoraj, where Bronia's maternal grandfather was born and Sally's grandmother lived when she was growing up.

Biłgoraj became better known in the twentieth century as the shtetl where Isaac Bashevis Singer lived as a teenager and heard the Yiddish folk tales that inspired some of his early fiction.[16] Singer later depicted the small town as a mythical paradise where "everything was green, . . . radiant with the light of the setting sun, and aromatic."[17] "I wished I could stay there forever," he wrote dreamily.[18] Bronia's grandfather apparently disagreed since he traded a life in Singer's rural paradise for a job manufacturing glass seltzer bottles in Lublin. Biłgoraj was a small enough town that Sally and Bronia wondered if perhaps they were distant relatives.

When the Germans liquidated the town's Jews in November 1942, Sally's parents gave her and her siblings a gold watch and some money and told them to hide in a nearby forest. She and her younger sister made it to Warsaw before eventually getting caught.[19] They were sent first to Majdanek, the concentration camp on the outskirts of Lublin, and then later to Auschwitz. Her sister became ill and died after being confined to the camp's infirmary. Like Dina, Sally felt guilty about not being able to save her sister and, in her grief, hoped she'd get sent to her death too. But Sally survived two more concentration camps, working as a slave laborer at an underground munition factory before liberation. She returned to Poland to discover her parents and the two brothers she'd fled with into the forest had all been murdered; three other brothers survived.

Sally had sailed to New York in May 1946 on the *Marine Perch*, the same ship Bronia and Nuchim took eight months later. She met her future husband Joseph at a Bronx night school.[20] Joey, as everyone called him, had moved as a boy from Poland with his father to Cuba, considered a backdoor to the United States for Eastern European Jews. In Cuba, Joey learned Spanish and developed a lifelong love of baseball along with skills as a diamond cutter. Sally and Joey wed in 1949 and had a son, Arnold, the same year.[21] Three years later, they settled in Vineland, sold on the idea of a chicken farm by friends who had moved there earlier.[22]

The Hymans and Greens moved to Orchard Road within months of each other. Half a century later, Sally still vividly recalled meeting Bronia for the first time and the impression made by both her new neighbor and the new house. The Greens' house—and the kitchen in particular—stood out as modern compared to Sally's musty seventy-five-year-old farmhouse. "It was really the nicest house in our neighborhood," Sally said.

Sally filled part of the void left now that Bronia no longer saw Dina every day. No matter how nice it was to have a house of her own, Bronia missed the companionship she had with Dina in their joint home. Bronia and Sally quickly dispensed with formalities, showing up on each other's doorsteps without an invitation. They talked in Polish about the chickens' health like Jewish mothers elsewhere might discuss their children's. "We had so much in common," Sally said. "We had so much to talk about."[23] Still, they didn't socialize together much outside their homes: having already lived in Vineland for more than four years, Bronia had already established her own circle of friends.

Bronia and Sally enjoyed cooking and baking together, especially around holiday time. Both had lost the mother and sister whom they might have worked with in the kitchen under different circumstances. They jointly bought ingredients—no egg purchases necessary—and together made hundreds of meat-filled raviolis called *kreplekh* for soup, and then split up and froze the finished product. "Food was a safe subject" for Grine, noted sociologist Arlene Stein, "a reminder of pleasant times and a source of comfort."[24] Food also became a fixation for many, given how most had starved during the war. What they planned to cook for dinner was the first thing Dina and Bronia talked about during morning phone calls that remained a daily routine for the rest of their lives.

Joey and Nuchim found their own common bond in baseball, which Joey had learned to love as a teenager in Cuba. Joey taught Nuchim about the sport, igniting a passion that lasted the rest of Nuchim's life. In the days before picture-in-picture televisions, Nuchim put one TV on top of another in order to watch Yankee and Met games simultaneously after he later moved to Brooklyn. Joey and Nuchim watched baseball games together with Ruth and Arnold on television and turned the grass between their properties into a playing field.

The adjustment wasn't easy for Ruth, who was six years old when they moved to the new house and missed having Dorothy around for comfort and constant companionship. "I was lonely," Ruth said of life without Dorothy. She soon found a new best friend in another daughter of Polish survivors, Helen Waiman, who lived on a farm just around the corner. Her parents, Zosia and Jerome, had grown up in the same small town but didn't meet until after the war. Zosia survived multiple slave labor and concentration camps, including Auschwitz. Jerome survived the Vilna Ghetto, thanks to a sympathetic German officer who looked the other way as Jewish workers built a false wall inside a factory to hide during liquidations.

Unhappily working at a Philadelphia shoe factory, Jerome relocated the family to Vineland shortly before Ruth moved to Orchard Road. Zosia came from a prominent family in her small town back in Poland and viewed poultry farming as a step down from her former life. She went to work at the Crown Clothing Company factory like Bronia. And like Bronia, Zosia found her own kreplach-making partner in another survivor wife with whom she also had a friendly rivalry over who made the best flourless Passover sponge cake.

On Orchard Road and similar streets around Vineland, these survivors found a new sense of security on their own land and a measure of comfort being surrounded by neighbors who had experienced similar horrors. They moved forward together, one batch of kreplach or farmyard baseball game at a time.

11 ▸ COMMUNITY BUILDING

ALLIANCE BEACH WAS a natural spot to host the annual picnic for Jewish farmers in south Jersey in August 1950. The site along the Maurice River, a "short, lazy squiggle" that eventually emptied into the Delaware Bay, was near the original Alliance Colony.[1] Half a century earlier, the first wave of Jewish settlers in the area washed their laundry here and swam in the tea-colored river water after long days of berry picking.[2] Settlers kept returning to the spot even after they moved to Vineland. Gas rationing during World War II made going to "the river" a favorite destination.[3] The Vineland chapter of a women's Zionist group held the first of what became an annual potluck at the site that became better known as Norma Beach in July 1945. Hundreds of people enjoyed hot dogs, roast corn on the cob, and giant watermelon chunks alongside traditional Jewish favorites like kugel and brisket.[4]

The survivors' presence at the 1949 farmers' picnic merited just a brief acknowledgment in the *Jewish Farmer*—and no mention at all in the *Times Journal*.[5] That changed in 1950, as a new face joined community pillars like Tevis Goldhaft of Vineland Poultry Laboratories and Theodore Norman of the Jewish Agricultural Society (JAS) in addressing the crowd. Speaking as a representative of the newer group of settlers, Miles Lerman described how recent arrivals like himself had adjusted to their new environment. "While some of them were confronted with a certain degree of growing pains, practically all of them are on solid ground and pulling along with the oldtimers to forge ahead," the *Times Journal* said in paraphrasing Miles's remarks.[6] Miles's upbeat message was welcome by JAS officials who sought to portray refugees as well-adjusted. "With the patience and perseverance forged in the fires of concentration camps these newcomers have bravely faced the inevitable hardships of beginners, overcoming them to a marked degree," the *Jewish Farmer* noted in recounting Miles's comments.[7]

The 1950 summer picnic was a coming out for Miles and the nascent Grine community. It had grown large enough to merit representation on the speakers' platform at events as survivors made their first attempts to organize themselves. Their model was the benevolent societies or *landsmanshaftn*, which earlier Jewish immigrants had established wherever they settled in the United States. Landsmanshaftn were usually organized around a common hometown back in Europe.[8] Others were tied to occupation, such as furriers in Manhattan's garment district. These organizations had helped newcomers find jobs and places to live and assisted those who got sick or lost their jobs. In addition to offering mutual aid, the landsmanshaftn also provided a venue for socializing and a forum to recall destroyed towns and villages that existed now only in their collective memories.

Survivors in New York joined existing landsmanshaftn, although they often felt a generational gap between themselves and "old-timers" who had arrived decades earlier and tended to look down on new arrivals.[9] For the same reasons, the Poultrymen's Club, established in Vineland by German Jewish refugees, didn't appeal to the Grine. At a typical talk in November 1950, a historian lectured club members in German on the late U.S. president Franklin Delano Roosevelt.[10] "Their needs were different from our needs. They were twenty years our seniors," Chris Lerman later recalled.[11] "Their entire outlook on life was different from ours. The German element and the Polish element were of a different mentality." She paused and then added delicately, "I'm not going to say who looked down on whom." So like the German Jewish refugees, the Grine opted to establish their own organization.[12]

The inaugural event of the Jewish Farmers Social Club in March 1950 at Vineland's H. L. Reber School featured a troupe of Yiddish performers, including singer Diana Blumenfeld, whose deep alto was a siren call to a lost world.[13] Blumenfeld and her husband, Yiddish actor and director Jonas Turkow, had performed in Poland's most famous Jewish theaters before the war and headlined in underground cabarets while trapped inside the Warsaw Ghetto, until the Nazis liquidated its residents. They performed together again in newly liberated cities almost as soon as the Germans retreated and in dozens of displaced persons camps where fellow survivors sought refuge.[14] Then, after deciding just like their audiences that the future lay elsewhere, they performed wherever the remnants of European Jewry had scattered, from Milwaukee to Miami Beach and Binghamton to Buenos Aires.

The war had aged Blumenfeld, who now in her mid-forties no longer resembled the young woman in the black-and-white headshot she still used to promote her concerts. But Blumenfeld's voice remained undiminished, instantly reconnecting these farmers to the lives and loved ones they'd lost. She might have sung "Kulis" (Coolies), which drew a parallel between Chinese forced laborers and Jews who had to pull rickshaws once trams stopped running inside the Warsaw Ghetto.[15] Or she might have chosen to perform another one of her standards—"Shoyn avek der nekhtn" (Yesterday Is Gone)—in which she sings, "Have fun brothers, this is how a Jew in exile dances."[16]

The sold-out crowd gathered this Sunday night became "gripped with tense emotion" during Blumenfeld's songs and "convulsed with laughter" during another cast member's comedy routine, according to the *Jewish Farmer*.[17] An accompanying editorial described the reactions of the audience as "gratifying for the buoyancy and cheerfulness," as if the editors were surprised to discover this particular audience was still capable of joy.[18]

Miles helped organize the event billed as "an evening of Yiddish talent and laughter" and did much of the talking on the new organization's behalf.[19] He explained that members were happy to have chosen farming and had come prepared to face any hardships. But Miles said they also wanted a satisfying social life.[20]

Miles impressed the next speaker to take the stage that night. Benjamin Stone led the JAS extension department and edited its monthly magazine, the *Jewish Farmer*. Stone, fifty-eight, was born in Ukraine and came to the United States as a teenager.[21] Miles clearly stood out among the thousands of Jewish farm families Stone had helped settle in more than thirty years with the JAS. The *Jewish Farmer*'s next edition described Miles as "one of the most progressive of the recent poultry settlers in the Vineland district," praise recycled in the next JAS annual report, which singled him out as its model survivor farmer.[22] An accompanying photo showed Miles standing on his outdoor poultry range in a sleeveless T-shirt. The story notes he "has proved so adept in the business that he was invited to speak before the Society's annual poultry conference in New York City." Later that year, the *Jewish Farmer* described Miles as a "public spirited, up-and-coming South Jersey poultryman."[23]

Taking a leadership role and making connections came naturally to Miles, and he put his networking skills to use almost immediately in Vineland, quickly drawing the attention of the local Jewish establishment. He was the sole Grine to attend a September 1950 organizing meeting of the local Vineland Allied Jewish Appeal that drew local Jewish community leaders such as *Times Journal* editor Ben Leuchter, Beth Israel rabbi Benjamin Teller, and feed company owner Edward Rubinoff.[24]

These American-born Jews probably found Miles's biography as appealing as his optimism and outgoing personality. An aura of mystery and bravery surrounded the former partisans. The *Times Journal* later referred to Miles's partisan unit as an "outlaw band."[25] Not that Miles told American-born Jews he'd just met much about his wartime experiences. Miles was still self-conscious decades later about how his exploits sounded in a world that prided itself on being civilized. But he had no regrets about what he had done, including the vigilante murder of the villager who had turned a Jewish mother and daughter into the Gestapo. Asked decades later whether he slept well that night, Miles replied, "Oh yes, oh yes."[26]

The survivors' community building started off slowly. After that initial March 1950 concert, the Jewish Farmers Social Club did little until the following year when members organized one of Vineland's earliest public memorials for the "six million Jews killed in Europe by the Hitler regime," as the *Times Journal* described it.[27] In July 1951, a group of survivors helped organize a chicken collection from area poultrymen for hospitals in Israel. A picture in the *Times Journal* showed Miles alongside Nuchim, who wore a sleeveless T-shirt and pants riding high on his waist as was his style. They posed with a group of eight men surrounded by cages holding some of the fifteen hundred birds taken to Lakewood, New Jersey, to be slaughtered, frozen, and transported to Israel via refrigerated cargo ship.[28]

The episodic community organizing effort finally took off in 1953 with Miles at the helm. He was installed as president at a February 1953 meeting of the latest incarnation of the survivors' group, one they named the Vineland Area Poultry Farmers Farband.[29] The Grine may have chosen the name "Farband" simply because it is a Yiddish word for association or union. They might have also been inspired by two earlier organizations with that name. The Farband—also known as the Jewish National Workers' Alliance—was an American Jewish fraternal organization founded in the early 1900s. Chapters provided mutual aid, education, and cultural programs to members and operated schools and summer camps for their children.[30] More recently, the first survivors attempting to organize themselves in the United States had named their group the Katsetler Farband.[31] This landsmanshaft founded in 1946 in New York, which was known in English as the United Jewish Survivors of Nazi Persecution, had branches in nine other North American cities and a thousand members. It organized sports groups, a drama circle, theater visits, and events to honor those lost during the war. The Grine farmers in south Jersey were aware of the Katsetler Farband's work. The two groups worked together to bring survivors' children living in New York to the Vineland area for summer farm vacations.

As Miles's prominence in the survivors' new organization grew, Nuchim's public profile shrank. Nuchim, who'd always expected to run his family business and led his small partisan unit in the woods, now seemed to have little interest in assuming any leadership roles in the community. He'd similarly receded into the background in Lublin, where he'd helped found a new Jewish organization to represent the first survivors to emerge in newly liberated Poland. He quickly disappeared from the group, a pattern that repeated itself with the survivors' organization in Vineland. Nuchim, like many other survivors, had no desire to draw attention to himself. Years of persecution and living in hiding had made them reluctant to stand out. Nuchim, as was also the case for Bronia, attended most Farband events and served on a few committees but rarely took on leadership roles. One of the few times he appeared in a photograph in the *Times Journal* came when the male survivors later organized a Mother's Day event for their wives.[32] Nuchim, with a bowtie and a handkerchief folded in his jacket pocket, held a platter in one hand like a waiter, as he helped serve the wives off "elegant silver service" borrowed from members' homes.

————◆————

At one of its first events, the farmers' Farband in February 1953 hosted Shmerke Kaczerginski, a forty-four-year-old poet and songwriter who lost his parents in the First World War and his wife in the second.[33] This former communist youth movement member turned against communism after witnessing how the regime of Soviet premier Joseph Stalin suppressed Jewish culture and purged intellectuals. At the Jewish War Veterans Hall, Kaczerginski told the poultry farmers "intimate details" about anti-Semitism in the Soviet Union, which had only intensified after the war.[34] Soviet anti-Semitism had peaked around the time he spoke in Vineland and then began to ebb two weeks later following Stalin's sudden death, which ended his nearly three decades of rule.

Kaczerginski's anti-Soviet message undoubtedly resonated with this audience. Most Grine, whom had lived under Soviet occupation during or after the war, had no love for communism. As one child of survivors who grew up on a Lakewood, New Jersey, chicken farm later put it, the Grines' "encounters with socialism and communism before and after the war left them skeptical and bitter." They were "anticommunist, and they tended to label any leftist movement as communist, to them a curse word."[35] Nuchim, for example, never forgave the communists for his arrest in Lodz while helping run a collectivized recycling business. He landed in jail shortly before Bronia was due to give birth in 1946. Nuchim harbored an intense dislike of the Soviet Union for the rest of his life, making clear to his grandsons how glad he was that President Ronald Reagan labeled the Soviet Union the "Evil Empire."

That's contrary to the warnings from members of Congress who opposed admitting more displaced persons. In 1948, Representative Ed Lee Gossett of Texas claimed the refugees included communist subversives, criminals, and other forms of "human wreckage."[36] "There can be no doubt but many of those registered as DP's awaiting passage to America have been schooled in subversive activities, and seek entry here to serve foreign ideologies," said Gossett, who estimated half of the refugees who arrived at displaced persons camps were communists.

Survivors in Vineland and beyond had long since cast aside any radical leanings of their youth. They were focused now on rebuilding their lives and the mundane work of eking out a living on a farm.[37] Given their experiences, many feared government authority of any kind. None wanted to stick out or be labeled disloyal foreigners, particularly now at the height of the Red Scare. Senator Joseph McCarthy, the Wisconsin Republican, hunting for what he claimed were subversive infiltrators throughout government, would soon begin focusing on alleged communists in the U.S. Army.

Americans lived in fear of a surprise Soviet atomic bomb attack. Nine days after Kaczerginski's talk, Vineland had a full-scale mock air raid drill. Local civil defense officials practiced responding to a "bombing" of a two-block section of downtown centered on Landis Avenue. After fire sirens sounded for three minutes, everyone in the affected zone was instructed to act as if the area had been hit by "incendiary and explosive missiles from the sky." Shoppers were directed to flee for cover while emergency crews practiced school evacuations.[38]

Left-wing politics never attracted many Vineland residents, perhaps because the area wasn't a leading destination in the 1920s and 1930s when the bulk of Jewish farmers drawn to "radical ideologies" settled in rural communities such as Petaluma, California.[39] Albert Ronis, a Vineland-area poultry farmer and perennial Socialist Labor Party candidate in the 1950s, garnered just twelve of eleven thousand votes cast locally when he ran for U.S. Senate in 1954.[40] In Petaluma, by contrast, a sizable faction of socialists and communists clashed with Zionists and religious farmers over whether the Jewish Community Center should have a separate entrance for the synagogue. The "red hots" didn't want to walk in the same door as people going to pray.[41] Tensions peaked during the Red Scare in the 1950s when allegedly "subversive organizations" like the International Workers Order and a Jewish folk chorus that sang "Happy Birthday" to Stalin in Yiddish got banned from the community center.[42] Similarly, in Farmingdale, New Jersey, neighbor turned against neighbor in 1953 when McCarthy led a spurious investigation of subversives at the nearby Army base, Fort Monmouth. FBI agents checked in on some farmers. Survivors in Farmingdale stayed on the sidelines, uninterested in ideological warfare.[43]

Anticommunist survivors in Vineland found a kindred spirit in Ben Leuchter, editor of the *Times Journal*, an orientation inherited from his father and predecessor, Max. His father used the paper's editorial page to fight back against alleged plans by communists and fellow travelers to seize control of the Vineland Egg Auction. Under Ben, the *Times Journal* vigilantly—and sometimes hysterically—reported on signs of nearby communist infiltration.

One August 1953 headline warned "Rutgers Prof. Suspected of Red Ties May Resign."[44] For a time in the 1950s, the paper also published a column by a Rutgers economist called "Microscope on Communism."

The survivors tended to shy away from politics when they selected events for the Farband, focusing instead on education and culture. More typical was the March 1953 children's show and party hosted by the Farband to celebrate Purim. Five hundred attendees listened to the trilingual program in English, Hebrew, and Yiddish and watched Israeli and Eastern European Jewish folk dancing performances. The farmers' children dressed like kings and queens, in honor of the heroes of the story, Esther, the secretly Jewish queen who convinces King Achashverosh that Haman, his chief adviser, is a threat. Fourteen smiling children posed for a picture published in the *Times Journal* in their costumes, including Jeanette Lerman, the daughter of Miles and Chris.[45] Jeanette, like all the other girls in the photo, dressed like Esther in homemade veils, the 1950s version of Princess Jasmine in the Disney cartoon *Aladdin*. Grine must have taken particular pleasure in this fictional revenge fantasy against a plot to wipe out the Jews that ended so differently than their own recent experiences.

12 ▸ NEW CONNECTIONS

Nuchim and Bronia had good reason to celebrate as they left Ruth home with a babysitter and departed for a rare midweek night out in April 1953. Egg prices in March had reached levels unseen for the month since 1909. They were about to build a thousand-dollar addition to their coop, according to a permit they submitted to the city a few weeks earlier. Still, even in flush times, the farm alone didn't produce enough revenue to support the family. Bronia had returned to full-time work at the Crown garment factory.

They were headed this Tuesday night to a Passover dance sponsored by the Jewish Farband. This was the first of many such gatherings where, for one night, the farmers and their wives could put on their best clothes and go out on the town.[1] The venue was the White Sparrow Inn on Delsea Drive, a thirty-year-old restaurant and nightclub nicknamed the Dirty Bird by servicemen who drank and danced there during the war while stationed at a nearby Army airfield.[2] These days, the Dirty Bird had mostly gone clean, hosting Chamber of Commerce lunches, wedding receptions, synagogue sisterhood shows, and Fred Astaire dance nights.

Nuchim and Bronia arrived at the White Sparrow Inn wearing their finest clothes, not that they had many to choose from: Nuchim owned only one suit. Bronia, who might have felt worn out after a full day at the garment factory, had to bundle up this early spring night with temperatures just above freezing even as a nearby town prepared to celebrate its blooming peach blossoms.

Even if it wasn't the last night of Passover, they almost certainly would have skipped dinner in the dining room downstairs, where they could order lobster or Chinese food prepared by chef Harry Wong. Nuchim and Bronia still couldn't afford to eat out. They climbed the steps upstairs to the catering hall, which doubled as a ballroom, and paid the admission fee, the proceeds helping buy an incubator for an Israeli agricultural school.[3] Bina Landau, a twenty-seven-year-old soprano and concentration camp survivor whose father operated a Vineland poultry farm, serenaded the crowd of three hundred farmers and wives with Yiddish folk songs. Then the band took over, transporting Nuchim and Bronia back in time to before the war when they first met as teenagers at a high school dance.

Nuchim and Bronia, who had turned thirty-nine and thirty-five, respectively, a couple of weeks earlier, were now more than twice the age as when they first saw each other at that Saturday night dance in the gym of their Lublin high school in 1932.

The setting might have also reminded the Lermans of the Lodz nightclub called Little Hell opened by Miles where he fell in love at first sight with Chris. They wound up dancing much of the night. Friends who'd been in the camp together told her not to marry Miles. He was too slick, they said. Her sisters split at first on his merits as a potential husband, but Regina ultimately came around.[4] Chris wore a blue dress to their wedding ceremony, where the Polish army's chief rabbi, who taught Miles Hebrew literature in Lvov before the war, officiated.

Even after all they'd been through, Bronia and Nuchim remained an attractive pair and danced just as well as when they were teenagers. When the evening's ballroom dancing competition started, they took to the floor. Other farm wives, themselves briefly recapturing their cosmopolitan prewar lives, might have turned and watched as Bronia, who usually hated to be the focus of attention, began dancing the Rumba. She moved side-to-side with Nuchim, their torsos erect in a series of two quick side steps and a slow forward step. They must have learned this Afro-Cuban ballroom dance back in Lublin before the war. They still performed it well enough this night to win the Rumba contest.

Three weeks later, in a courthouse in Bridgeton, the county seat located thirteen miles from Vineland, Nuchim and Bronia joined fifty-one other people, mostly from Germany and Poland, plus a smattering of other European countries, who became U.S. citizens.[5] David Horuvitz, a single-term Cumberland County judge, swore them in during an "impressive" ceremony inside one of two courtrooms in the clocktower-topped county courthouse. Horuvitz grew up in Bridgeton and would spend his whole career in south Jersey, ultimately buried in Alliance Cemetery right alongside survivors like these new citizens. If a ceremony Horuvitz conducted a few months earlier is any indication, he began by explaining the obligations of citizenship and warned that two criminal convictions could send them back from where they came. The county clerk then administered the formal oath of allegiance. This was a particularly proud moment for Nuchim, who had quickly fallen in love with the country that had offered refuge to him and his family.

——•——

In hindsight, the spring of 1953 that brought both the Rumba crown and American citizenship proved to be the highwater mark of prosperity for Bronia, Nuchim, and the community of survivor poultry farmers as a whole. No one knew the trouble to come at a time when egg prices—and the ranks of refugee farmers in the area—kept rising.

Roughly one thousand survivors had settled on south Jersey farms, an influx large enough that the JAS had opened an office in Vineland a few months earlier.[6] Local farm groups and community leaders urged the organization to provide more help to new arrivals "badly in need of instruction."[7] The volume of survivors seeking farms strained the resources of the Jewish Agricultural Society (JAS), which relied on growing subsidies and loans from the Baron de Hirsch Fund. In private, the JAS board of directors frequently debated whether to be more selective about who received loans. The *Jewish Farmer* "regretfully" reported in August 1953 that the JAS "will be unable to make loans except in cases of the direst emergencies" since "so much has been paid out in loans up till now, that the available loan funds are almost exhausted."[8] Nevertheless, the JAS still approved 90 percent of the one hundred loan applications submitted to its Vineland office in 1953.[9]

As the survivor community grew, their newly renamed Jewish Poultry Farmers Association of South Jersey (JPFA) began frenetically organizing activities.[10] In the months ahead, the JPFA would host modern dance performances and Yiddish folk concerts, as well as lectures on fowl cholera and the future of Jewish literature. The JPFA also hosted Tuesday night chess matches, an annual gala dance, and a New Year's Eve Ball at Vineland's National Guard armory complete with cocktails, a six-piece orchestra, and a turkey dinner. Events geared toward children included Hanukkah parties and a "Swedish gymnastics" class.[11] The JPFA established an arbitration committee that handled disputes between farmers when partnerships soured.[12] A mutual aid society funded by member purchases of five thousand dollars in bonds offered short-term, interest-free loans to farmers suffering temporary hardships.[13]

At the moment though, most survivors were doing well enough that they set up a summer program to host the children of urban Jewish survivors for a few weeks of country living in July 1953. The JPFA purposely created a separate program from the local Exchange Club, which brought underprivileged New York kids to Vineland under the auspices of the Fresh Air Fund. As Miles explained, many JPFA members didn't speak English fluently, and "their customs and language difficulties would make it awkward for them to serve as hosts" to children processed by the Fresh Air program.[14] Instead, they'd opted to partner with the Katsetler Farband, the survivor organization known in English as United Jewish Survivors of Nazi Persecution.[15] Miles explained that it made sense to host children with "the same speech difficulties and the same customs and dietary habits." "They need to be able to converse freely and easily if their visit to the 'country' is to be a success and we feel that the members of our association are the ideal group to help these children understand and appreciate rural life in America," Miles said.

Fifty-four children, many wearing Brooklyn Dodgers caps, exited two buses in Landis Park in July 1953 for two-week stays with their host families. The visitors included a ten-year-old boy who said that Vineland reminded him of Lund, Sweden, where he'd stayed for three and a half years after stops in Russia, Poland, and Germany. He matter-of-factly recounted his travails in a German prison camp and his liberation by American soldiers. The boy said he was very happy in Vineland and that his host family's cooking was "just like mother's."[16] A local feed merchant anonymously underwrote a picnic at Palatine Lake. Vineland Poultry Laboratories hosted a going-away party where a former Vienna opera baritone sang and all the kids received souvenirs.

A survivor named Musia Deiches organized many of the events for the visiting children along with much else of the JPFA's busy agenda. This former child dance prodigy born in Poland in 1921 stood out in her perfectly coiffed wavy hair and stylish dresses as the only woman in the group's male-dominated leadership. Deiches, who told her children she was born with the soul of a dancer, performed on the Warsaw stage by age six and starred in a Polish film at age eight.[17] She studied piano as a teenager at a Paris conservatory and ballet under a renowned Russian prima ballerina.[18] By the age of fifteen, she was choreographing operas in her native Vilna.

Confined to the Vilna Ghetto during the war, Deiches organized dramas, literary reviews, and dances before ending up in a concentration camp near Riga, Latvia. She lost her whole family—including a brother, two sisters, and the husband she had married months earlier.[19] She also lost her ability to dance due to wartime injuries. After the war, she married an old friend named Arnold who had lost his successful prewar hardware business and was as quiet as Deiches was outgoing.

They lived in Brooklyn for ten months before moving to Vineland in 1950 with their twins, Ruth and Harry, who turned four that year. They went into business with the family of another Vilna Ghetto survivor, Mira Swerdlin, who remembered seeing Deiches perform back in Europe as a child.[20] All Deiches had from her life as a child star were a handful of photos friends had given her after the war plus a program from one of her performances someone mailed her from Chicago.[21]

The Deiches and Swerdlin families amicably concluded that a single farm couldn't support all of them. But Musia and Mira remained close friends, connected by shared big-city roots and a love for the arts. Mira often accompanied on piano as Deiches channeled all her thwarted artistic ambition into her role as the JPFA's cultural chair. Deiches's own performances were limited to "dramatic monologues" in Yiddish at community memorials and JPFA events. Behind the scenes, though, she choreographed children's dance recitals and organized both a Purim show and a tribute to the Warsaw Ghetto uprising that spring. Deiches was a uniquely glamorous presence, particularly by the standards of Vineland. "She was so charming, funny, flirtatious, vibrant," recalled Mira's son, Ely Swerdlin.[22] "She always had jokes and stories and she was kind, such a kind heart." Afraid that anyone might accuse her of favoritism, Deiches always gave her daughter the worst parts in JPFA shows.

Deiches's efforts and unusual backstory attracted notice in the *Times Journal*, which published a profile of her in July 1953.[23] This being the 1950s, when a woman's appearance still seemed to matter above all, the story began by calling her "an attractive blonde with the pretty name" and went on to note her "lovely, graceful hands" and "large dramatic brown eyes." The profile of Deiches is one of the newspaper's first to describe a survivor's story in rich and often painful detail. The story recounted the "cruel head beatings" Deiches endured in a Nazi prison camp left her with "excruciating" migraine headaches. But the article focuses largely on the positive. "Now, the 'thousand years' in camp behind her, Musia Deiches is busy with plans for the happier present and future." A "huge bouquet of white gladioli" displayed on a vase on the television set along with "other beautiful gifts," marked her eighth wedding anniversary. In the accompanying photo, she is showing a picture from her days as a child ballerina to her twins, who were now seven years old.

Deiches seemed at peace about how her life had turned out. "She prefers things as they are now," the *Times Journal* said. "She and her family are very well adjusted and happy." Then Deiches says in conclusion, "When I was little I was big, now that I'm big I am little." In truth, Deiches struggled with her diminished, small-town life. While Deiches made great efforts to appear happy and composed in front of others, at home her daughter Ruth would hear her crying in the middle of the night.[24] Deiches never liked rural living and felt guilty about surviving when the rest of her family perished. She cycled in and out of the hospital with the terrible migraines alluded to in the profile.

The story about Deiches is just one of many about survivors that the *Times Journal* published in July 1953. Four days earlier, a story about a new poultry farmer and his wife noted had both survived concentration camps.[25] The next day, an article about Vineland residents becoming citizens noted, "Mrs. Rosalie C. Lerman . . . was in a Nazi concentration camp for three-and-a-half years."[26] Similarly, a story that month about two New York City children staying with JPFA families described them as survivors of a "prison camp in Germany."[27]

Since the first tentative stories in the fall of 1950, the *Times Journal* had slowly begun incorporating more explicit references to survivors' wartime experiences. A September 1951 story about a new synagogue in nearby Dorothy noted that "most of the members have arrived here within the last two years and are escapees of Nazi prison camps."[28] A March 1952 story about a fire that destroyed a newly constructed poultry house said it added "to the hard luck" experienced by the husband and wife. "Both were in a Nazi concentration camp for six years during World War II and when they came to New York, [his] health was so undermined that he was unable to continue his trade as a plumber." But the frequency of references accelerated in the summer of 1953.

In many respects, the *Times Journal* was ahead of more prominent media outlets in reporting on this trend. In June 1953, a *New York Times* story cited the JAS annual report in observing that "since the end of World War II there has been a large increase in the number of Jews on farms in the United States in contrast to the decline in farm population generally."[29] The story describes Vineland as "the center of an area containing 1,000 Jewish farm families, the majority of whom," the *Times* obliquely noted, "are newly arrived in the United States and newly settled." Another three years would pass before the *Times* more explicitly identified these new farmers as "victims of the Nazis" in an editorial on the JAS annual report.[30]

Why suddenly did the *Times Journal* start covering survivors so much more openly? In part, it's because there were more of them. The presence of so many survivors gave them "purchasing power, selling power, and voting power so that the community took note of us and of our activities," as Sol Finkelstein, who succeeded Miles Lerman as JPFA president, later observed.[31] Vineland's merchants came to recognize survivors as a distinct category of customers as evidenced by a local Purina feed dealer's ad that later ran in the *Times Journal*.[32] The ad features a product testimonial from Rubin Ausenberg that says, "Like many of his former countrymen, Mr. Ausenberg faced death many times during the Second World War. In the five years he was in a concentration camp, he was twice scheduled for the 'crematorium'—but escaped." The ad describes his trajectory from postwar Munich to raising twenty-five hundred chickens in Vineland before getting to the product pitch. "Purina helps us to raise good pullets and get good production throughout the year," says Ausenberg, who is pictured standing with baskets full of eggs. In Vineland's newspaper, being a Holocaust survivor was not a source of "stigma and shame" as was the case elsewhere: here, it had become marketing fodder.[33]

Pragmatism aside, the *Times Journal* stands out for its willingness to write about survivors vividly and humanely. Much of the credit goes to Ben Leuchter, who, by 1953, had found his voice as a small-town editor and front-page columnist. He was increasingly comfortable writing about Jewish Nazi victims in a way his father Max never was. Leuchter was a good listener by nature and profession, and he took seriously the role of editor that was thrust upon him far earlier than intended. Vineland residents—Jewish and non-Jewish, survivor and nonsurvivor—remembered his acts of kindness, large and small. If there was a function at his synagogue, Beth Israel, where new-comers stood off to the side, Ben was the one to go up to them and make them feel welcome. On Sunday nights, he chaperoned the synagogue's youth group, sitting in the corner writing editorials while the teens talked or danced.[34]

One survivor's son, Saul Golubcow, remembered dutifully reading the *Times Journal*, which, as an afternoon paper, arrived around the same time he got home from school. Saul thought the letters to the editor were an invitation to write the editor with questions of any kind.[35] Having just learned about the relationship between Congress and the president and fascinated by the concept of a veto, Golubcow mailed a handwritten letter to Leuchter asking the last time a veto had been overridden by Congress. This was long before the Internet would have provided the answer instantly. Leuchter took the time to type up a detailed reply about veto overrides through the Eisenhower administration. Leuchter encouraged Golubcow to write anytime—the start of a correspondence that would continue through high school. When Golubcow read Harper Lee's 1960 novel *To Kill a Mocking-bird*, Leuchter came to mind when he tried to picture Atticus Finch, the gentlemanly small-town southern lawyer who defends a Black man falsely accused of rape.

Ben displayed an early and unusual sensitivity to how survivors might perceive local events in Vineland. When crosses were burned on the lawns of two Jewish refugee families in January 1951, local police accepted explanations that at least one of the two incidents was a joke. Four local men, who ranged in age from nineteen to twenty-five, told police they had no idea who lived at the house and were just having "a little fun" after a night of ice skating.[36] Leuchter took a different view of the alleged prank in his daily column. "However playful the intent may have been," he wrote, "it must be regarded more than coincidental that the victims in both tactics were natu-ralized Americans of the Jewish faith to whom this country was a place of refuge from the extremes of Nazism," Leuchter wrote. "To dismiss these incidents blandly is to ignore historical realities."[37] He was even more forceful in his condemnation a few years later when vandals painted a swastika on the local Kingdom Hall of Jehovah's Witnesses. "The emblem's appearance was particularly cruel in this community, which has become a haven for the survivors of the barbarous butchery of some seven million human beings in Europe between 1937 and 1945," Leuchter wrote in his column. "It was a savage re-opener of emotional wounds, inflicting unnecessary hurt on innocent fellow men."[38]

Ben's wife, Magda, deserves much of the credit for Leuchter's heightened sensitivity. Magda, who grew up on the Jersey Shore steps from the Atlantic Ocean, was nineteen when they met on a blind date on Christmas Eve in 1947.[39] They married in August 1950, a year after she graduated from the University of Wisconsin. Magda, rather than Ben, connected with individual survivors first. She related to survivors more viscerally. It was mere luck, Magda told friends, that her mother had emigrated as a child from Hungary while family members remained behind in Europe. Magda got angry when Vineland's American-born Jews referred to survivors derisively as "Refs"—a dismissive shorthand for refugees.[40] She thought the American-born Jews in Vineland, many of whom came from working- or lower-working-class families and were trying to breach the upper middle class, feared the Grine might undermine their social standing. Leuchter, whose grandparents had emigrated from Austria but died when his father was a young boy, didn't feel the same direct emotional ties. "My mother educated my father," their daughter Janet said. "And my father was in a position to raise the consciousness of the rest of the community."

No American Jew in Vineland with the exception of attorney Harry Levin proved to be a better friend and ally to survivors than Ben Leuchter. And unlike Levin, born in 1905, who was a decade or more older than most of the Grine, Leuchter, born in 1926, was roughly their age. That made it easier for Ben and Magda to become a bridge to the survivor community. The Leuchters became one of the first and the most prominent members of Vineland's American Jewish community to reach out to the Grine person-to-person, starting with the Lermans. Miles recalled still feeling lost and a bit like strangers in town with a limited command of English when Ben and Magda were the first American-born Jews to invite him and Chris to their home.[41]

Magda and Chris initially found common ground with survivors over concerns about the fledgling Jewish state of Israel. At one early Hadassah gathering, a Grine teased Magda about whether she knew any Zionist folk songs. She began singing one and instantly established her credibility with everyone in the room.[42] Magda, like her mother, was a committed Zionist, who led a University of Wisconsin campus fundraising drive to help displaced persons settle in Israel.[43] As a young bride in Vineland, she joined the local chapter of Hadassah, the women's Zionist organization, along with survivors like Chris Lerman. As was the case with Magda, Chris's mother identified strongly as a Zionist, helping establish a local chapter of the Women's International Zionist Organization in their hometown in Poland.[44] Chris had joined the Zionist youth group back in Poland as soon as she was old enough.

The Zionist cause had similarly unified south Jersey Jews for decades.[45] "We saw it bringing the whole community together, the synagogue Jews and the non-synagogue Jews, the old-timers, and the German refugees and the Polish refugees," Arthur Goldhaft, the Vineland Poultry Laboratories founder, later observed.[46] In addition to Hadassah, Vineland was home in the 1950s to local chapters of Pioneer Women, Poale Zion, the Zionist Organization of America, and Mizrachi, a religious Zionist organization. A half-hour *Voice of Israel* radio show that aired on local WWBZ every Sunday morning since 1947. (A separate Yiddish radio show called *A Gut Vokh* [A Good Week] created by a survivor later aired on local WDVL for several years as well.) Vineland's mayors, like their big-city counterparts, had long recognized that identifying with Zionism was smart politics.

Two days after Israel declared its independence in May 1948, Vineland mayor John Gittone joined the standing-room-only crowd attending a celebratory rally at the H. L. Reber School. A color guard from Post 601 of the Jewish War Veterans of the United States of America presented arms. Then came the singing of both "The Star-Spangled Banner" and "Hatikvah," the Israeli national anthem and a reading of the Israeli Declaration of Independence. A local American-born Jewish attorney noted the "amazing rehabilitation" of Palestine's "barren land accomplished by Jewish pioneers in the face of taunts that Jews could not till the soil," a theme that undoubtedly resonated among Vineland's Jewish farmers.[47] Even Gittone, the Italian American mayor, got caught up in the moment. He declared that "every fighting person in the sovereign state of Israel is a Patrick Henry," invoking

the American Founding Father most famous for the phrase "Give me liberty, or give me death!"

Five months later, the local Poale Zion chapter displayed a mounted
tractor purchased as a gift for an agricultural community in Israel in the
annual Halloween parade on Landis Avenue.[48] It was just the first of many
times that Vineland's Zionists connected with Israel through agriculture. At
a 1950 appearance in Vineland, Levi Eshkol, a future Israeli prime minister,
noted the similarities between Israel's agricultural settlements and the colonies established around Vineland decades earlier.[49] The *Jewish Farmer's*
editor called Vineland "the Jerusalem of Jewish farming in the United
States," at an event there a few years later.[50]

Vineland became a natural training ground for novice American Jewish
farmers intent on settling in Israel. In 1949, a Zionist organization called
HeHalutz (The Pioneer) bought a dilapidated twenty-acre Vineland farm
as a training site for prospective Israeli settlers.[51] Its first mixed-sex class of
sixteen students who were mostly in their twenties and early thirties included
a physician, dentist, and a bookstore manager. The trainees repaired the farm's
buildings and grounds and lived in the eight-room farmhouse. They helped
out on Jewish-owned chicken farms and learned repair work at local garages.
The Sons of Jacob synagogue hosted a gala send-off in May 1950 attended by
two hundred people including Mayor Gittone where organizers thanked local
Vineland residents for donating money and helping train the students.[52]
After six weeks of Hebrew language instruction in New York, they set sail
for Israel in May 1950.[53] Subsequent classes continued to train at the site
through at least 1952 with less fanfare.

In 1950, some Vineland residents founded a separate group designed to
encourage resettlement in Israeli agricultural communities. A handful of
families—including at least two American-born chicken farmers—did
make *aliyah*, the term for immigration to Israel by diaspora Jews, in the early
1950s. They joined a new agricultural settlement named Orot in southern
Israel designed especially for middle-class American families and settlers
from other English-speaking countries.[54] Orot was a *moshav*, an alternative
to the *kibbutz*, the better known and more intensely egalitarian form of collective Israeli farm settlement. Farmland on *moshavim* were distributed
in equal measure rather than being operated collectively as on a kibbutz.
Nuclear families remained intact unlike on a kibbutz where children were
raised collectively. At the time Israel became a state its sixty or so moshavim

accounted for one-third of collective agricultural settlements.[55] The number of moshavim grew in the late 1940s and early 1950s, thanks to an influx of Eastern European survivors. When vegetable prices fell in the mid-1950s, some moshav farmers turned to raising chickens.[56] Each family that settled in Orot was allotted a well-stocked chicken coop along with five acres of land to grow vegetables, cotton, and fruit trees as well as a cow and a barn.[57]

Unlike the "young idealistic Zionists" who settled in Petaluma, California, two decades earlier, few, if any, Grine in Vineland viewed poultry farming as a springboard to a new life in Israel.[58] Events had already forced them to abandon earlier dreams of settling in Palestine. Bronia and Nuchim had considered immigrating to Palestine after leaving Poland but concluded it wasn't realistic at a time when she was pregnant. If not for the quirks of fate, Miles would probably have moved to Palestine before the war. As a teenager, he studied at a Hebrew junior college intent on following his older brother, Jona, who had already immigrated there.[59] Instead, after his father died of a stroke, he found himself back in the small town where he grew up in 1938 at the age of eighteen. The Lermans had hoped to go to Palestine while considering their future in a displaced persons camp. But Chris found the prospect of getting detained in Cyprus particularly unappealing given her wartime experiences. "We didn't need another prison," Miles said in explaining why they chose the United States instead.[60]

Much distinguished the survivors' individually owned farms from the moshavim in terms of ideological motivations, financials, and how land was allotted. But there are also similarities in terms of basic structure and the extent to which farmers acted cooperatively in the first years after settlement on the land, according to Hebrew University of Jerusalem historian Jonathan Dekel-Chen, who studies Jewish agricultural movements.[61] Grine felt a special camaraderie and emotional connection to Israeli farmers as they embarked on a common endeavor thousands of miles apart. "We were pioneers," said Chris Lerman in an interview decades later in which she compared the survivors' farms to a moshav.[62] The survivors looked for ways to support Israeli farmers from afar. The Grine joined the existing Zionist organizations and the JPFA also hosted Israeli-themed activities, including a three-day screening of an Israeli film at the Grand Theatre in June 1956.[63] That summer, children of JPFA members founded a new youth Zionist group and the organization sponsored a survivor's daughter's two-month stay in an Israeli village, a project designed "to strengthen the ties between the Vineland and Israeli farm youth."[64]

Miles often shared the stage with Ben Leuchter during Vineland events supporting Israel. At a February 1956 "Rally for Israel," Leuchter introduced the speakers, including Miles, who spoke to the crowd in Yiddish.[65] Two decades later, when Lerman was recognized at a dinner for his work on behalf of the local Israel Bond campaign, Leuchter gave the speech honoring him. "Thanks to giants such as Miles Lerman, the Jewish people rose from the ashes of history and took their rightful place in the family of nations," Leuchter said.[66] As with their wives, Miles and Leuchter grew close. Leuchter occasionally wrote about Miles in his column without any disclaimers about their friendship, a potentially unavoidable conflict of interest for small-town newspaper editors. When Miles left behind poultry farming a few years later and became a small business owner, their friendship took on yet another dimension as he became a small but frequent advertiser in Leuchter's newspaper.

Their "mixed" social circle grew to include both American-born Jews as well as survivors like Sol and Joseph Finkelstein, the poultry farming brothers who knew Chris before the war in Poland. Goldie Finkelstein remembered the Leuchters as "good friends" who might have viewed survivors as a "novelty" at first.[67] Likewise, Chris must have had Ben and Magda in mind when she told an interviewer in 1990, "People wanted to know more about us, reached out to us, and they became part of our immediate crowd and we became part of their immediate crowd and this is how we blended into the community."[68]

The Lermans and their friends remained outliers among survivors, in their eagerness to engage beyond their own community. The Lermans joined Beth Israel synagogue in 1953 at a time when most survivors preferred to pray with other Grine. Even as the Lermans still kept one foot firmly planted in the Grines' world, some survivors resented how the Lermans and their friends branched out. In this insular community, reaching out beyond their own could be perceived as an act of disloyalty or a sign someone thought themselves better than fellow survivors.

Miles and Chris occasionally escaped Vineland altogether. Two or three times a year, they took overnight driving trips to New York City. After finishing a full day's work on the farm, they'd leave the kids behind with a babysitter. Miles and Chris, who inherited a taste for high culture from her German-speaking father, then drove to New York, arriving just in time for the start of operas including *Porgy and Bess* and *Madama Butterfly*.

After the show, Miles and Chris drove drive as far back as Bordentown, New Jersey, and stopped at two o'clock in the morning for breakfast at a diner. They then finished the drive home, changed into their work clothes, and fed the chickens before going to sleep until eight o'clock. Chris did not have regrets about leaving New York behind for Vineland. "I loved it here. It was so easy to raise a family. It was just so peaceful and wonderful," Chris said later. "We didn't mind the hard work and we didn't mind all the struggles, all the hurdles that we had to overcome because life was simple." Asked if these whirlwind trips to New York were worth it, Chris replied, "You couldn't just live on the farm and be with the chickens all the time."[69]

13 ▸ FAMILY AND FRIENDS

RUTH WAS SIX or seven years old when Bronia began forcing her to write letters to a great uncle in Israel she'd never met. Under different circumstances, Ruth should have had five uncles and aunts, the youngest of which, Bronia's younger brother Monik, would still have been in his twenties in the early 1950s. Instead, Bronia's uncle Abraham Zylberlicht, who was her mother's brother, was the closest living relative she had left. Bronia did everything she could to build a connection with someone who otherwise would have been just a distant relation.

Bronia kept the postcards, photos, and letters Zylberlicht sent from Israel, where he moved after the war. One postcard with the Western Wall on the front wished the family a happy Jewish New Year in 1947, when Israel wasn't yet a state. Zylberlicht lost his wife, twelve-year-old son, and nine-year-old daughter during the war. In Israel he remarried, though he never forgot about the family that perished. He submitted records about all of the murdered Zylberlichts, including Bronia's mother, to Yad Vashem in November 1955, two years after its founding as Israel's official memorial to Holocaust victims.

Zylberlicht made a visit or two to the farm, during which Bronia and her neighbor Sally Hyman learned of their common roots in Biłgoraj. In a photo taken during one such visit, Zylberlicht stands stiffly and looks ill at ease in a coat, a tie, and baggy slacks. He later helped pay for Bronia's first trip to Israel in the early 1960s. Overall, though, the relationship proved a disappointment to Bronia, who idealized her uncle. Zylberlicht's new wife in Israel discouraged too deep a connection, perhaps concerned about what Bronia might inherit. Ultimately, Bronia got nothing when he died in the 1970s, although all she really wanted was a family connection for herself and Ruth.

Over and over again, Bronia and Nuchim would be disappointed by family. That was common among survivors, who discovered the difficulty of creating close bonds with distant relatives. At best, relatives were an exotic and fleeting presence in their lives, like Nuchim's cousin from New York who once visited Vineland and took them to Atlantic City for a daytrip. They walked on the Boardwalk, and the cousin treated them to dinner at a nice restaurant where Bronia ordered lobster for the first time in her life. It was, as far as Bronia could recall, the first and last time that cousin ever visited them.

One daughter of Grine recalled relatives from Philadelphia occasionally visiting her family's Vineland farm to pick up eggs and have a home-cooked meal. But they didn't reciprocate or introduce them to anybody when her family later moved to Philadelphia. She sensed her family embarrassed her relatives. "American Jews wanted to be accepted. You wanted to look like everyone else and talk like everyone else," she said.[1] "Having foreign relatives who didn't fit that mold and might make you look different and not as accepted."

Not all survivors in Vineland lacked extended families. The Lermans, for example, had five surviving siblings between them spread across four countries on three continents. One of Miles's brothers, Shlomo, had stayed in West Germany; a sister, Pesha, and second brother, Jona, lived in Israel, until he moved to the United States in search of better treatment for his polio-stricken son.[2] Chris's younger sister Regina, who stayed behind in Brooklyn when they moved to Vineland and attended Brooklyn College, finished her degree at Indiana University, where she helped teach Polish to U.S. Air Force officers. She got married in 1953 and settled in New York City. Chris and Miles would drive thirteen or fourteen hours to visit her older sister Anna, who lived in Toronto, singing Hebrew songs in the car with their children to pass the time.[3]

Perhaps no survivors in Vineland lived in as tight a web of family as the Lermans' friends, brothers Joseph and Sol Finkelstein. They settled on adjoining properties and jointly ran a farm. Their sister Ann and her husband also lived on a contiguous farm. Between their three properties, six survivors lived together in what Sol's son Joe described as a "Holocaust survivor kibbutz" as one big family, with seven children and twenty thousand chickens.[4]

Most survivors, however, had few if any close relatives nearby. Instead, they turned to each other. They offered one another the kind of support and kinship often lacking with scattered relatives who spurned attempts to connect. They socialized informally and gathered together on holidays and all the other Jewish life cycle events, from brises and bar mitzvahs to funerals, that they might otherwise have marked with murdered relatives. "All our friends were survivors," Bronia said. They were "like family."

The closest Nuchim and Bronia had to regular family visits didn't involve actual relatives. Chana Netzman, who went by Ann in America, and her husband Leon were fellow Lublin natives. Bronia and Nuchim met them during the war, when these two women forged the deepest of bonds in the worst of circumstances. In the fall of 1943, relief from the loneliness and tedium of life in the forest bunker came from Chana. She was born a couple years after Bronia and similarly was raised in a middle-class, observant but not quite Orthodox family in Lublin.[5] Chana was still a teenager when she married Leon, a livestock broker like her father, right before the war began. She gave birth to a daughter, Betty, in 1941 during the German occupation of Lublin. She wound up in a ghetto in Piaski and somehow managed to avoid a selection when German soldiers killed children the same age as Betty. "It was like devils came down from the sky," Chana said.[6]

She was hiding with Betty, who was about eight months old, with a group of sixty or so other Jews in a space for twenty during a selection when her daughter made a sound. Some in the hiding spot wanted to smother Betty to avoid discovery. They relented only when Chana threatened to scream and give away their location. That's when Chana realized she had to give up her daughter. She found a Polish couple who agreed to take Betty in exchange for her remaining possessions before escaping to the forest where Bronia and Nuchim were hiding. Leon went off with a mobile partisan group.

Their common grief made Bronia and Chana ideal companions. Chana was the same age as Bronia's younger sister Etka. They found some measure of escape by talking about food. In a dugout beneath a forest, years since their last full meal, Bronia learned to cook with nothing more than Chana's memories to guide her. Chana "could make a soup out of nothing and you would be licking your fingers," her daughter Tammy recalled.[7] Figuratively, that's exactly what she did in the forest, as she shared her chicken soup and roast beef recipes. Focusing on food might have inflamed their hunger, but it also let them imagine a future normal enough that they could cook in a kitchen again.

Bronia watched helplessly as Chana, who had become pregnant before Leon went off with other partisans, contracted typhus, just as Etka and her father had in the Lublin ghetto. The filth and crowding of the ghetto and underground bunkers provided perfect breeding grounds for the louse-born epidemic. Lice were so prevalent that Bronia, in her desperation, cut off her hair, a last vestige of her womanhood. Bronia helped nurse Chana back to health, and she miraculously gave birth to a healthy daughter, Tammy, in the spring of 1944. She had to give up Tammy to a Polish family after a German raid, just days before horse-mounted Russian soldiers brought news of their liberation.

Liberation was just the beginning of Chana and Leon's struggles to reclaim their daughters and then convince their older one, Betty, to accept them as her birth parents after three years apart. They came to the United States in 1948, settling in Philadelphia, where Leon's aunt sponsored them. Leon first found a job in a butcher shop and then eventually worked at Philadelphia's stockyard as a cattle buyer. That's how Chana, Leon, and their two daughters became frequent visitors at the Greens' farm on Sundays. Philadelphia is only about forty miles away from Vineland, close enough that some commuted by bus there every day. And yet for Chana and her family, the weekly trip to the country felt like visiting a world apart from their urban life.

Ostensibly at first, Leon came to buy cases of eggs from Nuchim and neighboring farmers to resell in Philadelphia, something he no longer needed to do once he'd gotten more secure work as a cattle buyer. Still, they continued to make these daylong trips on rural backroads. "We never had relatives," Tammy said.[8] "All my relatives were killed so when I came there, it was like family." Bronia put the forest cooking lessons to use, making Chana and her family all the recipes they'd talked about in the most hopeless moment of their lives. Chana was the only person besides Nuchim with whom Bronia could talk about the worst of what she'd endured during the war, perhaps because they'd experienced it together. The same held true for Chana, who shared a secret with Bronia that she couldn't bear to tell her own children.

A few days after her younger daughter's birth, German soldiers raided the forest, forcing everyone to flee the bunker. Fearful that a crying baby might reveal their position, Chana left newborn Tammy in a corner partially concealed by leaves. She returned a couple hours later to find Tammy unharmed and immediately sought out a Polish family to care for her daughter. But she found the idea of abandoning her newborn that way—even though she had no choice—so shameful that she never told her daughters about it. Tammy heard the story only from Bronia six decades later, long after her mother died.[9]

———•———

Bronia befriended another woman in Vineland who, like Chana, had to give her young daughter up during the war and then struggled to reintroduce herself when she returned. Lusia Igel grew up one of seven children of a dry goods store owner in Przemyśl, a city of about sixty thousand people in southern Poland.[10] She was married on August 27, 1939, the same night her new husband, Stanley, was called up for duty in the Polish Army.[11] The Soviet Union occupied most of the city, which was on the border with German-controlled territory, by the time their daughter Tonia was born in November 1940. Seven months later, the Germans took control of the entire city.

Confined to a ghetto, Lusia and Stanley managed to give their sixteen-month-old daughter Tonia to a Polish woman, who kept her for the next three and a half years. Stanley and Lusia escaped to the countryside, hiding in basements and attics. She returned to discover her family was wiped out and their daughter, nearly four years old, didn't recognize them. "I didn't want to go to strange people, why would I bother with them?," Tonia said later.[12] It took three months to reestablish ties.

Lusia, Stanley, and Tonia came to the United States in 1947, helped immeasurably by his brother.[13] He had traveled to New York for a medical conference and then got trapped in the United States when the war started. He married a wealthy American woman, who helped set the Igels up in New York with a fully furnished apartment. Their American relatives also helped them buy a farm.[14] Unlike so many other refugees, the Igels didn't end up as farmers by happenstance. Igel had entered the United States under a visa for skilled agriculturalists.[15] The Displaced Persons Act of 1948 subsequently gave preference to immigrants with agricultural experience, which proved a ticket to entry to the relatively few Grine like Igel with farming experience.[16] Stanley's family had farmed for generations back in Poland, and he had studied agronomy before the war. The Igels settled in Estell Manor, a more rural community roughly twenty miles to the east of Vineland. By 1953, Igel had amassed ten thousand hens—more than three times as many as Nuchim. Stanley and Lusia lived in a large, beautifully furnished farmhouse, with their two children, Toni, now a teenager, and son Stephen, who was two years younger than Ruth.[17]

Like Bronia, Lusia was quiet by nature and didn't like to talk about the many relatives she lost in the war or the gut-wrenching decision to give up her daughter.[18] Lusia enjoyed playing hostess on Friday nights for a half dozen or so guests and loved to cook, relying on her own instincts rather than recipes for dishes like stuffed veal breast, chicken soup, potato kugel, and stuffed derma. Almost every Friday night, the Greens drove forty-five minutes each way on dark rural roads for dinner at the Igels' farmhouse. It was purely coincidental that they gathered at the start of the Jewish Sabbath to socialize at the end of another week of farming.

Bronia's other recurring social engagement was a weekly card game, which became the centerpiece of many Grines' social lives. Every week, Bronia and four other Polish-born farm wives rotated among their houses for a night of five-cents-a-hand poker. Grine wives born in the same country often gravitated together this way when they socialized.[19] Their husbands had a separate game of seven-card poker—betting as much as twenty-five or fifty cents a hand—that might last until eleven thirty, a late night for poultry farmers who had to get up before dawn to feed their chickens.

It was important for the Jewish farm wives to dress well and never to cease "being ladies," as Eva Neisser, whose German refugee family settled on a Vineland poultry farm during the war, later put it.[20] "When they went across the street for a quart of milk, they put stockings and heels on and took their overalls off," Neisser wrote. "That was the way one behaved to show self-respect and respect to others" and show "they remained the same, unaffected by chicken or other manure: The table was always set nicely, the good porcelain was in use and the vase had fresh flowers." That was equally true for the Grine.

When it was Bronia's turn to host at her kitchen table, she baked blueberry pie, apple cake, or cheesecake, depending on the season. Bronia and her friends talked, mostly in Polish or Yiddish, about their children, cooking and baking, or local gossip while playing. What they didn't discuss much at Nuchim's—and particularly Bronia's card game—was the war. "Every one of us went through hell," said Nathan Dunkelman, one of the regulars at Nuchim's game.[21] "Everyone had a story—no more than a story, a book," Dunkelman said. "The truth is no one wanted to talk about it."

Not all survivors avoided the subject at social gatherings. "We always talked among our friends. No matter what the conversation, we could be talking about movies or the theater and we always come back to concentration camps," recalled another Grine farmer.[22] But many had no interest in talking about the war. Goldie Finkelstein had no idea where most of her friends came from or if they had siblings. They acted as if the years before the war "didn't exist," Finkelstein said. It was years before Finkelstein and her husband Sol even knew each other's stories, she later said.[23] Sol was more forthcoming outside their home. He described "the tortures of Nazi bestiality" he experienced in a German concentration camp at a 1951 Newfield Kiwanis Club meeting.[24]

Bronia couldn't even talk about her wartime experiences with Dina, whom she'd known since she was a child and who was the closest she had to a sibling. She certainly wasn't going to tell her poker partners over pie. Nor did she want to hear about others' experiences. "I really didn't like to listen to these stories," Bronia explained. "We didn't talk about the war." Having so many survivors living in one place meant they could sort themselves when socializing according to their particular preferences. Those who wanted to talk more or less about the war naturally gravitated toward each other, just as women who grew up speaking Polish or Hungarian tended to cluster together in their card games.

Something more than shyness or squeamishness explains the reticence of those who preferred not to talk about the war. It was important to their self-worth to see themselves as undamaged despite their wartime experiences. Some feared what would happen to their emotional well-being if they were to break the "internal silence" and talk about it. "The act of telling might itself become severely traumatizing, if the price of speaking is reliving; not relief, but further traumatization," wrote psychiatrist Dori Laub, who studied trauma and survivor testimonies.[25]

It was equally important to appear normal to others, as they sought to blend in rather than stand out. "They wanted to paint a great and wonderful picture to the outside world and make sure everyone looked at them in an approving way," said Lusia's daughter Toni. "They wanted to show they'd moved on and made things work and had a good and productive life." Survivors sought "to prove to others that they were not permanently contaminated by the Holocaust, that they were not less than others," wrote psychologist Aaron Hass.[26]

Only later did more survivors begin to feel comfortable speaking out and offering testimonies, often as they aged into retirement and faced questions from grandchildren.[27] They felt encouraged to open up by new projects that sought out their testimony such as the Survivors of the Shoah Visual History Foundation, established by film director Steven Spielberg. Historian Kenneth Waltzer explained that they did so "to combat Holocaust denial, to confront their own demons, to honor those who did not survive, and to make their stories and the wider history known. Some confronted their traumatic experiences for personal and therapeutic reasons, often to make peace with absent fathers whom they still dreamed of impressing or whom they worried they had failed or abandoned, while others sought to educate, bear witness, and tell the story for the others. Most did a combination of these things, making such testimonies complex indeed."[28]

Esther Raab, one of the regulars at Bronia's poker games, illustrates how survivors came to be more vocal with time. Her experiences as a war crime witness and public speaker also highlight the complex ways trauma affected what they remembered and later shared. Esther was four years younger than Bronia and grew up about forty-five miles east of Lublin in a small city called Chełm. In October 1943, Raab joined hundreds of Sobibor prisoners in the largest concentration camp uprising of the war. "Even if we killed one Gestapo, it was worth it," Raab later recalled.[29] "We were condemned people anyway. Why not try?" Of the three hundred prisoners who escaped, fewer than fifty survived the war, including Raab, who hid in a barn for months. After the war, she married Irving, who grew up near Chełm. As described earlier, the Raabs moved to Vineland after visiting the Lermans' farm.[30]

In 1950, not long before moving to the United States, Raab testified at the Berlin trial of Erich Bauer, alleged to be a "gassing officer" at Sobibor who took part in the killing of more than a quarter million Jews.[31] A photo of Raab standing and pointing with her finger extended at the defendant, who was seated next to two similarly dressed men, when asked to identify him during the trial appeared in papers throughout the United States.[32] The testimony of Raab, along with other Sobibor survivors, helped convict Bauer, who was sentenced to death for "crimes against humanity."[33]

Raab testified at another Sobibor war crimes proceeding in 1966 where she described seeing one defendant seize a baby discovered in a transport of Jewish detainees and then smash its head against a wall of the railcar.[34] The baby's head exploded from the impact, Raab recounted. The defendant's attorneys tried challenging Raab's account by noting she had recalled the incident differently on different occasions. The argument proved unpersuasive with the judges in the case, who found Raab had "a sound capacity for recollection and did not summarily or indiscriminately accuse the defendants."[35]

As historian Michael Bryant wrote in his account of the trial, "No instance of witness testimony, no matter how veracious the witness, is free of defects."[36] "This is especially the case when the witness is asked to recall traumatic events decades in the past, when the intervening years, the raw emotion aroused by the event, and exposure to the accounts of other victims have fretted holes in the texture of the witness's story," Bryant wrote. Holocaust survivor testimony taken years later "poses special challenges to history," warns historian Dominick LaCapra, who studies trauma and memory.[37] Such "critically tested memory may appear as the necessary starting point" in retelling survivors' stories "even though it is continually threatened by lapses, holes, and distortions."[38]

Raab's last attempt at helping identify a suspect proved unsuccessful. In 1993, Raab, who was one of the last fifteen Sobibor survivors still living, came forward to identify John Demjanjuk as a guard there based on old photos.[39] After World War II the Ukrainian-born Demjanjuk had settled in Cleveland, where he worked as an autoworker, but he had been stripped of his citizenship in 1981 and extradited to Israel. He stood accused of being

Ivan the Terrible, who murdered thousands at Treblinka.[40] He was sentenced to death in 1988 before his conviction was overturned in 1993 by the Israeli Supreme Court.

It was at this point that Raab emerged as the first Sobibor survivor to identify Demjanjuk as a guard there. But Raab had earlier failed to pick Demjanjuk's picture during a photo lineup session with U.S. government officials. As a result, after meeting with Raab at her Vineland home, staff of the Simon Wiesenthal Center, which helped tracked down Nazi fugitives, concluded the Israeli Supreme Court would be unlikely to consider her testimony.[41] Raab seemed to regret coming forward in an interview with a reporter. "It's not easy for me," Raab said.[42] "It was too much." She wasn't called to testify when Demjanjuk later went on trial in 2009 in Germany at age eighty-nine for being an accessory in the murder of 27,900 Jews at Sobibor. He was found guilty in 2011 and died the following year in a German nursing home.

Raab's heightened public profile from testifying against Nazi war criminals led to a different outlet for talking about the war. She began receiving invitations to speak at local schools in the 1970s.[43] Uneasy at first to talk with strangers, she eventually became more comfortable speaking publicly and served as a consultant at the set in a Slovenian forest where CBS re-created Sobibor for a 1987 television movie about the mass prisoner escape. For twenty years, she accepted invitations to attend screenings of the film and would stay afterward to talk about it, even though she couldn't sleep well for days after each viewing. Her life even inspired a two-act play, *Dear Esther*, based on the hundreds of letters she received from students who saw her portrayed in the movie. She answered every letter.

14 ▸ DOWNTURN

FIVE CHEFS CLUTCHING hoes served an egg breakfast on Saturday, June 19, 1954, out of what was billed as the world's largest frying pan at the corner of Landis Avenue and the Boulevard.[1] The thirteen-and-a-half-foot-diameter frying pan weighed half a ton and made enough egg sandwiches that morning for two thousand people at the kickoff of Vineland's first-ever Poultry and Egg Festival.

The daylong event featured south Jersey mayors facing off in a hands-free chicken eating contest, 4-H chicken competitions, and a keynote address by New Jersey governor Robert Meyner. The governor also had the honor of placing a crown on the head of the teenager coroneted as "New Jersey Poultry Queen."[2] A former blueberry queen won the crown and a four-piece matching luggage set.[3] Attendees could watch baby chicks born in a special glass incubator set up in the window of I. C. Schwarzman's department store on Landis Avenue. Door prizes entitled two lucky attendees to one thousand egg cartons each, although neither winner picked up the bounty by the end of the day.

Nuchim most enjoyed the chicken barbecue in Landis Park, a spot where he gave occasional tennis lessons. A broiler and all the fixings cost a dollar and twenty-five cents. All of downtown smelled like barbecue chicken as the two-hundred-foot barbeque pit under the supervision of a nationally known grill master served more than ten thousand pieces of chicken. Eight-year-old Ruth entered the "Miss Baby Chick" competition, which required "daughters of poultry industry-men" to come up with the "best costume based on a chicken motif."

At this moment in June 1954 poultry was still king in Vineland. Yet signs of trouble emerged that spring a few months before the first poultry festival. Unduly optimistic farmers enlarged their flocks just as a post–Korean War recession reduced consumer spending. Egg prices fell 13 percent in March compared to a year earlier while feed prices kept rising, prompting a prediction at an April industry conference in Philadelphia that "the honeymoon for poultrymen is over."[4]

Jewish Farmer editor Benjamin Miller sought to ease worries at a May 1954 Jewish Poultry Farmers Association (JPFA) meeting, three weeks before the poultry festival, the first of many times to come in which a Jewish Agricultural Society (JAS) official offered undue optimism in the face of economic collapse. Miller tried to dispel "the gloom and pessimism prevailing" in poultry communities.[5] The current lean times, he assured attendees, would be followed by a better future. But by the time the egg festival got under way in mid-June, egg prices had hit their second lowest mark for the month in a decade.

————•————

Exactly one month later, a forty-two-year-old Grine farmer entered his feed house not long after the sun came up. The farmer had arrived in the United States in 1949 on the *Marine Flasher*, a sister ship of the one the Greens and Lermans sailed to America. He moved to Vineland the previous year with his wife, around the same time they had their first child. The novice farmer tied one end of a new clothesline around the cable of an elevated automatic feeder and the other around his neck.[6] He was the third farmer to hang himself in ten days.

The first to end his own life was a forty-eight-year-old concentration camp survivor who'd bought a farm for forty thousand dollars a few weeks earlier with his son-in-law. He was discovered suspended from an electric cord in a chicken house. The *Times Journal* reported he "was believed beset by financial worries."[7] That same night, four hundred fifty poultrymen had gathered at the North Italy Club for a mass meeting "expressing growing concern over low egg prices that are threatening to 'force family-sized poultry farmers off the land.'"[8]

These two new poultrymen had arrived as the wave of refugee farmers had begun to crest. From a peak of 159 in 1951, the number of displaced persons the JAS helped settle on farms held steady at roughly ninety per year between 1952 and 1954. But only thirty-seven more would follow them onto farms with the help of the JAS in 1955 and 1956 combined. Farmers who started out in 1954 bought farms at peak prices, incurring even more debt than earlier arrivals. That seemed like a reasonable bet after three years of high egg prices. Then, as soon as they arrived, prices began to fall back to earth. Leuchter noted in his column that veteran farmers were better equipped to weather periods of low egg prices since they'd already paid off most of their debts and had lower interest expenses. "More recent additions to the ranks of poultrymen, however, particularly those who paid inflated prices for their farms, can easily be crushed by the squeeze of heavy fixed overhead and low income," Leuchter observed.[9]

In all, four farmers committed suicide in a grim five-week stretch that summer, two of them refugees and two of them widowers. One was a seventy-year-old who had lived by himself since his wife died two years earlier; another was a sixty-two-year-old "believed despondent" over his wife's death a month earlier. The sixty-year-old wife of another Jewish farmer hanged herself with a clothesline from a rafter in her Newfield farmhouse in mid-June.[10]

The deaths of two newcomers hit the Vineland survivor community hard, even though neither refugee had lived there long enough to befriend many other Grine. At a July 23 JPFA meeting, four days after the second survivor's death, Lerman all but pleaded that "suicide is no answer to a man's problems, particularly his financial ones, for by ending his own life he only dumps those problems on his family."[11] Lerman said that "in many cases, particularly when a man has young children, such an action is a terrible crime." He urged the two hundred fifty JPFA members present as paraphrased by the Times Journal "to share their problems with one another, talk over their difficulties and be genuinely interested in helping anyone unduly depressed by the current economic difficulties." The farmers formed a new "welfare committee" to offer "moral encouragement" on top of the mutual aid society they'd started a year earlier to provide small interest-free loans.

Miles and the other JPFA leaders were doing the best they could in the absence of any government or other mental health support for this trauma-tized population. Organizations such as the JAS and United Service for New Americans focused their energies almost entirely on making refugees economically self-sufficient and helping them assimilate fully. "It was so much simpler than confronting the messy, emotional, complicated needs of survivors," as historian Beth Cohen observed in her book about displaced persons.[12]

Seeking psychiatric help wasn't an entirely alien concept in rural New Jersey communities like Vineland at the time. Demand for therapy among Jewish poultry farmers in Lakewood, New Jersey, was so great that the com-munity supported two psychiatrists—one for adults and one specializing in children.[13] In Vineland, Rabbi Martin Douglas of Beth Israel delivered a sermon on "How Judaism Views Psychiatry" in January 1957, in the first in a series of sermons on the topic.[14] But survivors tended to be more hesitant about mental health treatment than American-born Jews, whether because they believed only the weak needed such help or out of fear of revisiting the past.[15] Even if they wanted help, finding a counselor in Vineland was harder than in Lakewood. The 1956 Vineland city directory included the name of only one psychiatrist among thirty-eight doctors listed under the category of "physicians and surgeons" and he worked in Philadelphia. "We didn't have anybody to talk to," Bronia said.

Regardless, agricultural training and assimilation—rather than mending mental wounds—remained the priorities when the JAS opened a Vineland office in 1952. The JAS representative in Vineland, Samson Liph, was born in Russia in 1888 and came to the United States as a teenager. He attended schools supported by the Baron de Hirsch Fund in Russia and Woodbine, New Jersey.[16] Liph, now bald and bespectacled, had worked for the JAS for thirty-four years by the time he arrived in Vineland. Liph enlisted a former high school teacher and local Hadassah president to help with a project he dubbed "spiritual Americanization."[17] They offered classes in conversational English and American Jewish history. He encouraged newcomers to embrace American arts and culture and "to enter into the civic and social lifestream of their adopted community." Doing so, he suggested, might help with the particular burdens this population brought with them from Europe. "He attempts to break down deeprooted feelings of insecurity and inhibitions born of mistreatment in the old country," the Times Journal noted.

Lerman understood the challenges farmers faced that summer. He served on an eight-member committee appointed by the local poultry industry that included such local eminences as vaccine maker Arthur Gold-haft and feed company owner Edward Rubinoff, as well as Martin Berwin, the longtime leader of the German refugee community. Their report starkly outlined the problem.[18] In the first six months of 1954 it cost farmers forty-eight cents to produce a dozen eggs, which earned only forty-three cents on the market. Farmers were losing money on every dozen eggs they sold.

The committee disagreed about the underlying causes or what to do about it. Berwin and Lerman, who together represented the bulk of Jewish farmers, wanted to press for immediate government aid, including urging the U.S. Department of Agriculture to release government-held grain to lower the price of their biggest expense: feed. Others argued government intervention would only exacerbate the problem of overproduction. "If the government helps us out, are we going to build more coops and make the situation even worse next year?," asked Herbert Wegner, the president of the New Jersey State Poultry Association.[19]

At the July 23 JPFA meeting, Lerman said they'd joined local industry asking for federal and state help to address the egg–feed ratio that put them in "a serious financial squeeze."[20] A month later, Lerman traveled to Washington, the first of many such delegations that pled for help. Still Lerman told his fellow farmers there was no reason to panic. "We had a bad period in 1950 when many of us thought it would be impossible for us to survive," he said. "Yet by the following year we had recovered financially."

15 ▸ RURAL CHILDHOODS

For THE SECOND summer in a row, dozens of New York City children arrived in Vineland in July 1954 to spend two weeks with Grine farm families. Despite the downturn and rash of farmer suicides, the hosts, including Bronia and Nuchim, carried on as if nothing was amiss.

At first, Ruth, now eight years old, didn't like playing host to a girl named Mina. She had grown accustomed to being the only child in the house and had no interest in sharing her parents' attention with someone else. Her jealously soon faded as Ruth realized how much she'd missed having the equivalent of a sibling in the house, something absent since moving out of the farm she shared with Dorothy. Ruth and Mina played together around the farm and attended all the events the Jewish Poultry Farmers Association (JPFA) organized for their young guests, including a "gala picnic" sponsored by the Rubinoff feed company.

Visiting New Jersey chicken farms challenged city-raised refugee children's notions of how Grine lived in America. "To me, they were urban animals who rode subways and took strolls on Broadway in topcoats and fedoras," journalist Joseph Berger, the son of survivors who grew up in New York, wrote of a visit to a poultry farm in Lakewood, New Jersey.[1] "Their accents seemed out of place on a farm, on the lips of men in denim and workboots." New York children enjoyed new experiences during these two-week stays on Vineland-area farms. Both the guests and the children they stayed with learned how much farm life differed from growing up in a big city. One eight-year-old girl explained to a *Times Journal* reporter she'd never seen a goat or cow before—except on television. She liked being around animals and having a chance to play outside all the time. Going home to Manhattan meant having to be quiet in their fifth-floor apartment or risk getting yelled at by the janitor in the apartment below for the slightest noise. "It's so nice here," she said with a wistful smile.[2]

Back in New York, the children of survivors and other working-class Jews had only intermittent and circumscribed exposure to nature. They played hopscotch on the sidewalk or stickball in alleyways.[3] The nearest park might be a bus ride or two away, and more sustained immersion came only in short bursts during the summer at sleepaway camp or a bungalow colony upstate. In contrast, the natural world—both idyllic and dangerous—was part of the daily lives of Grine children living on south Jersey farms. Ruth's earliest memories included petting soft baby chicks and the sight of the rifle her father kept handy to kill predators trying to snatch chickens. They had ample opportunity to explore their physical surroundings and were granted a great deal of freedom to do so.

From the earliest research into survivor well-being in the 1960s, a perception took hold that they tended to be "excessively overprotective, constantly warning their children of impending danger."[4] "This is quite understandable in that they witnessed death so frequently or lost previous children," wrote psychiatrist Bernard Trossman in a 1968 study of the adolescent children of concentration camp survivors. There is certainly evidence among the Grine in Vineland to support the idea that some survivors shared a fearful world-view with their children. Ruth remembered Bronia imparting the message that "the world was dangerous." But the labor-intensive work of running a farm meant many parents didn't have the time to watch over their children closely throughout the day. Children had to entertain themselves, particularly during summer breaks from school.

Ruth and Helen Waiman, the daughter of survivors who was the same age and lived around the corner, biked around the neighborhood, stopping for lunch at different friends' houses. "I loved roaming around, getting on my bicycle and being gone all day," Helen recalled.[5] They took inner tubes to a creek up the street and floated in the shallow waters. Others caught minnows or, if they felt particularly fearless, swam in a sand wash across the street. Ruth stayed back: she didn't know how to swim. The site also attracted unsavory gatherings, including teenagers whose bonfires occasionally scorched the adjacent farm's coops. The kids traded rumors that the site doubled as a mafia burial site.

Neighborhood kids even had their own haunted house on the block: an abandoned home once owned by an elderly Hungarian-born recluse, who died after a grass fire on the property.[6] Kids would sneak into the house for the ghoulish thrill of peeking at all the undisturbed abandoned property that made it seem as if he still lived there. Adding to the spooky effect, flowers still bloomed for years from the bulbs he'd planted outside. "It was Tom Sawyerish," said Aron Swerdlin, who recalled similar experiences growing up on a Landis Avenue poultry farm.[7] "For a kid, it was like a wonderland."

Ruth's childhood wasn't entirely idyllic. She often felt lonely at home and envious of friends who had brothers and sisters. Chris Lerman gave birth to their second child, David, in January 1951. Dorothy's baby brother Alex, born in 1953, was now a toddler. Ruth may have felt like the only one without a sibling, but that wasn't true. Older survivors, who may have lost their first family during the war, often couldn't start large second families. Leah Lederman, who lived directly across the street, didn't have any siblings either. But Leah had someone else in her life even more rare among survivors: a grandparent. Leah's grandfather moved from Israel and lived with her family on Orchard Road for about six or seven years. At first, Leah could barely communicate with her grandfather, who spoke only Yiddish and Hebrew. She learned Yiddish so they could talk.[8] A couple of Ruth's friends had grandmothers, and she once asked Bronia why she didn't have one. "I told her they didn't live through the war," Bronia said.

Ruth also struggled with her weight. Bronia loved to cook and made sure Ruth finished everything on her plate. Bronia served the carb-heavy dishes common back home in Poland like potted meat, perogies, stuffed cabbage, cheese-filled blintzes, and kishke, a stuffed beef intestine. Having gone so long during the war without enough food, Bronia couldn't bear to throw any out now and associated weight gain with health. Bronia couldn't find clothes Ruth's size in Vineland, so they took special bus trips to Philadelphia to shop in what Ruth described as a "chubette" store, which was an actual clothing category at the time.[9] Other survivors in Vineland and elsewhere had similar issues surrounding food.[10] Joe Finkelstein recalled being overweight because his mother would stuff him and his brother like geese. Food was both a way his mother expressed love and also represented something darker, Finkelstein later recalled.[11] "It was a pathology," he said. Finkelstein said his mother, who had starved during the war, wouldn't let the same happen to her children. They would have some extra weight to help them survive the next pogrom or ghetto.

—— · ——

Grine parents might have been hands-off about how their children spent the summer outdoors, but they actively encouraged participation in activities familiar from Europe or new ones that might help their children assimilate.

In the spring of 1954, Ruth and Helen joined Brownie Troop 82 that met every Saturday afternoon at a neighbor's home that doubled as their club-house. Their troop held an August cookout and hot dog roast followed by games and a pony ride. Bronia cohosted the installation that fall where other Grine daughters joined the troop. Ruth and Helen later graduated to the Girl Scouts at Beth Israel synagogue, earning storytelling badges and going door-to-door selling cookies on their rural road. The Grines' sons played baseball and joined local Cub Scout or Boy Scout troops, which added a Jewish twist: social awards to scouts who passed "special tests in Jewish history, customs, and ceremonies."[12]

When asked whether it was hard to become an American mother, Bronia explained, as was often the case, that she simply did "whatever we had to do." For Bronia, that meant serving as a hostess at Brownie meetings and joining the Orchard Road School PTA. Uncharacteristically for someone as shy and self-conscious about her accent as Bronia, she presented a report at an October 1954 PTA meeting. Bronia and Nuchim somehow managed to buy a used piano and scraped together money for lessons for Ruth, who attended alongside Dorothy. Ruth hated going to her piano teacher's musty-smelling home, yet she kept at it, at least for a year or two.

The Grine had learned piano and participated in gymnastics as children back in Europe. Some of the parents undoubtedly—and perhaps subconsciously—sought to recapture the lost innocence of their own child-hoods or make up for youths stolen by war. Survivors were also deeply invested in the development of children expected to fill the void of all those they'd lost. Both phenomena were evident among survivors beyond

Vineland as journalist Helen Epstein described in her 1979 book, *Children of the Holocaust*. Epstein's parents, both Czech concentration camp survivors, plied her with art, music, and dance lessons and took her to the opera, concerts, and the theater "on a budget that barely sufficed to pay the rent" for their New York City apartment.[13] "I could recapture the best of her past," Epstein wrote of her mother, who worked as a dressmaker.

Survivors also felt pressure to keep up with neighbors and provide whatever they imagined a proper American childhood required. One son of survivors, Saul Golubcow, recalled a community Hanukkah party where one boy played the accordion "beautifully."[14] Soon, all the other parents started lining up accordion lessons for their children too. Golubcow resisted, preferring to play baseball, but his parents went ahead and scheduled the lessons anyway, forcing him to miss his favorite TV show, *Wagon Train*.

The survivors' children lived in two worlds in Vineland—one full of JPFA Hanukkah and Purim parties and socializing with other farm families in Yiddish or Polish—and the other, American. Their parents encouraged them to cross the boundary, even if they still felt uncomfortable doing so themselves. Zella Shabasson, who was seven years younger than Ruth, recalled that she and a Jewish classmate, eager to be "good students," volunteered to say the Lord's Prayer during class at the Orchard Road elementary school.[15]

Helen Waiman was cast as Mrs. Claus in a Christmas play at the school, alongside Musia Deiches's son Harry as Santa. "I thought, 'ok, that's what we're supposed to do,'" Helen said.[16] It happened to be one of the few times her parents came to a school performance. They felt self-conscious having to talk to other parents in their heavily accented English. Seeing their daughter playing Santa's wife only heightened their discomfort. "They felt awkward even being there," Helen said. "I felt awkward having them there." Another daughter of survivors, who moved to Vineland at the age of eleven, cringed as her mother, a concentration camp survivor, tried bargaining with the clerk at a local clothing store.[17] She tried to explain to her mother that people didn't haggle like that in American shops.

Dorothy acutely felt as if she lived a dual life. Fewer survivors had settled near her family's Tuckahoe Road farmhouse, so she was among only a handful of Jewish students at the Richland School. Dorothy was seven when she portrayed a Christmas tree during the "Magic Christmas Bell" at a holiday program.[18] She is listed as among the students "feted" by the PTA at a party where Santa distributed gifts. It is more difficult to picture her younger brother, Alex, who grew up to be a strictly observant Orthodox Jew in Israel, playing the part of the sailor doll in a performance of "The Lost Reindeer."[19]

Dorothy hated being one of only three Jewish kids in her class and having to play "Jesus Loves Me" in school. She used to go to sleep at night thinking, "Why did I have to be Jewish?"[20] She tried playing with the Italian kids, but their lives revolved around church activities. She felt left out when they didn't include her. Just as her parents passed as non-Jewish during the war, Dorothy said she tried "passing" as non-Jewish in her school. "I didn't tell anyone I was Jewish."

Dorothy's Tuckahoe neighbor Lee Feinberg, one of the other two Jewish kids in the class, similarly felt like an outsider at school. "Not only didn't they have an idea what a Jew was, when I started school, I spoke no English," Feinberg said.[21] When his teacher asked him what religion he was, Feinberg blurted out the word "juice," rather than "Jewish," prompting laughter from the whole class. He remembered other kids picking on him and even beating him up. The other Jewish kids were a girl and a boy with hemophilia, so Feinberg became the target of choice. Feinberg gravitated toward the handful of Black kids in the school, who joined him in volunteering to clean out ash from the coal-burning stove to fill potholes in the courtyard since the white kids avoided the task. The bullying didn't just occur in outlying areas: Sam Feigenbaum, who was five years younger than Ruth and Dorothy, remembered being called "kike" and "dirty Jew" and getting spit on during bus rides or in gym class during junior high school after moving from Tuckahoe Road to a neighborhood closer to downtown Vineland.[22]

Some families avoided the dissonance by enrolling their children in the private Jewish day school that opened in the fall of 1953 in a renovated farmhouse.[23] Fifty-five students—mostly survivors' kids—filled the first through third grade classes that inaugural school year. No one had to fear getting awkwardly cast in a Christmas pageant at the Jewish day school, which hosted Purim and Sukkot parties, Hanukkah banquets, and model Passover seders.

The school day included religious instruction modeled on a European *kheyder* in subjects like Bible, Talmud, and Yiddish, in addition to secular classes. Joe Finkelstein recalled his parents enrolled him because they wanted him to "learn how to *daven*," or pray, which justified the sacrifice required to pay private school tuition. He remembered a good academic experience but not much of a social education, making the transition to public school challenging.[24] "It was a different world going from the very sheltered environment of the Jewish day school," Finkelstein said. It came as a surprise to learn that most parents hadn't survived a concentration camp when he went away to sleepaway camp. The subject never came up at the Jewish day school where everyone's parents seemed to be survivors, Finkelstein said.[25] At camp, he overheard his counselors sharing concerns that a discussion of the war that day might upset him. That's when it occurred to him that being the child of survivors was actually quite unusual, he said.

With the exception of a few non-Jewish teachers who taught secular subjects, the Jewish day school students lived entirely in a survivor bubble, at least during the school day. Rather than play cowboys and Indians, they pretended to be German and American soldiers on the playground. "No one wanted to be Germans, so we had to take turns," Golubcow said.[26] "We wanted to kill them, and sometimes we hit the Germans a little too hard." Only in a few New York City neighborhoods with equally dense concentrations of survivors like Williamsburg, Crown Heights, Flatbush, and Borough Park could their children feel so comfortable among themselves.[27]

Attending the Jewish day school could make life outside the survivor bubble even more jarring for these kids. Golubcow attended the Jewish day school yet lived in a mostly Italian neighborhood. Friendly neighbors plowed them out any time it snowed and came running to help put out a brush fire behind their coops.[28] At the same time, dead cats occasionally got dumped on their lawn and swastikas were scrawled on their coops. He asked his father whether the perpetrators were anti-Semites. His father replied, "Yes, but at least here they don't kill you." Around Easter time, some Italian boys from the neighborhood would jump Saul as he rode his bike while yelling "Christ killer" or "Dirty Jew." "They would hit me enough to bruise me a bit," Golubcow said. "Three hours later, they'd come by and say, 'You want to play ball?'"

Baseball became Saul's main point of contact with non-Jewish kids. He was about eleven years old when he joined a few dozen kids at a city park waiting to be selected by one of the Little League team managers. Sal, as the Italian kids called him, was small for his age but good at baseball, and the other players advocated on his behalf. "Pick the Jewish kid," they yelled. There were twenty-five kids left, then twenty, and then ten. Finally, Saul stood alone, the last player chosen.

A few days later, Saul rode his bike to his first Little League practice straight from the Jewish day school. The manager handed the team their uniform tops and asked all the boys to put them on. The problem was Saul had on his *tzitzit*, the ritual fringes worn by observant Jews, beneath his shirt. He froze as his teammates took off their shirts and put on their jerseys. He wondered what to do, afraid everyone would make fun of his unusual undergarment. Eventually, he took off his shirt. If his teammates saw his tzitzit, nobody said a word.

———•———

There was one spot where both the Grine and their children recalled feeling completely at ease: Norma Beach. By 1953, the stretch along the Maurice River ten minutes from downtown Vineland where the original colonists once skinny-dipped and two subsequent generations of local Jews and swam and sunned had become the closest the Grine came to an oasis. David Lerman, the son of Miles and Chris, called it their "Riviera."[29]

Nuchim would drop Bronia and Ruth off with a lunch pail, usually tuna sandwiches or leftovers. Other mothers who had to work just left the children for the day. Older siblings watched younger brothers and sisters, their parents assured that there were always a couple of mothers around to keep an eye out.[30] Ruth and her friends gravitated toward the acre or two of coarse, sandy beach. The younger kids had mud fights, built sandcastles, or climbed on each other's backs in a game called "buck buck." As the temperature rose in the afternoon, the kids waded into the river for a swim, emerging from the water covered in reddish-brown flecks that fell from adjacent cedar trees.

The women could always find company among the wives who spent the day talking among themselves in Polish. As one survivor wife explained, Norma Beach was *heymish*, the Yiddish word for a cozy, warm place.[31] "Everybody was there," Bronia recalled. "Everybody knew everybody." The women played poker or fourteen-card rummy, just like at home. Their husbands might stop by during afternoon breaks on the farm, for a round of poker or pinochle. Some played chess instead. The men were all in the same business but never felt like competitors, unless they were playing cards or chess. As was the case in the home-based games, the men and women didn't mix at the card table here either.

Grine living in New York City in search of a similar spot where "they would find affirmation and comfort" in a "bucolic setting" traveled upstate to the Catskill Mountains.[32] Wives and children—often joined on the weekend by husbands—spent part of their summers staying in bungalow colonies where they could laugh, play cards, and swim surrounded by other survivors. "Here was a place where our parents were able to relax together with people like themselves and really let their guards down," Brooklyn-born author Jake Ehrenreich wrote of his summers in Catskill bungalow colonies with fellow survivors' families.[33] "Somehow the fresh air and the freedom of the setting made everything and everybody just seem happier—more joyful and carefree."

At Norma Beach, Louis Goldman, a Polish-born teenager living on his parents' poultry farm at the time, watched the men, often shirtless in shorts and slippers, play knock rummy for fifteen or twenty-five cents a hand.[34] They'd complain in Yiddish about hens that laid too few eggs or talk about current events. Sometimes, they'd comment about the figures of women passing by on the beach. "It was fun just to listen to them," said Goldman, whom the men gave a quarter to fetch sodas from the concession stand. Eventually, the game broke up as the men left for their farms to make sure the chickens had enough water to get through a hot summer day.

At the open-sided concession stand everyone called the "hut," children dropped off with a nickel or a quarter for the day faced the dilemma of choosing between the pinball machines or the snack counter.[35] Kids could buy ice cream, hot dogs and hamburgers, or, most affordably, pretzel rods (two for two cents and a penny more if you wanted mustard). Savvy kids increased their buying power by collecting soda bottles and redeeming them for a deposit at the snack counter.[36] Teenagers gathered near the jukebox when they weren't playing football on the beach.

Toward evening, mothers who worked outside the home showed up with picnic dinners while husbands who couldn't get away from their farms earlier played some poker, setting up flashlights so they could see their cards as the sun set.

16 ▸ HURRICANES

Bronia, nuchim, and Ruth rushed down into their cellar on Friday, October 15, 1954, carrying candles, canned food, and water. Hurricane Hazel, which had already battered Haiti, the Bahamas, and the Carolinas, was barreling north with ninety-mile-per-hour winds.[1]

They took shelter in the cellar, which smelled like dill from the pickles Bronia cured there. A small window provided some natural light and perhaps intermittent glimpses of the chaos outside, at least until the sun set. They could hear the wind uprooting trees and peeling the roofs off chicken coops like lids off tin cans.

The storm passed around nine o'clock in the evening. Nuchim and Bronia considered themselves lucky to emerge and find only one coop's roof damaged. All the chickens huddled inside survived. The Hymans next door lost a coop, as did Helen Waiman's family around the corner. Helen's father Jerome had gone outside to check on the chickens in the middle of the storm, and the roof of the coop collapsed just as he was about to step inside. He returned to the cellar ashen faced and said he'd almost been killed.[2]

Vineland residents woke up the next morning and discovered the full extent of the damage caused by what at the time was one of the most powerful storms ever to hit the U.S. mainland. Downtown, downed trees blocked Landis Avenue, and the windows caved in at I. C. Schwarzman's department store that held the glass incubators four months earlier during the poultry festival. Hazel destroyed or heavily damaged hundreds of coops— including one hundred owned by farmers supported by the Jewish Agricultural Society (JAS).[3] Dead chickens littered farmyards. Hundreds of thousands more were left homeless and without ready access to water since electric pumps on most farms lost power. The city opened fire hydrants, and some farmers resorted to fetching water from the Maurice River using pails.[4]

Things could have been worse: Hazel wiped out as much as a quarter of the broilers raised for meat in Delaware and Maryland in a single day.[5] The fact that the storm hit Vineland at night when chickens were roosting rather than in the morning when they were outside on ranges limited losses. Most roosts were on the south walls, which remained largely intact or toppled outward due to the direction of the winds.

The Jewish Poultry Farmers Association (JPFA) quickly organized volunteer crews to help collect and house the homeless birds. Teams of four to six went out each night at seven o'clock and worked until as late as two or three in the morning. In one week, the crews relocated sixty thousand displaced birds.[6] Given the hard times ahead, the lucky ones might actually have been the farmers who lost everything and used insurance proceeds to start over in a new business—or in an entirely different place.

———•———

The mood was understandably gloomy when farmers gathered three weeks after Hazel hit at North Italy Hall for the annual meeting of Jewish poultry farmers in south Jersey.[7] The event, which opened with the singing of both "The Star-Spangled Banner" and "Hatikvah," included all the usual elements of the farmers' community meetings: a moment of silence in memory of the Nazis' victims, odes to the American way of life, and some Old World entertainment, in this case in the form of a fading vaudeville comedian.

Before the comedy started, Judge Harry Adler, a scion of one of the original Russian Jewish immigrant families that settled the area decades earlier, began with what amounted to a pep talk. The forty-nine-year-old former state assemblyman, appointed a state judge earlier this year, still woke up at six o'clock in the morning to drive around the county to visit with the farmers with whom he felt a deep kinship.[8] He told those gathered that they should feel proud to be in south Jersey, an area that had been a stretch of wilderness when the original settlers arrived with no schools, mail delivery, telephone lines, or electricity. "Life was primitive and hard, but their spirit was undaunted," Adler said, and their "patience, perseverance, love for their homesteads and a vision of a better world" helped them "weather many a storm."

Adler eventually turned to the present difficulties, urging the audience to have the same fortitude and vision as the earlier pioneers. He said he was "certain that they would overcome their difficulties in time." Adler then summed up his American credo: "An honest dollar, an honest friend, an honest neighbor, respect for God, for oneself, compassion in one's soul, sharing and participating in the democratic process."

What would the survivors in the audience have made of Adler's upbeat speech? Unlike the idealistic colonists, these survivors had no interest in building a "better world." They wanted only to make a living and support their families. This audience, so many of whom had been betrayed by neighbors—and in the view of some of them, God, too—had seen the worst of human nature and certainly didn't need any lessons on the importance of resilience. What did Adler or any of the other American-born Jews in the audience know about hardships? It seems like Adler, though well meaning, delivered the wrong message for the wrong crowd at the wrong time. Or maybe hearing encouragement from a local luminary provided some measure of comfort at a difficult moment.

Two weeks later, Lerman laid out just how "desperate" a situation the farmers faced in a letter pleading for help to the Conference on Jewish Material Claims Against Germany.[9] Twenty-three major international Jewish organizations formed the conference in 1951 to negotiate with the German government for indemnification for the material losses suffered during the war. The Claims Conference funneled the proceeds into compensation for survivors and funded social service agencies that helped them. The letter, cosigned by the JPFA mutual aid society's president, noted economic hardship in the poultry industry "has already caused two suicides of Jewish poultrymen due to financial difficulties." Hazel had compounded farmers' problems, forcing many who lost poultry houses to sell their laying hens at "ridiculously low prices" due to a lack of housing. Now, farmers had no funds to raise replacement birds.

Many JPFA members couldn't apply for long-term government loans because they weren't yet U.S. citizens, the letter said, and the nearly eighty

loan applicants sought more than the JPFA mutual aid society could provide. "You are the only organization to whom we can turn for help which is
so badly needed," the letter said in requesting seventy-five thousand dollars.
A "farmers aid committee" of the Vineland B'nai B'rith chapter, which
included attorney Harry Levin, wrote the Claims Conference in support of
the JPFA request.[10] "Coming to America in a depressed frame of mind, suffering from the severe economic reverses of the poultry business, Hurricane
Hazel did all but drive them into a psychological depression," the B'nai B'rith
committee reported in an eight-page memo. "All of them have been through
the hell and terror of concentration camps and all they want is an opportunity
to make good. They do not want charity. They do need some help."

The request bounced among the Jewish organizations within the Claims
Conference. One official noted a hesitance to provide funds to organizations "in self-supporting areas like the U.S."[11] Another official explained
the difficulty of "raising funds in Europe for a cause in the U.S.A., however
deserving, which does not appear to be supported by the American institutions."[12] The Jewish Colonization Association, another entity created by
Baron Maurice de Hirsch, ultimately agreed to contribute thirty-five thousand dollars, while two other organizations contributed an additional fifteen thousand.[13] The fifty-thousand-dollar loan provided at a minimal
interest rate allowed the JPFA's mutual aid society to increase the size of the
interest-free loans it offered members from five hundred to one thousand
dollars.

———•———

Vineland's refugee farmers struggling to recover from Hazel later joined the
larger Jewish community in rallying around a single family for whom misfortune compounded on misfortune. The hurricane destroyed the poultry
house of Isak Michnik and his wife Toni, two concentration camp survivors
who had lived in Vineland since 1950, and scattered four thousand of their
chickens.

The natural disaster came at a particularly bad time for Michnik, who
turned forty-seven in 1954 and had been hospitalized and unable to work
with a serious illness. Toni had to take care of their three-year-old son as
well as what little remained of their farm. She sold off their chicken flock for
pennies on the dollar as Isak endured what would eventually total ten surgeries in Philadelphia hospitals. Without an income, the Michniks were on

the verge of losing their home. A feed mill sought a sheriff's sale to recover thousands of dollars the family owed.[14] The Michniks had no choice but to begin bankruptcy proceedings.

That's when the JPFA welfare committee intervened, negotiating with creditors and helping the Michniks rebuild. Eleven contractors volunteered to reconstruct their coops using supplies donated at cost. Twenty-two JPFA members signed up for half-day construction shifts.[15] To restock the farm, the JPFA organized a "chicken drive," asking members to donate a crate or two of birds.[16] Nathan Wernicoff of Vineland Poultry Laboratories warned that collecting live birds from so many farms increased the risk of poultry illness. The JPFA collected cash instead, and then local hatcheries donated twelve hundred baby chicks.

Help came from the broader community, too. Members of the local Hebrew Women's Benevolent Society assisted Toni with household chores. Other volunteers drove her to Philadelphia during Michnik's many hospitalizations. When after three years Michnik was finally well enough to raise chickens again, he was nothing but optimistic and grateful for how his neighbors had rallied behind his family. "There are so many people that we owe so much to," Michnik said. "We are the happiest people in the whole world that we are in this country."[17]

There wasn't much reason for optimism as 1955 began. In January, Miles suggested every local farmer needed to "help pull himself up by his own bootstraps" by finding ways to help better promote their eggs.[18] He proposed putting advertising panels on trucks leaving Vineland and windshield stickers that could highlight the nutritional value of Vineland eggs. Within weeks, Miles found a way to diversify his income by becoming a chick salesman. In a February 1955 ad in the *Times Journal*, Miles urged fellow Vineland poultryman to buy "Hy-Line 934" chicks, which he described as the "bird of the future."[19]

Samson Liph, manager of the JAS's Vineland office, discovered the depth of poultrymen's worries during visits to area farms that winter. "They all were anxious to tell in detail of their difficulties, pleading for leniency in collection and appealing for additional help," Liph wrote.[20] "The people needed sympathy and understanding of their problems to give them courage to go on with their farm activities and face the future with confidence." Still, Liph remained optimistic. "The poultry industry is here to stay, to grow and to develop," he wrote.

As the year progressed, ever more farmers sought help from the JPFA's mutual aid society. The number of outstanding loans to JPFA members rose from 31 to 181 by year's end.[21] Struggling farmers must have watched with some envy as the rest of the local economy continued to flourish. Vineland's glass plants, clothing factories, and food processors added thousands of jobs during the 1950s.[22] In 1955, the ranks of the city's food processors grew to include the B. Manischewitz Company. The company that billed itself as the world's largest year-round producer of kosher food began manufacturing borscht at a Delsea Drive site where workers previously packed sweet potatoes and manufactured dog food.[23] Vineland municipal leaders who hosted a welcome dinner at the White Sparrow Inn for Manischewitz executives made sure to serve kosher food from a Philadelphia caterer.[24] The Manischewitz plant employed only fifty workers at first, but came to be far more well-known than the survivor farmers among American Jews.[25] The plant soon added gefilte fish to its product lineup, and Manischewitz ads that ran in Jewish weekly newspapers around the country before Passover in March 1956 boasted that they were made of eggs from "the famous Vineland, New Jersey egg farms." The ads made no reference to the unusual backstory of the farmers raising most of those eggs.[26]

———·———

Nuchim and Bronia's friends, Stanley and Lusia Igel, stood out as the rare poultry farmers who continued to thrive. The Igels started out with three thousand birds and now had twenty-one thousand chickens. Igel boasted of his eye-popping capital improvements to the *Times Journal* in June 1956.[27] Automatic waterers and aluminum-covered roofs and sprinklers in his coops had eliminated most heat-related chicken deaths on their farm. A cooler-dryer could hold sixteen baskets of eggs at once, allowing him to dry in ten minutes what used to take five or six hours. These investments gave farmers such as the Igels an advantage in competing against emerging southern megafarms that produced eggs more efficiently on a much larger scale.

Everything wasn't quite as blissful as it seemed for the Igels, particularly their fifteen-year-old daughter Toni. She had long since gotten reacquainted with the parents she rejected as a young girl after being hidden by a Christian family during the war. But Toni had an unhappy childhood isolated on the Estell Manor farm. She had commuted ninety minutes to two hours each way via car, bus, and jitney every day to attend a Jewish elementary school in Atlantic City. She didn't have any kids to play with near her farmhouse except her brother, who was eight years younger.[28] Toni was the rare child of survivors born during the war, so even when friends like the Greens visited on weekends, Toni was much older than any of the other children. Her father was serious and strict and brooked no dissent. Her parents had little empathy for her growing pains given their wartime experiences.[29] "For them, it was not an issue," Toni recalled. "What is happy? What does that mean? I'm alive, what is happy?"

A year earlier, Toni and her younger brother Stephen, who was six and a half at the time, had endured a harrowing ordeal while at sleepaway camp. Stephen and Toni were at Camp Massad in the Pocono Mountains in Pennsylvania when Hurricane Diane, the second major storm in a week, swelled a local creek and caused catastrophic flooding. A thirty-foot wave of water washed away homes and tourist cottages and killed nearly forty women and children at nearby Camp Davis.

Electricity cut out at Camp Massad, which was arrayed like a horseshoe around a lake on slightly higher ground, and a fire broke out in the bakery. During the night, the lake broke through a retaining wall, overturning twelve cabins that had been evacuated earlier. Word of what happened at Camp Davis circulated among the older kids Toni's age, who talked about it in horrified whispers. She recounted to a reporter how for three days the five hundred campers had no electricity and little cooked food and had no way of finding out whether their parents knew they were safe.

In Vineland, Stanley and Lusia were frantic, seeing no reference to Camp Massad in newspaper accounts of the flood. "For four days, I could not rest. How did I feel? I cannot explain it but I don't have to tell any parent."[30] Between them, Stanley and Lusia estimated they'd lost more than four hundred family members during the war. Now, the daughter whom they'd had to give up and who didn't even recognize them when they returned was missing along with her brother. He called the police in Stroudsburg, the nearest town of any size, several times a day, each call taking hours to get through. Each time, the police assured him the children at Camp Massad were safe.

On the fourth day, the children of Camp Massad walked three miles to a small town called Tannersville. Stephen ignored directions to take nothing with them and smuggled out a small suitcase with a Davy Crockett belt, a Western storybook, and a book on insects. On the way, they saw cars overturned and a home broken in half. At Tannersville, Toni and Stephen boarded a bus to New York City, where they reunited with their father. "I was never so glad to see anybody in my life," Toni said. Of those five days, Toni added, "It was terrible . . . one cannot imagine . . . one cannot believe."

17 ▸ COPING

Ruth was about ten years old when she went around the
corner one Saturday night to her best friend Helen's house for a sleepover
that she'd never forget. Over breakfast the next morning, Helen's mother
Zosia described in passing how she had her fingernails pulled out and suffered other forms of torture during the war. Helen was used to these off-
hand references to her mother's wartime experiences. If Helen complained
about having to do something as a child, her mother might say, "At least
you're not moving rocks from one side of a field to another."[1] Many years
later, Zosia and Helen watched a television program about other Auschwitz
survivors returning to visit the concentration camp where a green lawn was
visible. Zosia pointed out that no green grass grew during her time there:
starving prisoners like herself would have eaten it.

Zosia never offered her daughter a full account of her wartime experiences. Only later did Zosia testify during a West German investigation of a
Nazi official's role in liquidating a Jewish ghetto in south-central Poland and
sending sixteen hundred Jews to slave-labor camps in Starachowice.[2] Zosia
was first imprisoned in Starachowice, which was located near her hometown. She described to German investigators indiscriminate killings and

women forcibly torn from their children. After several escape attempts, guards threw grenades into underground burrows prisoners dug beneath the barracks to hide in, Zosia's testified.[3] Between twelve- and fourteen hundred Starachowice prisoners were transferred to Auschwitz-Birkenau in July 1944 as the Soviet Army closed in from the east.[4] Only half were still alive at the end of the war.[5]

Helen didn't remember her mother mentioning torture during a sleepover, though it didn't surprise her either. "That's how she would talk about it," Helen said.[6] Zosia's aside made Ruth deeply uncomfortable, in part because such a dark comment seemed so out of context at the breakfast table. It also stuck out because Zosia's openness about her wartime experiences contrasted with how little Ruth's parents said about theirs. Zosia's extreme candor and Bronia's silence encapsulate the polar extremes in how survivors in Vineland and elsewhere chose to talk about the war with their children. Some, like Zosia, spoke openly, if casually. Others talked about the war to excess, as was the case with Musia Deiches, the former child star.

Musia filled her children's bedtime stories with tales of wartime abuse and insisted her twins accompany her to the annual memorial service she helped organize. Her daughter Ruth was about twelve years old when a teacher asked her class to write an essay describing what period in history they would live in if given the chance. Ruth wrote that she'd choose the Nazi era to take some of her parents' pain away. The concerned teacher called her parents in for a meeting. "It was never forget, never forget," said Ruth Deiches, which had the effect of repelling her and her twin brother.[7] "Right now, me and my brother don't want to hear anything about the Holocaust," she said.

At the other extreme were survivors like Bronia, who chose to stay silent around their children. Bronia told Ruth nothing more than their family hadn't survived the war. "It was too painful" to say more, Bronia said. She couldn't even bear to hang any of the few pictures of her family that she'd carried with her from Europe. She kept the photos in a cigar box and never looked at them in Ruth's presence. Bronia's approach might have been more typical among survivors who "above all, wished to foster a normal family life once again," according to psychology professor Aaron Hass.[8] Likewise, Chris Lerman mostly avoided talking about the war with her children when they were young, in part to shelter them. Chris never dodged the topic if her children asked questions, including about the numbers tattooed on her arm.[9] Her son David recalled his parents keeping a book about the camps, which included pictures of the victims' skeletal corpses "stacked like wood" at the time of liberation "high up" on a shelf and out of reach. He looked at the book only later as a teenager.[10]

———•———

The Grine couldn't shield their children altogether from hearing about the war, no matter how hard they tried. The kids overheard snippets, typically when families gathered to socialize at one another's houses and the talk turned to the war or their early lives. At this time in the mid-1950s, there was no single word used by survivors—or journalists, novelists, or anyone else, for that matter—to refer to the Holocaust, as historian Hasia Diner has observed. In Yiddish, some called it the destruction, the third destruction, which referred to the destruction of the First and Second Temple in ancient Jerusalem, or Hitler times.[11] While the term "Holocaust" wasn't widely used until well into the 1960s and 1970s, the Jewish Agricultural Society occasionally referred to the "Nazi holocaust" and "Hitler holocaust"—never capitalized and always as a compound noun—as early as 1954 in its publications.[12]

Ruth first heard about her parents' experience at the age of five or six on the joint farm when family friends came over. Ruth remembered these as generally happy gatherings, full of laughter and vodka. Sometimes, though, talk turned to the war as she and Dorothy listened from their room right next to the kitchen. Bronia would refer to the *milkhome*, the Yiddish word for war. Ruth heard only fragments; never anything close to a full chronicle.[13] "I couldn't understand," she said. "It was all a mystery." Saul Golubcow similarly heard snippets about the war while hiding under his family's Vineland kitchen table as his parents and their friends talked in Yiddish.[14] He particularly liked the partisans' stories. "It was wistful, it was sad, it was somewhat angry," Golubcow said. "It was resigned in a way: 'Could you believe we're farmers?'"

Inside their farmhouse, the only formal acknowledgment of what Bronia and Nuchim lost came each spring when they lit *yortsayt*, or memorial, candles to commemorate their relatives' deaths. They didn't know the exact date their families died, choosing as a rough approximation the date on which the liquidation of Lublin's ghetto began, which also corresponded to when they got married.

When I started this project, I identified more with Bronia's younger sister Etka, who was roughly my age, and whose olive complexion I share. By the time I write this, my thoughts turn more often to their younger brother Monik, who was not much older than my son is now when the war began. From the age of seven, he lived the rest of his short life confined first to his family's apartment, and then the ghetto. He should have been about the age I am now when I was born; in some alternative universe, he should have been just seventy-seven at my wedding. Instead, he was frozen in Bronia's memory forever as the little boy with the sunburn so bad during a summer in the country that they used sour cream as a balm. At the time her siblings got deported from Lublin's ghetto to Belzec, Bronia remained trapped in Nuchim's family recycling plant with no way—and nowhere—to mourn. Just more rags to sort and more worries about what might happen next.

Bronia and Nuchim shared none of those details of what they experienced or lost with Ruth as they lit the memorial candles in their families' honor. Ruth noticed Bronia grew particularly withdrawn some days, which she guessed corresponded with family birthdays. Regardless of the day, however, the tone inside the house "was somber, very somber," Ruth said. Even as Bronia insisted that Ruth take piano lessons, she never played any records or listened to music on the radio at home. Guests didn't see that side of their private life. David Lerman recalled that "some survivors' houses understandably felt like a perpetual *shiva* house so deep and lasting were the losses and the pain," referring to the weeklong mourning period following a death. In contrast, David remembered the Greens' home as "a very happy place" where there was plenty of laughter and Bronia always had a smile on her face.[15]

Ruth found it a little easier to coax Nuchim into talking about the war as she got older—particularly if she asked about his exploits as a partisan. He took pride in how he protected Bronia, their neighbor Sally noted. "Otherwise, I don't think she would have survived," Sally said.[16] But Nuchim found it all but impossible to talk about the family he lost. That was often the case. Orchard Road neighbor Zella Shabasson remembered how her father, who survived several concentration camps, occasionally sang songs from childhood or talked generally about how things were "in the home" growing up but never talked about his family.[17] It wasn't until a few weeks before he died at the age of ninety-two that Shabasson could talk to his daughter about his sister, revealing she'd had a baby who also got murdered.

———•———

Bronia tried not to dwell on the war, as if it was merely a matter of will-power. "If you think about it, there would be no life," she said. Despite her best efforts to put it out of mind, Bronia undoubtedly suffered from the lingering effects of wartime injuries both physical and psychological. She didn't talk much about it beyond saying she was more anxious after the war than before. Bronia provided the most comprehensive catalogue of her injuries in applications she submitted for reparations from the West German government, the first of which she filed in June 1956. The challenge is disentangling what's true in her applications from the fabrications that had compounded on top of one another for more than a decade.

West Germany's reparation law, first enacted in 1953 and then revised in 1956, aimed to compensate Nazi victims for losses of liberty, for injuries, as well as for damage to their ability to earn a living. Some survivors refused to accept what they considered a form of blood money. For most south Jersey Grine—and the German refugees who settled here earlier—the prospects of reparation payments were of intense interest. One of Ruth's friends recalled her German-born grandmother who came to the United States in 1940, and lived with her family part-time in Vineland, would carry her reparations papers in her pocketbook at all times.[18]

In June 1956, the German refugees' Poultrymen's Club hosted a talk by former war crimes prosecutor Robert M. W. Kempner about the latest revisions to the reparations law. Kempner, a German-born Jew, was a prominent Berlin attorney in the 1920s when, as chief legal adviser to the Prussian police, he helped prosecute Adolf Hitler for attempting to overthrow the German government.[19] He was arrested, imprisoned, and finally forced to leave Germany after the Nazis took power. He returned after the war as a prosecutor at the international military tribunal at Nuremberg, where his knowledge of the German legal system and police methods proved particularly useful.[20] In 1951, Kempner resumed practicing law in Germany, and he spent the next four decades representing Jewish clients in restitution cases. Bronia's reparation records indicate she was among Kempner's clients.

Kempner's June 1956 talk at North Italy Hall was at least the third he had delivered on the subject of German restitution laws to the Poultrymen's Club in Vineland. The fact that the talk was held at the North Italy Hall rather than the Poultrymen's smaller Landis Avenue clubhouse suggests the event was aimed at a much wider audience then the club's German Jewish members.[21] Kempner explained to attendees that they could receive up to thirty-five dollars per month under the new law, a not inconsiderable sum for struggling farmers—or any Americans, really—at a time when the median U.S. household income was forty-eight hundred dollars per year.[22] Nazi victims would ultimately be entitled to much more, depending on the extent of the physical injuries and other losses they suffered during the war.

Bronia filed a deprivation of liberty claim under the provision of the reparations law that allowed for recovery by those who had been in police or military custody, detained or imprisoned, or forced into a ghetto. Her application and an accompanying affidavit in German from her childhood friend Dina Liverant attested to the fact that she was in the ghetto in Lublin that was "closed off completely" from December 1939 until November 1942. Bronia received notice in April 1957 that she was entitled to six thousand deutsche marks for the forty months of lost liberty. That's roughly fifteen hundred dollars in 1957 or fourteen thousand dollars today, a sum that undoubtedly cushioned their income as egg prices remained low.

In 1958, Bronia filed a separate health claim. The relevant part of the German reparations law was modeled on a worker's compensation system, with awards based on the extent to which wartime injuries reduced earning potential. At the time Bronia initially applied, only physical—rather than psychological—injuries qualified for compensation, although that would later change.

Bronia explained in her application that she was "greatly hindered" and "hardly able to work" due to "severe pain in all the limbs," particularly when the weather changed. She also said she suffered from dizziness, exhaustion, headaches, irritability, insomnia, crying, and shouting, with palpitations and stomach discomfort. When asked to describe specific circumstances that brought about this damage, Bronia recounts how an SS guard once struck her with the tip of his gun. She also described living in a "cold and damp" pit in the forest with little to eat and said that at the time of liberation she weighed as little as sixty-five pounds, a shockingly low weight more common among emaciated concentration camp victims than those who survived in the woods.

An accompanying letter from Dr. G. Anthony Mascara of Vineland provided more detail about Bronia's health. Mascara, an Italian American World War II veteran who opened his Vineland medical practice in 1946, attested to having begun treating "Bertha Green" in 1947. Among her symptoms were "severe nervousness (shakes continuously)" plus loss of appetite, insomnia, and "a severe sense of exhaustion" that means she "cannot work nor perform her daily duties as a housewife." "There is no doubt that patient has a very severe anxiety state incurred while being persecuted by the Germans," Mascara wrote, before concluding that Bronia was 65 percent disabled. To assess claimants' disability, the German consulate appointed doctors who were usually German-born themselves, since they needed to provide a written report in German.[23] Bronia's reviewer classified her as 35 percent disabled, above the 25 percent threshold that qualified for compensation. She received an initial lump sum payment and a monthly pension of roughly one hundred deutsche marks, which increased over time.

There is much in the 1958 application that's at odds with Bronia's actual history, starting with her birthdate. She listed her birthdate as March 18, 1922—the right month and day but four years after the actual date. She'd shaved four years off her age as early as the summer of 1946 when she registered for the first time as a displaced person upon arriving in the American occupation zone in Germany. Nuchim similarly shifted his birth year from 1914 to 1919 on their registration cards. He also listed Ruth's birthplace as Frankfurt, Germany, rather than Lodz and his as the Soviet city of Minsk. In a letter to his uncles in New York, Nuchim explained that he registered as a Jew raised in the Soviet Union, rather than Poland, in an attempt to expedite their arrival in the United States. "Maybe that will be quicker that way," Nuchim wrote.

Jews had no choice but to lie as a matter of survival, both during and after the war. Those who passed as Gentiles lied about their religion. The old and young alike tried obscuring their true ages during selections that culled those who weren't fit enough to be worked to death. During an early ghetto selection, Chris Lerman's mother tried to make her scrawny, younger sister look older by stuffing her chest with rags and applying rouge to her cheeks.[24] Older concentration camp prisoners dyed their hair with shoe polish to look younger. After the war, "for large numbers of DPs, lying was a necessity," historian David Nasaw has noted.[25] In just one example, the Displaced Persons Act of 1948 set December 22, 1945, as the date by which refugees had to have entered the American zone of occupation in order to qualify for a visa, even though the mass migration of Polish Jews didn't occur until the following year.

Nuchim and Bronia had arrived in the United States before the DP Acts went into effect, but also felt compelled to embellish their biographies in ways they thought would make them more attractive refugee candidates. That's probably why they claimed Ruth was born in Germany. Existing U.S. immigration laws designed to limit new arrivals from undesirable Eastern and Southern European countries set a higher quota for Germany than Poland or the Soviet Union. Nuchim, who prided himself on his honesty, continued fudging once in the United States. He and Jack exaggerated the extent of their prior farming experience when seeking help from the Jewish Agricultural Society.

These strategic and necessary fabrications often took on a life of their own and later caused unexpected complications. As the volume of claims and the size of potential payouts increased over time, German reparation authorities looked more closely for discrepancies in applicants' place of birth or age and reexamined those already receiving pensions for health reasons.[26] Decades later, survivors had trouble collecting Social Security benefits because they had claimed to be younger when they came to the United States.[27] The Social Security Administration later revised its rules to help an estimated ten thousand survivors who had lied about their age.[28]

Bronia later struggled to explain to reparation administrators why she couldn't provide any official documentation of Ruth's birthplace in Germany. Having listed Ruth's birthplace as Frankfurt, she couldn't change course. In a subsequent reparations filing, Bronia claimed she gave birth in a private apartment in "a small town close to Frankfurt." "I have tried to remember the place where my child was born; I have not succeeded," Bronia said in the affidavit. She remained fearful that the lie might catch up with her and worried she'd get deported. Bronia never felt entirely comfortable telling the truth, even to her own family. Ruth learned of her true birthplace only as an adult. Bronia's continued discomfort was still evident on a tape-recorded family history interview Ruth did with Bronia around 1980. When Ruth asked where she was born, Bronia replies, "You were born in Germany." At that point, Ruth turns off the tape and everyone is laughing when they resume the interview. "Alright, you can say where I was born?" Ruth asks. Only then does Bronia reply, "Lodz."[29]

A close childhood friend of Bronia who settled in Israel after the war weaved a more elaborate web of fabrications. Bronia's friend claimed to have survived the war hidden in Poland in information submitted to the U.S. Holocaust Memorial Museum and during an interview she did with a Polish organization committed to preserving her hometown's Jewish history. In fact, Bronia's friend and her father had fled to Soviet-occupied territory, exiled first to Arkhangelsk, a port city in the far north on the White Sea, and then relocated to Samarkand, Uzbekistan, on the southern edge of the nation. Bronia's friend made clear she didn't want any identifiable information published about her time in the Soviet Union. She probably had submitted a liberty claim for reparations as someone who survived under German rule, which she wouldn't have qualified for since she'd escaped soon after the occupation began.[30]

Bronia's fibs aren't quite on the same scale but still make it difficult to figure out how much her health was actually damaged during the war. It is hard to reconcile accounts provided by Bronia and her Vineland physician that give the impression she was incapable of working full-time when she was employed at a garment factory off and on for years while raising Ruth and helping out on the farm. In all likelihood, a sympathetic doctor helped survivors like Bronia game a system that couldn't possibly compensate them for all they had lost or for their continued anguish. Bronia may not have weighed sixty-five pounds when she emerged from the forest. But she still struggled with wartime injuries, including a melancholy that never really lifted. That is not to say she never experienced joy in Vineland, whether on the dance floor at the White Sparrow Inn during Jewish Poultry Farmers Association dances, while playing cards with friends at their kitchen tables, or while sunbathing at Norma Beach. But the sadness was always there too, and only grew worse in the years ahead.

———•———

In the early 1960s, a German Jewish refugee psychiatrist named William Niederland would coin the term "survivor syndrome" to describe a set of symptoms common among survivors, ranging from isolation and withdrawal to depression, anxiety, and agitation.[31] A whole body of research in subsequent decades examined the survivors' long-term mental well-being with mixed conclusions.[32] Accounts by social scientists and journalists later challenged the tendency to overpathologize victims and instead focused on the survivors' "flexibility and resilience," while skeptics questioned whether the prevalence of those who easily transcended trauma were overstated.[33]

The American Psychiatric Association incorporated the constellation of symptoms associated with "survivor syndrome" and earlier forms of wartime trauma such as "shell shock" by adding posttraumatic stress disorder to its official manual of mental disorders in 1980.[34] Researchers studying trauma have since noted the commonalities among trauma survivors, whether they endured concentration camps or rape, political terror or domestic abuse. Survivors of all kinds vary widely in how they react to trauma, often continuing to feel the effects for years after the fact. "No two people have identical reactions, even to the same event," wrote psychiatrist Judith Herman in her groundbreaking 1992 study of trauma and recovery.[35] "The traumatic syndrome, despite its many constant features, is not the same for everyone."

Survivors in Vineland, as was also the case elsewhere, for the most part can't be neatly typecast. They varied as widely in how well they dealt with their emotional wounds as in how much they told their children. It is too simple to say concentration camps survivors, who endured so much, found it harder to cope or to keep the details to themselves. True, Zosia Waiman and Musia Deiches were both concentration camp survivors. Then again, so was Chris Lerman. So many factors played a role, including their individual disposition, their prewar upbringing, the extent of their wartime suffering, and whether they lost everyone or had surviving family members for support.

Even the seemingly most well-adjusted like Chris and Miles didn't escape entirely unscathed. Chris found positive outlets to channel her wartime trauma. After surviving on thin soups with potato peels and bread with more sawdust than flour, Chris particularly enjoyed cooking a barley soup nearly thick enough to hold up a spoon.[36] After the filth of Auschwitz, she relaxed by ironing crisp, clean sheets.[37] Still, Chris later said, "The terrible things are there all the time and they will always remain deeply rooted."[38]

What survivors attempted to hide from their children during the day often surfaced in the middle of the night.[39] Miles yelled in his sleep in Russian and Polish and dreamed of running away from pursuers without gaining any distance. In his nightmares, he struggled to reload the clip in his gun.[40] Chris dreamed of running away from Nazis with her two children—both born after the war—in her arms. She made a joke out of it, telling people who asked why she didn't have more children that the reason was "because I only have two arms" to carry them if they needed to flee.[41]

Well into her seventies, more than a half century after her mother's murder at Treblinka, Chris still woke up in the middle of the night screaming, "Momma!"[42]

18 ▸ GRIEF AND FAITH

Vineland hosted two very different Memorial Day events in the span of three days in May 1956. First came the annual bilingual memorial for the "Martyrs of Nazi Tyranny" at Vineland's junior high school where Rita Karin, a survivor and star of the Yiddish stage, performed in Yiddish. Then, on Memorial Day itself, the Vineland Riding Club's annual one-day horse show opened on a site around the corner from Bronia and Nuchim's farm on Orchard Road, starring Sally Starr, a gun-toting cowgirl who hosted Philadelphia-area Western TV and radio shows.[1]

The two events—attended by some of the very same people—had become late May fixtures in Vineland by the mid-1950s. They were just one of many such incongruous juxtapositions between Jewish and rural life possible in Vineland at this moment in time. Name another small town in 1950s America where a horse show shared the same stretch of rural road with a Jewish day school and a *shtibl*, the sort of small synagogue common in Eastern European communities before the war.

The evolution of Vineland's memorial event in the years since it began five years earlier is a window into the uneasy way survivors coexisted with the broader local Jewish community. This kind of memorial ceremony and

the mourners' service during the High Holidays took on outsized importance to survivors. They lacked any of the normal ways to mourn for relatives
murdered in concentration camps and disposed of in crematoria or mass
graves.[2] They never had a chance to bury their loved ones or sit *shiva* during the traditional weeklong mourning period that followed; they didn't
know the exact day of death on which to say Kaddish, the Jewish mourning
prayer. They couldn't visit a gravesite.

Commemorating the monthlong Warsaw Ghetto uprising that began in
April 1943 became a popular way to highlight Jewish resistance and strength
as well as the broader "immense, impenetrable tragedy."[3] At these events,
survivors and nonsurvivors helped create a "memorial culture" designed to
"keep alive the memory of the Jews who had perished."[4] The raw emotion
survivors displayed at Vineland's memorials could leave American-born
Jews in attendance shaken or uncomfortable. Magda Leuchter, the wife of
the *Times Journal*'s editor who went out of her way to befriend survivors,
told her daughters about the heart-rending scenes full of "shrieking and
wailing" she witnessed there.[5]

At the 1951 event sponsored by the predecessor of the Jewish Poultry
Farmers Association (JPFA), both of Vineland's establishment rabbis spoke,
and a Brooklyn cantor and his wife sang "Ani Ma'amin," a mournful dirge
American Jewish groups had begun including in songbooks because it was
said to have been sung by "Nazi victims who were about to be cremated."[6]
The following year, the local Beth Israel synagogue hosted a community-
wide event featuring the U.S. Navy's highest-ranking chaplain, which didn't
include any survivor representation.[7] Perhaps that explains why the Jewish
community hosted two different memorial events in 1953: one organized by
the survivors in April held two days after the tenth anniversary of the start of
the Warsaw Ghetto uprising; twelve local Jewish organizations held a
community-wide event at the Beth Israel synagogue in May.[8]

In an oral history interview decades later, Annette Greenblatt, whose
Philadelphia-born parents opened I. C. Schwarzman's department store in
Vineland in the 1930s, recalled that "the survivors would not allow anyone
other than a survivor" to come to their commemorative services.[9] "They
held them themselves, and it was secretive, and it was their thing," said
Greenblatt, who graduated high school in 1941. Greenblatt's recollection
provides insight into how American-born Jews perceived survivors, but is at
odds with the contemporary record. In fact, the community had coalesced

around a single event in 1954, although the survivors still stood apart to some extent; the portion under Miles Lerman's direction didn't begin until after intermission.[10] Finally, in 1955, they unified, just as other communities throughout America moved away from smaller separate programs to massive city-wide memorials.[11] For one day at least, descendants of the original Russian Jewish settlers, German Jewish refugees, and postwar survivors came together even if they weren't yet entirely comfortable with one another the rest of the year.

For the second year in a row, attendees at the 1956 event gathered before twilight on a Sunday night in late May at Vineland's Memorial Junior High School, one of the few venues in town capable of hosting a crowd of more than five hundred people. The two-story school had opened less than two years earlier, and the auditorium's antiseptic light-colored wall panels and checkerboard floor tiles still gleamed like new. Audience members in folding mahogany seats that matched the woodwork on the elevated stage heard attorney Harry Levin, chairman of the Vineland Jewish National Fund Council, announce a goal of planting ten thousand trees in the Jerusalem hills.[12]

The ceremony had many of the elements common among Warsaw Ghetto commemorative events held elsewhere at the time, including stirring speeches, prayers, canonical ghetto hymns, and the lighting of six candles to honor those lost.[13] JPFA president Chaim Gruenfeld, a dark-haired forty-four-year-old survivor whose drawn face made him look much older, lit the memorial candles. A Philadelphia cantor delivered a memorial prayer, and a Yiddish poet recited some of his work before Yiddish actor Rita Karpinovitch depicted "Nazi oppression and life in the Ghettos."[14]

Karpinovitch, a Vilna native, managed alongside her husband to make a living by entertaining fellow survivors in Yiddish, first in displaced persons camps in Europe and then in the United States.[15] Karpinovitch, or Karin as she came to be known during a decades-long stage, film, and television career in the United States, later recorded a Yiddish song for the U.S. Holocaust Museum. She sang "A Yidish Kind" (A Jewish Child) about a Jewish mother forced to leave her child with a Gentile family, a recording that went off flawlessly, even as she sobbed between takes at the bitter memories the song evoked.[16]

Visiting Vineland could be an emotional experience for New York–based Yiddish artists. Isaac Shmulewitz, editor of the Yiddish daily *Forward* newspaper, recalled the "excited anticipation" he felt before his many appearances at

JPFA events and the "longing" when it was time to leave.[17] This was a chance to see "the rare new Jewish settlement on American soil" where farmers had created a "warm, truly Jewish" environment, Shmulewitz later wrote.

To survivors, the Yiddish-speaking singers, poets, writers, and actors offered much more than an occasional evening of entertainment. These performances provided a way to stay connected to a language with deep emotional resonance. Yiddish reminded some of lost childhoods, families, and hometowns. For those who had survived ghettos and concentration camps, where Jews of many nationalities wound up confined together, Yiddish became a "lingua franca," at least among Eastern European Jews.[18] More assimilated Jews who didn't speak Yiddish regularly before the war embraced the language as an expression of solidarity while in hiding. Nuchim and Bronia, who grew up speaking mostly Polish, learned Yiddish fluently in the woods. They joined their fellow partisans in renouncing their mother tongue of Polish in protest against a homeland they believed had betrayed its Jewish citizens.

For all those reasons, survivor poultry farmers held onto Yiddish tightly. Yiddish—or what some survivors like Bronia referred to as Jewish— became the primary language at JPFA meetings and in its newsletter.[19] Members could borrow Yiddish translations of world classics, part of a lending library of five hundred books by Jewish authors available Sunday nights at the Veterans of Foreign Wars hall on Plum Street.[20] (Circulation was only "fair," one organizer noted with sadness.)[21] Just as survivors in New York helped breathe new life into Yiddish theater, the Grine in Vineland helped revive Yiddish culture in an area where attorney Harry Levin said "many of our so-called 'Native American Jews' had almost forgotten what a Yiddish word was, a Jewish play, a Yiddish concert."[22]

The *Times Journal* didn't mention what songs Karin performed in Vineland at this memorial event, nor did the paper offer an estimate of the crowd, which usually totaled between four hundred and six hundred people. Bronia and Nuchim—or at least Nuchim—were probably in the audience that Sunday. Given his fascination with cowboys, he was also likely in attendance three days later at a far more festive occasion right around the corner from his farmhouse on Memorial Day itself.[23]

Each Memorial Day for the previous decade or so, the largely empty lot at the corner of Orchard and Elm transformed into a scene out of the Wild

West, or at least Hollywood's version of it. On every other day, this site occupied by the Vineland Riding Club was a quiet patch of dirt where neighborhood kids played baseball or rode their bikes. Riding club members occasionally gathered there for early breakfasts at the modest clubhouse before setting off on morning rides or came late at night for campfire music and "moonlight rides" that started at ten o'clock.

The riding club's membership rolls included few survivors. Horse riding reminded survivors of the hapless cavalry units from their days in the Polish Army. Horses—whether in the flesh or as depicted by Hollywood—appealed more to the survivors' children in an era when cowboys dominated pop culture. *Gunsmoke*, the CBS radio Western drama set in Dodge City, Kansas, had made the leap to television a year earlier, prompting NBC to follow with its own Western, *Wagon Train*, in 1957.

All through the summer of 1956, television station Channel 12 aired weekly rodeos held twenty-five miles away at Cowtown in Pilesgrove, New Jersey. Closer to home, the Rocking R Ranch on West Oak Road hosted pony rides every night from five o'clock until dark all summer. One of Bronia and Nuchim's neighbors who led Ruth's Girl Scout troop, occasionally allowed the girls to ride her horse. In this era of Davy Crockett and Westerns on television, "everyone wanted a coon skin cap and a gun and a holster," recalled Ruth's friend and neighbor Helen Waiman, who was in the same Girl Scout troop.[24]

The gates at the Memorial Day horse show opened at nine forty-five in the morning, and the one-dollar admission fee for adults and fifty cents for kids gave attendees access to a daylong series of thirty attractions. This year's performers included "Uncle Elmer" Hines, who circled the oval in a two-wheel racing cart pulled by his favorite black mule.[25] Living nearby had advantages. Helen Waiman, who lived next door, could sneak in through the back. Leah Lederman, who lived across the street and loved horses, watched for free some years by climbing atop a wooden fence on the Hymans' property abutting the horse club. Leah had no choice but to pay the admission fee in order to enter the raffle to take home a pony at a subsequent year's show; much to her parents' relief, she didn't win.[26]

The horse show held little appeal to Ruth, who had just turned ten. She mostly remembered the noise—and the smell—of so many horses and hundreds of people on a hot summer day. The event was of greater interest to Nuchim, given his love of Westerns. Nuchim had also developed a taste for kitschy Americana in his first decade in his adopted country, enjoying visits to Vineland's most bizarre year-round attraction: the Palace of Depression. George Daynor, who claimed to be a former Alaskan gold prospector, constructed a mansion made out of trash on the site of a swampy automobile graveyard.[27] Daynor built the eighteen-spired castle-like house with odd pieces of cement, rocks, and scrap metal plus everything from a baby's crib gate to a wagon wheel. Tours cost twenty-five cents at what became a famous enough draw to be included on Esso gas station maps of New Jersey.[28] "It gave me the creeps," Ruth recalled.

Nuchim was probably drawn less to the formal riding and jumping competitions than the performance by Joanna and Wilson Mathis, a married rodeo trick duo and their white albino horse Chico.[29] Perhaps Wilson performed his favorite routine, the Roman ride, in which he rode two horses with a foot on each's back while they jumped hurdles in unison.[30] For the children, the big draw of this year's show came when the thirty-three-year-old Starr entered the parade circle around eleven thirty.[31] Starr had started hosting an evening television show at six o'clock on Philadelphia's WFIL that soon morphed into *Popeye Theater*. She introduced cowboy Western movies and the famous animated sailor's cartoons in her signature fringed cowgirl outfit, complete with tall boots and a white cowboy hat that covered her long blond hair. She wore the same getup for public appearances like this one.

Starr's TV show stayed on the air until the early 1970s, and an entire generation of Philadelphia-area children grew up watching every night after school. Decades later, survivors' children shared warm memories of Starr, who signed off every night by saying, "Love, luck and lollipops." "She was my first crush," said Ely Swerdlin.[32] At the riding club this day, Starr undoubtedly charmed adults and children alike. She made—and lost—a fortune off just this kind of personal appearance headlining at pig farms and Kentucky Fried Chicken grand openings. By late afternoon, the concession stand had sold out of ice cream and soda.[33] The crowds thinned, and the performers and their horses left the site for another year.

———•———

The horse club's site had long since gone quiet by the time a new synagogue came to life on the opposite corner at Orchard and Elm in early September. With its triangular roof and residential window frames, the synagogue looked more like just another farmhouse than a house of worship, except for the tablet with Hebrew letters above the door capped by a crown and two lions.

This modest one-story sandy brown clapboard building was a shtibl, the type of small house of prayer common in Europe before the war that had been more recently transplanted to the United States. Observant Jews don't drive or use public transportation on Shabbat or holidays and need a communal place to pray within walking distance of their homes. They opened shtiblekh in converted houses or semi-renovated storefronts in American cities.

Perhaps only in Vineland, though, could a shtibl open directly across the street from the site of a horse show. If that wasn't unusual enough, a motor raceway had opened about two miles south of here on Delsea Drive on Palm Sunday in April 1955.[34] As many as three thousand fans gathered Saturday nights as stock cars raced around the Vineland Speedway's track.

The average survivor found auto racing about as appealing as horseback riding as a leisure activity, though congregants at the shtibl couldn't avoid the racing experience altogether. The speedway was close enough that anyone walking home from Shabbat services at the shtibl could hear the stock cars in the distance during occasional Fright night races. Another staple of 1950s Americana was even closer: the Delsea Drive-In movie theater. It sat just a mile away on South Delsea Drive. On the night the shtibl held its first service in September, *Away All Boats*, about a U.S. Navy amphibious troop transport in the Pacific during World War II, premiered at the drive-in.

Other, less religious poultry farmers later recalled feeling more comfortable among themselves rather than in one of Vineland's two biggest establishment synagogues, Beth Israel and Sons of Jacob.[35] "They treated the Holocaust survivors like inferiors," Nella Juffe, who was born in Poland and fled to the Soviet Union after the German invasion, recalled in a memoir decades later that provided no further explanation of why she felt unwelcome.[36] Her husband, Leon, who survived the war hiding for sixteen months in a bunker covered with boards, straw, and manure under a horse stable, helped found another survivor shtibl, Agudath Achim, on South Main Road.[37] "We were proud of our synagogue and felt comfortable there with the other Holocaust survivors," Juffe wrote. Barbara Werner, a daughter of survivors who was born in the early 1950s, stopped going to Hebrew school at Beth Israel because "American Jews made my life miserable."[38] One of the

American Jewish girls taunted her for living on the wrong side of the tracks and made fun of her parents' accent. "It was horrible, and finally I said I didn't want to go back." (Barbara's cousin, Mark, who was roughly the same age and also grew up in Vineland, remembered no such negative experiences.)[39]

Some American and German Jews recalled sometimes feeling just as unwelcome at Beth Israel as the Grine. There was a class dimension to who felt out of place at the establishment synagogue where Jewish professionals and businesspeople congregated. The American-born owner of an auto shop once went to Beth Israel to say Kaddish in his mechanics overalls. He was told he wasn't dressed appropriately and never went back.[40] Some German Jewish refugees broke off from Beth Israel to establish their own synagogue right near Agudath Achim. The two congregations located within feet of one another remained strictly separate. One son of survivors whose family attended Agudath Achim didn't enter the nearby German Jewish synagogue, Shaare Tikvah, until he was a teenager, and then only because his friend, a talented dancer, went to the German synagogue to teach a youth group a popular dance move called the "strand."[41]

Early on, the survivors had prayed in farmhouses and even a firehouse. As their numbers grew, they eventually established at least five shtiblekh around Vineland. Most became known by the name of the street on which they were located, such as Mill Road, Main Road, or, in this case, Orchard Road. The Orchard Road congregants chose a formal name for their shtibl rich with meaning: Shairit Haplaite—the surviving or spared remnant.[42] In 1944, an underground newspaper in a Dachau subcamp had used the term, which has biblical origins, to describe those who might survive to see Germany defeated.[43] The term stuck after the war. American Jews also used it as a shorthand for those who had survived.[44] The 1952 annual report of the Jewish Agricultural Society (JAS) described the new wave of émigrés who had taken up farming in New Jersey as "'the surviving remnant' of the Nazi holocaust, who had been through the 'seven flames of hell.'"[45]

Abraham Tauber, a former Polish yeshiva student who survived as a forest partisan and operated a feed mill on his Vineland poultry farm, found the piece of land he described as a *lokh*—hole, in Yiddish.[46] The owner, a non-Jewish Hungarian immigrant, sold them the parcel in 1955 for one dollar, according to the deed, in a transaction handled, of course, by attorney Harry Levin. Tauber told his children that Mayor John Gittone sent, at no cost, city dumpsters filled with dirt to help level the site. Starting with sixty dollars, Tauber and a few dozen fellow farmers and other Grine who lived around Orchard Road had come together to fund and build the shtibl themselves. Wives sold cakes at a bake sale. Their children donated a few coins each. A *Times Journal* story inviting readers to send contributions noted "the birth of this synagogue was based upon the founders' dream for religious belief, a right denied them when they were displaced persons in Nazi concentration camps."[47] By late August, the structure was mostly complete, with just heating, plumbing, and other interior installations left to finish before Rosh Hashanah and Yom Kippur, referred to as the High Holidays, began.

A photo accompanying the *Times Journal* story about the new shtibl showed a five-man choir rehearsing for High Holiday services. Helen's father, Jerome Waiman, is among those pictured holding siddurs and wearing bowties, yarmulkes, and *tallit*, the fringed garment worn by men over their clothing while praying. In the center of the group stood thirty-five-year-old Irving Schock, dressed in the black robe he would don as the shtibl's lay cantor on many High Holidays and Shabbats to come. Schock, who lived on an Orchard Road poultry farm near Bronia and Nuchim, was a former yeshiva student who came from a long line of scholars. The noise of New York City repelled Schock after he arrived there in 1949, and he opted for a quieter life in Vineland.[48] Schock found peace on his own bit of land and in the routine of farmwork. He found a sense of mission in helping build this shtibl, an outlet for the great joy of his life: cantorial singing.

When congregants entered the shtibl for the first time at the start of Rosh Hashanah services at seven o'clock on the evening of September 5, the most observant kissed the *mezuzah*, the decorative case containing a parchment inscribed with Torah verses hung on doorposts. Inside, the *bimah*, or raised platform where the Torah is read, stood against the left wall facing east toward Jerusalem. A mahogany cabinet—the ark—housed the velvet wrapped Torah. Both the ark and the bimah had been rescued from a Philadelphia synagogue being closed to make way for a factory.[49] This was a "no-frills" Orthodox shul with room to seat a few dozen congregants, an informal, homey atmosphere, with no sermons, just *davening*, or praying. Tauber, who served as the congregation's first president and sang melodies from Hebrew prayers to his daughter as bedtime lullabies, often led the davening. The women sat in fold-up chairs and chatted in the back behind the curtain that divided them from the section up front where the men prayed.

Children played outside and ate homemade fried chicken cooked by their mothers.

Sometime that fall, the new congregation took to the street to celebrate the arrival of the synagogue's Torah, which, like its members, was a refugee from the war in Europe. Three men in suits and ties and one equally formally dressed woman each carried a rod above their heads that held up a dark sheet. It was a mobile version of the *chuppah*, the canopy under which a bride and groom stand at their wedding ceremony. Underneath this canopy, an older man in a suit, tie, and fedora carried the Torah itself. Three dozen men, women, and children, all formally dressed for the occasion, made up the rest of the procession. The man holding up the canopy in the foreground with a yarmulke on his head and a handkerchief in his suit pocket is Nuchim, evidence that he was front and center at the shtibl, at least for its opening. He must have been proud to participate, celebrating his religion so openly on their street, an act of defiance in a city where a cross was burned on the lawn of Jewish refugees just a few years earlier.

Nuchim's prominent role at the celebration didn't carry over into regular attendance on the Jewish Sabbath or holidays, unlike some neighbors who attended services at the shtibl dutifully every Saturday. Ruth had to all but drag her parents to the synagogue even though it was just a few feet from their farmhouse. "I forced the issue," Ruth said. "I would make a big deal of going, so we would go, just on holidays." At the time, Ruth couldn't understand her parents' indifference about religious observance. "I knew I was Jewish, we spoke Yiddish," she said. They still celebrated holidays, and Bronia faithfully lit *yortsayt* candles to honor the memory of family members she lost. Nuchim remained as committed a Zionist as ever. But when it came to religious practice, Nuchim "really gave up," Ruth recalled. Only later did Ruth come to understand the extent to which the war had tested their faith. As Bronia explained, she had lost her observant parents and saw "the best rabbis" die, so she couldn't help but be less observant.

It was an attitude shared by many survivors, but certainly not all. While Bronia and Nuchim lost faith in equal measure, the phenomenon was more uneven in other survivor households in Vineland. Aron Swerdlin recalled his mother, Mira, a Vilna Ghetto survivor, "lost her belief in God" entirely and "was agnostic."[50] Yet his father, Herman, continued to attend services regularly at Sons of Jacob, where he read Torah portions in Hebrew, as much for the comfort of maintaining a routine from childhood as an expression of devotion.[51] The Swerdlins didn't keep a kosher house or observe the Sabbath, although both sons went to Hebrew School and had bar mitzvahs. Even Mrs. Swerdlin went to services on the High Holidays.

What's perhaps more surprising is just how many of the survivors in Vineland and elsewhere didn't give up on religious observance, no matter how much they'd suffered during the war. Survivors belonged to synagogues, kept kosher homes, and observed the Sabbath more often than other American-born Jews and were three times more likely to identify as Orthodox.[52] In 1954, the *Times Journal* told the story of one such observant survivor, Chaim Lindenblatt, a fifty-five-year-old former rabbinical student who the paper said "has one burning desire in this world that overshadows anything else"—to establish a synagogue near his poultry farm in Landisville, a small town just east of Vineland.[53]

Lindenblatt had lost his first wife, two sons, and a daughter to the Nazis, and yet went back to Poland after liberation from Buchenwald to retrieve his father's Torah scroll that he'd buried in the woods for safekeeping. He set up a makeshift synagogue on his poultry farm in Landisville and bought Jewish prayer shawls for youngsters and refreshments out of his own modest pockets for as many as thirty people who attended. He had so much trouble at first gathering a *minyan*, the quorum of ten needed to conduct communal Jewish worship, on High Holidays, he wrote other survivors from his hometown in Wolen, Poland, who lived in Baltimore. Several traveled to Landisville for Yom Kippur. "Religion is life itself to Lindenblatt," the *Times Journal* noted.

The ranks of survivors included enough believers like Lindenblatt to fill five shtiblekh and expand the Jewish day school, which moved into a new forty-thousand-dollar, eight-classroom schoolhouse on three and a half acres on Orchard Road in early 1957. Enrollment had tripled from 55 in 1953 to 164 students as the school expanded from kindergarten through third grade to kindergarten through eighth grade. Most were the children of survivors. Vineland mayor Frank Testa was among seven hundred people who attended the opening ceremony for the new school building.[54]

The Jewish day school's student body ultimately included the children of Moses and Leah Silberberg, both the sole survivors in their families. Moses lost his first wife and two children; Leah lost all six of her sisters. Still, both

remained intent on marrying someone *frum*, the Yiddish word for observant Jews. They met after the war in Germany and settled in Vineland as one
of the few strictly Orthodox families on a poultry farm there. Leah covered
her hair and wore modest clothing. Neighbors teased Leah about her
daughters' old-fashioned clothing, warning that no one would want to
marry them. One daughter ultimately married an ultra-Orthodox rabbi and
settled in Israel.[55]

Harry Golubcow also enrolled his son at the Jewish day school even
though he lost his first wife and the rest of his family during the war. Still,
Golubcow wrestled with his faith within earshot of his children. His son
Saul was about eight or nine years old when he heard his father, in Yiddish,
tell fellow survivors gathered at their house that Hitler had made him into
an *apikoyres*, or nonbeliever.[56] The comment left Saul both upset and angry.
His father sent him to the Jewish day school, an experience that filled him
with "a belief in God and fear of God," and here was his father saying what
to Saul was one of the worst things anybody could say. "It made no sense to
me because I saw him every morning putting on *tefillin*," Saul said, referring
to the set of small leather boxes containing Torah verses worn during week-
day prayers. "That was so bewildering to me."

Only as an adult did Saul come to understand that verbalizing a lack of
faith was more an expression of anger than a rejection of God. He was saying, "Show me why I should believe in you, God," Saul said. "To me, it was
almost a challenge to God, a desperate plea." Saul once asked him whether
he believed in God, and Harry just shrugged. "I don't know for sure, but if
you live a good life and at the end there is no God, then you've done right
and it makes no difference. And if there is a God, even better for you."

———— • ————

In the summer between the annual Warsaw Ghetto memorial service and
the opening of the Orchard Road shtibl, the JAS published its annual report
with a newsworthy statistic. "Perhaps as many as ten percent" of Jewish displaced persons who arrived in the United States since the war had settled on
farms.[57] The finding was noteworthy enough to merit both a news story and
an editorial in the *New York Times*, which reported that of twenty-three
thousand families of displaced persons, more than two thousand had settled on farms that produce eggs, broilers, and milk.[58] "The rehabilitation of

these newest immigrants, victims of the Nazis, has been the most important phase of this organization's work," the *Times* editorial noted approvingly.[59]

The 10 percent figure is a striking statistic, but one not necessarily supported by JAS records. As the *Times* also noted, the JAS had assisted 830 refugee families, a figure consistent with statistics provided in the organization's annual reports. If two thousand displaced person families had settled on farms, that would mean roughly twelve hundred of them did so without JAS assistance. Few survivors had the financial wherewithal to purchase farms without the aid the JAS provided, let alone six out of every ten of them. What's more, there's little evidence that volume of refugee families settled on south Jersey farms or anywhere else. At its peak, the JPFA would boast of 708 members in 354 families in 1955.[60] Not every survivor who settled on a south Jersey farm joined the JPFA, so the actual total was undoubtedly higher. It is possible to identify approximately one thousand survivors in as many as five hundred families who settled on farms in Vineland and the surrounding area by searching JAS records, local phone directories from that era, and digital newspaper archives.

The JAS archives and research done by scholars about other rural Jewish farming communities provide no evidence that another fifteen hundred families of displaced persons settled elsewhere. In all likelihood, the actual total is probably in the range of one thousand to fifteen hundred rather than two thousand families. Sociologist William Helmreich, who interviewed some former Vineland farmers as part of an exhaustive study of Holocaust survivors, put the total at fifteen hundred.[61] Both spouses in Grine farm families were often survivors, and many had married in Europe and come to the United States with a child. Given those patterns, three thousand seems like a reasonable estimate of the total number of individual survivors who settled on American farms. They would have accounted for 2 percent of the 140,000 Jewish displaced persons who came to the United States between 1946 and 1954. That is roughly the same proportion of the Jewish American population engaged in farming earlier in the twentieth century, but far higher than the share in the 1950s. Only one-tenth of 1 percent of Jews identified as farmers or farm managers, according to the Census Bureau's 1957 Current Population Survey.[62]

Regardless of the exact number, the survivors who settled on farms in south Jersey had a tremendous impact on the Jewish community there and New Jersey's poultry industry as a whole. New Jersey had become the nation's fifth-leading egg producer by 1956, and poultry was the top agricultural enterprise in the state.[63] Four New Jersey counties—including Cumberland County, where Vineland is located—ranked in the top ten nationwide for its chicken population, and the state's farmers supplied nearly one out of every five eggs eaten in the New York City market.[64] "Poultry farming in the Garden State is Big Business," concluded Rutgers University economists in a 1958 report.[65] The report confidently predicted that "the poultry industry in New Jersey is almost certain to expand in the years ahead."

19 ▸ FEED MEN AND A RECORD-BREAKING HEN

IN DECEMBER 1956, the Jacob Rubinoff Company held a banquet at Glover Caterer, a North Main Road reception hall, which for two decades had hosted weddings, Christmas parties, and Rotary Club luncheons with the promise of "every meal a pleasant memory." The occasion this day was the company's "golden jubilee," although technically back in 1906, the firm known as Shenberg & Rubinoff did as much business selling horse blankets, harness oils, and carriage robes as chicken feed.[1] That didn't matter to the two hundred fifty employees and distinguished guests at the banquet, including Vineland's mayor, New Jersey's agriculture secretary, and the local U.S. congressman.

They heard Edward Rubinoff, the founder's son and the company's current president, boast about the two and a half million dollars in wages, taxes, and utility payments the business pumped into the local economy. Rubinoff emphasized the overriding principle that guided his father in running the company: service to the community, employees, and customers. "Their welfare is the final product of our efforts," Rubinoff told the crowd.[2]

The company had survived the Great Depression and a giant explosion at its mill in 1951, which blasted out the corrugated metal walls and injured twenty-three workers, five of whom suffered severe burns.[3] In a stroke of luck, Arthur Kuhnreich, then twenty-seven years old and one of the few Grine working at the mill, overslept that morning for perhaps the only time in his life. "It was a miracle," said Genia Kuhnreich, who at the time was his girlfriend and soon became his wife.[4] Within three weeks of the fire, the Rubinoffs had opened an auxiliary mill at its Delsea Drive warehouse and resumed full-scale feed mixing and deliveries.

The feed mill business afforded the Rubinoff family a lifestyle the likes of which its Grine clientele could only dream about: vacation spots on the Jersey Shore and an exclusive boarding school for Edward's nephew, Bernard Bress. Bernard's father had a top leadership role at the feed company. Edward hoped Bernard, now a student at the University of Virginia, would become the third generation to join the family business. His parents discouraged that career path, which proved to be good advice, given the local poultry industry's trajectory. In an early sign of trouble for the company, Rubinoff soon shut down its retail store on Landis Avenue, which Kuhnreich took over and turned into a combination feed and home pet supply store.

Kuhnreich was among the employees honored at the banquet with a length-of-service award and was perhaps the only Grine on the long list of attendees. There wasn't much love lost between struggling farmers and feed dealers, who were often their biggest creditors. Even in good years, poultry farmers found themselves dependent on feed dealers. Farmers, who had to provide food to young hens for months before they started producing eggs, found themselves in perpetual debt to feed suppliers. When farmers got paid for their eggs, the first thing they did was go pay the feed man. "Sometimes, he delivered the feed and he said, 'You owe me,'" said one Polish survivor. "We used to owe a lot of money [to] the feedman."[5] This sort of codependent customer-supplier relationship was common in other economic niches where Jews occupied multiple roles. Earlier generations of Jewish peddlers and small shopkeepers "on the bottom rung of an integrated Jewish economy" had depended on credit from Jewish wholesalers and other business owners further up the chain.[6]

The relationship between feed dealers and chicken farmers grew more fraught as egg prices dropped. This year had proven to be another difficult one for Vineland egg farmers. Low egg prices meant they could barely cover operating costs, making it hard to meet living expenses and pay interest and mortgages on their farms. Irving Raab, a Grine farmer, later recalled mediating between his fellow poultrymen who couldn't pay their bills and a local family-owned Purina dealer that had been selling feed since the 1890s. Raab could see both sides. "The farmers did not like to be thought of as dishonest and they were angry."[7] On the other hand, the feed dealer "was trying to run a business and wanted the bills to be paid." Raab tried to explain to the feed dealer that "these are not dishonest men. They want to pay their bills. Sometimes, they just need more time." He attempted to negotiate so that farmers could stay in business and the feed men got paid at least part of what they were owed.

Other feed dealers also worked to accommodate farmers. Ryna Alexander, whose family operated the Berkowitz feed mill in Norma, later found German bonds while cleaning out her father's house.[8] When she asked about it, her parents said people gave them whatever assets they could to pay the bills. One survivor recalled his father going to "Mr. Rubinoff" and explaining that he didn't want to go into bankruptcy but couldn't pay his debt. They came to terms at roughly ten cents on the dollar, which his father was eventually able to pay off while avoiding bankruptcy.[9] The negotiations didn't always work out. Families would sometimes pack up the night before the feed man came around to collect—and leave the farm with the lights and television on so no one would know they'd fled.[10]

Morton Gordon, who served as secretary-treasurer of his family's feed company in rural Connecticut in the mid-1950s, provided insight into how feed companies viewed themselves as a benevolent force toward Grine. In a 1974 doctoral thesis, Gordon described how feed merchants extended credit "without which the farmer could not remain in business" while baby chicks matured or when farmers needed loans to build new coops and had no collateral.[11] "While the feed merchant profited in the sale of his feed during this process, in terms of Jewish tradition, his aid to the farmer was truly an act of Gemilus Chesed," Gordon wrote, referencing the Jewish concept of acts of loving kindness.[12] The aid enabled "the farmer to become established in his own business and thus support himself and his family." Gordon included a lengthy excerpt from a letter he wrote accusing the Jewish Agricultural Society (JAS) of giving short shrift to feed merchants in a book on Jewish farmers. "You above all should recall how my family helped to establish the many Jewish D.P.'s who arrived in the area penniless."

Most farmers, to put it gently, saw things differently. Struggling poultry-men who had no control over poultry diseases, weather, and the whims of distant commodities traders directed much of their frustration at the feed man they knew by name and saw every week. Feed dealers actually had no control of what angered farmers the most: federal price supports that kept the cost of feed ingredients high even as egg prices dropped. Ben Leuchter explained in a July 1954 column that the impact of high feed prices was felt most keenly by "more recent additions to the ranks of poultrymen," who had paid top dollar for their farms and "can easily be crushed by the squeeze of heavy fixed overhead and low income."[13]

To be sure, the Rubinoffs made a fine living off their mill and hardly suffered as much as their customers when egg prices sank. Ultimately, however, the fortunes of farmers and feed dealers—along with the hatch-eries, egg dealers, and all the other businesses dependent on the poultry industry—rose and fell together. As a pamphlet the Rubinoffs published to mark the golden jubilee put it, "that which is good for the poultryman is good for the Jacob Rubinoff company."[14] Events would prove that the con-verse was equally true. Feed companies like Rubinoff's understood they needed egg farmers to thrive and did what they could to help boost Vine-land's struggling egg industry. Edward Rubinoff joined a variety of efforts to market Vineland eggs, including an ad campaign that began a month after the banquet that featured a smiling cartoon egg saying, "Eat More Eggs, They're Your Biggest Food Value." The ad also noted, "Eggs are Vineland's Leading Product and What Helps Our Farmers Helps Our Community Too!"[15]

Phillip Alampi, the New Jersey state secretary of agriculture, emphasized the importance of aggressive promotion and marketing when he spoke at the Rubinoffs' golden jubilee banquet. What neither Alampi nor anyone else at the banquet realized is that, at that very moment, a Vineland hen was already on her way to becoming the most famous chicken in America, eclipsed perhaps only by Foghorn Leghorn himself.

———•———

Meggi O'Day, as she came to be known, was a contestant in an egg-laying contest supervised by a Rutgers University poultry science professor. Egg-laying contests became popular throughout the country early in the century. The contests helped poultry scientists study how efficiently chickens could produce eggs; farmers and hatchery owners liked to submit their hens for bragging rights. One of the first, starting in 1916, was hosted at Vineland, where Arthur Goldhaft's son Tevis first cared for chickens as a teenager.[16]

Gus Stern, the son of Romanian Jewish immigrants, grew up mostly on Staten Island and in the 1920s moved to Vineland, where he opened a hatchery with his brother. Stern bought newspaper ads boasting about how his "Longevity Leghorns" performed in the contests.[17] By 1956, Vineland's egg-laying contest was waning, and Gus entered a four-pound, average size, single comb leghorn in the competition in northern New Jersey. Stern's hen quietly began what would become a record streak of consecutive laying days on November 3.

Each morning, an attendant walked along the row of henhouses at Rutgers University's experimental farm, checking whether the thump of a dropped egg had triggered a lightbulb to illuminate.[18] Like clockwork, Stern's hen laid an egg every morning by seven o'clock, day after day, month after month, except for one morning in May when she waited until eight o'clock before emitting her telltale cackle that signaled she'd laid an egg. By late May 1957, her streak had reached 240 days—shattering the previous record of 146 set in 1946—a particularly impressive feat given the average hen produced only 180 eggs in an entire year.[19]

Her streak became the object of intense fascination. When reporters started asking if she had a name, a quick-thinking Rutgers public relations representative came up with "Meggi O'Day"—a play on an "egg a day," which some reporters shortened to "Meg O'Day." By July, the New York Times had written about Meg's streak, as did papers as far away as Glasgow, Scotland, and Belfast, Northern Ireland, perhaps drawn to her Irish-sounding name.[20] Rutgers turned down television and newspaper photographer requests, fearful she'd get stage fright and stop laying. At one point in July, an upstart in Santa Rosa, California, claimed to have a hen with a 275 consecutive day streak. By early August, Meg had passed that mark, too.

The contest was set to end in September, but Meg didn't quite make it. On August 14, the attendant hadn't heard a cluck or seen the light bulb illuminate.[21] He poked around Meg's nest and the corners of her coop, hoping to find an egg, to no avail. He called in the news. Meg's streak had ended at 284 days, eliciting headlines in hundreds of papers in just about every state. Her streak tapped into the American fascination with breaking competitive records in this era when the New York Yankees' Roger Maris and Mickey Mantle would soon dual for the record of most home runs in a single season. She went on to make news again in September when she broke the record for most eggs in a one-year span. Dubbed the Mickey Mantle of poultry, she'd laid 354 eggs in 357 days.[22]

The contest closed its doors for good soon after Meg ended her streak. Organizers cited the expense of maintaining the contest. "There'll never be another Meg O'Day," one New Jersey newspaper noted.[23] Meg then set out on a victory tour, stopping first at a poultry industry conference in Harrisburg, Pennsylvania, where she was displayed in a gilded cage, before making her way home to Vineland. Stern's wife had a fit when Meg laid an egg inside their house. Meg soon returned to Rutgers, where scientists were eager to figure out how she could lay so many eggs.[24]

All the publicity around Meg's record-breaking streak didn't do much to boost sales of Vineland eggs. Nor did all the other marketing and promotional efforts launched by Rubinoff and other local poultry businesses, which later launched a "saturation advertising and merchandising campaign" aimed at getting New Yorkers to eat more eggs.[25] The campaign focused on the New York metro area's foreign-born residents with ads in eight foreign-language newspapers and radio stations, including the Yiddish daily newspaper the *Forward*, plus Spanish and Italian ethnic newspapers.

When Meg died in 1959 at age two and a half, Gus had her stuffed and mounted on a wooden base with an inscription on a bronze plate noting she'd worked her tail off (she was missing many of her tail feathers at the end).[26] He gave her a place of honor in his living room right above the TV.

20 ▸ LABORERS

CELINA ROSENBLUM WAS a twenty-seven-year-old Polish survivor, and her husband Idek was just under three weeks shy of his thirty-fifth birthday on July 1, 1957. Both survived Auschwitz and had the tattoos on their arms to prove it: 174242 for Idek; A-22025 for Celina.[1] He survived the war as a slave laborer unloading coal and later manufacturing ammunition at an Auschwitz satellite camp. She was first put to work as a slave laborer at fourteen, so hungry she was forced at one point to eat acorns. Celina prayed for Allied planes to end her suffering by bombing the ammunition factory where she worked.

Around midnight on July 1, Celina awoke with a start in the bedroom of their farmhouse. When she opened her eyes she saw her farmhand of three years, Juan Rivera Aponte, standing in her bathroom holding a flashlight shaded by a piece of clear plastic.[2] Celina yelled for Idek, who confronted Aponte and wound up with two blows to his head from a club.

Vineland police soon arrived at the Rosenblum farm and arrested Aponte outside the chicken house, which contained his living quarters. To the arresting officers, this was just another altercation involving poultry farmers and the itinerant men they hired as farmhands. South Jersey poultry farmers relied on staffing agencies that recruited Baltimore and Philadelphia men, often down-on-their-luck vagrants and alcoholics, and provided them with one dollar and a bus ticket to Vineland.[3] "They came with no clothes, nothin', you know, they were hungry," one Grine farm wife recalled.[4] Survivors had no choice but to take whoever stepped off the bus. They could neither afford experienced workers nor do all the work themselves.

Laborers could become belligerent when drunk—or sober—as Sam Wasserstrum, a thirty-nine-year-old survivor, learned during a 1954 dispute with his farmhand over whether he was working on a particular day. The laborer cut off part of Wasserstrum's ear, which, his son recalled, was gobbled up by a chicken before he could retrieve it.[5] One laborer wound up jailed on his first day on the job when a farm wife spotted a revolver in the man's pocket after discovering one dollar missing from the house.[6] Another survivor's daughter recalled her father tried heading off trouble by telling a laborer who asked how he wound up on a farm that he'd murdered someone in France.[7]

One employment agency owner later testified at a New Jersey State Department of Labor hearing that he never knowingly placed workers with criminal records in jobs in Vineland or elsewhere.[8] A state official then described thirteen arrests of the agency's clients, none of whom had a fixed address, for disorderly conduct. All of them were subsequently placed in new jobs by the agency.

Nuchim and Bronia had their own troubles with farm laborers. In August 1955, their former worker was arrested for stealing a clock, mirror, and stove from their home. Bronia stopped feeling safe at home alone with laborers after an incident inside her farmhouse that may have involved an attempted sexual assault against her. She ran across the road to the Ledermans' farmhouse so visibly upset that Mrs. Lederman had to calm her down.[9] Bronia only hinted to Ruth at what had happened, but that was the last time either Bronia or Ruth ever stayed home alone with a laborer present. The same farm laborer charged with robbing Bronia and Nuchim in 1955 was charged at the same time with molesting his most recent employer, another survivor wife.[10] The victim told police the laborer called her into his quarters, made inappropriate advances, grabbed her, and tried to force her to the floor. She managed to free herself and escape.

The Ledermans' trouble with laborers never seemed to end. One was jailed for disorderly conduct in a dispute over cab fare after Lederman fired him for drinking too much.[11] Three months before Aponte's arrest, another one of the Ledermans' laborers received sixty days in jail for striking Lederman's father and breaking his glasses. A few years later, his pickup truck, fifty dozen eggs, and the laborer who had worked for him for two weeks all went missing at the same time.[12]

Given the often unpredictable and short tenures of farmhands, Johnny— as the Rosenblum family referred to Aponte—stood out for his steady three years on their farm. They trusted the forty-seven-year-old Puerto Rico native enough to leave him in charge of the farm when they went away on a rare vacation. Johnny also played with their two sons, now five and seven years old, in the nearby woods.

———•———

Aponte's arrest came to the attention of two Vineland detectives investigating the disappearance nine months earlier of a thirteen-year-old neighborhood boy. His abandoned bicycle was discovered in the woods across the road from the Rosenblum farm. Investigators had spent months searching without success for the boy, even dragging portions of the Maurice River with a hook. Fearful parents warned their children not to ride their bikes alone. The detectives remembered that Aponte had been friendly with the boy, so they brought him to police headquarters for questioning.[13]

Through a Spanish interpreter, Aponte accused Rosenblum of murdering the boy. He told the detectives that on the night the boy disappeared in October 1956, Rosenblum forced him to help bury the body and threatened that he'd suffer the same fate if he told anyone. Aponte told the detectives fear and a lack of money made him stay on the farm rather than return home to Puerto Rico. He said he'd come up to the farmhouse earlier that night at Rosenblum's invitation and that Celina struck him with a chair and Idek hit him with a club.

Aponte volunteered to lead police to the boy's body. Returning to the farm, Aponte pointed to a spot in the dirt floor along the west wall separating the chicken house from his living quarters. Road department workers uncovered the boy's body in a shallow grave. The farm was one hundred yards south of the boy's house and across the street from the wooded area where his bicycle was found after his disappearance. Some of the boy's clothes were missing, which Aponte claimed were later burned in a pit on the farm. Also missing: the top of the boy's skull as well as his left foot and left hand.

Police detectives detained Rosenblum and, after a nine-hour interrogation, informed him he was being charged with murder. Rosenblum appeared bewildered and "stoutly" denied the accusation.[14] Celina was also taken into custody as a material witness and then released after two thirty in the morning when her mother, who also lived in the Vineland area, posted a twenty-five-hundred-dollar bond.

Front-page news of Rosenblum's arrest in the next day's *Times Journal* triggered anxiety throughout Vineland's Jewish community. Jews in small towns never felt "completely secure," sociologist Benjamin Kaplan noted in his 1957 account of three Jewish communities in Louisiana.[15] "Outwardly they may be calm but inwardly they are worried," Kaplan wrote. Sociologist Ewa Morawska later observed the same pattern in her study of the Jewish community in Johnstown, Pennsylvania, where she noted a form of "civic insecurity," particularly during confrontations with the dominant society. These small-town Jews preferred to remain inconspicuous, adopting a "'Shah! Be quiet! Don't call attention to us' approach," Morawska wrote.[16] Rosenblum's arrest made Vineland's Jews stand out in the worst possible way. What's more, the lurid details might have reinforced suspicions among Vineland's American-born Jews that the Grine—particularly those, like Idek, imprisoned in concentration camps—came out of the war damaged.

News of Rosenblum's arrest must have come as a particular shock to survivors, who as a general matter lived with a "perilous uncertainty."[17] Bronia, for example, harbored a perpetual fear of "not feeling secure, or rooted—that something could happen," Ruth said. Ruth, who was eleven at the time, had no recollection of the boy's disappearance or Rosenblum's arrest. But another child of survivors who grew up on a Vineland poultry farm recalled overhearing his parents talk about the murder of a non-Jewish child whose body was recovered in a Jewish farmer's coop. Mark Werner misremembered some of the details but provided a sense of how the survivor community reacted to the news. His parents talked in hushed tones about the murder and fears that the body had been dumped in the coop to frame a Jew, evoking parallels to European blood libels that were often pretexts for anti-Jewish violence. "While American-born Jews probably would not have been afraid of this possibility, my parents and their peers envisioned a repeat of what they hoped they had left behind in Europe," Werner later wrote.[18]

Every survivor remembered the July 1946 pogrom that erupted in the Polish town of Kielce, ninety miles from Lodz, where Bronia, Nuchim, and three-month-old Ruth were living at the time. A Polish boy left home without telling his parents to visit friends and pick cherries in a nearby village. After he returned to Kielce two days later, Jews were accused of kidnapping him. A mob stormed a group house where survivors lived, dragging Jews out and beating them with rifle butts. Forty-two Jews died in the violence that followed, a massacre that convinced many survivors they'd never be safe in Poland.[19] Nuchim and Bronia joined the mass migration that followed into the American occupation zone in Germany.

Survivors' wartime experiences made encounters with any government authority figures—and uniformed ones in particular—intensely anxious. The parents of Ruth's childhood friend Helen Waiman were reluctant to tell anyone too much and inadvertently provide information that could be used against them. "You could say things to other Jews, but not to anybody else, especially authorities," Helen said.[20] "You had to be very circumspect in what you said, particularly to the government, which was not your friend, ever."

Imagine how Celina felt, home alone in Vineland with their five- and seven-year-old sons, while Idek remained detained thirteen miles away in a hot third-story jail cell in Bridgeton, the county seat. Celina had been raised in cosmopolitan Krakow and probably would have never met Idek, a small-town religious boy seven years her senior, if not for the war. They met and married at an Austrian DP camp where she wore a hand-me-down dress and traded cigarettes for butter to make their wedding cake.[21] They'd settled first in Cleveland, where she had family and they both got factory jobs. Then, like so many others, Idek heard from a friend living in Vineland, took a Greyhound bus on Thanksgiving Day, and put the two thousand dollars he had saved up since arriving toward the purchase of a poultry farm.[22] Her mother soon followed them to Vineland.

Idek had adjusted more easily to life in Vineland than Celina, both because he'd grown up in a small town and because he tended to put a positive gloss on life no matter the circumstances. Asked decades later how locals treated him in Vineland, he replied, "very nice."[23] Get-togethers with fellow Polish Jews were "very nice." And initially at least, he was "making nice money." It wasn't nearly as nice for Celina, who chafed at farm life from the beginning. Now, look where farm life had gotten them.

Nearly hysterical, Celina sent her sons to stay with her mother a mile away, desperate to shield them from the police investigation unfolding on their farm. The trauma was manifold, starting with the event that had started it all in her bedroom. The version of the story she later shared with her sons was even more harrowing than newspaper accounts at the time.[24] She told them she woke up that night and saw Aponte clutching a club and rope as he stood over her son's bed, situated in his parents' bedroom. She tried calling police. Aponte kicked the phone away before Idek was able to fight him off. In her memory, Aponte hadn't just broken into their home—he'd tried to kill their son, and Idek was the one now charged with murder.

On the morning of July 8, Celina visited Idek in the Bridgeton jail and found him understandably depressed about their rapid shift in fortunes. And then, just as quickly, their luck changed again. By the time Celina reached their lawyer's office back in Vineland, she found out Aponte had confessed to murdering the boy whom he falsely accused Idek of killing.[25] Idek learned of his exoneration from relatives who heard the news on the radio.

Celina wore "a grin a mile-wide" as she awaited her husband's release that afternoon.[26] They reunited that night at City Hall and posed for photographers. Idek, whose face is covered in a five o'clock shadow from not shaving in jail, planted a kiss on the cheek of Celina, who looks exhausted with dark bags under her eyes. "How do I feel? How do you think I feel?," she said. "I knew that he didn't do it but the last few days have been like living in hell." Celina and her mother told reporters they bore no ill will toward Aponte, whom they described as a loyal employee. "Three years he was here," Celina's mother said while shaking her head. "He never bothered anyone. So quiet, too."

The *Times Journal* observed "the experience of the past week was another heartache in her 28 years of heartache" for Celina and Idek, whom the paper noted had both survived Auschwitz.[27] Celina, who knew firsthand the pain of losing family violently, got emotional as she expressed sympathy for the boy's family. "I feel sorry for them, and for the child," she said. But the *Times Journal* noted, "The worst was over now. Idek was home again, the accusations had been proved false and time would ease the memory of the past few days."

It wasn't quite that easy to forget, particularly as they learned the grisly details of Aponte's crime. Aponte confessed the boy had come to his quarters in the chicken coop asking for a cigarette. He proceeded to strike the boy on the back of his head, knocking him unconscious and then strangling him with a cord. The reason, Aponte explained to police, was that he had been doing a lot of reading about "black magic" and he needed the powder from a human skull for a potion in order to cast a spell over women.[28] He killed the first person that proved convenient, waiting until the Rosenblums went to bed that night before burying the boy's body. He watered the gravesite and then covered it with chicken litter to hide the fresh dirt. Seven months later, Aponte opened up the grave and used a small paring knife to remove a portion of the skull.

Following his confession, Aponte led police to the skull, which he'd hung to dry for two months on a string in a two-burner kerosene stove inside his living quarters. Aponte told police he had nothing against the Rosenblums; he just needed someone to blame, and they made logical suspects. He showed little remorse but seemed relieved to have the matter behind him.

Vineland detectives said Aponte was under suspicion from the outset since he had led police directly to the body and it was known that the boy had gone to see Aponte before he was last seen. Discrepancies in his story made the police only more suspicious. That was, of course, of little solace to Idek, who spent five days in jail wrongly accused of murder. Grateful to be free, Idek expressed nothing but appreciation to the police for working hard to identify the real culprit and clear his name.[29] He shook hands with investigators and personally thanked Vineland's public safety director as a crowd of reporters and photographers recorded the scene. The case proved irresistible to newspaper editors nationwide. Associated Press wire stories about the crime appeared in newspapers in at least twenty-five states and dominated the front page of the *Times Journal* for days.

Just as survivors worried about how Rosenblum's arrest would reflect on them, leaders of Vineland's budding Puerto Rican community now feared the lurid details of Aponte's crime would tarnish their image. Marcelino Figueroa, the president of the local Puerto Rican Social Action Club, founded a year earlier, put out a statement saying Puerto Ricans living in Vineland "are just as horrified as anyone else" about the crime.[30] "The fact that Juan Rivera Aponte was attempting to practice so-called 'black magic' is hard for Puerto Ricans to understand," said Figueroa, a U.S. Army veteran who worked at Kimble Glass. "'Black magic,' is not practiced by Puerto Ricans in their native country, nor, for that matter, anywhere else in the world."

Vineland's Puerto Rican community took root around the same time as the survivors arrived in the area and felt even less secure. The estimated four hundred Puerto Ricans living in Vineland in the mid-1950s were part of a much larger migration from the Caribbean territory fueled by high unemployment at home, the lure of plentiful low-skill jobs, and cheaper air travel.[31] Most lived in New York City, while some settled in other cities, including Camden and Newark, New Jersey, where they were confined largely to densely populated neighborhoods with substandard housing and low-paying jobs in factories or personal service. Others found work as farm laborers, harvesting potatoes on Long Island or cranberries on Cape Cod.[32] As was the case with survivor farmers, south Jersey was "the center of Puerto Rican farm-labor migration."[33] But unlike Jewish refugees, who had institutional support from organizations like the Jewish Agricultural Society, Puerto Rican migrants lacked access to credit and couldn't afford to buy their own farms.[34] The government of Puerto Rico could only help them find jobs as laborers.

Thousands of Puerto Rican men landed every spring at an airport a few miles south of Vineland in Millville as part of an organized airlift to supply farmworkers for New Jersey truck farms.[35] They began picking asparagus in early spring and worked through the fall as other vegetables, berries, and small fruit ripened. Puerto Rico's sugar cane season ran roughly from January to July, so migrant workers could work both harvests. Most of these laborers worked under contracts regulated by the Puerto Rican government that were designed to prevent exploitation. Some stayed permanently, abandoning contract work in favor of more informal arrangements on truck or poultry farms or, as in the case of Figueroa, found factory jobs. This was the beginning of a Latino presence that would eventually far exceed the size of Vineland's Jewish community.

Some Vineland Jews saw the future earlier than most, whether for altruistic or self-interested reasons. In 1951, two nonsurvivor Jewish brothers who jointly operated a local farm successfully lobbied Vineland's evening adult education program to start Spanish-language classes. Albert and Alfred Stern wanted "to be able to have their workers understand their directions" and recounted how "strange things can happen when sign language has to be depended upon."[36] The eight who enrolled in the course included Sam Sabul, an American-born Jewish merchant who owned a menswear store on Landis Avenue. In 1952, the bow-tied haberdasher put up a sign in the window in

Spanish offering copies of *El Diario*, a Spanish-language newspaper.[37] The sign didn't result in a stampede of new business, but some migrant farm laborers, desperate for news from back home, asked in Spanish for a copy of the newspaper. "Just the fact that someone is making an effort to make them feel at home here" has generated good will, Sabul said.

Few in Vineland or elsewhere in New Jersey made such efforts to connect with Puerto Rican residents. "The Puerto Rican, like the American Negro, is a second class citizen" discriminated against "in churches, schools, homes, places of public accommodation and employment," a 1955 report by the New Jersey State Department of Education concluded.[38] The report found widespread "attitudes of mistrust, misunderstanding, and dislike toward Puerto Ricans" who, even in churches, were tolerated "but were not really accepted." "The Puerto Rican has felt that he was not being treated as a man," the reported noted.[39] Just as survivors and German Jewish refugees before them in Vineland had turned inward, so did Vineland's Puerto Rican community. The new Puerto Rican Social Action Club soon purchased a clubhouse on Third Street and hosted its first formal dance on July 4, 1958, a not-so-subtle reminder to the broader community that they too were patriotic Americans.[40]

———•———

Farmhand crime was a recurring concern in Vineland's courts long after Aponte's arrest, as when the case of a poultry farm laborer charged with vagrancy came before a municipal judge in October 1959. The judge complained something had to be done to stop employment agencies from sending "human derelicts" to Vineland from big-city "skid rows" to work cheaply for the economically depressed poultry industry.[41] The judge also expressed sympathy for farm laborers living in conditions akin to "slavery." The laborer charged with vagrancy worked seven days and as many as 112 hours a week. He earned about nineteen cents an hour while living in a converted coop with a cot and propane gas stove for cooking. One Vineland attorney later described accommodations of laborers on south Jersey poultry farms as "pre–Civil War."[42]

The references to "slavery" and "pre–Civil War" living conditions hinted at the unacknowledged racial dimension to the relationship between survivors and their farmhands. Few survivors had much prior experience interacting with Blacks and Puerto Ricans at the bottom of the U.S. caste system. Bronia and Nuchim's neighbor Joey Hyman, who had spent much of his youth in Cuba, was the rare Grine farmer who could speak fluent Spanish and communicate well with Puerto Rican laborers, who often spoke English no better than the survivors.

Their experiences with discrimination back in Europe didn't automatically make survivors more sympathetic to the plight of workers lower on the American social hierarchy. One survivor was later sued for labor exploitation.[43] A complaint filed in Vineland municipal court alleged that the farmer had made illegal deductions from employees' wages and violated the state's minimum wage law. The farmer also lacked a permit to house employees in his coop. Vineland's director of inspections and permitting said "no one should be residing there."

Just as the Grine integrated into American society and the poultry economy, they also assimilated into the existing racial and labor hierarchies. As farm owners, even struggling ones, they stood above the farm help, who occupied the lowest rung on the labor ladder. The exploitative nature of agricultural work meant even farmers who were victims of horrific abuses themselves, might still subject farmhands—many of whom were Black or Latino—to subpar working and living conditions. Urban Jews had similarly "deeply unequal" interactions as Black migrants "moved into Jewish neighborhoods and met Jews as employers, teachers, landlords and shopkeepers, not as fellow oppressed people."[44]

Ben Leuchter, who was deeply sympathetic toward the farmers' plight, seemed torn when state and federal investigators investigated the treatment of laborers.[45] While "there undoubtedly are many ways in which farmers" could improve migrant living conditions, Leuchter also noted how little help the average farmer had received as their income plummeted. "It's no wonder he questions how it will be possible to pay for the better living conditions sought for the itinerant farm employees," Leuchter wrote.

Some Grine found Puerto Rican workers to be a more reliable source of labor than what agencies in Baltimore or Philadelphia provided.[46] Some Puerto Rican laborers recalled feeling welcome on south Jersey farms, particularly by truck farmers from Sicily with whom they shared common island backgrounds and food traditions and the same Catholic faith.[47] A few would return to the same farm summer after summer for decades, and so would their children.[48] More typically, however, farm owners groused that workers skipped out on the job, while laborers complained about mistreatment, poor accommodations, and terrible working conditions. "The farmers don't try to understand the Puerto Rican," one minister in a farming community said.[49]

———·———

Aponte was sentenced to life in prison in October 1959. By then, the Rosenblums had left Vineland behind and moved to Canada. An acquaintance in Toronto who had gotten into real estate development invited Idek to become partners. Idek welcomed the chance to put some distance between him and what had happened on the farm. He loaded up a moving van and relocated his family that had expanded to include a daughter. A few years later, they moved back to the United States, settling in northern New Jersey this time.

By the time Idek and Celina sat down for separate oral history interviews about their lives, forty years had passed since they'd left Vineland. In the interim, he'd built a successful real estate business, which had grown to include his son. Idek and Celina lived in an apartment in Fort Lee, New Jersey, and also had a home in Bal Harbour, Florida. Neither made any reference to the murder in their oral history interviews. The closest Celina came was when she observed that, except for her imprisonment in concentration camps, their period on the farm was "the worst time of my life."[50]

21 ▸ THE GOLDEN EGG

THE MURDER HAD exposed social hierarchies and tensions in Vineland between laborers and survivors, and survivors and other Vineland residents. Three months later, the publication of a memoir by Arthur Goldhaft provided written proof of the low regard American-born Jews had for the Grine. Goldhaft, the seventy-two-year-old founder of Vineland Poultry Laboratories, was an elder statesman of both the international poultry industry and the local Jewish community by the time he published his memoir, *The Golden Egg*, in November 1957. He'd long since handed over the reins of the business to the next generation of his family as he traveled to Israel and poultry conferences abroad and wintered near Miami. Goldhaft was old enough now that two of his granddaughters had become the third generation in his family to attend an Ivy League college—Cornell, just like their parents.

Not bad for the son of Russian Jewish immigrants, which is the overarching theme of Goldhaft's self-effacing memoir, starting from the first page. He begins by questioning why a "plain citizen" of Vineland had the nerve to write about himself.[1] (He refers to himself as an "old horse doctor" throughout.) Goldhaft notes the world didn't need another rags-to-riches tale before launching into just such a tale, describing how he opened his first laboratory on the spot in Vineland where his struggling parents once picked strawberries for fifty cents a day.

The book is well written, with the tone of a professional writer rather than a veterinarian who showed no similar gift for words in decades of forgettable public remarks. The title page says it was "edited with an introduction by" journalist and novelist Meyer Levin, a description that obscured his true role as ghostwriter. Levin had signed an agreement with Goldhaft in 1955 to write a book about his life and career in exchange for five thousand dollars.[2]

Survivors are only a small piece of Goldhaft's narrative, occupying a dozen or so of the more than three hundred pages. Not until page 263 does Vineland's most famous Jewish citizen describe survivors as "touchy," "demanding" and much worse.[3] "They were bitter, angry, hurt people, suspicious of the whole world," Goldhaft explained.

The callous depiction of survivors is all the more striking given that Goldhaft portrays himself as deeply sympathetic to the plight of European Jewry in general and the earlier German Jewish arrivals in particular. Goldhaft recounts the horror he felt seeing pictures in newspapers of German stormtroopers forcing Jewish women on their knees to scrub the street. "Now for the first time we could understand" the way his parents "described their childhood, and the pogroms in Russia," Goldhaft wrote. Convinced something had to be done to assist refugees, Goldhaft recounts helping revive "the back-to-the-soil" plan for German refugees and his efforts to train them.

Goldhaft often typecasts the German Jews, almost entirely in a good way. In his telling, the Yekkes, as the German Jews were nicknamed, were hardworking "high grade fugitives." He praised these former doctors and lawyers known for their "super-orderliness." "The German refugees were mostly older people, who had been persons of importance in their native land, and who hoped only, in the poultry industry, to find a safe corner to complete their shattered lives, in peace and obscurity," Goldhaft wrote.

Contrast that with how he talks about the Grine, who he writes "were different from those who had come before.... These people had been through everything. If they had been in the slave camps they had survived because of superior strength or cunning. If they had been hidden, they had been through years of silent fear, buried alive in a closet, or a garret, or a space between two floors, half starved. If they had been among the parti-sans, they had lived as wild hunted things, and as killers." They arrived in Vineland as new poultry farmers "to do work that none of them had ever done and for which many were unsuited. The first months were filled with quarrels, and accusations and disasters." Goldhaft's relentlessly negative por-trayal of the Grine unintentionally echoed anti-Semitic tropes that depict Jews as cunning, crafty, and less than fully human. "They demanded credit from everyone, and played off one feed dealer against another; they had learned every commercial trick in the D.P. camps, and we feared they would end by giving all Jews a bad name," Goldhaft wrote.

In one of several anecdotes that portray Grine in the worst possible light, Goldhaft recounts how one survivor sold another Grine chickens advertised as twelve weeks old and thus about to produce eggs. The chickens turned out to be six weeks younger. "Yes, the refugees would even do such things to each other in the beginning," Goldhaft wrote. "That was what it meant to have survived Hitler's camps." He recounted that "much, much work had to be done to bring them back, to make human beings out of them again."

Yet among these angry, maladjusted Grine, Goldhaft could find one who stood out as exemplary: Miles Lerman. Goldhaft recounts an early gathering of newcomers where he gave a lecture in his halting Yiddish that immediately got interrupted by "questions, angry remarks, even accusa-tions" from the audience. Then, "a young fellow" with "a leader's personal-ity" jumped up and quieted the crowd with a soliloquy on why they should listen to what Goldhaft had to say. This "remarkable young man," Goldhaft writes, "became not only a leader in their own community of survivors, but in the entire city of Vineland." If you looked at Miles "and his beautiful wife, and their healthy children, you would never imagine they are any-thing but a couple of fine people from good families, who had had no evil experiences."

Singling out Miles for praise while insulting everyone else brought to the surface resentment toward the leader of their community that some Grine had harbored quietly for years. Almost from the beginning, Miles had been cited by the Jewish Agricultural Society (JAS) as the model survivor farmer. Then along comes this book holding him up at everyone else's expense. "That was one of the things that really stoked the jealousy," recalled Janet Leuchter, the daughter of the *Times Journal*'s editor and a close friend of the

Lermans.[4] "The rest of the survivors were furious" and labeled the Lermans "traitors to our community," she said.

Survivors directed much of their fury about Goldhaft's book at Lerman.[5] Some boycotted his new home oil business or cut themselves off socially from him and his wife. Chris later recalled feeling ostracized for a time after the book's publication even though Miles had "nothing to do with" how Goldhaft portrayed him. "It was like a mob psychology," Chris said.[6] Chris chalked up any jealousy of Miles to the perils of being a natural leader. "All I can tell you is that if one has leadership ability, one always come to the forefront, no matter what." She added, "The man has done so much in his life for people in general and for the Jewish people in particular that he has quite a record, that he does not have to explain anything."

In the view of Ben Leuchter's daughter Janet, so much of the resentment toward Miles "had to do with who was still poor and who was becoming less so, who was able to get off the farm successfully."[7] Lerman's friend and fellow survivor Sol Finkelstein similarly alluded to how what had started out as a "very tight community" began to splinter. "It was later, when somebody got a little bit more money, or somebody got a little less money, that we started to have some social difference," Finkelstein said.[8] Farmers had more or less started in the same place. But their fortunes had begun to diverge, all the more so as some began abandoning farming for more lucrative pursuits. The sense of equality that earlier allowed Grine to identify with collective agricultural settlements in Israel had begun to dissipate.

Survivors had only more reason to resent Miles that fall as they watched how easily—at least from a distance—he seemed to have transitioned into a new business. Miles had increased the size of his flock to close to forty thousand hens but concluded he'd need to expand to a hundred thousand birds to succeed.[9] Instead, Miles started delivering home heating oil and repairing broken furnaces. In preparation for the career shift, Miles had taken classes at a trade school while Chris studied bookkeeping and accounting.[10] They enclosed a screened-in porch in their farmhouse to serve as the start-up office. What detractors didn't see was that the hours were no better than farming, which Miles also continued to do while building the new business. Miles's ads in the *Times Journal* promised "emergency service, day and night," and he went out in the middle of the night on house calls when he couldn't find mechanics.[11] His children served as the informal answering service as teenagers when Miles and Chris went out on Saturday nights.[12]

Branching out into the oil business is another example of how Miles benefited from developing relationships beyond the survivor community. Miles's experience working in an Italian food importer's warehouse in his early months in New York proved useful in Vineland. "I learned to curse in Italian before I could speak English," he later recalled.[13] Just as when he befriended American-born Jews, Lerman's business associations in the broader community also might have generated resentment from those who remained in the poultry business and did not yet feel quite as comfortable making similar connections. Irving Raab later recalled how Miles "started mingling" with the American-born businessmen and professionals at the local synagogue. "He was promoted and they helped him," Raab said.[14]

Lerman found a mentor in George Rossi, an Italian American Vineland native ten years older than him who had operated a Landis Avenue gas station before becoming an Amoco fuel distributor. Rossi had no qualms about explaining the business to a potential competitor and sold Miles his first piece of equipment. "He remembered what it was like to be an immigrant, either the child or grandchild of one and had memories of how tough it was," said Miles's son, David.[15] Rossi's sister Mary was vice principal and then principal of Vineland High School when the first German and Austrian born refugees' teenage children enrolled there. She insisted on calling them "new Americans" rather than "refugees" so they didn't feel stigmatized.[16]

Other Italian American families in Vineland also went out of their way to help Jewish refugees. Spartico "Duke" Renzulli, whose parents had emigrated from Italy, first hired survivor Chaim Lindenblatt to work on his farm.[17] Then, after Lindenblatt bought his own property, Renzulli lent a hand on his former employee's farm during Lindenblatt's frequent illnesses. Renzulli's wife Josephine drove Lindenblatt's wife Rifka to Vineland to light *yahrtzeit* candles at a synagogue in memory of those she lost during the war. Both Renzullis also took the Orthodox family's lambs to get slaughtered in a kosher manner. Renzulli also drove another family of survivors whose child was born with a congenital heart defect to a Philadelphia hospital several times, his son recalled.[18]

Miles felt a particular debt of gratitude to Vineland's Italian community. When an earthquake hit near Naples, Italy, two decades later, Miles joined the Italian Relief Fund of South Jersey as vice president. Asked why he participated, Miles told a reporter, "So what if I'm Jewish, not Italian?"[19] Rossi and other Italian American leaders were just as generous during the Six-Day War in 1967 and the Yom Kippur War in 1973, offering unsolicited donations to Israel during local fundraising drives. To Miles, his Italian Catholic neighbors were "'landsmen'—Yiddish for 'my people,'" his son David explained in a tribute after Miles died.[20] "For so it was that they treated him and others who came to Vineland seeking to rebuild their lives."

———•———

Anger about *The Golden Egg* only intensified in the months following publication. At a September 1958 Jewish Poultry Farmers Association (JPFA) meeting, a survivor farmer accused Goldhaft of having "besmeared and blackened in an unparalleled way all—in a lump—post war Jewish refugees from Poland."[21] "It is deplorable that we have to meet tonight—13 years after the end of the War, when the nightmarish experiences of our past history seemed to be a bad memory—that we have to meet to voice our indignation and our condemnation of a so-called reputable gray-haired Jewish resident of this community," the Grine farmer wrote in typed remarks she either distributed as a flyer or prepared for delivery at the meeting. She demanded Goldhaft apologize and "destroy" the section of his book that most offended the Grine community, by removing those pages from existing copies and leaving them out in any future printings.

Levin saved a signed copy of the survivor's remarks in his personal papers, along with a revision he drafted to the offending section that treated the postwar refugees much more gently. In an October 17, 1958, letter to Goldhaft, Levin wrote that a JAS official had told him of lingering unease within the refugee community about the language and noted they'd committed to removing that portion from the book.[22] Levin suggested it might be best to remove the passage to leave no questions about whether they were keeping their word. Subsequently printed copies of the book contained the revised language.[23]

Goldhaft and Levin also publicly apologized. The *Jewish Farmer's* October 1958 issue included a special insert headlined "Recent Controversy Settled."[24] The accompanying editor's note observed that "certain passages" in *The Golden Egg* had caused "considerable dissatisfaction among the Jewish farmers in the South Jersey area." The *Jewish Farmer's* editors wrote that accompanying letters by Goldhaft and Levin had satisfied the JPFA. Levin took much of the blame in his letter. "In trying to sharpen and make effective Dr. Goldhaft's portrait, I took too much for granted, and cut out too many of his qualifying statements," Levin wrote. "As a result, too much can be taken out of context, and it is even quite easily possible to misunderstand the passage as a whole, and to see it as a criticism of the very group we meant to show as equal with any other." Goldhaft, in his shorter apology letter in the *Jewish Farmer*, wrote, "I had no intention of offending anyone at any time but, quite to the contrary, I tried to portray the qualifications, courage, and fortitude of all those brave people who were successful in overcoming their previous horrible suffering and experiences." He added, "I am sorry that in showing the dark side from which they had to emerge I made some statements in such a way that their intent could be misinterpreted."

Goldhaft and Levin had merely said publicly in print what many American-born Jews in Vineland and beyond thought but wouldn't necessarily say out loud at the time. Nearly everything Goldhaft wrote about survivors in 1957 got repeated in an oral history published in 1993 chronicling Petaluma's Jewish poultry farming community. "The ones who survived were not the best of Jews, believe me," one Petaluma resident told author Kenneth Kann.[25] "I tried to work with them, but they wanted everything. Aggressive! Demanding! Greedy! Unethical! They were out for themselves and no one else." Another Petaluma resident explained to Kann that the survivors had left Europe with black-market fortunes and only grew wealthier in America. "The Jewish Agricultural Society presented them to us as poor, but these people knew how to fool officials," the man said.[26] His wife added, "The postwar refugees were a completely different element from the pre-war refugees." Similarly, American-born Jewish farmers in Farmingdale, New Jersey, described the community of Grine who settled there as conniving, cheating liars as historian Gertrude Wishnick Dubrovsky detailed in her 1992 book about the farming community there.[27]

Even the refugee farmers' biggest supporters weren't above the regrettable typecast. At a June 1956 JPFA meeting, Herman Levine, a thirty-seven-year JAS employee, recalled first encountering many of those in the audience years earlier at the agency's home office in New York not long after their liberation from concentration camps. "Broken physically as well as spiritually, forlorn and despondent, they looked with little hope to the future," he said.[28] Levine used similar language a few years later in a salute to the farmers on the occasion of the JPFA's tenth anniversary when he noted survivors who had "suffered unheard of horrors and persecutions before reaching our shores" had been left "broken in body and spirit."[29] At least, Levine ended on an upbeat note when he addressed the JPFA in 1956: as he visited the south Jersey area, Levine noted he was happy to see how the vast majority of them were "successfully settled."

For Vineland's survivors, it must have seemed particularly cruel that *The Golden Egg* was penned by Goldhaft, the city's most illustrious Jewish citizen. He chaired the local United Jewish Appeal campaign to help survivors reach Palestine and helped organize the local State of Israel Bond Drive. When survivors including Stanley Igel built a Jewish Center in nearby Dorothy, they asked Goldhaft to cut the ribbon at an October 1956 ceremony.[30] Seven months before *The Golden Egg* debuted, Goldhaft received an award recognizing him as the biggest buyer of state of Israel bonds in the community at a rally. He was handed the bronze plaque by Eleanor Roosevelt, the former first lady and wife of the late president Franklin D. Roosevelt.[31] Goldhaft was no self-hating Jew who abandoned his Jewish identity as he became more successful. If anything, his Jewish identity, if not his religious observance, had deepened with age.

Decades later, Louis Goldman, who was a twenty-year-old son of Grine poultry farmers in Vineland when *The Golden Egg* came out, noted the irony of Goldhaft insulting the farmers off of whom he'd gotten rich—or at least richer. Who, wondered Goldman, were these American Jews like Goldhaft to judge them? They'd lacked for nothing during the war, didn't have to fear for their lives or worry about how they'd scrounge for their next piece of bread. The Grines had, with only a few exceptions, come with nothing and were desperate to make a living. "Some of these Grines exerted pressure, they tried so hard. They didn't do anything wrong," Goldman said.[32] "And the Americans took it wrong. They said the Grine are over-aggressive, they want to be richer than us."

———·———

There is another possible explanation for the vitriol directed at survivors in *The Golden Egg*, one that puts the onus on Levin. Goldhaft's ghostwriter brought an epic grudge to the project, one that had already triggered a ruinous, lifelong obsession and may have also curdled his view of survivors.

Levin, the son of Lithuanian Jewish immigrants, grew up in Chicago's slums before graduating from the University of Chicago. He started out as a journalist in college and also later became a novelist. As a correspondent for the Jewish Telegraphic Agency during World War II, he was among the first Americans to enter Nazi concentration camps. Newly liberated prisoners desperate to share word of their survival wrote their names in pencil on his Jeep until the entire surface was covered. "From the beginning I realized I would never be able to write the story of the Jews of Europe," Levin wrote in a 1950 autobiography. "This tragic epic cannot be written by a stranger to the experience."[33]

In 1950, Levin found what he thought was the perfect person to give voice to the war's Jewish victims when he read the diary of a German-born teenage girl soon to be known around the world. Anne Frank began writing a diary at the age of thirteen, shortly before going into hiding in 1942 with her family in the secret annex of an Amsterdam building where her father Otto had worked. The hiding place was raided two years later. Anne, who was not quite sixteen, and her older sister died of typhus at the Bergen-Belsen concentration camp in early 1945. Only after his liberation from Auschwitz did Otto, the sole surviving member of the family, find Anne's moving account and publish it as a book in 1947 in the Netherlands.

Levin, who was living in France, immediately recognized the book's tremendous potential back home. Levin persuaded Otto Frank to let him help find an American publisher and negotiate theatrical and film rights, and thought he'd gotten assurances that he would write the stage adaptation.[34] Levin convinced the New York Times to assign its review of the Diary to him without disclosing his potential commercial interest. His June 1952 review helped boost American sales of a book that became a global cultural phenomenon.[35] The Diary would ultimately be translated into seventy languages and sell thirty million copies.[36] But Levin's draft script for the play got rejected, an outcome that he viewed as a deep betrayal.

Levin had worked hard to promote the Diary, and he believed his script faithfully captured Anne's spirit, only to find himself cut out in favor of non-Jewish writers. He was appalled that the play and movie largely minimized Anne's Jewish identity. Otto Frank wanted to tell a universal story, whether because he thought that's how his daughter saw the world or because it would appeal to as broad an audience and make as much money as possible.

Levin, however, saw more sinister forces at work. He nursed suspicions that he was the victim of a communist plot that sought to minimize the Jewish dimension of Frank's story, as Ralph Melnick recounts in his book about Levin and the *Diary*.[37] Levin's rage only grew when he saw the similarities between his version and the play that premiered on Broadway in October 1955, which ultimately won a Tony and a Pulitzer Prize and was later turned into an Oscar-winning movie. For his part, Otto Frank was angry that Levin thought he understood Anne better than her father did.[38] Whatever sympathy he had waned as Levin's sense of victimhood intensified.[39]

Levin sued Otto Frank and two others involved in turning the *Diary* into a play, claiming, among other things, that Frank had reneged on their agreement and that the staged play appropriated his ideas. Levin sought more than a million dollars at a trial that began in a New York courtroom in December 1957, just two weeks after *The Golden Egg's* publication.[40] Levin spoke of the legal battle in moral terms, convinced he was fighting on behalf of the Jewish community's right to own its cultural material and for "the voice from the mass grave to be fully heard."[41] The jury returned a verdict in favor of one of Levin's claims that the adaptation had used material he originated, although the judge threw out the damage award and ordered a new trial. Two years later, Frank agreed to pay fifteen thousand dollars in an out-of-court settlement in exchange for Levin handing over any rights, although Levin kept trying to stage his version.[42]

Both Frank and Levin have attracted their share of prominent defenders in subsequent decades, as Ian Buruma detailed in a 1998 account of their "sad story" in the *New York Review of Books*.[43] What's most relevant here is that Levin began work on *The Golden Egg* while embroiled in this legal dispute with one of the Holocaust's most famous survivors over the diary of its most famous victim. Levin, consumed by rage, self-pity, and a sense of injustice, may have allowed his anger about the *Diary* to color how he thought about survivors and portrayed them in *The Golden Egg*. The battle distorted Levin's thinking and hardened his feelings about survivors, Lawrence Graver notes in a book about Levin and the *Diary*. He appeared "at times to be more wounded by, or at least more entangled with, the harm that had been done to his career than he was with the atrocities committed against the Jews, or with the misrepresentation of Anne Frank's words in the theater."[44]

In his correspondence with Goldhaft, Levin seemed anxious to resolve the controversy surrounding *The Golden Egg* out of fear it might be used against him in his litigation with Frank. Levin wrote the Frank case was occupying much of his time in his October 1958 letter urging Goldhaft to excise the offending section of the book immediately.[45] Levin suggested to Goldhaft that his foes were even planting unflattering items about him in newspapers. Levin also cited the Frank case in his letter of apology that appeared the same month in the *Jewish Farmer*. "Had I not been dreadfully preoccupied with a court case at the time, and with the production of a play, I would probably have sensed the danger in these passages when I saw the material in proof," Levin wrote.[46]

Levin's grievances aside, it's impossible to overstate the significance of Anne Frank's diary, which proved to be a watershed in raising the profile of Holocaust victims and survivors alike. It was not the only cultural depiction of the Holocaust in the 1950s—multiple books were published in this decade about the Warsaw Ghetto and concentration camp memoirs.[47] Survivors appeared in three episodes of *This Is Your Life* in the 1950s, while another show, *Queen for a Day*, awarded an Auschwitz survivor plastic surgery to remove her tattoo.[48] The television anthology series *Playhouse 90* averaged one Holocaust-related drama per season.[49] But none had the resonance of Anne Frank, and this was true in Vineland as well.

The week *The Diary of Anne Frank* movie premiered in March 1959, her diary was still ranked ninth on the ten most sought-after nonfiction books at the Vineland Public Library seven years after its American debut (*The Golden Egg* was ranked first).[50] That same week, the local YMCA's community drama club staged a performance of the play at a local high school.[51] The film played at the Landis Theatre in Vineland and then later at the Delsea Drive-In. Bronia and Nuchim probably didn't see it at either venue. While Nuchim read books about the war, Bronia avoided all cultural representations of what by the late 1970s became known as the Holocaust. Ruth did read Anne Frank's diary as a teenager—although her parents weren't the ones who gave it to her.

———•———

Goldhaft merited attention far beyond Vineland when he died three years after *The Golden Egg*'s publication in April 1960 at the age of seventy-four.

The *Philadelphia Inquirer* described him as "one of the Nation's first veterinarians to specialize in poultry pathology."[52] And the hometown *Times Journal* lauded him as "one of Vineland's most honored citizens."[53] His family business continued to thrive in his absence. Within a few years, Vineland Poultry Laboratories would also have facilities in Mexico City, the Virgin Islands, and Israel.[54]

Levin nursed his obsession about Frank for another two decades, writing a 1973 book about the topic, *Obsession*, which a *New York Times* reviewer described as a "disturbing, strangely involving" book by an author who "sees the world from the cave of his preoccupations."[55] He remained a significant enough literary figure at the time of his death in 1981 to merit obituaries in both his hometown *Chicago Tribune* and the *New York Times*. In 2011, Mandy Patinkin played a character based on Levin alongside a marionette depicting Anne Frank in an off-Broadway play.[56] Levin finally received at least some of the credit he thought he was due on the website of the Anne Frank House, the Amsterdam museum that Otto helped establish at the site of the family's hiding spot that became a popular tourist destination. The Anne Frank House credits Levin's "enthusiastic review" in the *New York Times* with helping launch American sales of the diary and, in what can be described only as a considerable understatement, notes that Frank's rejection of his script "caused a lot of bitterness."[57]

The same could be said of *The Golden Egg*.

22 ▸ SEEKING HELP

FOR FIVE YEARS, Vineland's poultry farmers had suffered through lean times largely unnoticed, drawing little attention beyond south Jersey. That changed in the spring of 1959 as the bottom fell out of the egg market, the beginning of a poultry depression severe enough to prompt national press attention and a series of congressional hearings.

The trouble began in early March, when the price farmers could earn from a dozen eggs stood at thirty-eight cents—25 percent lower than a year earlier. The price of eggs kept falling as the month went on and into April, prompting Ben Leuchter to write, "All of us view this prolonged period of low egg prices and high costs of production with genuine horror."[1] None of the survivors had ever seen prices like these—60 percent lower than what Nuchim and Bronia earned when they arrived in Vineland twelve years earlier, without even controlling for inflation.

The last time farmers earned less than thirty cents a dozen was 1941, the *New York Times* noted in an April 25 story, the first of seven articles the paper published that spring on the plight of egg farmers.[2] The story cited overproduction as the culprit, reporting that occupants of New Jersey hen houses were "laying with a zeal that borders on the fanatic."

Sydney Goldberg witnessed the impact at his Vineland real estate office at Landis Avenue and Sixth Street as he fielded inquiries from poultry farmers desperate to sell their properties. The problem: no one wanted to buy a poultry farm as egg prices plummeted. Goldberg hadn't sold a single one in twelve months. "I could list 10 a week, but I don't bother," he said in June 1959. "There are no buyers."[3] With no other way out, many farmers found their only remaining escape just up Sixth Street at the office of attorney Philip Lipman where poultry farmers came every day seeking to file bankruptcy.

Lipman was a fifty-year-old lawyer who like Harry Levin had returned to Vineland after law school and opened up his first law office on Landis Avenue in 1932. Lipman sympathized with the poultry farmers; his older brother operated poultry farms and a feed mill. There just wasn't much he could do to help these farmers, whose property had as many as four mortgages attached.[4] The state's farm bankruptcy rate was soon the highest in the nation.[5]

In late April, a contingent of Jewish Poultry Farmers Association (JPFA) members traveled to Washington for two days of hearings on poultry and egg prices before the U.S. House Agriculture Committee. JPFA president Irving Schock, the chicken farmer and lay cantor who lived on Orchard Road near Bronia and Nuchim, led the Vineland delegation and would testify on their behalf. Schock must have felt a bit awed as he arrived for the first day of hearings April 30 and walked into the marble-floored lobby of the seven-story New House Office Building directly across Independence Avenue from the U.S. Capitol.

Leuchter captured the wonderment these political neophyte farmers experienced in their first visits to the nation's capital in an August 1954 column that recounted a trip to Washington with the Greater Vineland Poultry Council. He sat beside Miles Lerman in the public gallery above the Senate floor as senators Hubert Humphrey and Joseph McCarthy delivered speeches about price support legislation. After making their respective speeches, McCarthy, the conservative Republican red-baiter from Wisconsin, walked over to the Democratic side to talk strategy with Humphrey, the Minnesota liberal and future vice president. "At this, Miles Lerman's eyes almost popped out of his head," Leuchter recounted.[6] "Why, they're supposed to be such bitter enemies," Miles said. Another member of the 1954 Vineland delegation, Tevis Goldhaft, told Leuchter, "Where else can a bunch of poultrymen, for example, hop into a car, go to their capital, storm into a Congressman's or Senator's office and give him hell, if they want to, without having to worry about having police at the door during the middle of the night?"

It wasn't quite in mild-mannered Schock's nature to give anyone hell, let alone members of Congress. Schock might have had reason to feel optimistic after being personally welcomed to the Capitol a day earlier by Agriculture Committee chairman Harold Cooley. He came from Nashville, North Carolina, a town of fourteen hundred, and representing a district filled with tobacco farmers for twenty-five years had made Cooley sympathetic to small farmers of all kinds. But we can only wonder what he made of the witness list for these hearings, which left the impression that Jews owned nearly every small chicken farm in America.

The most eloquent and homespun testimony came from a survivor from Lakewood, New Jersey, named Rita Brandenburg. She had woken up at four thirty that morning for a bus ride to Washington along with more than one hundred other farmers and their wives. Many of them wore signs on their lapels reading, "Do Not Let the Family Farmer Die!"[7] Brandenburg, who led her local equivalent of the JPFA, had taught English in prewar Poland and was more comfortable speaking in English than most other Grine.[8] "Our life has never been peaches and cream, but we could put ends together," Brandenburg said. "We don't want charity. We don't want to go into bankruptcy." "Murmurs of approval" followed Brandenburg as she left the witness stand.

Schock had the misfortune of testifying right after Brandenburg. He certainly knew how to perform, albeit on the smaller stage of his Orchard Road *shtibl* or the other synagogues in south Jersey and the Philadelphia area where he'd serve as an itinerant High Holiday cantor in the decades to come.[9] On the *bimah*, the raised platform in a Jewish house of worship where the Torah is read, he cut a majestic figure in his long black robe he donned on Rosh Hashanah.[10] Off the bimah, however, he felt more comfortable poring over the text of the Torah and Talmud. He probably wasn't as comfortable in the public spotlight as Stanley Igel, who sat silently at this hearing behind the mayor of Estell Manor. Igel had emerged as one of the poultry farmers' most vocal advocates in New Jersey's capital, Trenton, and in Washington, D.C., now that Miles Lerman had transitioned into the oil business.

Of all the Jewish witnesses that day, Schock was the only one to identify as such explicitly, perhaps unavoidable given the name of the organization he came to represent. He explained the JPFA "is comprised of displaced persons from various parts of Europe who sought refuge and freedom from oppression and persecutions."[11] Unlike Brandenburg, Schock didn't dwell on his own *tsores*, or troubles, although he had plenty himself. Instead, he presented a six-point plan for how the federal government could help small family farmers, including a minimum floor on prices for small egg farms. Most of his suggestions aimed at bringing more transparency to the mercantile exchanges that set prices and that farmers long suspected of fixing prices. "Our industry is sick, and radical surgery is required at once," Schock said.

It's probably not a coincidence that Schock, the foreign-sounding immigrant representing a Jewish farmers group, paired up at the witness table with Hirsch Nadel, a U.S. combat veteran. Nadel arrived in the United States from Poland at age nineteen in 1938 and served six years in the U.S. Army. Nadel explained to the committee that he spent two and a half years in veterans' hospitals after getting wounded. "Now I am fighting to make a living on my poultry farm," Nadel said. The final member of their panel was Lipman, the Vineland lawyer who described farmer bankruptcies that produced "a sum total of nothing net." "There is nothing but broken hearts in some of these small poultry farms that are in existence in the Vineland area," Lipman said.

The farmer witnesses like Schock elicited sympathy from lawmakers, particularly Chairman Cooley, but got little else. Cooley said there wasn't much lawmakers could do while putting the blame squarely on President Dwight Eisenhower's agriculture secretary, Ezra Taft Benson. Cooley charged that Benson was driving farmers into bankruptcy by refusing to help buy surplus eggs or set a minimum floor on egg prices. Benson, fifty-nine, was born on a family farm in Idaho and spent his career in agriculture, including stints as a county agricultural agent and as leader in the National Council of Farmer Cooperatives.[12] This future president of the Church of Jesus Christ of Latter-day Saints was both deeply religious and a devout disciple of laissez-faire economics.

Benson believed markets should be left alone to work and distrusted both economic planning and farm subsidies. Those views made him perhaps the most polarizing agriculture secretary ever, earning the enmity of small farmers across America.[13] He dodged a half dozen eggs thrown at him during an appearance at a 1957 South Dakota mechanical corn picking contest.[14] Vineland farmers never had a chance to throw their eggs at Benson, who remained the hidden hand as far as they were concerned. They had more contact with Hermon Miller, head of the U.S. Department of Agriculture's (USDA) poultry division. Miller had long insisted—including at a 1956 appearance at the Vineland Egg Auction—that the industry's problem was oversupply.[15] He argued additional government support such as lowering the price of feed would only induce farmers to produce more eggs and further depress egg prices.

Miller testified at this hearing that the USDA had done all it could to aid poultrymen and said the industry needed to cut production voluntarily. One incredulous congressman asked whether the only way to help the government balance supply and demand was to let farmers "all go broke." Miller replied, "I do not know that I should answer that."[16] (At a subsequent hearing a few months later, busloads of farmers "had nothing but jeers" for Miller when he testified that the poultry situation is "adjusting itself.")[17]

The Eisenhower administration's do-nothing approach didn't dim the optimism of Schock, the cantor-farmer, and Lipman, the small-town lawyer, buoyed perhaps by lawmakers' sympathetic platitudes and this rare chance to be heard. The *Times Journal* reported Vineland's delegation left the Capitol "convinced help might be on the way."[18] A week later, Schock reported back to the JPFA at a well-attended meeting in Vineland. He noted four different lawmakers had complimented the group's plan. Lipman said he expected action would be taken—although he didn't specify by whom or what form it might take—due to the pressure exerted by poultrymen.[19]

Schock submitted written testimony rather than returning to Washington when the committee convened its next hearings on egg prices in mid-June.[20] By then, egg prices had bottomed out in May at twenty-five cents a dozen, down 60 percent from the peak for this time of year during the Korean War. In his written testimony, Schock said the situation had "gotten worse" since his appearance as more families abandoned their farms and bankruptcies increased. The Eisenhower administration still refused to intervene by buying up hens, fresh shell eggs, or broilers. Agriculture Secretary Benson agreed to increase purchases only of dried and frozen eggs while encouraging Americans to eat an extra egg a day.

Survivors found no more sympathy among public officials back home. That was evident at a special meeting to discuss the poultry crisis in mid-May

convened by the Cumberland County Board of Freeholders, which func-
tioned as the administrative and legislative governing body of the county
that encompassed Vineland. Joseph Hancock, a Democratic Freeholder
and truck farmer, rejected calls for price limits on feed. "The truth is there are
too dog-gone many eggs," Hancock said, and he knew just whom to blame.[21]
"We have supported refugees who have come into the area and put them in
the poultry business," Hancock said. "The poultryman should solve his own
problems."

Hancock backtracked slightly in a letter to the editor a few days later,
insisting that he hadn't intended to be derogatory in his choice of words. "If
the word 'refugee' offended, I'm sorry," Hancock wrote.[22] Harry Rothman,
the associate Cumberland County agricultural agent, later rejected as
"absurd and ridiculous" the suggestion that refugees were to blame for the
poultry depression in south Jersey. The survivors had purchased farms from
Vineland-area farmers who were on the verge of retirement. "Had there not
been any customers for these farms, the poultry industry of the area would
have gone to nothing," Rothman said.[23]

Equally unfair was blaming survivors' extravagant lifestyles for their
troubles.[24] One Vineland survivor interviewed decades later by sociologist
William Helmreich pointed to his fellow farmers' profligate spending. "A lot
of the survivors who did well got too cocky," Louis Goldman said.[25] "They
weren't happy just making a living. This guy wanted a new car, that guy
wanted a new mink and furniture. But there's just so much you can get out
of a farm. A lot of them didn't figure on that and they thought it would
always be blue sky." To Helmreich, this "tendency toward an extravagant
lifestyle" in reaction to "extended deprivation" was the sort of individual
failing that explains why some survivors didn't succeed economically.[26] In
fact, personal thrift alone made little difference in the face of structural economic changes buffeting small poultry farmers at the time.

The biggest threat to Vineland's poultry farmers, as a January 1959 editorial in New Jersey Farm and Garden warned, were "factory-size" farms in low-
cost southern states.[27] These southern farms produced eggs on such an
efficient a scale that even Vineland's biggest small farmers with ten- or fifteen thousand birds couldn't compete. Within a decade, successful egg
farmers would need fifty- or a hundred thousand layers, and most New Jersey
survivors couldn't afford to expand on that scale. As it happens, the most
famous exemplar of the coming era of industrial-scale poultry farming was

also a survivor. German-born "egg kingpin" Julius Goldman, whose family was killed during the war, started out with three thousand birds in Van Nuys, California, and ultimately housed a flock of three and a half million hens on 205 acres he dubbed "Egg City" in the Santa Susana Mountains. At his peak, Goldman's hens laid two million eggs a day in the 1970s, emitting odors that offended much of Ventura County.[28]

These mega operators were far better equipped to cater to the demands of giant supermarket chains. Farmers also had to contend with changing consumer tastes. Homemakers had embraced box baking mixes that required fewer eggs and served fewer eggs in the morning under the influence of a barrage of breakfast cereal ads. Consumers also worried more about calories and a new health concern: cholesterol.[29]

Most farmers interviewed by the New York Times in the spring of 1959 understood the complexity of the situation, suggesting it was a "gross oversimplification" to blame overproduction or reduced consumption alone for their woes.[30] They knew full well, the Times reported, that in the previous twelve months "a major portion" of the New York market "has been seized by farmers of the South." "Northern producers, even the efficient ones, are expected to be squeezed tighter and tighter because of the competitive advantage that the South has from lower labor and flock housing costs," the Times noted.

————·————

Survivor farmers tried hiding their economic troubles from their children as best they could, with mixed success. Eight-year-old Ely Swerdlin realized how much trouble poultry farmers were having when he visited Vineland's newest supermarket that opened on Landis Avenue in August 1959. The giant new A&P—just the sort of chain that preferred giant suppliers over small farmers—boasted two hundred parking spots and "seeing-eye" doors that opened without being touched.[31] At the opening, Ely's father Herman gravitated to the shelves of eggs where A&P charged nineteen cents per dozen. "I remember him saying it cost him more as a farmer to put that out as a product than what they were selling it at the supermarket," Ely said. "That always stuck with me. I could feel his angst."

By the end of 1959, the number of chicken farms in New Jersey had fallen 20 percent. An unfortunate if fitting coda to a difficult year came in December when the Jewish Farmer told readers that this issue would be its last. It ceased publication after fifty-one years.[32] The editors said there were "many reasons" for the decision, including the fact that "practically no Yiddish speaking immigrants" had come to the United States for several years and almost all Jewish farmers, having been here for five or more years, "understand English fairly well" and didn't need a Yiddish section. It became "highly questionable" whether the Jewish Agricultural Society should incur the "considerable expense" required to publish it only in English, given the availability of many other English-language farm publications. Thus ended the last surviving agricultural paper in the United States with a non-English section.

The collapse of Vineland's egg industry soon claimed victims closer to home. In March 1960, the Jacob Rubinoff Co. announced it had been sold to a Philadelphia stock holding company, Son-Mark Industries, for more than two million dollars. Edward Rubinoff was to stay on as general manager. "The long-depressed state of the poultry industry has been no secret to us who have lived outside of Greater Vineland," said Abe Goldman, president of Son-Mark Industries. "We have every reason to believe that under the stewardship of Mr. Rubinoff coupled with our own experience, varied interests and keen sense of responsibility to the people of this community, a stronger poultry industry and more stable local economy will ultimately emerge."[33]

In just fourteen months, Goldman, a forty-three-year-old cigar-chomping Philadelphia native who talked "like an itinerant evangelist," had built a thirty-million-dollar business after buying nineteen firms across eight states. His acquisitions included a New York installment furniture chain and a clothing store in Mobile, Alabama. "What we do," Goldman explained, "is take a going business that has become a little complacent and give it an injection of Son-Mark juice."[34] The latest to get that "Son-Mark juice" injection would be the Rubinoffs in Vineland, the site of what Goldman claimed was his first business success: a grocery store he opened on Delsea Drive at the age of eighteen. It was an instantaneous success—for two weeks—until business quickly trailed off. Perhaps Goldman's track record should have given the Rubinoff family pause, but they were just relieved to get such a good price for the company as the poultry industry faded.

One day after Son-Mark's purchase of the Rubinoffs' business was announced, Leuchter noted the first reaction among readers—particularly farmers—"might naturally have been one of panic, as if to say 'the poultry industry must be heading nowhere if the Jacob Rubinoff company is getting out of it." Leuchter chose to put a positive spin on the news as "a happy move for all the participants."[35]

————•————

As the Rubinoff Feed Company looked to Son-Mark for relief, some Vineland farmers turned to an even more unlikely savior: America's most notorious labor leader, James Hoffa. A Jewish farm wife, Miriam Katz, deserves much of the credit for coaxing the International Brotherhood of Teamsters into taking up the farmers' cause. Katz, a prewar immigrant from Poland, and her Romanian-born husband Charles stood out as two of the few non-refugees to buy a Vineland chicken farm in the 1950s. They'd followed her cousins, including a Buchenwald survivor who left his job in a New York tailor shop for a farm near Vineland.[36]

Miriam and Charles, a sheet-metal plant foreman who hid the fact he couldn't read or write in English from his children, traded Bayside, Queens, for Vineland.[37] Their timing was terrible. Eggs were selling at sixty-three cents a dozen when they bought the farm; by the time their chickens laid their first dozen eggs the price had dropped to thirty-five cents. Their troubles worsened as the decade progressed. Katz's oldest daughter dropped out of school for a time to help support her teenage sister and younger brother.[38]

Frustrated with their lot, Miriam joined a protest at the Mercantile Exchange in New York and became a leader in a poultry farmers' association that was founded in Vineland and affiliated with the AFL-CIO.[39] "They didn't help us at all," Katz recalled. "It was a small, weak union with nothing behind it."[40] She traveled to Washington pleading for help from their congressman. He didn't do anything, either. That's when Katz and another poultry farmer, Thomas Leone, sent a letter to Hoffa. "We figured 1,777,000 people in the Teamsters make a living under Hoffa, and maybe we could too," she said.

Within three days, the Teamsters had invited Katz and Leone to Washington, the start of a lightning-fast courtship between Hoffa and Vineland's poultry farmers. Their first public meeting in Elizabeth, New Jersey, in mid-February generated headlines nationwide. Hoffa pledged to aid farmers and promised to recommend establishing a Teamsters local for poultry farmers in New Jersey "if things work out satisfactorily."[41]

The forty-seven-year-old union chief was at the height of his powers in 1960, having organized a union of mostly truckers into the nation's largest. Few Teamsters were agricultural workers. But Hoffa, who grew up in a coal mining town of ten thousand in Indiana before moving to Detroit at the age of eleven, had a genuine affinity for both small-town America and "individualistic and resilient workers," a description that certainly applied to Vineland's poultry farmers.[42]

Hoffa also had less than altruistic reasons for helping. By 1960, he'd already been tried—and acquitted—for bribery and wiretapping. He had been the target of a long-running Senate corruption investigation led by Robert Kennedy, the brother of Massachusetts senator and presidential candidate John F. Kennedy.[43] Robert Kennedy published a book that spring suggesting that Hoffa's tactics and underworld ties constituted a "conspiracy of evil."[44] Just a few days after meeting with Katz in Elizabeth, Hoffa was scheduled to appear before a federal judge who would determine whether he should be removed as Teamsters president.[45] On February 24, a half dozen Teamsters officials, including Hoffa's "right-hand man," were indicted for illegal political contributions.[46] None of that mattered to Katz, who told reporters Hoffa is "a wonderful man. So sympathetic, so interested, a human being. He doesn't give anyone the brush off."[47] Asked by reporters what she thought of the Senate investigation of corruption among the Teamsters, she replied, "I don't believe everything I read. What about the corruption in Washington?"[48] As she told reporters, "He gives us hope, he's the only one that does."[49]

On March 29, one thousand New Jersey poultry farmers crowded into a large conference hall at the Ambassador Hotel on Atlantic City's Boardwalk. Hoffa, wearing a suit and tie, railed in an hour-long speech against the press and the "phonies . . . and the intellectual geniuses in Congress" who he said had "abandoned the poultry farmer."[50] (Hoffa had particular reason to be angry at Congress: a Senate panel wrapped up its three-year investigation with a report issued one day earlier portraying him, in the words of the Associated Press, as "an ally of gangsters, a betrayer of his fellow unionists and a corrupter of men.")[51] The only hope for farmers is to organize, Hoffa said. The audience was convinced. With only a single dissenting vote, the farmers appointed a committee headed by Katz to work out the details of organizing with the Teamsters.

Hoffa's appeal in Vineland piqued the curiosity of newspapers around the country. The Associated Press sent a reporter to Vineland, and the resulting story on Hoffa's organizing efforts ran in newspapers from Akron to El Paso. The AP's reporter described Katz as an "attractive blonde" and "vocal member" of the organizing committee. The story depicted her cousin Paul Flumenbaum as a "sad-eyed little man" who had survived a German concentration camp, employing the sort of insensitive characterization of survivors avoided by Vineland's local paper.[52] In "heavily accented English," Flumenbaum said he'd been a member of the garment workers union in New York but was reluctant to join a union in Vineland at first, viewing himself more as an independent businessman than a worker. "I don't feel that way anymore," said Flumenbaum, who operated a farm in Buena. "Nobody else wants to help us." Flumenbaum said Hoffa's reputation didn't concern him. "He hasn't been proven guilty of anything." Flumenbaum's twenty-five-year-old Philadelphia-born wife Audrey was an even bigger believer. Her father was a Teamster, and she saw "what a strong union can do." As for Hoffa, Audrey said, "He looks out for his own."

Others remained skeptical about what Hoffa could offer Vineland's chicken farmers. Carleton Heritage, president of the New Jersey Farm Bureau, warned the Teamsters couldn't help boost low farm prices since antitrust laws prevented them from bargaining collectively over the price of farm products. "Many poultrymen are desperate for a chance to get out of the economic poorhouse," Heritage said. "But the Teamsters can't lead them out. If they say they can, they are practicing a fraud on the unsuspecting."[53] An even more strident warning came from Leuchter the day after Hoffa won over so many Vineland farmers with his speech in Atlantic City. Leuchter, who gave Son-Mark Industries the benefit of the doubt as the Rubinoffs' rescuer, didn't extend Hoffa the same courtesy. "What Jimmy Hoffa is peddling to desperate poultrymen is on a par with the traveling medicine quacks of old who went from town-to-town peddling magic pills that would cure anything from athlete's foot to cancer," Leuchter wrote in his column.[54]

Leuchter's warnings went unheeded among many desperate south Jersey farmers. Three hundred signed up to join the Teamsters once it opened an office on Landis Avenue. Over three hundred fifty farmers attended a May 1960 ceremony formally establishing Teamsters Local 530: the New

Jersey Poultry Farmers Union.[55] A Teamsters official almost certainly exaggerated the following month when he boasted the union local had signed up one thousand of the area's seventeen hundred poultry farmers. The highest figure otherwise referenced in press accounts is seven hundred members paying three dollars in monthly dues. In part, the Teamsters didn't do better in their recruiting drive because most survivors stayed away.

Some Jewish farmers participated. Katz was installed as the temporary vice-president, pending elections, and a German Jewish farmer, who like Katz had come to the United States before the war, was named a trustee. But the committee notably included no survivor farmers, and only one survivor was elected a local officer later that year. It wasn't that survivors were averse to collective action. The JPFA had created its own mutual aid society and a cooperative association to negotiate better contracts than farmers could get individually with egg dealers.[56] But survivors who feared government authority and drawing attention to themselves didn't want to associate with Hoffa, who was under constant law enforcement scrutiny.[57]

At a June 1960 meeting, organizing committee chairman Irving Goldstein, a Vineland insurance agent, unintentionally provided insight into why the organizing drive hadn't made greater inroads among survivors. Goldstein, an American-born Jew and president of a local insurance workers union, "laughed off rumors that membership in the Teamsters Union would end in 'deportation.'"[58] The prospect of deportation was no laughing matter to survivors, who had only recently become citizens and worried about the permanence of any safe harbor after what happened in Europe. Igel, increasingly one of the poultry farmer community's most visible advocates, demurred when asked his position on Hoffa. Still, he understood the appeal. If the state and national organizations do nothing to improve the farmers' conditions, poultrymen have no other choice than to seek out someone like Hoffa.[59]

Teamster officials referred to Local 530 as a "pilot" program, yet by June Hoffa had already shifted his attention north to another poultry farming community in central New Jersey.[60] He told a June 1960 gathering of Lakewood-area poultrymen he wasn't going to "promise the moon" but agreed to organize a local there as well.[61] Letters of interest about organizing similar locals arrived from poultry farmers from as far away as Mississippi and California. The Teamsters opened an office in Lakewood. In October, Jackson

Township poultry farmer Samuel Elperin noted the Lakewood office was painted but hadn't yet opened. The union "has fallen asleep," Elperin said.[62]

By that point, Hoffa could be forgiven for not paying much attention to the troubles of New Jersey poultry farmers anymore. He had plenty else to worry about, particularly when John F. Kennedy was elected president in November 1960. For attorney general, President Kennedy chose his brother Robert, who pursued Hoffa relentlessly. The local continued meeting periodically in 1961 and pressed for a congressional investigation of the Mercantile Exchange, to no avail. Katz had scaled back her involvement in the local after receiving some nasty phone calls and developing health problems.

In the end, Hoffa had proven a false savior, and things only got worse for Katz and her family. When her daughter Sharon went off to Temple University in the fall of 1961, her father couldn't afford a new pair of shoes for four years.[63] Miriam found work as a hatchery sales representative.[64] Eventually, she and her husband declared bankruptcy.[65] Schock didn't fare much better as a farmer. He moved to Philadelphia in the mid-1960s and opened an Army-Navy store.

23 ▸ ALTERNATIVE
LIVELIHOODS

THIRTEEN-YEAR-OLD ARNOLD GLANZ had just returned to Vineland from a Passover-week trip to visit family in New York along with his mother and younger sister when his father calmly shared some bad news.[1] A fire had gutted about three-quarters of one of their chicken coops.

The fire, which killed twenty-four hundred chickens, had started just before midnight. Vineland's fire chief concluded the fire had originated in a propane stove used to warm laying chickens or from a short in the electrical wiring. It could have been worse. Three companies of Vineland firefighters backed up by reinforcements from two neighboring towns managed to protect the farmhouse, garage, and their other two coops on the Landis Avenue property.

Many years would pass before Glanz, which is not his real name, began to wonder if good planning rather than good fortune explained why their house survived unscathed. Could his father have set fire to the coop for insurance money? His father certainly didn't say anything at the time to

Glanz, who had celebrated his bar mitzvah less than two months earlier. Nor would either of his parents ever talk about the fire later.

Glanz's father did seem very calm when he delivered the news. Then again, what's a destroyed chicken coop after all he'd been through? Glanz's father lost his first wife and son after the Germans occupied their village in Belarus. He survived Auschwitz in a unit of prison laborers forced to work in a crematorium disposing of the bodies of gas chamber victims. He started his second family after moving to New York, where he met a woman nearly a generation younger who grew up in his hometown and came to the United States before the war. He was past fifty when Glanz was born, in his mid-fifties when Glanz's sister arrived. Glanz's father was now well into his sixties and still doing the hard labor poultry farming demanded. One clue embedded in Glanz's memory, only to prompt questions many years later, was the odd location of his bicycle along with his sister's at the time of the fire. In hindsight, Glanz wondered why the bikes, which usually got stored in the garage, wound up burned in the coop, making it possible to buy new ones.

It's also entirely possible that the fire really was just an accident. Fires were common in the coops, including at the Tuckahoe Road farm that Bronia and Nuchim used to share with the Liverants. In January 1959, the Liverants' farm laborer woke them up in the middle of the night after noticing a fire in their coop.[2] The blaze that firefighters believed started in a kerosene brooder stove used to keep the chickens warm at night left 6,500 ten-week-old broilers dead. The loss was only partially covered by insurance. Lightning later struck another coop on the Glanz property, causing a fire that destroyed a third of it.

Regardless, the possibility that Glanz's father might have successfully pulled off an insurance fire makes another incident that happened around the same time all the more ironic. His mother happened to wake up in the middle of the night, look out the window, and notice a neighbor's coop in flames. She called the fire department, which arrived in time to put out the fire. The next morning, Glanz was sitting at the kitchen table eating breakfast when the neighbor angrily burst into the house. Rather than offering a thank-you, he yelled, "Can't you mind your own business?"[3]

Some farm owners found other unsavory ways to make money off their properties. In 1958, federal agents and Vineland police raided an Oak Road chicken farm, confiscated a six-hundred-gallon moonshine still, and arrested the man—not a Grine—who leased the property and lived in the farmhouse.[4] Desperate farmers also proved easy marks for the unscrupulous. A survivor couple in Toms River, New Jersey, that had abandoned egg farming later supplemented their income by leasing two acres of their property as a temporary storage site for five thousand steel drums they were told were empty.[5] They had unwittingly allowed their property to be used as a dumping ground for toxic chemicals that seeped into the groundwater.

Most Vineland farmers never turned to arson, moonshining, or toxic waste storage, but almost all sought new ways to make a living in the early 1960s. Some chose to abandon Vineland altogether, even if they couldn't sell their farms. By December 1960, more than two hundred Vineland poultry farms sat empty, and the vacancy rate in some neighborhoods reached 50 percent.[6] No one even wanted to buy the coops for scrap. A *Times Journal* classified ad offered, "Chicken coops, free for the lumber."[7]

Real estate development and operating motels proved particularly alluring, at least to those with enough capital to start their own businesses. Several bought motels in Vineland or Atlantic City or as far away as Miami Beach. Others became small shopkeepers, opening a printing business or grocery store in Vineland. Some switched from selling eggs to related businesses. Brothers Sol and Joe Finkelstein and their brother-in-law Norbert Berman realized they could earn more processing eggs than selling them by the dozen. They established an egg breaking and freezing business on their adjoining Newfield farms, filling thirty-pound brass cans for wholesale purchase by bakeries in Philadelphia and New York.[8] Irving and Esther Raab first branched out into chicken vaccinations, and later opened a poultry processing plant, Vineland Kosher Poultry.

A few farmers tried to scale up and compete with bigger southern operations, taking advantage of cheap land to buy up abandoned farms. One family rented out coops on five other properties, raising fifty thousand chickens at their peak, before giving up altogether and opening a menswear store near Philadelphia.[9] But few of the survivors, most of whom had multiple mortgages that left them deep in debt, had the kind of capital needed to scale up operations and cut operating costs by automating chicken feeding and egg handling. A few chose a less risky alternative called contract farming. Feed distributors bought and stocked farms with hens and then contracted with families to manage the operation in exchange for a set price for each dozen eggs. The arrangement provided some measure of stability, but the *New York Times* noted many farmers equated these contracts with becoming "sharecroppers on acreage they only recently proudly possessed."[10]

Bronia and Nuchim witnessed the exodus firsthand as friends and neighbors started moving away. In early 1960, Dina and Jack sold the Tuckahoe Road farm and moved north to Brooklyn. Jack went first, partnering in a grocery with survivors he'd met in night school when they'd first arrived from Europe. Nuchim and Bronia remained behind in Vineland, still trying to eke out a living with their small poultry operation.

Why did small farmers like Nuchim stay in a business that was so obviously failing? "You think it was so easy to find something to do?," Bronia said simply. "It wasn't easy to move," explained Nathan Dunkelman.[11] "I had no trade and not enough money to do something else." One farm wife who later bought a motel with her husband said, "You were afraid to take a chance when you have a family."[12] Some older survivors felt like it was too late to start all over once again. Ely Swerdlin cited his father as example. He'd come to the United States in his mid-forties, was nearing fifty when his younger son was born, and was approaching sixty as the poultry business collapsed. "Imagine trying to determine what you're going to do at that point with no financial means and limited education?," Swerdlin asked.[13] "So they stayed with what they knew at the time." For younger farmers, "time was more on their side," Swerdlin said. But younger survivors had their own disadvantage: teenagers when the war started, some hadn't even finished high school, let alone college.

Survivors who had lost so much and found some measure of stability in Vineland, no matter the economic hardships, didn't want to give it up. Zosia Waiman, the mother of Ruth's friend, Helen, would have loved to move and pointed out all the people leaving to her husband Jerome.[14] But Jerome, who turned fifty in 1960, was happy with his modest, quiet life. He had his friends and his autonomy, even if the family didn't always have enough money to buy food and ate eggs three times a day in the worst of times.

In Nuchim's case, his innate optimism played a role in keeping him on the farm. This trait had served him well during the war, buoying Bronia's spirits in the worst of times when they had no good reason to be hopeful about their chances of surviving. That same optimism proved less useful in Vineland, making it harder for him to see just how grim the future was on the farm. Nuchim "would not see bad things," Ruth said. "'Things would get better,' he would say. He would not see the negative." Nuchim was hardly the only farmer guilty of undue optimism or wishful thinking. "I don't share the gloom and predictions of doom" for the poultry industry, Martin Berwin, the longtime president of the German Jewish refugees' Poultrymen's Club, wrote in the much-diminished pages of the *Times Journal*'s poultry section in March 1963. "Contrary to those prophets of doom, I believe more than ever in a bright future for our New Jersey poultry industry."[15]

——•——

Even the most optimistic farmers who tried sticking it out as small farmers realized they needed to find ways to supplement their income. Next door, Joey Hyman went to work at a garment factory while Sally stayed home managing the farm. Around the corner, Jerome Waiman started a route delivering eggs directly to independent grocers and restaurants in Philadelphia and the Jersey Shore. Nuchim also took to the road for new opportunities. Starting sometime in 1960, Nuchim loaded up his green and white finned Oldsmobile with cardboard boxes every Friday, Saturday, and Sunday. He crossed over the Delaware Memorial Bridge, ending his roughly two-hour commute at a windowless, one-story, c-shaped market in New Castle, Delaware.

Nuchim came to the New Castle Farmers Market to sell leather handbags and belts he displayed on a wooden table and hung from makeshift walls and on hooks from a beam below the ceiling. Leather goods was something of a family business to Nuchim. His grandfather had a tannery in Poland; the uncles who initially assisted him when he first arrived in New York had their own wholesale hide business. Nuchim, desperate for a way to earn extra money, fell into the business when their neighbor Sally Hyman connected him with a *landsman* who was a leather goods wholesaler in New York. Later, Nuchim expanded his offerings to include fabrics, the giant bolts filling what little empty space remained in the booth.

Nuchim could tend to the chickens early in the morning and still make it to New Castle for the market's noon opening. In the course of a workday, he transitioned from squawking hens to a cacophony of cash registers and merchants selling everything from women's blouses to goldfish and roast beef in the warren of dozens of booths. The smell of cotton candy and popcorn replaced the smell of chicken feces.

Ruth, who joined Nuchim on weekends when she didn't have too much homework, glimpsed an entirely different side of her father at the farmer's market. At home, she knew him only as a solitary chicken farmer with little contact with anyone during the workday other than the laborers who helped with the chickens. Here, he had an easy manner with customers and fellow merchants. He befriended the meat salesman across the aisle. "He liked people, was good with customers, they liked him," Ruth said. On the way back home, Ruth and Nuchim might stop for a rare meal out: a steak dinner in their car at a farmer's market near the Cowtown Rodeo back on the New Jersey side of the bridge.

Once home, Nuchim put the cardboard boxes full of his pocketbook inventory back in the living room, which remained largely barren nearly a decade after they'd moved into the house. Nuchim and Bronia's small third bedroom still doubled as the common area where they kept a desk, couch, and their black-and-white television. Ruth and her parents often ate dinner together there while watching *The Huntley-Brinkley Report*, NBC's evening news show. Nuchim watched intently, grousing about the Soviet Union's continued stranglehold on Eastern Europe and communist advances in Southeast Asia. Bronia, as was her habit, stayed quiet.

This was a particularly difficult time for Bronia, whose health issues compounded the family's financial worries. Bronia was suffering from a benign condition. But she was medically unsophisticated and hadn't gotten the chance to watch her own parents age and get sick, so she thought she had a life-threatening malignancy. With Nuchim tending to the chickens and away three days a week at the farmer's market, it was Sally next door who helped Bronia recuperate from surgery.

———•———

As Bronia and Nuchim struggled, their lives diverged further from the Lermans, who had begun transitioning out of the poultry business at just the right time. Miles did well enough with the home heating oil business to build a fuel storage plant for home heating, kerosene, and industrial oil on Weymouth Road, not far from his home. An October 1959 *Times Journal* story, which reads more like a press release, noted the plant "was made necessary by the growth in sales" of the Miles Lerman Oil Co., as the firm was known.[16]

In August 1961, the Lermans were nominated for the "Family-of-the-Year" award by the South Jersey Modern Living Show, a short-lived annual exposition at Vineland's Armory. A *Times Journal* story announcing the nomination included a photo of the family in what the article described as their "large two-story" Weymouth Road home.[17] The article lists their many good deeds on behalf of local Jewish community causes: United Jewish Appeal bond drives, B'nai B'rith, Beth Israel congregation for Miles; Hadassah for Chris.

The story noted Chris "serves as secretary for her husband's growing fuel oil business," a typical undervaluing of a woman's contributions at a time when women of a certain class were supposed to limit themselves mostly to the domestic sphere. In that vein, the *Times Journal* wrote that Chris "takes charge" at home raising David, a sixth grader, and thirteen-year-old Jeanette, who the story notes had "achieved one of the highest ranks in Girl Scouting." The foursome is all smiles and look relaxed in the photo, seated on a couch in front of a floral-patterned curtain.

The story begins by noting that the Lermans "began life anew here after being liberated from Nazi concentration camps," which wasn't actually true in the case of Miles, who ended the war as a partisan. A few months before their nomination as family of the year, Miles and Chris had a chance to observe a top Nazi up close. Their first trip to Israel in the spring of 1961 coincided with the trial of Adolf Eichmann, the German official responsible for drawing up the plans for the mass deportation of Jews to extermination camps. In May 1960, Israeli agents grabbed Eichmann, the most senior Nazi official responsible for the Holocaust ever captured, outside his home in Argentina, where he'd hidden since the war. They drugged Eichmann and disguised him in an El Al uniform before secreting him out of the country on a flight of the Israeli national airline. His capture generated international headlines. A year later, reporters from around the globe packed the Jerusalem courtroom where Eichmann went on trial on multiple counts, including crimes against humanity and crimes against the Jewish people.

The trial was front-page news worldwide, including in Vineland, at least until the unsuccessful CIA-backed invasion of Communist Cuba at the Bay of Pigs pushed it to page two in the *Times Journal*. In an April 11 column, Leuchter made no reference to Vineland's survivors as he wrote, "If it serves to strengthen mankind's resolve to prohibit genocide in the future, if it makes the world a little less cruel and a little more understanding, then this strange trial will have served a useful purpose."[18] The trial proved momentous for many reasons, putting the Nazis' Jewish victims front and center for the first time. Eichmann's trial also elevated in the public consciousness the idea of the Holocaust and even the word itself, which was used by court translators throughout the proceedings.[19]

Neither Chris nor Miles is among the list maintained by Yad Vashem of more than one hundred witnesses who testified at the trial.[20] Nor is it clear whether they planned their visit to Israel to coincide with Eichmann's trial or, as was so often the case, they simply had good timing. Miles attended a number of sessions of the trial, but they were already back in Vineland by the time Eichmann testified on his own behalf.[21] Eichmann argued he was just carrying out orders rather than acting on his own initiative.[22] Upon returning to Vineland, Miles and Chris posed for a *Times Journal* photo holding a picture of Eichmann in the glass cage where he spent the trial dressed in a suit and tie surrounded by uniformed Israeli police.[23] Miles spoke about the Eichmann trial at a May Hadassah meeting at Beth Israel synagogue.[24] Miles told the audience that the trial had helped "chisel into the memory of mankind the brutal and destructive deeds a dictatorship makes possible." Another year passed before Israel erected its first-ever gallows and executed Eichmann.

The Lermans lost out on the family-of-the-year title—and the one-hundred-dollar savings bond prize—to a family of a longtime Rubinoff employee, which was just as well given how the feed company was struggling. The company's situation had only grown more dire under the direction of its purported rescuer, Son-Mark Industries. Son-Mark had seemed like a miniature version of the conglomerates that snapped up disparate businesses in the 1960s, but turned out to be the forerunner of another corporate archetype: the 1980s raider that looted its acquisitions. Son-Mark became the target of multiple lawsuits alleging the businesses it bought had made loans to the parent company and then wound up in trouble or failing.[25] By the spring of 1961, Son-Mark had gone bankrupt, and the Rubinoff company owed the IRS more than $180,000 in unpaid back income taxes.[26]

Rubinoff employees launched an eight-month campaign to wrest control of the mill. One hundred employees mortgaged their homes, borrowed from friends, and skipped at least one payday, although they turned down offers of help from sympathetic customers and suppliers. The company's original owners regained title to the property in a foreclosure sale and then leased it to employees with an option to buy. In January 1962, employees finally succeeded in taking control via a stock purchase.[27] The *Philadelphia Daily News* called the mill "the innocent victim of the collapse of a financial house of cards."[28]

24 ▸ TEENAGERS

VINELAND CELEBRATED ITS centennial in August 1961 in a monthlong burst of civic pride complete with parades, historical pageants, pie-eating contests, and three-legged races. The men of Vineland were encouraged to grow beards or at least a mustache to join the "Brothers of the Brush," a fellowship meant to evoke the time of Abraham Lincoln here in the clean-shaven Camelot era of President John F. Kennedy. The "Centennial Belles" donned bonnets for their photos.

The celebrations began with a reenactment of founder Charles Landis driving a railroad spike at Landis Avenue. During the first of many parades to come, Mayor Albert Giampietro wore a top hat and beard for the occasion and rode in a horse and carriage, accompanied by a 1913 Ford and other antique cars. The centennial celebration culminated over Labor Day weekend with a beard-judging contest and communal shaving, plus the obligatory appearance by television cowgirl Sally Starr and a chicken barbecue, evoking Vineland's long-since-faded poultry festival.

Vineland's Jewish residents weren't much of a presence during the centennial programs. Still, Ruth, then fifteen years old, and her friends were eager to march in one of the parades. Bronia sewed Ruth a long, red, nineteenth-century-style calico dress trimmed in lace with a matching bon-net. Her friend wore a matching blue one. "I loved small town life," Ruth said. "That was so typical." The dress was important enough to Ruth that she saved it and, forty years later, could readily retrieve from her basement the box in which it was carefully folded. Perhaps the dress had so much sen-timental value because the preteen "chubette" Ruth had blossomed into a svelte, head-turning adolescent. Nearly every male former classmate or neighbor noted without any prompting how pretty she was—or how much of a crush they had on her. "She was a standout," one said.[1]

Rather than Bronia's fair skin and light hair, Ruth had inherited the dark complexion of Etka, who should now have been her forty-year-old aunt. It is striking how much teenage Ruth looks like Bronia's sister in the one surviv-ing photo of her as an adolescent. In the picture, Etka's straight black hair is tucked behind her ears and beneath a beret that sits at an angle on the side of her head. She is wearing fashionable boots rising above her ankles, reveal-ing just the hint of leg beneath her skirt. A white blouse is barely visible beneath her dark dress and overcoat. She is, like Ruth now, on the cusp of adulthood, one she never had a chance to live. If Bronia found it either unnerving or a source of joy to be raising the spitting image of her lost sister, she never said so, at least to Ruth. She noted the similarity to Ruth only a single time.

———•———

Ruth and her high school classmates born in 1946 were the first members of the baby boomer generation. In the United States, this term referred to the large number of children born after World War II to the families of return-ing service members. Ruth was an early part of another sort of postwar baby boom: the survivors' first post-liberation children. Her high school class included at least twenty-five children of Grine born in Europe who came to the United States as displaced persons. They accounted for roughly 6 percent of their high school class of approximately 430 students. The number might have been even higher if refugee families hadn't begun mov-ing away from south Jersey after abandoning chicken farming.

Just like their parents, the Grines' children often felt more comfortable among themselves and recalled American-born Jews treating them differ-ently. "Their parents didn't speak with an accent, weren't on chicken farms. They had money," recalled Ruth's classmate Lee Feinberg in describing

American-born Jewish classmates. "All of a sudden they had somebody to look down at." Ruth's friend and neighbor Helen Waiman recalled, "We knew who the Grine were. You just had this commonality that drew you together."[2] Waiman inverted the sense of inferiority some survivors' children experienced. "I felt we were better," she said. "We had this wonderful community and our parents had gone through hell and survived and we had each other. We had all this extended family that was not family but friends you could always go to."

But Ruth and her classmates also show how divisions among Jewish refugees began to fade in their children's generation. Unlike their parents, the children of Yekkes and Grines formed close friendships. Ruth's clique of girls consisted of six daughters of survivors and two daughters of German Jewish refugees. Marjie Low was the only one in Ruth's circle of friends born in the United States. Her parents had come to the United States in 1939 and worked as servants in the homes of upper-class New York Jews—one of whom told her father to change their name from Levy to something less Jewish—before saving enough to buy a farm in Vineland. Marjie was drawn to this "cool group" of Grine kids, who were less serious than the children of her parents' German Jewish friends.[3] Her mother didn't like her hanging out with the Grine at first, although she grew to love them.

Distinctions between the children of refugees and American-born Jews similarly faded with time. The Grines' children began dating American-born Jews, although it could be awkward at first. Barry Kanner, who graduated Vineland High School in 1967, recalled dating an American-born Jewish girl whose family owned a Vineland's menswear store.[4] "It took them awhile I think to accept a chicken farmer's son," Kanner said. Such courtships got easier as the 1960s progressed. Sam Feigenbaum, for example, remembered American-born Jews always declined date invitations from Grines' children; his younger brother Jim felt much more accepted by the time he was in high school. Some of Ruth's Grine friends also dated Italian American classmates, a choice that could infuriate survivors sensitive about intermarriage.

Outside of school, her clique couldn't afford to spend much time at Vineland teenage hangouts like Nucci's Diner or the Roll-O-Rink and Spiegel's bowling alley but joined all the other teenagers cruising up and down Landis on weekends. This sort of small-town scene out of the coming-of-age movie *American Graffiti* bored some survivors' kids. Others fled what they found a stifling, insular community. "I had to get out," said one son of survivors, who attended high school at a New York yeshiva.

Ruth, by contrast, preferred not to venture too far. One summer, Ruth and her friends got jobs at a Jewish girls' camp in the rural northeastern corner of Pennsylvania that drew heavily from upper-middle-class families in the New York metropolitan area. Ruth was hired as a camp waitress in her first summer away from home. She wound up homesick and left midsummer along with one other friend. Unlike her friends, she never got a waitressing job at an Atlantic City rooming house or worked as a mother's helper on the shore at Margate or Ventnor during other summers in high school. She liked her summer in Vineland better.

Ruth's summers in Vineland still revolved around Norma Beach. When not in the sun tanning, Ruth and the other teenagers gravitated to the jukebox inside the concession stand known as "the hut" or a table under the trees outside where they could hear the music.[5] All afternoon, rain or shine, they'd dance the shuffle, the stomp, or the horse with their shoes off on the wood floor. "It was like having a party twenty-four hours a day," Ruth said.

Ruth and her classmates, like most American teenagers at the time, learned about the latest rock-and-roll songs and dance moves by watching *American Bandstand*, the Philadelphia-based television show hosted by Dick Clark. Just as the Grine had relied on early television stars like Milton Berle to help them assimilate into American culture, their children turned to *American Bandstand* and other shows for insights into fashion, dance, and music. Lee Surwit, who grew up on Orchard Road near Ruth, watched old movies and sitcoms like *Father Knows Best* and *Leave It to Beaver* for a "clue to what an American household was like."[6] How did they eat? How did they live? "I enjoyed them but also I was looking for information," Surwit said. No source was more important than *American Bandstand*, comparable as a cultural lodestar for teens to MTV in the 1980s or Instagram today. "It was the bible," Helen Waiman said.[7]

Affording the newest fashions spotted on *American Bandstand* such as poodle skirts and Ben Casey shirts required a great deal of ingenuity given how little they had to spend on clothes. That explains why, five months after Vineland's centennial celebrations, Ruth and Bronia were at the front of the line when the Colony Shop, a dress shop on Landis Avenue, had a literal fire sale. A fire in the oil burner in the basement of an adjoining corset shop filled the Colony Shop with dense smoke.[8] They waited for hours in line to buy clothes that smelled like smoke at a discount. They had to wash the new clothes to get rid of the smell before she could wear them to school.

Grine parents like Bronia wanted their daughters to look good and have a proper American teenage experience. The impulse to make sure their children fit in mixed with the desire to show that the whole family was well adjusted. Hosting a sweet sixteen party became just as important to some mothers as signing up their daughters for the Girl Scouts or music lessons had been earlier. One of Ruth's friends found her mother crying in their kitchen because she couldn't afford to throw her any kind of sweet sixteen party. Three months after the Colony Shop fire, Bronia proudly threw Ruth a surprise sweet sixteen party at their house. On the day of her party, Ruth was shocked to see all her friends in their living room. Ruth later admitted with some shame that she was mostly embarrassed at the time to have her friends inside her living room, which remained unfurnished. The self-consciousness was misplaced. Her friends didn't remember Ruth's house being any emptier or more threadbare than anyone else's in their circle. "Everybody was poor," said Helen, who lived around the corner with her two sisters and parents in a tiny two-bedroom house with a single bathroom.[9] "You didn't think about it."

Ruth generally stuck close to home as a teenager, with one exception: every Christmas recess she traveled by herself to visit Nuchim's aunt Alexandra Frydman in Manhattan. This holiday-time ritual began when she was just twelve years old. Bronia's desire to find ways for Ruth to connect with relatives outweighed whatever worries she had about putting Ruth on a bus to New York by herself at such a young age.

Alexandra was the sister of Noah and Morris, who had sponsored Nuchim's immigration to the United States. Nuchim had distanced himself from his two uncles after the disappointing early months in New York. But Bronia and Ruth grew close to their older sister. Born in 1895 in Poland, Alexandra was a modern, independent woman, by any standard. She was trained as a dentist in Europe and came to the United States with her daughter Nadia, born in 1916. They'd settled on Riverside Drive in Manhattan at 138th Street near the Hudson River. Nadia, who was roughly the same age as Nuchim and Bronia, was a psychologist who had married and then divorced and had no children of her own. In the absence of grandchildren, Alexandra took great joy in hosting Ruth each December.

The trip was both scary and exciting, particularly at first, for Ruth, who had never traveled by herself, let alone to a city as big as New York. "The tunnel terrified me, I was alone, it was scary," Ruth said. The smells of city life—garbage on the streets and all the different cooked foods inside Alexandra's building—overpowered her senses. Still, she loved these visits, which exposed her to urban life for the first time. She was amazed at the skyscrapers that towered over anything on the horizon back home in Vineland. They went to the movies and to Radio City Music Hall to see the Rockettes perform in their annual Christmas pageant. They visited the Rockefeller Center Christmas tree and the holiday decorations in fancy shops along Fifth Avenue. More than just an opportunity to sightsee, these visits were the only time of the year when Ruth felt what it was like to have a grandmother or an aunt. "She was the only relative I felt I had," Ruth said.

———•———

Ruth's December trips to Manhattan were an escape from life at home, where the burden she felt as the only child of two survivors grew heavier as an adolescent. Ruth knew in the most abstract sense that her parents suffered during the war and more concretely about their struggles on the farm. Like many Grines' children, Ruth was determined not to add to their troubles. Ruth felt like she couldn't share her feelings and "had to make everything good and perfect." "I kept everything in," Ruth said. "I never shared anything negative." She did it because she knew they'd been "through enough" and she didn't want to bother them. "They wanted to hear about good things," Ruth said.

Bronia—and Nuchim in particular—had a rigid sense of how things should be done due to their strict European upbringing and expected Ruth to act accordingly. Neither Ruth nor Bronia could do anything that contradicted him. "Everything had to be his way," Ruth said. Looking back, Ruth came to see that Nuchim had a lot of anger, regarding both what he'd lost during the war and how life had turned out since. His uncles had disappointed him when they'd first arrived in New York. And he had watched fellow Grine who started out in the egg business at the same time like Miles Lerman and Stanley Igel thrive while he continued to struggle on the farm. Difficulty making a living was particularly upsetting for male survivors who wanted to protect and provide for their families. Hard work and accomplishment helped renew their sense of agency.[10]

Dorothy contended with a different manifestation of her parents' anger at home.[11] It would be many decades before Dorothy told Ruth of the time on the Tuckahoe Road farm before her family moved to Brooklyn when she liked to escape from her house by climbing a tree and reading. Dorothy pretended she didn't hear when her mother Dina called her to dinner. When she finally came down, Dina chased her around, hitting Dorothy with her hand covered with a dish towel to lessen the blow. Then Dina told Jack how terrible Dorothy had behaved, and Jack would dutifully hit her with a strap. Corporal punishment reflected the strict style of child-rearing they'd grown up with themselves back in Europe. "I got hit all the time," Dorothy said. And yet, Dorothy never understood how Jack, who recounted being beaten in the Majdanek concentration camp with seventy-five lashes, "hit his daughter with a belt."[12]

In the face of Nuchim's anger and her parents' rigid expectations, Ruth says she grew up "suppressed and repressed." She never spoke up or back to her parents, other than to insist on losing weight and keeping it off when she reached adolescence. She never rebelled by dating one of her many non-Jewish classmates like some of her friends did. She tried her best to be the perfect daughter. What else could you do when your mother tells you, as Bronia once did, that you gave her a reason for living?

The burden Ruth felt as the daughter of survivors was one shared by other Grine children on south Jersey farms and elsewhere. In the 1970s, doctors who had treated survivors' adolescent children began publishing studies chronicling the psychological toll of their upbringing. Researchers found they suffered from greater behavioral problems and had more difficulty coping than the general population. Researchers theorized that survivors suffering from the lingering effects of war transmitted the trauma they experienced to their children. Subsequent research questioned those findings or instead emphasized the achievements of survivors' offspring who came to self-identify as the "second generation."[13]

Film professor Sharyn Blumenthal highlighted the second generation's emotional wounds in an early 2000s documentary called *The Phoenix Effect* about the children and grandchildren of Vineland's poultry farmers.[14] The documentary intersperses individual and group interviews with images of concentration camp victims' corpses, 1950s Vineland farm life, and abandoned chicken coops. Many of the survivors' children, now parents and grandparents themselves, described in the film how they felt pressure to achieve and tried never to be sad or angry in front of their parents.

At the most extreme, survivors in Vineland—still deeply traumatized by what they'd experienced—wound up terrorizing their children. Blumenthal focuses on Edith Hirshtal, a child piano prodigy who grew up in the Vineland area where her parents operated a small grocery store. Hirshtal describes how her father, an Auschwitz survivor who lost his first wife and three daughters during the war, woke up screaming every night. He insisted that Edith sleep on a cot on her mother's side of her parents' bed until she was eleven or twelve years old. Hirshtal wondered if that was connected to the idea that you had to spend every minute with your family out of fear someone could snatch them away at any time. Hirshtal was terrified that she'd never manage to live like a normal person because she couldn't sleep without her parents. Hirshtal went on to become a classical pianist who performed at New York's Lincoln Center.

Other survivors' children recounted in the documentary how their parents' fears became their own. One remembered hearing a helicopter fly overhead one night, convinced the SS was coming for her parents. Another recalled seeing men with rifles and German Shepherds on her family's property as she walked home from school one day. She became terrified they were going to take her to a concentration camp. Turns out they were hunters, just passing through.

The survivors' trauma and its impact on their children are undeniable. Grine who settled on farms were no different in that respect, and their children carried the same burdens as the offspring of displaced persons raised in cities. Yet that wasn't the whole story, which is something you don't get a sense of watching The Phoenix Effect, and that's why not all the survivors' children who participated in the documentary liked the finished product. "I would have a different vision," said Harry Furman, the son of survivors who grew up on a Vineland poultry farm.[15] As a Vineland High School social studies teacher, Furman later taught one of the first classes on the Holocaust in the 1970s.[16] He rejected the "Mark of Cain" prism, as he put it, through which The Phoenix Effect explored the survivor experience. "I would have preferred a movie about the whole anomaly of very sophisticated urban Jews coming to this very rural area and the process of assimilation," said Furman, who later became an attorney and served on a state commission on Holocaust education. "These people were so scarred and yet they gradually were able to reemerge and become very successful in many ways, not just economically, building families, spawning an entire generation of children who did very well and have gone on to very constructive lives. That to me is a very positive story."

Saul Golubcow noted the subtler reality that survivors like his parents were people of "extraordinary contradictions. . . . They were people who were so shattered and sad, and yet they could feel exhilaration, too. They were people who thought about all they lost and invested so much in their kids, in their future. They saw themselves as heroic, and they saw themselves as cowardly."[17] To speak only about their losses is to tell only part of the story.

25 ▸ VALEDICTORY

THE JEWISH POULTRY FARMERS ASSOCIATION (JPFA) was a shell of its former self by the time current and former members gathered for a tenth anniversary banquet on June 9, 1962. Membership and its robust schedule of social and cultural activities had been shrinking for years. But the few Grine still farming and many more who had left in favor of steadier income reunited here at Sons of Jacob for what must have felt like a valedictory for a moment in time.

Musia Deiches, the former child dance prodigy who had organized so many JPFA events, stood surrounded by beautiful floral arrangements on the podium handing an engraved gavel to the outgoing JPFA president.[1] Toastmaster Hirsch Nadel praised former JPFA presidents, including Miles Lerman and Irving Schock, the *shtibl* cantor who testified before Congress in 1959. Stanley Igel, who had since picked up the mantle from Lerman and Schock during trips to Washington, was recognized during introductions. The JPFA presented a special award and commemorative clock to the defunct *Jewish Farmer's* former editor.

Times Journal editor Ben Leuchter praised the JPFA as "a considerable force for good in the Greater Vineland community," while attorney Harry

Levin, who had done so much to help the survivors, credited its members with giving "a boost or a shot in the arm to all the other Jews living in our vicinity."[2] In remarks in Yiddish included in the written program, Miles Lerman credited the Grine with bringing new life to Vineland's existing Jewish community that had become "Americanized" and had only a weak interest and limited understanding of the Jewish people around the world. Under the influence of the newcomers, "the pulse of the local Jewish life has begun to beat with a stronger tempo."

The Miles Lerman Oil Co. purchased an ad in the program along with Vineland Poultry Laboratories, which continued to thrive. In just a few weeks, the vaccine maker was scheduled to finish construction on a plant in Israel on the main highway between Haifa and Tel Aviv.[3] The Goldhafts' business was a rare bright spot in the local poultry industry. Few, if any, of the many hatcheries and feed mills that advertised in the JPFA anniversary program would survive much longer.

Theodore Norman, the general manager of the Jewish Agricultural Society (JAS), noted the poultry industry's troubles in his contribution to the JPFA anniversary program. "The last ten years have been by and large years of violent change and severe stress for poultry farmers," Norman wrote before concluding with the JAS's typical optimism.[4] "I do believe that the industry is gradually approaching a state of stability, so that those who have been able to carry on thus far will still continue to operate successfully in the future." Similarly, Norman didn't dwell much on structural changes that had made small-scale poultry farming unsustainable in his monthly reports to the JAS board of directors. Instead, Norman focused on seasonal price changes and wrote "we can't complain about the year so far" in a February 1962 report.[5] Little could justify the rosy predictions. The JAS's own financial statements showed how its accounts suffered along with the farmers. The society faced steady 55 to 60 percent delinquency rates in the early 1960s, and the organization's budget was down nearly a third between 1958 and 1962.

Vineland's poultry leaders kept trudging down to Washington to plead for federal aid, with little success. Igel made trips to the capital in both May and June 1962 as vice president of the state poultry association. Egg prices that spring were down 20 percent compared to a decade earlier and, except for the depression years of 1959–1960, were the lowest since the early 1940s.[6] In a meeting with U.S. Department of Agriculture (USDA) officials, Igel all but begged for increased government purchases of eggs. He again reminded them that poultrymen suffered from having to buy feed that's subject to price supports while selling their eggs on the free market. USDA officials were unmoved, suggesting that small farm operators were on the way out.

Three weeks later, Igel was right back at it, this time pleading with lawmakers for help. He came back in July to ask the USDA to buy more dried eggs and in October to meet with the president of the American Farm Bureau. He left that meeting and called it "one of the most fruitful" in which he'd participated in the past five years, although, once again, not much came of it.[7] Igel returned to Washington at least a half dozen more times in the next two years, with no greater success. Eventually, he would narrow his request, asking USDA officials to provide just enough support that egg farmers could exit the business gracefully, rather than being forced into bankruptcy.

———•———

By the end of 1962, Bronia's neighbor and close friend Sally had given up on farming. She and Joey were nearly bankrupt when they moved north with their two children to New York, settling in the Forest Hills neighborhood of Queens.[8] The Hymans traded a big farmhouse for a three-and-a-half-room apartment, but Joey's factory job could support them all, and, as Sally said, "we didn't have to worry about the chickens."[9]

Sally's departure—on top of Dina's two years earlier—was surely a blow to Bronia, who by the end of 1962 was working again full-time at the Crown Clothing Company factory. At forty-four, she was more than a decade older than when she'd gone to work there the first time. She still wasn't in the best of health. All their money troubles only compounded her anxiety. Dr. Anthony Mascara noted Bronia "is still under my care for a very severe anxiety neurosis" in a January 1963 submission to the German reparation authorities. Offering a convenient diagnosis designed to help ensure the reparation payments continued, Dr. Mascara wrote that "she cannot work nor even perform her ordinary household duties," although Bronia continued to work at the garment factory throughout 1963.

Bronia and Nuchim stayed on the farm, in part because they didn't want to disrupt Ruth's high school experience. After having their early twenties upended, they wanted to provide a more stable childhood to Ruth. She'd made clear to her parents she had no interest in moving away even as so many of their friends did. "I carried on so, I didn't want to move," said Ruth, who was a high school junior in early 1963. "I had fits."

The Lermans were doing well enough in the oil business that they could finally give up poultry farming entirely in 1962.[10] In selecting the oil business after leaving poultry, Miles figured that "people always needed to stay warm and drive," as his daughter Jeanette later said.[11] The gamble had begun to pay off handsomely. In February 1963, the American Oil Company named Miles's firm its exclusive distributor in Vineland and a large swath of southern New Jersey.[12]

Nothing better symbolized the diverging trajectories of survivors than Nuchim and Miles, two forest partisans who walked off the same ship and started life out in America on the exact same day. Miles wasn't even the biggest success story among passengers on their voyage on the *Marine Perch*. That distinction belongs to Leon Joselzon, a concentration camp survivor from Warsaw who disembarked with six dollars in his pocket. He built a sewing machine empire each year doing seven million dollars in business— more than seventy million in 2021 dollars—by the time he became a citizen in 1952 at the age of thirty-nine. Jolson, as he became known in America, became a symbol of survivor rags-to-riches success, often profiled in newspapers and magazines. Asked the secret of his success, Jolson had a simple answer, "Forget the past, forget what you have lost and start afresh."[13]

What explains why some survivors struggled while others did so well? It's a question I posed to many of the farmers' children. Harry Rosenblum, whose father was falsely accused in the farmhand murder case before leaving Vineland to become a thriving real estate developer, credited some of their success to luck and being at the right place at the right time—and mostly to drive. He said his parents and many of their friends who did well "could think on their feet and despite their education being taken away from them, had a certain innate intelligence of being able to pick up a business and run with it." There were others, he noted, "who were not quite as adept as them."[14]

Lee Feinberg, who grew up on Tuckahoe Road near the farmhouse that Ruth and Dorothy once shared and watched his survivor parents struggle, thought it came down to a matter of mindset. Some of the survivors "had their mindset stuck; they were still 20 years old and never overcame it," Feinberg said.[15] "Another group said, 'I'm going to show them, I'm not only going to survive but will succeed and thrive.' They were motivated as much by the war as other people were destroyed by the war." Feinberg, who went on to a successful career on Wall Street, said his parents—and his mother in particular—"still talked about the old country forever." "She was stuck," Feinberg said. "She couldn't leave it. She couldn't emotionally move on whereas others got into all kinds of opportunities and took advantage of it."

David Lerman said his parents never stopped thinking about the war, but it wasn't the "organizing point for the balance of their lives."[16] They took the attitude that they've "experienced the worst life can dish out, and it can only get better," David said. As Chris Lerman put it in a 1998 oral history interview, "Don't forget the past, but don't live in the past. Whether it was good or whether it was bad, it just doesn't make any difference, the past is the past and for as long as you live, you have to . . . deal with the present and look to the future."[17]

Resilience has become a popular explanation for why some people manage to overcome past trauma. It is a quality Chris Lerman alluded to in a 1979 interview.[18] "My experience in life was such that I can easily adapt myself to any situation," Chris said. In her youth, she elaborated, "I had to do things, forced labor, under such terrible conditions, that anything I did later in life to build a future for myself, as long as it was solid, honest, good work" before trailing off. The reporter noted that "the end of the sentence eludes her, but her meaning is clear." That same inner strength was on display that same year when she returned to Auschwitz for the first time since the war, recalled her daughter Jeanette. "I was sort of expecting my mother to fall apart" with emotion, Jeanette said.[19] Instead, she returned "with a sense of triumph" because "she survived; the Nazi regime did not."

Sociologist William Helmreich came up with a list of ten factors that explain why some survivors "were able to lead positive and useful lives": flexibility, assertiveness, tenacity, optimism, intelligence, an ability to distance themselves from what had happened, group consciousness, assimilating the knowledge that they survived, finding meaning in one's life, and courage.[20] Many of those who "fared poorly" shared a similar trait as well: "excessive caution, a reluctance to take chances."[21]

Vineland's most successful Grines, epitomized by Lerman, knew when to get out of farming and, whether by dint of good fortune, ambition, or some combination of both, seized new opportunities. But as Helmreich also notes, making it in America also required good health and good luck.[22] The mere act of survival meant every one of these poultry farmers had been fortunate, at least compared to all those who perished during the war. But enduring unimaginable suffering proved no protection against future misfortune. Time and time again, Vineland's survivors fell victim to accidents, illnesses, and untimely deaths.

Sometimes, early deaths resulted directly from wartime injuries. In January 1957, for example, one thirty-four-year-old survivor died from a kidney ailment attributed to her jumping from a moving train headed for Auschwitz.[23] She left behind a poultryman husband and a ten-year-old daughter. Some deaths were sudden and inexplicable, like former JPFA president Chaim Gruenfeld, felled by a heart attack in April 1957 at the age of forty-five. More than three hundred attended his funeral, and Miles Lerman delivered the eulogy at Alliance Cemetery, the one place where survivors could achieve full equality with earlier generations of Russian and German Jews buried there.[24] Ben Leuchter described Gruenfeld's death as "a bitter pill for hundreds of farm families who already have experienced far more than their rightful share of tragedy. And the non-poultry community, though it might not have known it, lost a good and a valuable American."[25] Other declines were drawn out, as was the case with Isak Michnik, the poultryman who had undergone countless surgeries and faced financial ruin after Hurricane Hazel until the entire community rallied behind him. Michnik died midway through Passover in 1959 at the age of fifty-two, almost exactly two years to the day after resuming operations on his farm.[26]

As events proved during the war and then many times in Vineland, so much in life is random, and who succeeded—or even just survived in America—could be just as inexplicable as during the war. Bronia and Nuchim's neighbor, David Liebel, had the good sense to get out of chicken raising early, branching out to become a middleman with poultry processors, including the Campbell Soup Company. David and his wife, fellow survivor Sylvia, had two daughters, and "life was good," as Sylvia later put it.[27]

Then on a Sunday in February 1963, the same month Lerman landed his exclusive oil distributorship, David got in the car with his nine-year-old daughter Shirley and picked up another nine-year-old girl who also lived on Orchard Road. Snow and freezing rain fell overnight, and there was still a little snow on the ground. They reached an intersection in downtown Vineland just south of Landis Avenue at the same time as one of Ruth's Vineland High School classmates. The teenage driver thought Liebel's car was farther away than it was. She kept driving through the intersection and collided with his car.[28]

Shirley, still in the backseat, and their neighbor, who got thrown from the car, were admitted to Newcomb Hospital in shock, but miraculously suffered only scrapes. Liebel, forty-nine, was ejected clear from the car and found six feet from the intersection. He was taken to the hospital with a concussion and internal injuries and died two hours later. The teenage driver, a merit roll student and girls' basketball team captain, was charged with careless driving and failing to stop for a stop sign and had her license suspended for a year. Friends of Liebel's wife Sylvia slept over at the family's Orchard Road farmhouse for weeks to keep the grieving widow company.[29] Sylvia, who had survived part of the war passing as a Pole in Germany as a farmhand, at first pledged to keep running the business.[30] But she couldn't bear the thought of staying alone on the farm anymore. She soon sold the house and moved into an apartment in Vineland before leaving a few years later for the Philadelphia suburbs with her two teenage daughters.

Moving closer to Philadelphia meant a jarring transition from the bubble of survivors in which they'd lived, recalled her daughter Harriet, who was sixteen when they left Vineland. Most of Harriet's Vineland friends were the children of Grine. She had good memories of life before her father died. "I felt secure," Harriet said. "I felt I had everything I needed." In Philadelphia, she wasn't even sure if her new friends knew what had happened to Jews during the war. Harriet, who went on to earn a doctorate in school psychology, later wondered if her mother had benefited from spending all those years among fellow survivors or whether being exposed to a wider world might have been better preparation for life after Vineland. "I don't know," Harriet said. But at the time her mother suffered the loss of her husband, "it was a very good place to be."

———•———

The end finally came for the Rubinoff feed company in April 1964. The two-year experiment in employee ownership had failed, and the company filed for Chapter 11 bankruptcy protection. An attorney appointed as receiver unsuccessfully tried to convince the firm's former owners to reorganize the company on a sound basis, which "would assure poultrymen of this area of continued quality feed and service with which the Rubinoff name has been associated for 58 years."[31]

Within a week, any hopes for another rescue had been dashed. The company's receivers reported that they "were unable to prepare a feasible reorganization plan" since Rubinoff's assets were "only a fraction" of its $1.4 million in liabilities.[32] The mill, which still had about sixty-five employees and five hundred customers, ceased operations altogether on April 13.

Exactly a month later, Ruth donned a white floor-length dress and waited for her date to escort her to their senior prom at the local National Guard armory. By the time she and 431 members of the class of 1964 graduated on June 16 at Gittone Stadium, Nuchim and Bronia were poised to leave Vineland and move that summer to Brooklyn, the same New York City borough where their former housemates, Dina and Jack Liverant, lived.

They sold the farm to a Jewish family, which operated a discount clothing store on Landis Avenue and had a son who had just graduated Vineland High School along with Ruth. There would be no more poultry farming done on the property, although a laborer who worked on another survivor's farm got arrested a couple years later for allegedly breaking into the house through a cellar window and stealing a bottle of cognac and seven dollars from a money jar.[33]

26 ▸ AFTER FARMING

IN 1966, THE Jewish Agricultural Society (JAS) published an elegy for the American Jewish farm movement that proved to be the organization's own eulogy. The two authors of the one-hundred-page monograph, who had served a combined seventy-nine years with the JAS, laid out all the changes in the poultry industry that had made it so difficult for small farmers to survive. "Large numbers of Jewish farmers, especially immigrants who settled on chicken farms since the end of the war—with little capital of their own and big mortgages on the farm and livestock—were caught in the squeeze and could not carry on."[1] Half of the Jewish farmers in New Jersey had left their farms or dismantled their coops and sold their farm equipment in the past decade. The "largest number of defections" occurred in south Jersey, where the ranks of Jewish farmers had fallen from eleven hundred to about three hundred and the JAS "suffered large financial losses."

There is a funereal tone to the monograph. Gone are the usual hopeful words about better days ahead. It focuses instead on the organization's legacy. "While it deeply regrets the decline in the number of Jewish farmers," they conclude, "the Society is proud of the part it played in helping thousands of immigrants become independent citizens of the United States and it is for this achievement that it hopes to be remembered."[2] Ultimately, placing refugees on individual farms—at a time when family poultry farming was collapsing—proved no more sustainable than maintaining colonies in the nineteenth century. JAS officials, many of whom had spent their entire professional lives with the organization, couldn't see—or at least chose not to acknowledge publicly—the poor prospects for the farmers they had helped settle.

Survivor poultry settlements—like the earlier colonies before them—proved to be a waystation rather than a permanent destination. What historian Ellen Eisenberg wrote of south Jersey colonists also held true for the survivors: "They hoped to establish themselves economically, to escape the city, and to live in a Jewish community with a Jewish cultural life while easing their way into American society."[3] By that measure, even if poultry farming wasn't particularly lucrative, the Grine still achieved their other adjustment goals. Besides, survivors wouldn't necessarily have been much better off in cities. "If you came over with no family whatsoever, no connections to anybody, then going to a colony like this could be a more welcoming way to land in a new country and a new society," said Jonathan Dekel-Chen, a historian at the Hebrew University of Jerusalem who studies Jewish agricultural settlements.[4] "There was already in place functioning synagogues, Jewish welfare organizations, mutual credit associations, cultural activities and a sense of community that someone alone and anonymous in the Bronx wouldn't necessarily feel."

————•————

Nuchim and Bronia certainly didn't have an easy time after they moved to New York in July 1964 at a particularly chaotic moment for the city and urban America as a whole. New York was "a city destroying itself," as *Fortune Magazine* put it in a 1964 cover story that portrayed it as a declining, dirty, poorly run city beset by pollution, crime, and racial strife.[5] Anger about northern racial discrimination and police brutality exploded into rioting that began in New York in July 1964 and spread elsewhere in the first of what became known as the long hot summers of the 1960s. Riots broke out first in Harlem after an off-duty police lieutenant shot a fifteen-year-old Black youth.[6] The unrest soon spread to the Bedford-Stuyvesant section of Brooklyn, New York's largest and poorest Black neighborhood, about four miles from where Bronia and Nuchim moved that same month in East Flatbush.

Bronia and Nuchim were unaware of the upheaval in New York when they arrived there. "I don't think they knew. I don't think they cared," Ruth said. They had to leave the farm, and given his innate optimism, Nuchim probably wanted to see the best in the situation. Plus, as Ruth pointed out, "Where was he going to buy a cheap business? Not on Broadway in Manhattan." Bed-Stuy was where Nuchim soon opened the first in a series of unsuccessful small businesses, using the meager proceeds from the sale of their farm. He first tried opening a convenience store and later had more success with a children's clothing store, until he lost that business, too, after a fire in the building. "He had lousy luck, no luck," Ruth said.

Some survivors who opened similar inner-city businesses after leaving Vineland-area poultry farms fared even worse. One who traded a farm in Norma for a liquor store in Los Angeles's Compton neighborhood was killed in 1967 during a holdup, the first in the eight years he operated the store.[7] The next year, another former farmer who left Vineland in 1959 and opened a grocery store in a northeast Washington, D.C., neighborhood was killed after being shot in the chest during a September 1968 holdup.[8] He had reopened the store three weeks earlier after it had been looted and burned during the rioting that followed Martin Luther King Jr.'s assassination.

Jack Liverant enjoyed much more success as a small businessman in New York than did Nuchim, his former poultry farm partner. Jack had a false start in the grocery store business with partners he'd met in night school after first arriving on the *Marine Perch*. One grocery store burned down, and the second one ran into trouble. That's when Jack connected with someone he knew back in Lublin who had gone into the muffler business on Long Island.[9] Jack apprenticed there and went to franchise training in Chicago before opening his own Midas muffler shop in the Bronx, a business that, combined with some real estate in Brooklyn, provided a steady income for decades to come.

After growing up on a farm, Ruth felt claustrophobic at first in their new home, a small second-floor apartment in a two-family brick rowhouse. She spent most nights sitting out on the tiny balcony that offered some fresh air and a view of the sky. Two months later, she moved to Fairleigh Dickinson's campus in New Jersey. Moving even this short distance couldn't have been easy for Ruth, who found a summer away at a sleepaway camp waitressing to be too long away from home. Ruth's departure for college proved even more difficult for Bronia. As Helen Epstein writes in *Children of the Holocaust*,

"Family separation was more than separation for survivor households. It carried implications of impotence and loss, sometimes death."[10] Bronia had to simultaneously adjust to her daughter moving away and their alien surroundings in Brooklyn. Even being in the same city again as Dina and Sally wasn't enough to fill the void. Bronia sank into a deep depression, which left Nuchim feeling helpless.

The sense that she was so far from Bronia while her mother was in distress only compounded Ruth's homesickness and guilt about living away from home. She went back to Brooklyn to see her parents most weekends, and her Vineland friends at Fairleigh Dickinson could tell she wasn't happy away at college. She transferred by the end of the first semester to Long Island University's Brooklyn campus, living at home and taking the subway to class. She'd come to enjoy urban life, a chance to broaden her horizons and meet different kinds of people. She made the Dean's List. Bronia, too, began commuting to work at a midtown Manhattan women's clothing store as she started to feel better after receiving psychiatric care for the first time.

In the summer after her freshman year, Ruth got set up on a blind date with a Yeshiva University student eight months her junior named Harvey Stern. Three years later, Ruth and my father Harvey, who was a medical school student at the time, got married on Christmas Day 1968.

———•———

As Ruth moved back to Brooklyn after her first semester of college, Jeanette Lerman traveled from Vineland to Los Angeles in December 1964. She delivered the keynote speech at the western regional convention of Young Judaea, a national Zionist youth group. Jeanette then flew to Texas, to give the keynote speech to the group's chapters in Texas, Oklahoma, and Louisiana.

A Times Journal story about the trip described Jeanette, who was about to turn seventeen, as "one of those rare combinations of beauty, brains, and personality."[11] She was a "consistent honor student" who edited her high school's monthly newspaper and was a member of both the debating team and French Club. She also spoke Hebrew fluently and had made use of that knowledge the previous summer when she flew to Israel for a seven-week Young Judaea tour of Israel that included ten days working on a kibbutz. "In a world whose distances seem to shrink every year, Jeanette Lerman seems to be right at home," the Times Journal said.

Jeanette enrolled in Brandeis University while her younger brother David went on to Harvard College after graduating high school in 1968. Just like the Goldhafts and Rubinoffs before them, the Lermans had gone from immigrant to Ivy League in a single generation. David later joined his father in real estate development after first practicing law in Houston.

——•——

In June 1965, just short of one year after Bronia and Nuchim moved away, Philadelphia television station WFIL aired a boosterish "Salute to Vineland."[12] The sonorous announcer describes a "growing" city that's full of "the spirit of youth" and "is a good place to live at any age." Vineland's mayor predicted the city would be bigger than Atlantic City and Trenton within twenty years. And as the film ends, the announcer intones that Vineland is "growing fast and has plenty of room to grow."

In fact, the local economy's long decline was well under way. All the pillars of what was once "a balanced economy, one based upon thriving glass and clothing factories, on the one hand, and upon eggs, poultry and other farm products" soon crumbled.[13] First to falter after the poultry farms were the garment factories, followed by many of the region's food processors. Last to go were the glass manufacturers. Kimble Glass was sold repeatedly in the decades to come, its Vineland workforce shrinking to a fraction of its former size.

Vineland's once-bustling shopping district anchored by Landis Avenue declined right along with the local economy. It was undone, like so many small-town main streets, by a mall, which opened just a couple miles south in 1973. Many shops along Landis Avenue either moved to the Cumberland Mall or closed down entirely; those that remained operated between boarded up and abandoned buildings.[14]

Jewish farmers still produced 75 percent of New Jersey's eggs in the mid-1960s, but the contraction accelerated as the decade progressed.[15] The JAS ceased operations in 1972.[16] Its remaining functions were absorbed by the Baron de Hirsch Fund. There was still a number listed for the JAS in the 1973 Vineland phone directory, which rang in Harry Levin's law office, although no one had called him on JAS business for years.[17] Only half a dozen or so Jewish farmers remained by 1973.[18] "Most of the forest of chicken coops that once dominated the Vineland area has been razed," the *New York Times* observed in 1975. "Scores that remain have been abandoned."[19]

Few of the survivors lamented that poultry farming declined before their children could take over. Even if poultry farming had proven a sustainable business, it's unlikely many farms would have continued operating with a second generation in charge. The Grine shared middle-class American-born Jews' aspirations that their children would go to college and become professionals or entrepreneurs. Choosing farming didn't seem to diminish the prospects of their children, many of whom went on to become successful doctors, lawyers, executives, business owners, and professors.

Even Vineland's most successful poultry business-owning family got out, too. The Goldhafts sold Vineland Poultry Laboratories in 1970, and the company changed hands two more times before the plant closed in 2007.[20] In the mid-1970s, Vineland High School's sports teams changed their name from the "Poultry Clan" to the "Fighting Clan."

—————•—————

A harbinger of the Vineland Jewish community's future came in October 1966 when vandals set fire to a chapel at Beth Israel synagogue. They destroyed a Torah scroll, prayer shawls, and one hundred fifty prayer books and scribbled anti-Semitic slogans on a classroom blackboard.[21] The Jewish day school also became a target of vandalism, at least a dozen times in the 1970s.[22] The Orchard Road *shtibl* was similarly ransacked in 1980 by vandals, who threw the Torah scroll and prayer shawls on the floor and scratched the words "I will return to kill you" on the podium.[23] The shtibl staggered along for years until religious services ceased in 1999. Its ark, *bimah*, and seats were ultimately donated to a Jewish day school in Yardley, Pennsylvania.[24]

The Jewish community's exodus continued unabated in the seventies. As many as one in nine of the twenty-five hundred who remained planned to move away, a demographic study conducted in 1976 found.[25] It was a pattern repeating itself throughout the country as "once thriving Jewish communities in small and medium-sized cities have become merely the skeletal remnants of their former self," sociologist Eugen Schoenfeld observed in 1977.[26] The survivor influx had only temporarily delayed a similar decline in Vineland.[27]

The outflow in Vineland made it ever harder to maintain Jewish institutions, like the Jewish day school, which closed by the early 1980s, or even a nursery school, which stayed open longer with an increasingly non-Jewish student body. The kosher delis were long since gone, and the last of three kosher butchers closed in the 1980s.[28] By 1988, only thirty-five of Vineland High School's sixteen hundred students were Jewish, although a course on the Holocaust and genocide was the school's most popular elective.[29] As the Jewish community shrank, distinctions between American-born Jews and refugees faded further. The old divides mattered even less to their children, who joked about their "intermarriages" into American-born Jewish families.

Harry Levin did his best to preserve the area's Jewish past, writing a history of the original Alliance colony his family helped found. He collected synagogue charters and old farm tools and served as a source for researchers and scholars studying the region's Jewish agricultural past. He admitted that he wished it wasn't just history. "I'd like to see more Jews living here," Levin said.[30] His days as the "marrying judge" ended in 1982 when he wasn't reappointed municipal court judge in Pittsgrove, but he kept on practicing law until a few months before his death in 1988 at age eighty-three.[31]

———•———

Ruth had little interest in returning to Vineland, even to visit, after settling on Long Island and going to work as a social worker. Her friends had all moved away, and so much of what she remembered fondly was gone. Even Norma Beach had disappeared. The hut where they'd danced to the jukebox and played pinball burned down in 1971, by which point contamination had made the Maurice River unsafe for swimming.[32] The scenic swimming hole became a "trash-littered, disgusting mess" with beer bottles, tires, and plastic bags all along the banks and sunk on the river bottom.[33] What ultimately drew Ruth back at least one time was a "Norma Beach Reunion" in June 1986 organized by children of survivors who still lived in the area.[34]

By then, Nuchim was dying of colon cancer. The man who faced down Nazis as a partisan was afraid to go to the doctor and sought treatment too late, the sad ending to his post-Vineland life. He and Bronia tried their luck in Binghamton in the early 1970s, before returning to Brooklyn, where they wound up with a small stake in a nursing home. The plaque he received in 1980 "in appreciation of dedicated service to Queens-Nassau Nursing Home" hangs on my wall beneath my diplomas, a reminder that the full measure of a man isn't where he went to school or what job he holds. Nuchim's last job was as a security guard in a Brooklyn supermarket. His biggest regret was being unable to provide more for Bronia materially. His passing in

October 1986 on my eleventh birthday went unnoticed in the press, except for the replica "Person of the Year" *Time* magazine cover I created that fall for a sixth-grade social studies project. "During the war, he was always brave and never afraid to die for his wife," I wrote.

————•————

Miles and Chris had stayed in Vineland, loyal to a community that had given them so much, even as it changed around them. "I will be a Vine-lander as long as I live," he said. "I am so proud."[35] They split their time between Vineland and Palm Beach, Florida.

His prominence in Jewish causes grew, including trips to Israel for gatherings of important Israel bond fundraisers and donors. Days after the Yom Kippur war ended in 1973, he flew to Israel on a special El Al flight to attend an emergency economic conference with Prime Minister Golda Meir.[36] Pictures of Miles with Meir, David Ben-Gurion, and Moshe Dayan, a top Israeli military commander who later served as both defense and foreign minister, hung on the wall of his Vineland office.[37] In 1979, he was among guests invited to witness the signing of a peace treaty between Israel and Egypt at the White House.[38] And in 1982, when former—and future—Israeli prime minister Yitzhak Rabin visited Vineland for a community Israel Bond Drive rally, the Lermans hosted him at their home for a reception before he spoke at Beth Israel synagogue.[39]

By the time Miles sold his company—then known as Miles Petroleum—in 1984, it owned or supplied sixty-seven gas stations throughout south Jersey and pumped twenty-five million gallons of gas per year.[40] His friend Ben Leuchter had already sold the *Times Journal*, which was ultimately purchased by the Gannett newspaper chain in 1985.[41] Leaving the newspaper was hard for Ben. He became a president of a group of weekly newspapers in Massachusetts. His daughters joked he hoped that one of them might work at the paper and meet a nice Jewish husband. The strategy worked when his daughter Lisa met her husband on a blind date.[42]

Like Miles's, Ben's prominence in Jewish groups only increased over time. In 1988, he became president of the Hebrew Immigrant Aid Society, the organization that had helped many survivors settle in the United States.[43] He later was diagnosed with ALS or Lou Gehrig's disease, a progressive nervous system condition that causes loss of muscle control. When he died in 2001, a family friend read a note he'd written earlier when he thought the end was near. "I'm not afraid of death," Leuchter wrote. "I've had the most wonderful life."[44]

Selling Miles Petroleum left Miles more time to focus on what proved to be the great mission of his life: building the U.S. Holocaust Memorial Museum in Washington. His interest in commemorating the Holocaust first took root in Vineland. In 1969, he spoke in Yiddish at the dedication of a granite monument shaped like "a tree trunk whose limbs had been sawed off but was still growing" at Alliance cemetery.[45] Miles and Chris later commissioned a metal memorial sculpture that debuted in the lobby of Beth Israel synagogue at the April 1976 annual memorial for the "six million Jewish victims of the Nazis." He started speaking out more widely, bringing New Jersey state lawmakers to tears in an April 1979 address during a Holocaust memorial ceremony in the assembly chamber.[46]

President Jimmy Carter appointed Miles to a twenty-four-member federal commission tasked with coming up with recommendations for commemorating the Nazis' victims.[47] Miles and Chris flew to Europe in 1979 to visit existing memorials at the site of concentration camps, including Auschwitz, which Chris visited for the first time since she was a prisoner there. The visits to Auschwitz, where her father was killed, and Treblinka, where her mother died, were particularly wrenching for Chris. "But my daughter is the proof that the Nazis didn't succeed in what they set out to do," Chris said during the trip.[48] "We go on."

Miles shuttled back and forth to Eastern Europe in the eighties, negotiating a series of agreements with communist regimes on the verge of collapse and their newly liberated successors eager to build goodwill with the United States.[49] The agreements made it possible to bring thousands of artifacts and documents to the future museum. He asked for human hair, suitcases, concentration camp uniforms, children's shoes, and torture equipment so that the horrors became real to museum visitors. "To say, 'I want human hair, I want children's shoes'—it tears your guts out," Miles said in 1989. "It drains your energy, your strength, your emotions. But the reward that will come out of this is so substantial that it's worth the physical and mental abuse."[50] He also led the museum's capital fundraising campaign, which ultimately raised $190 million.[51] He put the networking skills honed in Vineland as a poultry farmer to use. On one flight to Utah, he struck up a conversation with his Mormon seatmate and landed a million-dollar pledge to the museum before the plane was back on the ground.[52]

When the Holocaust Museum opened in April 1993, Miles, then seventy-three years old, joined President Bill Clinton and twelve foreign heads of state before the crowd of ten thousand. "It's a dream come true," Miles said. "It is a miracle."[53] President Clinton appointed him chairman of the museum's governing council, a position that he held until 2000.[54] Four years later, Lerman traveled once again to Poland for the dedication of a memorial he helped spearhead at the site of the former Belzec camp. The group of family accompanying him spanned four generations, ranging from his ninety-four-year-old brother Jona to his seventeen-year-old great-grandnephew.[55]

Shortly after the dedication, I first wrote Miles's daughter Jeanette. She connected me with her father, who spoke with me briefly on the phone. "I was very fond of your grandfather," he told me. Miles and Chris were in Florida at the time, and he said they'd be back in the spring and that he came to Washington quite often for Holocaust Museum business. He gave me the name of someone at the museum to contact about scheduling a time to talk, but we didn't end up meeting.

Miles never stopped speaking publicly about the Holocaust. "There are those who counsel us to forget the past and move on with the future," Miles, then eighty-five, said in a lecture at a Palm Beach synagogue in 2005.[56] "This advice may be well meaning, but it is fallacious and we reject it vehemently." In an interview the same week with a local newspaper reporter, Miles "with a small mordant smile," introduced his wife as "an Auschwitz alumnus." "If you don't have a sense of humor, you lose your mind," Miles said. He died in January 2008, two days after his eighty-eighth birthday, and was buried in Alliance Cemetery near Vineland.[57] Miles merited obituaries in the *New York Times* and other newspapers across the United States. The *Daily Journal*, as Vineland's newspaper was now known, published pictures of Miles with Pope John Paul II, with President Jimmy Carter at the Holocaust Museum, and, as a younger man, as a guard outside the Berlin displaced persons camp where he lived after the war.

His time as a poultry farmer was mentioned in passing, at best. And yet chickens were still on his mind at the end. In a Holocaust Museum tribute, David Lerman described how as his father grew weaker in his final two weeks and had difficulty staying awake, Miles said things that provided insight about what he wanted nailed down before his death, concerns that spanned his lifetime.[58] In his semi-slumber, he worried about the chickens. "We assured him that the chickens were well taken care of," David said.

Chris lived another eight years, dying peacefully at ninety in her home in Philadelphia, where she'd finally moved from Vineland. She was surrounded by David, a successful Philadelphia real estate developer, and her daughter Jeanette, a prominent Philadelphia philanthropist, as well as their spouses and children. At the time of her death, Chris had five grandchildren and seven great grandchildren. Her death attracted widespread media attention, including in the *Philadelphia Inquirer*, which noted Miles Lerman considered Chris his "secret weapon."[59] "She was equally strong, but in different ways," Sara Bloomfield, the director of the U.S. Holocaust Memorial Museum, said. The same could be said of Bronia.

Even Ruth couldn't imagine how Bronia would survive without Nuchim. And yet, as so often was the case, she surprised everyone with her resilience. The grandmother I knew looked fragile and had a habit of falling and breaking something every decade or so; an arm in her sixties after I was born, her hip on a trip with Ruth to the beauty parlor to celebrate her seventieth birthday, and then a rib the year she turned eighty just a few weeks before my older brother's wedding. Even that broken rib didn't prevent her from traveling from New York to the wedding ceremony in Montreal, no matter how much it hurt, just as she started anew after the war and resettled in Vineland without complaint.

She survived Nuchim by twenty-eight years, outlasting both Dina and Jack and nearly every friend she'd made in Vineland. She lived long enough to know two of her three great-grandchildren, and she had no regrets about settling in Vineland. "The business got bad, but we lived a very good life," she told me. Only in her nineties did she start to fade away with dementia, her addled mind recalling Italian phrases she'd learned from coworkers at the Crown garment factory in Vineland. Her long-lost sister Etka was the last person she remembered by name. She died in 2014 at the age of ninety-six in a Far Rockaway, Queens, hospital room with a view of the same stretch of the Atlantic Ocean where the *Marine Perch* sailed on its way to New York Harbor with the Greens, Liverants, and Lermans aboard sixty-seven years earlier.

POSTSCRIPT

BY THE TIME I first drove into Vineland in October 2004, only a few relics remained from the city's poultry past. Sixty-foot-high gray concrete grain silos still stood at the site of a feed mill that turned out fifteen tons of mash an hour off Delsea Drive before shuttering in 1966. Chicken coops still littered the area "like flotsam from a ship sinking."[1]

In a sign of Vineland's changing demographics, the Landis Avenue storefront where Goldstein's kosher delicatessen once operated had become a Mexican restaurant. Hispanic residents accounted for 30 percent of Vineland's population in the 2000 census and almost 40 percent a decade later. Just as Italians and Jews shaped Vineland's first one hundred years, the *Daily Journal* predicted in 2001 that Hispanics may shape the second century. "Just like them, we used to be farm workers," noted Ruperto Figueroa, a U.S. Army veteran born in Puerto Rico, who opened Los Amigos Furniture in Vineland in 1968. "Things change."[2]

I visited the South Main Road home of Phil Snyder, where he'd operated Snyder's Hatchery until 1998.[3] His was the last of roughly two dozen hatcheries in town to close and the last commercial hatchery in New Jersey. His father had started the business in 1926, and Snyder joined two decades later.

At its height, Snyder's hatched tens of thousands of chicks a week. By the end, he'd stopped hatching chickens altogether, focusing instead on wild game for hobbyists and egg embryos for swine flu vaccine manufacturers. What remained of the hatchery was out behind the family farmhouse, in which he'd grown up and later inherited. Adjacent farmland was now occupied by a school and a strip mall, its video rental shop soon to go the way of Vineland's poultry industry.

Inside the former hatchery sat the surplus military generator that helped Snyder through the four-day power outage that followed Hurricane Hazel. His old delivery van, a 1960 white Ford F-100 panel truck emblazoned "Snyder's Hatchery" with a license plate that read "PEEP," still ran. In one room sat vintage plywood and redwood incubators circa 1951. Originally, the entire room's walls were lined with eight of these incubators, capable of hatching eighty thousand chicks a week in a space no larger than the typical suburban garage. In the backroom, painted a light blue, musty with cobwebs and dust, was the closest Vineland had at the time to a museum or archive of its poultry industry: one hundred pound feed mill sacks from the Berkowitz feed mill and yellowed ads from other hatcheries. There were tiny metal scales for eggs and old fountains and water pans from which chickens once drank.

I returned to Vineland a few months later and stopped by the home of Nathan Dunkelman, who was then seventy-six years old and may well have been the area's last active Jewish poultryman. We talked in his kitchen where he once played poker with my grandfather. Dunkelman arrived in Vineland in 1953 and had, by the time I visited, been in the poultry business for a half century. An elevated highway ran along what used to be part of his property. "Everyone thought we'd get so much money from the highway," Dunkelman said.

He guided me outside to the coop where he still conducted his wholesale egg business as a middleman, buying eggs from a farm in Pennsylvania that dropped off about 360,000 eggs every Monday. The eggs sat on pallets inside the windowless cement-block coop that had a dank odor and air cold enough that he didn't need to turn on the refrigerators in winter. A series of laborers once lived in an adjacent piece of old barn whose windows were now boarded up.

Until a year or two earlier, Dunkelman drove the white truck emblazoned "Dunkelman Farms" on the cab that's parked outside the coop to deliver the eggs to Philadelphia five days a week. Now, he had a driver and helper who made the trips. "I'm getting older," he told me. Still, he had no plans to quit any time soon. "When I retire, I'm dead. I talk on the phone with customers. I feel like I'm somebody yet." His work took up about four hours a day, then he went to the YMCA to exercise. He was still operating the egg business when he died five years later at the age of eighty-one. His wife Phyllis, a concentration camp survivor, and daughter Eve took over the wholesale business, which still delivered eggs and chickens two times a day when we talked in 2020.

Most of the farmers had passed away by the time raising chickens became a popular hobby in the early 2010s among urban hipsters overcome by what the leader of an fowl rescue organization calls a "misplaced rural nostalgia."[4] How-to guides described chickens as "great pets" who have a "certain kind of grace and can be truly beautiful" and are "just plain fun to be around!"[5] Interest faded as disillusioned city dwellers discovered that "actually raising the birds can be noisy, messy, labor-intensive and expensive," NBC News observed. Owners dumped unwanted hens on animal shelters and sanctuaries.

Vineland looked a little bit more forlorn each time I visited over the course of a decade. The Raab family's Vineland Kosher Poultry plant where, at its height, *shochtim* or ritual slaughterers, killed thirty thousand chickens a day ceased operations in December 2010.[6] The Manischewitz plant closed and later got demolished in 2015, and the Progresso factory shut down two years later.[7] No wonder Barbara Kingsolver picked Vineland as the ideal setting for her 2018 novel about a downwardly mobile family. Kingsolver portrays Vineland as a bleak, empty-pocketed city full of broken sidewalks and too many houses for sale that no one wants to buy.[8]

On one trip, I walked down Orchard Road, the street where my grandparents and mother lived, passing the former riding club site at the corner of Orchard and Elm since replaced by Christlike Ministries of Deliverance International, which described itself on as a "Pentecostal Deliverance Ministry." Across the street the building that once housed the Orchard Road *shtibl* had long since been converted into a private home. As I approached Bronia and Nuchim's former farmhouse, I heard what sounded like a rooster. There, in front of the house next door to where the Hyman family once lived, a chicken strutted in the front yard.

Only one place remained mostly the same: Bronia's former workplace, the Crown Clothing Company, which was located in the same white, one-story, block-long building on Paul Street. A sign out front had a gold crown and the motto, "Maker of Fine Uniforms for the U.S. Armed Forces." A sign on the front door that read "Operadores de Máquina Necesitada"—machine operators needed—made clear how Vineland's demographics had changed since Italian and Jewish immigrants like Bronia worked here.

I had to visit Philadelphia to see the most famous artifact of south Jersey's Jewish poultry farming past. Meg O'Day, the record-setting egg layer, had found a permanent home at the National Museum of American Jewish History. After Gus Stern died in the 1980s, his daughter donated Meg, now long-since stuffed, to the museum, where she was part of a small temporary exhibit on New Jersey's Jewish farmers in 2016.

———•———

Fittingly, the only sign of Jewish farming left in the Vineland area is at the site of the original Alliance Colony. And the person trying to restart a farm is none other than the grandson of Harry Levin, who had done so much to preserve the history of Vineland's Jewish agricultural past. William Levin, who was sixteen when his grandfather died, graduated from Vineland High School in 1989. He ultimately landing in Brooklyn, where he worked as a writer for *Shalom Sesame*.

In 2014, William and his wife Malya, a New York attorney, were inspired during a visit to a Jewish spiritual retreat in rural Connecticut to try to restart farming on the New Jersey property his family still owned. They spent roughly half a million dollars to acquire property, mostly from family members, and hired an experienced farmer to help clear and cultivate their fields.[9] Their project, dubbed the Alliance Community Reboot, hosts Jewish community events and student tours of the seventy-acre property, which included brunches of bagels and smoked fish from Brooklyn at the farmhouse where his grandfather lived. "Jewish farming is not just touchy-feely hippie B.S.," William told a visiting reporter in 2017.[10] Malya added, "Farming is a way to create a meaningful, modern-day community."

The challenge remains figuring out what crop could make the operation economically viable, William and Malya told me when we spoke in 2020.[11] They'd worked with a young *shochet*, who had ambitions of starting a heritage poultry operation. That fell through after a year, although the schochet met his *bashert* or soulmate there and got married in 2020. William and Malya connected with another experimental farmer growing pest-resistant strains of sorghum, but that couldn't sustain a business. They investigated hemp but didn't have the capital required to make it work.

Other recent attempts to preserve the history of Alliance and other early colonies have had mixed success. In 2007, around the 125th anniversary of the original Alliance colony, the Jewish Federation of Cumberland County studied the idea of building a Jewish Heritage Center there.[12] Separate buildings would focus on different eras: the original colony, Jews who arrived before the war as refugees, and the survivors who came after. The five-million-dollar project never got off the ground. In 2019, Stockton University teamed up with the Jewish Federation to establish a new Alliance Heritage Center, which is developing a virtual museum.[13]

By the time we talked by phone in the middle of the COVID-19 pandemic, the idealistic couple sounded a little dispirited. "It's taking longer than we thought because we're not farmers and we're learning a lot about the business and what's involved," William explained. For the time being, they were growing turnips, collard greens, and zucchini and exploring "value-added" products like kombucha plus agritourism. At a minimum, they projected it would take another five years to become profitable. "Right now, we don't even break even," William said. They weren't sure whether they would be able to host any of their usual fall High Holiday programming or their annual Hannukah party that includes a concert inside the Alliance synagogue. "It's an awkward time," William said.

The same week I first talked to William and Malya, I also happened to speak with Herb Bierig, a former president of Vineland's Sons of Jacob synagogue whose family had operated a local meat processing business for more than half a century. I mentioned Harry Levin, and, unprompted, he questioned the wisdom of William's effort to revive Jewish farming in the area.

"That's all history," Bierig said.[14]

ACKNOWLEDGMENTS

This book wouldn't have been possible without the many refugee farmers and their children who generously shared recollections with me. I would particularly like to thank Eva Neisser and Leah Lederman, who welcomed me into their homes during many visits to Vineland. The individuals involved in the local poultry industry who spoke with me during early visits included Sam Crystal, Nathan Dunkelman, Phil Snyder, William Snyder, and Herbert Wegner.

Many others in the Vineland area provided vital assistance, including Kirk Wisemayer, formerly of the Jewish Federation of Cumberland, Gloucester & Salem Counties, Christine Koehler and other current and former staff of the Vineland Public Library, Patricia Martinelli, curator of the Vineland Historical and Antiquarian Society, Dorris Hecht of Vineland's Hebrew Women's Benevolent Society, Vicky Johnston and Lauren Camille Holden of the Cumberland County Clerk's Office, and Frank DeMaio Jr. of the Friends of Historic Vineland.

I have been working on this long enough that many people who assisted me have left or retired from the institutions identified here. Thank you to Vincent Slatt, Liviu Carare, and Michlean Amir of the U.S. Holocaust Memorial Museum; Dan Yalovsky of the Survivors of the Shoah Visual History Foundation; Derek Merleaux of the Yale University Library's Manuscripts and Archives; David Rosenberg of the Center for Jewish History; Gunnar Berg of the YIVO Institute for Jewish Research; Michael Hayse, Gail Rosenthal, and Irvin Moreno-Rodriguez of Stockton University; Ronald Becker, Bonita Craft Grant, and Soo Lee of the Rutgers University Libraries' Special Collections and University Archives; Misha Mitsel of the American Jewish Joint Distribution Committee; Ellen Kastel of the Jewish Theological Seminary; Jennifer Manuel of the American Jewish Archives; Franz-Josef Herlt of the Darmstadt, Germany, Regional Council's Department of Social Affairs, Integration, and Refugees; as well as the staff of the National Archives and Records Administration in Washington, D.C., and College Park, Maryland, and the Paley Center for Media in New York. I would particularly like to thank the staff of the Center for

Jewish History's Lillian Goldman Reading Room and Katie Fortier at Boston University's Gotlieb Archival Research Center who provided access to materials housed there at a time when the COVID-19 pandemic made visiting impossible.

A number of professors generously shared their expertise about American Jewish history, Jewish agricultural settlements, farm laborers, displaced persons, and Yiddish, including Beth Cohen, Jonathan Dekel-Chen, Hasia Diner, Ellen Eisenberg, Gabriel Finder, Ismael García-Colón, Miriam Isaacs, Ellen Kellman, Avinoam Patt, Miriam Udel, and Lee Shai Weissbach.

Oliver Althoff translated German reparation records, and Pamela Russ provided Yiddish translations. Among those who offered feedback on manuscript drafts are Ronald Becker, Jonathan Dekel-Chen, Karen Ertel, Joe Finkelstein, Saul Golubcow, Keith Perine, Diane Schilit, and Kim Silver. Joseph Dahm, Molly Beckwith Gutman, and Pamela Haag provided invaluable edits. Thank you to Peter Mickulas, Cathy Denning, and their colleagues at Rutgers University Press for agreeing to publish this book and seeing it through to fruition.

Of the many children of survivors who spoke with me, I would particularly like to thank David Lerman, Dorothy Goldberg, and my mother. I was unable to share this book with my grandmother but hope all three of her great-grandchildren, Aaron, Kayla, and Ezra, will read it one day. Thank you most of all to my wife, Claire, for her patience and wisdom throughout.

NOTES

ABBREVIATIONS

Archives

CJH   Center for Jewish History, New York

Egg Basket oral histories, JFCC
       Oral Histories: Egg Basket of the Nation, Jewish Federation of Cumberland
       County (NJ)

Geneva Collection, JDC Digitized Archive
       Records of the Geneva Office of the American Jewish Joint Distribution
       Committee, 1955–1964, Georgette Bennett and Leonard Polonsky Digitized
       JDC Text Archive

Gotlieb ARC
       Howard Gotlieb Archival Research Center, Boston University Libraries

Herr Archive, USHMM
       Jeff and Toby Herr Oral History Archive, U.S. Holocaust Memorial Museum,
       Washington, D.C.

JAS Board Meeting Minutes
       Minutes of the Board of Directors of the Jewish Agricultural Society
       Board Meetings

USF OHP
       University of South Florida Holocaust Survivors Oral History Project

VHA, USC Shoah
       Visual History Archive, USC Shoah Foundation

Newspapers

DJ   Vineland Daily Journal
NYT   New York Times
TJ   Vineland Times Journal

PROLOGUE

1. The city of Vineland resulted from the 1952 merger of Vineland Borough (population 8,155 in 1950) and Landis Township (population 21,418 in 1950). U.S. Department of Commerce, Bureau of the Census, "Population of New Jersey: April 1, 1950," in *1950 Census of Population: Advanced Reports* (Washington, DC, 1951).

2. *Spokane (WA) Daily Chronicle*, "Life among the Exiles," August 14, 1891.

3. Eva Neisser, "Chicken Farming: Not a Dream but a Nightmare," in *Between Sorrow and Strength: Women Refugees of the Nazi Period*, ed. Sibylle Quack (Cambridge: Cambridge University Press, 1995), 286.

4. *New York Times*, "Jewish Refugees Take up Farming," June 17, 1956.

5. Jonathan Dekel-Chen, "Putting Agricultural History to Work: Global Action Today from a Communal Past," *Agricultural History* 94, no. 4 (Fall 2020): 514.

6. Joan Rubinstein Barch, "Jewish Egg Farmers in New Jersey" (master's thesis, Northeastern Illinois University, 1977), 27.

CHAPTER 1   PASSAGE

1. *New York Times*, "800 Nazi Victims Sail for Shelter in U.S.," May 12, 1946.

2. *Berkshire (MA) Evening Eagle*, "310 Jewish Refugees Due in New York," February 11, 1947.

3. Irene Eber, email message to the author, May 11, 2005.

4. Roland W. Charles, *Troopships of World War II* (Washington, DC: Army Transportation Association, 1947), 213; Associated Press, "PreChristmas Troop Arrivals Are Due to Exceed 40,000," *Sacramento Bee*, December 24, 1945.

5. Yitzhak Arad, Israel Gutman, and Abraham Margaliot, eds., *Documents on the Holocaust: Selected Sources on the Destruction of the Jews of Germany and Austria, Poland and the Soviet Union* (Jerusalem: Yad Vashem, 1981), 269–270.

6. Robert Kuwalek, interview by the author, May 31, 2005.

7. Kuwalek interview.

8. Gershon Greenberg, "The Theological Letters of Rabbi Talmud of Lublin (Summer–Fall 1942)," in *Ghettos 1939–1945 New Research and Perspectives on Definition, Daily Life and Survival* (Washington, DC: U.S. Holocaust Memorial Museum Center for Advanced Holocaust Studies, 2005), 113–129.

9. Nuchim Green, interview by Ruth Stern, 1980 (in the author's possession).

10. Dina Fogelgaren, interview by the author, July 1999.

11. Gertrude M. Ruskin to Nuchim Grin, September 29, 1948, Nuchim Grin case file, Records of the United Service for New Americans, YIVO Institute for Jewish Research, Center for Jewish History, New York (hereafter cited as Grin case file, CJH).

12. Charles, *Troopships of World War II*, 213.

13. Irene Eber, *The Choice: Poland, 1939–1945* (New York: Schocken Books, 2004), 174.

14. Regina L. Gelb, interview by Regine Beyer, March 23, 2001, RG-50.549.03.0002, Jeff and Toby Herr Oral History Archive, U.S. Holocaust Memorial Museum, Washington, DC (hereafter cited as Herr Archive, USHMM).

15. Rosalie L. Lerman, interview by Joan Ringelheim, December 1, 1998, RG-50.030.0396, Herr Archive, USHMM.

16. Lerman interview.

17. Rosalie L. Lerman, interview by Joan Ringelheim, January 13, 1999, Herr Archive, USHMM.

18. Joyce Vanaman, "Holocaust Revisited by Someone Who Was There," *Press of Atlantic City*, September 16, 1979.

19. Rosalie Lerman, January 13, 1999 interview, Herr Archive, USHMM.

20. Vanaman, "Holocaust Revisited," September 16, 1979.

21. Rosalie Lerman, January 13, 1999 interview, Herr Archive, USHMM.

22. Vanaman, "Holocaust Revisited," September 16, 1979.

23. Anna L. Wilson, interview by Joan Ringelheim, February 21, 2001, RG-50.030.0411, Herr Archive, USHMM; Chris Lerman, December 1, 1998 interview, Herr Archive, USHMM.

24. Eric Moss, "He Fights to Ensure World Won't Forget," *Jewish Floridian* (Miami), February 7, 1986.

25. Jim Perskie, "A Survivor's Search for Holocaust Memorial," *Courier-Post* (Camden, NJ), March 2, 1979.

26. Joyce Vanaman, "He Saved the Last Bullet for Himself," *Press of Atlantic City*, February 18, 1979.

27. Miles Lerman, interview by Joan Ringelheim, July 17, 2001, RG-50.030.0413, Herr Archive, USHMM.

28. Perskie, "A Survivor's Search," March 2, 1979.

29. Miles Lerman, July 17, 2001 interview, Herr Archive, USHMM.

30. Regina L. Gelb, interview by Regine Beyer, March 18, 1998, RG-50.549.02.0013, Herr Archive, USHMM.

31. Regina L. Gelb, March 23, 2001 interview, Herr Archive, USHMM.

32. Miles Lerman, July 17, 2001 interview, Herr Archive, USHMM.

33. Lerman interview.

34. Eber, email to the author, May 11, 2005.

35. Carl Schmelzer, interview by the author, November 2006.

36. *New York Mirror*, "Warm Welcome After Rough Trip," February 12, 1947.

CHAPTER 2   NEW YORK

1. Lyman Cromwell White, *300,000 New Americans: The Epic of a Modern Immigrant-Aid Service* (New York: Harper, 1957), 136–137.

2. *New York Times*, "Second Contingent of Refugees Here," May 22, 1946.

3. Norma Feder, interview by the author, November 13, 2006.

4. "One Early Morning" (United Service for New Americans, 1947), 30 min., 21 sec.; from New York Public Radio Archive Collections, https://www.wnyc.org/story/one-early-morning/.

5. Beth B. Cohen, *Case Closed: Holocaust Survivors in Postwar America* (New Brunswick, NJ: Rutgers University Press, 2007), 47.

6. Memorandum by A. F. Heller, October 2, 1947, Nuchim Grin case file, Records of the United Service for New Americans, YIVO Institute for Jewish Research, Center for Jewish History, New York (hereafter cited as Grin case file, CJH).

7. Memorandum by A. F. Heller.

CHAPTER 3   FINDING A FARM

1. Gabriel Davidson, "The Jew in Agriculture in the United States," in *American Jewish Year Book, September 28, 1935 to September 16, 1936* (New York: American Jewish Committee, 1936), 101.

2. Ellen Eisenberg, *Jewish Agricultural Colonies in New Jersey, 1882–1920* (Syracuse, NY: Syracuse University Press, 1995), 38–39.

3. Leonard G. Robinson, "Agricultural Activities of the Jews in America," in *American Jewish Year Book, September 12, 1912 to October 1, 1913* (New York: American Jewish Committee, 1914), 61.

4. Joseph Brandes, *Immigrants to Freedom: Jewish Communities in Rural New Jersey since 1882* (Philadelphia: Jewish Publication Society of America, 1971), 51.

5. Brandes, *Immigrants to Freedom*, 51.

6. I. Harry Levin, "History of Alliance, New Jersey: First Jewish Agricultural Settlement in the United States," *Vineland Historical Magazine* 54, no. 1 (1978): 4.

7. Brandes, *Immigrants to Freedom*, 10.

8. *Courier-Post* (Camden, NJ), "The New Jerusalem," June 10, 1882, 1.

9. *Spokane (WA) Daily Chronicle*, "Life among the Exiles," August 14, 1891; Brandes, *Immigrants to Freedom*, 55.

10. Levin, "History of Alliance," 5.

11. Brandes, *Immigrants to Freedom*, 76.

12. Eisenberg, *Jewish Agricultural Colonies in New Jersey*, 136–137.

13. *Spokane (WA) Daily Chronicle*, "Life Among the Exiles," August 14, 1891.

14. Eisenberg, *Jewish Agricultural Colonies in New Jersey*, 87.

15. M. D. Hirsch, "Refuge for Russian Jews," *Forum*, 11 (August 1891), 631, quoted in Samuel Joseph, *History of the Baron de Hirsch Fund: The Americanization of the Jewish Immigrant* (Philadelphia: Jewish Publication Society, 1935), 12.

16. Robert Alan Goldberg, *Back to the Soil: The Jewish Farmers of Clarion, Utah, and Their World* (Salt Lake City: University of Utah Press, 1986), 38.

17. Janet E. Schulte, "Proving Up and Moving Up: Jewish Homesteading Activity in North Dakota, 1900–1920," *Great Plains Quarterly* 10 (Fall 1990): 228–244.

18. J. Sanford Rikoon, ed., *Rachel Calof's Story: Jewish Homesteader on the Northern Plains* (Bloomington: Indiana University Press, 1995), 89.

19. Sophie Trupin, *Dakota Diaspora: Memoirs of a Jewish Homesteader* (Lincoln: University of Nebraska Press, 1984), 102.

20. Adam D. Mendelsohn, *The Rag Race: How Jews Sewed Their Way to Success in America and the British Empire* (New York: New York University Press, 2015), 207; Hasia R. Diner, *Roads Taken: The Great Jewish Migrations to the New World and the Peddlers Who Forged the Way* (New Haven, CT: Yale University Press, 2015).

21. Davidson, "The Jew in Agriculture," 103–104.

22. Michael Hoberman, *How Strange It Seems: The Cultural Life of Jews in Small-Town New England* (Amherst: University of Massachusetts Press, 2008), 78–82. Hoberman provides an account of Jewish potato farming in Aroostook County, Maine.

23. Davidson, "The Jew in Agriculture," 119.

24. Morton L. Gordon, "The History of the Jewish Farmer in Eastern Connecticut" (DHL diss., Yeshiva University, 1974), 161. Gordon provides an account of the Central Connecticut Farmers' Cooperative Association.

25. Brandes, *Immigrants to Freedom*, 319.

26. Gabriel Davidson, *Our Jewish Farmers and the Story of the Jewish Agricultural Society* (New York: L.B. Fischer, 1943), 132.

27. Gabriel Davidson, "Jews Become Good Farmers," *American Jewish World* (Minneapolis), September 8, 1939.

28. Davidson, *Our Jewish Farmers*, 137.

29. Minutes of the Board of Directors of the Jewish Agricultural Society Board Meeting (hereafter JAS Board Meeting Minutes), February 11, 1947, box 74, Records of the Baron de Hirsch Fund, Center for Jewish History, New York (hereafter cited as Baron de Hirsch Fund records, CJH).

30. *Annual Report of the Managing Director, 1947* (New York: Jewish Agricultural Society, 1948), 9.

31. Davidson, "The Jew in Agriculture," 119.

32. *Report of the Managing Director for the Period 1900–1949* (New York: Jewish Agricultural Society, 1950), 20.

33. Jonathan Dekel-Chen, "Putting Agricultural History to Work: Global Action Today from a Communal Past," *Agricultural History* 94, no. 4 (Fall 2020): 525.

34. JAS Board Meeting Minutes, December 9, 1947, box 74, Baron de Hirsch Fund records, CJH.

35. Gertrude Wishnick Dubrovsky, *The Land Was Theirs: Jewish Farmers in the Garden State* (Tuscaloosa: University of Alabama Press, 1992), 67.

36. JAS Board Meeting Minutes, October 15, 1947, box 74, Baron de Hirsch Fund records, CJH.

37. JAS Board Meeting Minutes, September 28, 1948, box 74, Baron de Hirsch Fund records, CJH.

38. Herman J. Levine and Benjamin Miller, *The American Jewish Farmer in Changing Times* (New York: Jewish Agricultural Society, 1966), 35.

39. Davidson, *Our Jewish Farmers*, 128–129.

40. Levine and Miller, *American Jewish Farmer*, 35.

41. Memorandum by A. F. Heller, October 2, 1947, Nuchim Grin case file, Records of the United Service for New Americans, Archives of the YIVO Institute for Jewish Research, Center for Jewish History, New York (hereafter cited as Grin case file, CJH).

42. Aaron S. Negin to Herman J. Levine, October 7, 1947, Grin case file, CJH.

43. Memorandum by E. Merer, January 2, 1948, Grin case file, CJH.

44. Jewish Agricultural Society to Nathan and Bertha Green, December 5, 1947, Grin case file, CJH.

45. Memorandum by E. Merer, January 2, 1948, Grin case file, CJH.

CHAPTER 4   SETTLING IN

1. *The Egg and I*, DVD, directed by Chester Erskine (1947; Universal Pictures; Universal Studios, 2012).

2. Paula Baker, *Looking for Betty MacDonald: The Egg, the Plague, Mrs. Piggle-Wiggle, and I* (Seattle: University of Washington Press, 2016), 45–47.

3. Memorandum by E. Merer, January 2, 1948, Nuchim Grin case file, Records of the United Service for New Americans, Archives of the YIVO Institute for Jewish Research, Center for Jewish History, New York (hereafter cited as Grin case file, CJH).

4. Selma Robinson, "New Seed on American Soil," *PM Daily*, May 23, 1948.

5. "Work Sheet for Estimating Cost of Furniture, Furnishings & Equipment," January 27, 1947, Grin case file, CJH.

6. *Better Farming: A Series of Lesson Units* (Urbana-Champaign: University of Illinois, 1947), 5.

7. Leslie Ellsworth Card and Melvin Henderson, *Farm Poultry Production* (United States: The Interstate, 1948), 25.

8. Phillip R. Naftaly, "Jewish Chicken Farmers in the Egg Basket of the World: The Creation of Cultural Identity in Petaluma, California, 1904–1954" (PhD diss., New School for Social Research, 1999), 99.

9. Robinson, "New Seed on American Soil," May 23, 1948.

10. *This Is New Jersey* (New Jersey Department of Economic Development, 1947), 14 min., 34 sec.; from YIVO Institute for Jewish Research, MP3, https://exhibitions.yivo.org/items/show/6396.

11. *Jewish Farmer*, "Jewish Farmers Start Season in High Gear," May 1943.

12. Gabriel Davidson, *Our Jewish Farmers and the Story of the Jewish Agricultural Society* (New York: L.B. Fischer, 1943), 37.

13. *Jewish Farmer*, "Poultry Pointers," January 1948.

14. This newspaper section grew in size and frequency as the local poultry industry boomed, becoming a weekly Friday feature in March 1950.

15. *TJ*, "The South Jersey Poultryman," January 31, 1948.

16. Goldie Finkelstein, interview by Effie Mayerfeld, August 19, 1996, interview 18729, Visual History Archive, USC Shoah Foundation.

17. *TJ*, advertisement, August 7, 1961, 28; *Press of Atlantic City*, "Obituaries," June 14, 1995.

18. *TJ*, "Paul's Delicatessen Opens Thursday at 321 Landis Ave.," January 21, 1948.

19. *TJ*, advertisement, March 1, 1957.

20. Charles K. Landis, *The Founder's Own Story of the Founding of Vineland* (Vineland, NJ: Vineland Historical and Antiquarian Society, 1903); *New York Times*, "A Quaint Town Where Everybody Minds His Own Business," September 11, 1904.

21. Kenneth T. Jackson, *Crabgrass Frontier: The Suburbanization of the United States* (New York: Oxford University Press, 1985), 85.

22. Landis, *Founder's Own Story*, 11–12.

23. Salvatore J. LaGumina, Frank J. Cavaioli, Salvatore Primeggia, and Joseph A. Varacalli, eds., *The Italian American Experience: An Encyclopedia* (New York: Routledge, 1999), 8.

24. W. P. Dillingham et al., *Report of the U.S. Immigration Commission, Immigrants in Industries (in Twenty-Five Parts), Part 24: Recent Immigrants in Agriculture* (Washington, DC: Government Printing Office, 1911), 47.

25. Dillingham et al., *Report of the U.S. Immigration Commission*, 51.

26. *NYT*, "A Quaint Town Where Everybody Minds His Own Business," September 11, 1904.

27. *Vineland and Vicinity New Jersey: Its Advantages as a Place of Residence, Profitable Investment, Unexcelled Facilities for Agricultural Pursuits on Its Many Attractive Farms* (New York: E. A. Strout, 1893), 7, Rutgers University Libraries Special Collections & University Archives.

28. *TJ*, "Welch Developed Famed Grape Drink in Vineland in '69," August 5, 1986.

29. "Pathfinder Visits Poultry Center of Eastern United States," *Pathfinder*, August 18, 1927, reprinted in *Vineland Historical Magazine* 64, no. 1 (1989): 34.

30. Joel Denker, *The World on a Plate: A Tour through the History of America's Ethnic Cuisine* (Cambridge, MA: Westview, 2003), 24.

31. General Mills, "Progresso Soup Cooks Up 'Soup Worth Talking About' for Coming Soup Season," news release, September 30, 2010.

32. Harold Brubaker, "Now With Owner No. 6, Progresso Still Cooking," *Philadelphia Inquirer*, October 25, 2002.

33. Bill Snyder, "Vineland Was Egg Capital of the East Coast," *DJ*, November 13, 2003.

34. *TJ*, "Wholesale Sales on Upswing in Vineland Area," October 22, 1955.

35. *Poultryman*, "Egg Prices Reach Highest December Figure since 1920," January 2, 1948.

CHAPTER 5   SMALL-TOWN JEWS

1. Deborah R. Weiner, *Coalfield Jews: An Appalachian History* (Urbana: University of Illinois Press, 2006), 9–10.

2. Hasia R. Diner, *Roads Taken: The Great Jewish Migrations to the New World and the Peddlers Who Forged the Way* (New Haven, CT: Yale University Press, 2015).

3. Adam D. Mendelsohn, *The Rag Race: How Jews Sewed Their Way to Success in America and the British Empire* (New York: New York University Press, 2015), 196.

4. *Beautiful Vineland New Jersey: Souvenir of 50th Anniversary and Old Home Week, August 6 to 12, 1911* (Vineland, NJ, 1911), Rutgers University Libraries Special Collections & University Archives.

5. *Vineland (NJ) Evening Journal*, "Local News," October 11, 1898, quoted in Joseph Brandes, *Immigrants to Freedom: Jewish Communities in Rural New Jersey since 1882* (Philadelphia: Jewish Publication Society of America, 1971), 237.

6. *Evening Journal*, "Public Path," August 12, 1909.

7. *Evening Journal*, "Jewish Down," March 29, 1879.

8. *Evening Journal*, "Civic Matters Before Chamber," April 17, 1920.

9. Brandes, *Immigrants to Freedom*, 286.

10. Brandes, *Immigrants to Freedom*, 285.

11. *TJ*, "Jacob Rubinoff, Vineland Feed Manufacturer and Civic Leader, Dies at Home," November 24, 1948.

12. Arthur D. Goldhaft, *The Golden Egg* (New York: Horizon Press, 1957), 45–53.

13. Goldhaft, *Golden Egg*, 133.

14. Stephen B. Hitchner, "Poultry Vaccine Laboratories in the United States: A Historical Perspective," *Avian Diseases* 40, no. 2 (1996): 256.

15. Jacob M. Maze, "Farming by Jews in New Jersey: A Historical Review," in *Annual Report of the General Manager 1952* (New York: Jewish Agricultural Society, 1953), 26.

16. Gabriel Davidson, *Our Jewish Farmers: And the Story of the Jewish Agricultural Society* (New York: L. B. Fischer, 1943), 130.

17. Davidson, *Our Jewish Farmers*, 127.

18. Eva Neisser, "Chicken Farming: Not a Dream but a Nightmare," in *Between Sorrow and Strength: Women Refugees of the Nazi Period*, ed. Sibylle Quack (Cambridge: Cambridge University Press, 1995), 286; Steven Hamburger, interview, July 15, 2003, transcript, Oral Histories: Egg Basket of the Nation, Jewish Federation of Cumberland County (NJ) (hereafter cited as Egg Basket oral histories, JFCC).

19. Maze, "Farming by Jews in New Jersey," 25. Most accounts refer to this group as German Jews, although a significant share were born in Austria. Stockton University's Sara and Sam Schoffer Holocaust Resource Center identified 453 German-born Jews and 36 Austrian-born Jewish refugees who settled in Cumberland, Atlantic, and Cape May counties in south Jersey. Some arrived after the war ended. Michael Hayse, email message to the author, February 3, 2022.

20. Eva Neisser, interview, July 17, 2003, transcript, Egg Basket oral histories, JFCC.

21. Hans Fisher, interview by the author, March 13, 2006.

22. Bernard D. Weinryb, "Jewish Immigration and Accommodation to America," in *The Jews: Social Patterns of an American Group*, ed. Marshall Sklare (New York: Free Press, 1958), 17; Irving Howe, *World of Our Fathers* (New York: Harcourt Brace Jovanovich, 1976), 31.

23. Renee Kreisworth, interview by the author, August 13, 2020.

24. "It's because": Ruth Bickhardt, interview by Susan Douglass, January 20, 1997, interview code 24918, Visual History Archive, USC Shoah Foundation.

25. Neisser, interview, July 17, 2003, transcript, Egg Basket oral histories, JFCC.

26. Neisser, "Chicken Farming," 287.

27. Steven M. Lowenstein, "The German-Jewish Community of Washington Heights," in *Leo Baeck Institute Yearbook* 30 (1985), reprinted in Jeffrey S. Gurock, ed., *American Jewish History*, vol. 4, *American Jewish Life, 1920–1990* (New York: Routledge, 1998), 215–233.

28. Gertrude Wishnick Dubrovsky, *The Land Was Theirs: Jewish Farmers in the Garden State* (Tuscaloosa: University of Alabama Press, 1992), 61–63; Rhonda F. Levine, *Class, Networks, and Identity: Replanting Jewish Lives from Nazi Germany to Rural New York* (Lanham, MD: Rowman & Littlefield, 2001), 125.

29. *TJ*, "Poultrymen's Club to Present Movies," January 9, 1948.

30. Regina L. Gelb, interview by Regine Beyer, March 18, 1998, RG-50.549.02.0013, Jeff and Toby Herr Oral History Archive, U.S. Holocaust Memorial Museum, Washington, DC (hereafter Herr Archive, USHMM).

31. Gelb interview.

32. Rosalie L. Lerman, interview by William B. Helmreich, January 12, 1990, RG-50.165.0064, Herr Archive, USHMM.

33. Rosalie L. Lerman, January 12, 1990 interview, Herr Archive, USHMM.

34. A 1979 newspaper story said "Mrs. Lerman and her husband" visited Vineland together. Julia Klein, "The Long Journey into the Light on Jersey Farmlands," *Philadelphia Inquirer*, August 12, 1979. In the January 12, 1990, oral history interview with Helmreich, she said she stayed in New York with their baby daughter.

35. Miles Lerman, interview by Joan Ringelheim, July 17, 2001, RG-50.030.0413, Herr Archive, USHMM.

36. Rosalie L. Lerman, January 12, 1990 interview, Herr Archive, USHMM.

37. Klein, "Long Journey."

38. Rosalie L. Lerman, January 12, 1990 interview, Herr Archive, USHMM.

39. Dorothy Goldberg, interview by the author, May 22, 2005.

40. Dorothy Goldberg, interview by the author, March 1, 2020.

41. Davidson, *Our Jewish Farmers*, 106.

42. William Kahane, interview by Sandra Stewart Holyoak, Shaun Illingworth, and Gino Namur, March 5, 2007, Rutgers Oral History Archives, https://oralhistory.rutgers.edu/images/PDFs/kahane_william.pdf.

43. Israel Goldman and Louis Goldman, interview by William B. Helmreich, June 12, 1990, RG-50.165.0033, Herr Archive, USHMM.

44. Herman J. Levine and Benjamin Miller, *The American Jewish Farmer in Changing Times* (New York: Jewish Agricultural Society, 1966), 35.

45. Herbert Kolb, "Our Chicken Farm," Birnbaum Wildmann family website, https://wildmannbirnbaum.com/wp-content/uploads/Our-Chicken-Farm-by-Herbert-Kolb.pdf.

46. Joyce Vanaman, "He Saved the Last Bullet for Himself," *Press of Atlantic City*, February 18, 1979.

47. Rosalie L. Lerman, January 12, 1990 interview, Herr Archive, USHMM.

48. Lerman interview.

CHAPTER 6   WORD-OF-MOUTH MIGRATION

1. Lee Shai Weissbach, *Jewish Life in Small-Town America: A History* (New Haven, CT: Yale University Press, 2005), 45.

2. Harvey M. Choldin, "Kinship Networks in the Migration Process," *International Migration Review* 7, no. 2 (1973): 163–175; John Bodnar, *The Transplanted: A History of Immigrants in Urban America* (Bloomington: Indiana University Press, 1985), 57–58; Leonard Rogoff, *Homelands: Southern Jewish Identity in Durham and Chapel Hill, North Carolina* (Tuscaloosa: University of Alabama Press, 2001), 58; Alejandro Portes and Rubén G. Rumbaut, *Immigrant America: A Portrait* (Oakland: University of California Press, 2014), 83–84.

3. William B. Helmreich, *Against All Odds: Holocaust Survivors and the Successful Lives They Made in America* (New York: Simon & Schuster, 1992), 108, 170.

4. Marvin Smith, "Many in Vineland Lived Tragedies Brought by War," *TJ*, September 1, 1959.

5. Irving Raab, interview by Janie Brown, November 23, 1997, interview 35757, Visual History Archive, USC Shoah Foundation (hereafter cited as VHA, USC Shoah).

6. Irving Raab with Carol Cunningham Suplee, *99 Years: The Remarkable Story of Irving Raab* (Columbus, OH: Gatekeeper Press, 2018), 251–252.

7. Sol Finkelstein, interview, July 17, 2003, transcript, Oral Histories: Egg Basket of the Nation, Jewish Federation of Cumberland County (NJ) (hereafter cited as Egg Basket oral histories, JFCC).

8. Finkelstein interview.

9. Jacob Kahan, interview, April 21, 1998, interview 40789, VHA, USC Shoah.

10. Kenneth L. Kann, *Comrades and Chicken Ranchers: The Story of a California Jewish Community* (Ithaca, NY: Cornell University Press, 1993), 75.

11. Eva Neisser, "The Benevolent Revue: 75 Years of Non-Trivial Pursuit" (in the author's possession).

12. *Jewish Farmer*, "J.A.S. Loan Policy," June 1953.

13. David Nasaw, *The Last Million: Europe's Displaced Persons from World War to Cold War* (New York: Penguin, 2020), 427.

14. *Annual Report of the Managing Director for 1950* (New York: Jewish Agricultural Society, 1951), 8.

15. Phillip Naftaly, "Jewish Chicken Farmers in the Egg Basket of the World: The Creation of Cultural Identity in Petaluma, California, 1904–1954" (PhD diss., New School for Social Research, 1999), 1; Phillip Naftaly, "Jewish Chicken Farmers in Petaluma, California, 1904–1975," *Western States Jewish History* 23, no. 3 (1991): 242.

16. Kann, *Comrades and Chicken Ranchers*, 178.

17. Herman J. Levine and Benjamin Miller, *The American Jewish Farmer in Changing Times* (New York: Jewish Agricultural Society, 1966), 86.

18. Levine and Miller, *American Jewish Farmer*, 37; 60–70: Morton L. Gordon, "The History of the Jewish Farmer in Eastern Connecticut" (DHL diss., Yeshiva University, 1974), 65.

19. Jacob M. Maze, "Farming by Jews in New Jersey: A Historical Review," in *Annual Report of the General Manager 1952* (New York: Jewish Agricultural Society, 1953), 27.

20. Abraham D. Lavender and Clarence B. Steinberg, *Jewish Farmers of the Catskills: A Century of Survival* (Gainesville: University Press of Florida, 1995), 143; Levine and Miller, *American Jewish Farmer*, 37–38.

21. Maze, "Farming by Jews in New Jersey," 26.

22. Joseph Greenblum and Marshall Sklare, "The Attitude of the Small-Town Jew toward His Community," in *The Jews: Social Patterns of an American Group*, ed. Marshall Sklare (New York: Free Press, 1958), 288.

23. Greenblum and Sklare, "Attitude of the Small-Town Jew."

24. Weissbach, *Jewish Life in Small-Town America*, 18–28.

25. Weissbach excludes "agricultural colonies and rural localities" such as Norma and Rosenhayn near Vineland from consideration "because the experience of Jews in agrar-

ian environments has received a fair amount of attention in recent years." Weissbach, *Jewish Life in Small-Town America*, 28.

26. Weissbach, *Jewish Life in Small-Town America*, 29.

27. The average was 176,427 if New York was excluded. Weissbach, *Jewish Life in Small-Town America*, 35.

28. John P. Dean, "Jewish Participation in the Life of Middle-Sized American Communities," in Sklare, *The Jews*, 305.

29. Only in a few small rural communities such as Bennington, Vermont, and Rockland, Maine, did the Jewish population account for 7 or 8 percent of residents in 1927. Michael Hoberman, *How Strange It Seems: The Cultural Life of Jews in Small-Town New England* (Amherst: University of Massachusetts Press, 2008), 15.

30. Weissbach, *Jewish Life in Small-Town America*, 30.

31. Weissbach, *Jewish Life in Small-Town America*, 338–348.

32. One parallel is Johnstown, Pennsylvania, where the interwar Jewish community of roughly twelve to thirteen hundred accounted for less than two percent of the city's population and grew to a postwar peak of two thousand. Ewa Morawska, *Insecure Prosperity: Small-Town Jews in Industrial America, 1890–1940* (Princeton, NJ: Princeton University Press, 1996), 76, 246.

33. Toby Shafter, "The Fleshpots of Maine," *Commentary*, January 1949.

34. Lee J. Levinger, "The Disappearing Small-Town Jew," *Commentary*, August 1952.

35. Eugen Schoenfeld, "Small-Town Jews' Integration into Their Communities," *Rural Sociology* 35, no. 2 (June 1970): 175–190.

36. Peter I. Rose, *Strangers in Their Midst: Small-Town Jews and Their Neighbors* (Merrick, NY: Richwood, 1977), 77.

37. Louise Laser, "The Only Jewish Family in Town: In Rural Ohio," *Commentary*, December 1959.

38. Renee Stern, interview by Dawn Horwitz, January 30, 1997, interview 25239, VHA, USC Shoah.

39. Barbara Werner Schwarz, interview by the author, September 8, 2015.

40. Schoenfeld, "Small-Town Jews' Integration," 181.

41. *Trenton Evening Times*, "New Jersey Egg Center Was Started by Jewish Society," October 4, 1950.

42. Gertrude Wishnick Dubrovsky, *The Land Was Theirs: Jewish Farmers in the Garden State* (Tuscaloosa: University of Alabama Press, 1992), 121.

43. Maze, "Farming by Jews in New Jersey," 26.

44. Helmreich, *Against All Odds*, 60.

45. Helmreich, *Against All Odds*, 62.

CHAPTER 7   MIXED RECEPTION

1. I. Harry Levin, "History of Alliance, New Jersey: First Jewish Agricultural Settlement in the United States," *Vineland Historical Magazine* 54, no. 1 (1978): 4.

2. Levin, "History of Alliance."

3. Ron Avery, "The Last Remnants of South Jersey's Alliance Colony of Jewish Farmers," *Courier-Post* (Camden, NJ), October 27, 1973.

4. Adrienne I. Possenti, "'Marrying Judge' Ends Career," *TJ*, February 8, 1982.

5. Marsha Schumer, interview by the author, August 30, 2015.

6. Eli Kuhnreich, interview by the author, May 22, 2020.

7. Schumer, author interview, August 30, 2015.

8. Possenti, "'Marrying Judge' Ends Career," February 8, 1982.

9. Susan (Dover) Rosen, interview by the author, August 17, 2020.

10. Selma Robinson, "New Seed on American Soil," *PM Daily*, May 23, 1948.

11. I. Harry Levin to United Service for New Americans, November 26, 1947, Nuchim Grin case file, Records of the United Service for New Americans, Archives of the YIVO Institute for Jewish Research, Center for Jewish History, New York.

12. *TJ*, "William H. Levin, 95, Dies; Last of 1882 Alliance Colony," March 11, 1969.

13. *TJ*, "Manuel Levin, 86," November 20, 2001.

14. Ron Avery, "The Last Remnants of South Jersey's Alliance Colony of Jewish Farmers," *Courier-Post* (Camden, NJ), October 27, 1973.

15. Levin, "History of Alliance," 13.

16. Ron Avery, "Judge Still Expert on Marriage," *Courier-Post* (Camden, NJ), January 14, 1980.

17. Aharon Pelc, "Greetings," in *Tenth Anniversary Journal of the Jewish Poultry Farmers' Association of South Jersey* (Vineland, NJ: Jewish Poultry Farmers Association, 1962), U.S. Holocaust Memorial Museum Library and Archives, Washington, DC.

18. Hasia R. Diner, *We Remember With Reverence and Love: American Jews and the Myth of Silence after the Holocaust, 1945–1962* (New York: New York University Press, 2009), 152.

19. The UJA raised $750 million between 1945 and 1952, including more than $150 million in 1948 alone. Rachel Deblinger, "Purim, Passover, and Pilgrims: Symbols of Survival and Sacrifice in American Postwar Holocaust Survivor Narratives," in *Reconstructing the Old Country: American Jewry in the Post-Holocaust Decades*, ed. Eliyana R. Adler and Sheila E. Jelen (Detroit: Wayne State University Press, 2017), 259.

20. *TJ*, "Arrange Campaign For Jewish Relief Aid in Europe," June 5, 1947.

21. *TJ*, "South Jersey Zone Rally for United Jewish Appeal Planned for October 27 at Reber School," October 19, 1949, 3.

22. *TJ*, "Economic Plight of Refugees to Israel to Be Described by Lerner at Vineland AJA Dinner," October 16, 1950, 3.

23. Helen Kejzman, interview by the author, September 16, 2015.

24. Israel Goldman and Louis Goldman interview by William B. Helmreich, June 12, 1990, RG-50.165.0033, Jeff and Toby Herr Oral History Archive, U.S. Holocaust Memorial Museum, Washington, DC (hereafter cited as Herr Archive, USHMM).

25. Goldie Finkelstein, interview by Effie Mayerfeld, August 19, 1996, interview 18729, Visual History Archive, USC Shoah Foundation (hereafter cited as VHA, USC Shoah).

26. Finkelstein interview.

27. Hasia Diner, interview by the author, September 14, 2021.

28. *Battle for Survival*, a 1946 UJA-produced film narrated by Orson Welles, opened with "barefoot Jews marching aimlessly down a dusty road." Deblinger, "Purim, Passover, and Pilgrims," 261.

29. Aaron Hass, *The Aftermath: Living with the Holocaust* (New York: Cambridge University Press, 1995), 91.

30. Jay Greenblatt, interview by the author, May 26, 2020.

31. Ursula Bernstein, interview by Merrill Grumer, August 12, 1997, interview 31911, VHA, USC Shoah.

32. "Robinson, "New Seed on American Soil," May 23, 1948. German and Polish Jews constituted the two largest blocs of refugees who settled in south Jersey according to research by Stockton University's Sara and Sam Schoffer Holocaust Resource Center. Of approximately 1,400 refugees whose place of birth could be identified, 83 percent were born in Germany or Poland. Another 7 percent were born in Austria and Czechoslovakia. The remainder were born in thirteen other Western and Eastern European countries. This includes both refugees who came prior to the U.S. entry into World War II or after the war ended and both farmers and nonfarmers. Michael Hayse, email messages to the author, January 21, 2022 and February 3, 2022.

33. Jack Blumenthal, interview by the author, September 10, 2021.

34. Eva Neisser, interview by the author, February 20, 2005.

35. Irving Raab with Carol Cunningham Suplee, *99 Years: The Remarkable Story of Irving Raab* (Columbus, OH: Gatekeeper Press, 2018), 259.

36. Yisroel Leifer, Esther T. Raab, and Izzy Raab, interview by William B. Helmreich, June 6, 1990, RG-50.165.0062, Herr Archive, USHMM.

37. German- and Austrian-born Jews accounted for approximately one hundred of the refugee farmers who settled in south Jersey after the war, according to the author's research. Some had arrived in the United States prior to its entry into the war, while others came after the war ended.

38. Ron Schwarz, interview by the author, August 26, 2021.

39. Murray and Fay Chamish interview, July 17, 2003, transcript, Oral Histories: Egg Basket of the Nation, Jewish Federation of Cumberland County (NJ).

40. Barbara Stern Burstin, *After the Holocaust: The Migration of Polish Jews and Christians to Pittsburgh* (Pittsburgh: University of Pittsburgh Press, 1989), 122–123.

41. Richard Flaim, interview by the author, September 17, 2015.

42. Ira Rosenblum, "State Backs Holocaust Course," *New York Times*, February 17, 1985.

CHAPTER 8   GETTING NOTICED

1. *TJ*, "Latvian Family Hopes for New Life in America after Fleeing War Torn Homeland," October 25, 1949.

2. Bert Vorchheimer, "Russian Youth Attending Vineland High School Tells of Escape from Odessa," *TJ*, October 27, 1949.

3. *TJ*, "New Chicken House Gives Birds Plenty of Room in 40-Foot Square Coops," October 29, 1949.

4. *TJ*, "Max Leuchter, Publisher of Times-Journal, Dies of Auto Crash Injuries," May 16, 1949.

5. John Garrahan, "Keeping up with the Leuchters," *DJ*, September 22, 2000.

6. *DJ*, "Officer's Letter Home Recounts Destruction at Sea," November 10, 2007.

7. Ben Zion Leuchter, *How a Small-Town Editor Saw the World: The Story of Max Leuchter and the Vineland Times Journal* (Coconut Grove, FL: TreisterWilkins Communications, 2000).

8. Leuchter, *How a Small-Town Editor Saw the World*.

9. Joanne Palmer, "Remembering Vera Greenwald of Presov, Vineland, Milford—and Teaneck," *Jewish Standard* (NJ), February 18, 2016.

10. *Jewish Farmer*, "South Jersey Jewish Settlers Meet," September 1949.

11. *TJ*, "$600,000 Worth of Poultry Houses Built Here in '49," January 12, 1950.

12. Stephen Davis, *Say Kids! What Time Is It? Notes from the Peanut Gallery* (Boston: Little, Brown, 1987), 58.

13. *TJ*, advertisement, September 6, 1949.

14. Lawrence Van Gelder, "Milton Berle, TV's First Star as 'Uncle Miltie,' Dies at 93," *New York Times*, March 28, 2002.

15. Milton Berle with Haskel Frankel, *Milton Berle: An Autobiography* (New York: Delacorte Press, 1974), 29–36.

16. Randy Roberts and James Stuart Olson, *John Wayne: American* (Lincoln: University of Nebraska Press, 1997), 5.

17. Jeffrey Shandler, *While America Watches: Televising the Holocaust* (New York: Oxford University Press, 1999), 28.

18. Andrew Yarrow, "Paul Kohner, Hollywood Agent and Film Producer, Is Dead at 85," *NYT*, March 19, 1988.

CHAPTER 9   VICISSITUDES

1. Herbert J. Gans, "Park Forest: Birth of a Jewish Community," *Commentary*, April 1951.

2. Ben B. Seligman, "Some Aspects of Jewish Demography," in *The Jews: Social Patterns of an American Group*, ed. Marshall Sklare (New York: Free Press, 1958), 93; Barry R. Chiswick, "The Postwar Economy of American Jews," *Studies in Contemporary Jewry* 8 (1992), reprinted in Jeffrey S. Gurock, ed., *American Jewish History*, vol. 4, *American Jewish Life, 1920–1990* (New York: Routledge, 1998), 215–233.

3. Joseph Berger, *Displaced Persons: Growing Up in America after the Holocaust* (New York: Scribner, 2001), 108.

4. Barbara Stern Burstin, *After the Holocaust: The Migration of Polish Jews and Christians to Pittsburgh* (Pittsburgh: University of Pittsburgh Press, 1989), 157–158.

5. Herman J. Levine and Benjamin Miller, *The American Jewish Farmer in Changing Times* (New York: Jewish Agricultural Society, 1966), 34.

6. Leslie E. Card and Melvin Henderson, *Farm Family Production* (Danville, IL: Interstate, 1948), 28.

7. Joseph Schepps, interview by Pearl Taylor, July 19, 1995, interview 4120, Visual History Archive, USC Shoah Foundation (hereafter cited as VHA, USC Shoah).

8. Julia Klein, "The Long Journey into the Light on Jersey Farmlands," *Philadelphia Inquirer*, August 12, 1979.

9. *TJ*, "104 Expensive Chickens Killed by Marauding Dogs, One of Which Is Slain," September 29, 1952.

10. Murray Ressler, interview by Harry Furman, August 7, 1996, interview 18299, VHA, USC Shoah.

11. Klein, "Long Journey."

12. William B. Helmreich, *Against All Odds: Holocaust Survivors and the Successful Lives They Made in America* (New York: Simon & Schuster, 1992), 88.

13. Helen Epstein, *Children of the Holocaust: Conversations with Sons and Daughters of Survivors* (New York: G.P. Putnam's Sons, 1979), 52.

14. Helmreich, *Against All Odds*, 102.

15. Arthur D. Goldhaft, *The Golden Egg* (New York: Horizon Press, 1957), 264.

16. Ben Leuchter, "Rotten Roof Racket," *TJ*, September 22, 1950.

17. Jonathan Mark, "The Country Life," *Jewish Week*, June 17, 2004.

18. Edward L. Schapsmeier and Frederick H. Schapsmeier, "Eisenhower and Agricultural Reform: Ike's Farm Policy Legacy Appraised," *American Journal of Economics and Sociology* 51, no. 2 (1992): 147–159.

19. *TJ*, "Poultrymen's Resolution, Adopted at Mass Meeting, Asks Egg Support of 90%," December 14, 1949.

20. *TJ*, advertisement, December 13, 1949.

21. Martin J. Gerra, *The Demand, Supply, and Price Structure for Eggs*, Technical Bulletin No. 1204 (Washington, DC: U.S. Department of Agriculture, 1959), 136.

22. *TJ*, "Keeping Up with the Times," January 26, 1950.

23. Lee Shai Weissbach, *Jewish Life in Small-Town America: A History* (New Haven, CT: Yale University Press, 2005), 134.

24. Lorraine J. German, *Soil and Shul in the Berkshires: The Untold Story of Sandisfield's Jewish Farm Colony* (Troy, NY: Troy Book Makers, 2018), 29; Abraham D. Lavender and Clarence B. Steinberg, *Jewish Farmers of the Catskills: A Century of Survival* (Gainesville: University Press of Florida, 1995), 36.

25. Deborah R. Weiner, *Coalfield Jews: An Appalachian History* (Urbana: University of Illinois Press, 2006), 75.

26. *TJ*, "Two New Clothing Shops to Replace Bankrupt Plants," April 24, 1940; *TJ*, "Sydney Levin, 76, Dies; Clothing Firm Founder," July 17, 1984.

27. William Kahane, interview by Sandra Stewart Holyoak, Shaun Illingworth and Gino Namur, March 5, 2007, Rutgers Oral History Archives, https://oralhistory.rutgers.edu/images/PDFs/kahane_william.pdf.

28. Helen Waiman Rasner, interview by the author, August 17, 2020.

29. *Jewish Farmer*, "How Far Is Korea?," August 1950.

30. *Jewish Farmer*, "Egg and Poultry Outlook," April 1951.

31. *TJ*, "Dr. Goldhaft Plans $100,000 Expansion of His Laboratories," March 23, 1951.

32. *TJ*, "Goldhaft House is Modern Yet Easy to Maintain," October 6, 1951.

CHAPTER 10   COMFORT ZONES

1. *Annual Report of the Managing Director, 1951* (New York: Jewish Agricultural Society, 1952), 11.

2. *Jewish Farmer*, "Look to Lower Egg Prices Next Year," October 1951.

3. Judith Jurysta Feinstein, "To Be the Daughter of Holocaust Survivors (and Chicken Farmers): The Beginning in America," *Medium*, April 15, 2015, https://medium.com /@roberTJordan33/to-be-the-daughter-of-holocaust-survivors-and-chicken-farmers -the-beginning-in-america-72d71fae8d6a.

4. Joseph Berger, *Displaced Persons: Growing Up in America after the Holocaust* (New York: Scribner, 2001), 81, 171.

5. Berger, *Displaced Persons*, 98, 102.

6. Berger, *Displaced Persons*, 83.

7. Berger, *Displaced Persons*, 175.

8. Ronald Becker, email message to the author, December 13, 2021.

9. Kenneth T. Jackson, *Crabgrass Frontier: The Suburbanization of the United States* (New York: Oxford University Press, 1985), 234–235.

10. Jackson, *Crabgrass Frontier*, 240.

11. Jackson, *Crabgrass Frontier*, 239.

12. Françoise S. Ouzan, "New Roots for the Uprooted: Holocaust Survivors as Farmers in America," in *Holocaust Survivors: Resettlement, Memories, Identities*, ed. Dalia Ofer, Françoise S. Ouzan, and Judy Tydor Baumel-Schwartz (New York: Berghahn Books, 2012), 252.

13. *DJ*, "Rosa Lederman, 75," February 3, 1995. They moved: *DJ*, "Herz Lederman, 86," February 12, 2001; *TJ*, "Landis Issues 97 Bldg. Permits," May 16, 1951.

14. Leah Lederman, interview by the author, May 4, 2014.

15. Sally Hyman Birnbaum, interview by Max Pearl, August 10, 1995, interview 4036, Visual History Archive, USC Shoah Foundation (hereafter cited as VHA, USC Shoah).

16. Paul Kresh, *Isaac Bashevis Singer, the Magician of West 86th Street* (New York: Dial Press, 1979), 75.

17. Isaac Bashevis Singer, *In My Father's Court* (New York: Farrar, Straus and Giroux, 1966), 269.

18. Bashevis Singer, *In My Father's Court*, 275.

19. Sally Hyman Birnbaum, interview by Max Pearl, August 10, 1995, interview code 4036, VHA, USC Shoah.

20. Arnold Hyman, interview by the author, December 22, 2013.

21. Hyman interview.

22. Sally Hyman Birnbaum, interview by the author, August 25, 2006.

23. Hyman Birnbaum interview.

24. Arlene Stein, *Reluctant Witnesses: Survivors, Their Children, and the Rise of Holocaust Consciousness* (New York: Oxford University Press, 2014), 54.

CHAPTER 11   COMMUNITY BUILDING

1. Ruth Weinstein, *Back to the Land: Alliance Colony to the Ozarks in Four Generations* (Galloway, NJ: South Jersey Culture & History Center Regional Press, 2020), 149.

2. Bluma Bayuk Rappoport Purmell, *A Farmer's Daughter: Bluma* (Los Angeles: Hayvenhurst Publishers, 1981), 93.

3. Bennett Bardfeld, "Oh, to Swim at Alliance Beach," *DJ*, August 15, 2002.

4. *TJ*, advertisement, July 28, 1945; *TJ*, "Annual Beach Picnic for Sunday, July 16," June 22, 1961; Louis Goldman, interview by the author, May 18, 2006.

5. *Jewish Farmer*, "South Jersey Jewish Settlers Meet," September 1949.

6. *TJ*, "South Jersey Jewish Farmers Hold Annual Summer Meet at Alliance Beach Party," September 1, 1950.

7. *Jewish Farmer*, "Jersey Settlers Foregather at Regional Meets," September 1950.

8. Michael R. Weisser, *A Brotherhood of Memory: Jewish Landsmanshaftn in the New World* (New York: Basic Books, 1985), 4–5.

9. William B. Helmreich, *Against All Odds: Holocaust Survivors and the Successful Lives They Made in America* (New York: Simon & Schuster, 1992), 152.

10. *TJ*, "Poultrymen's Club to Hear Lecturer," November 17, 1950.

11. Julia Klein, "The Long Journey into the Light on Jersey Farmlands," *Philadelphia Inquirer*, August 12, 1979.

12. Survivor farmers in Farmingdale, NJ, similarly formed the New Americans Club. Gertrude Wishnick Dubrovsky, *The Land Was Theirs: Jewish Farmers in the Garden State* (Tuscaloosa: University of Alabama Press, 1992), 83.

13. *Jewish Farmer*, "Recent Jewish Settlers Form Club," March 1950, 30; *TJ*, "Jewish Farmers Club Plans Entertainment; To Aid New Growers," March 7, 1950.

14. *Jewish Criterion* (Pittsburgh), "Famous European Jewish Troupe to Appear Here Soon," April 2, 1948.

15. "Kulis," Stonehill Jewish Song Archive, Center for Traditional Music and Dance, https://stonehilljewishsongs.wordpress.com/2018/04/18/0146-coolies/.

16. "S'iz avek der nekhtn," Stonehill Jewish Song Archive, Center for Traditional Music and Dance, https://stonehilljewishsongs.wordpress.com/2018/04/17/0079-siz-avek -der-nekhtn-yesterday-is-gone/.

17. *Jewish Farmer*, "Recent Jewish Settlers Form Club," March 1950.

18. *Jewish Farmer*, "Allegiance to Triangular Basis of Americanism," March 1950.

19. *TJ*, "Jewish Farmers Club Plans Entertainment; To Aid New Growers," March 7, 1950.

20. *Jewish Farmer*, "Recent Jewish Settlers Form Club," March 1950.

21. *TJ*, "Benjamin Stone, JAS Farm Editor Dies in New York," March 13, 1953.

22. *Jewish Farmer*, "Recent Jewish Settlers Form Club," March 1950.

23. *Jewish Farmer*, "Farmers Collect Chickens for Israel Children," August 1951.

24. *TJ*, "Goal of $100,000 Set for '50 Allied Jewish Appeal Drive in Greater Vineland," September 19, 1950.

25. Marvin Smith, "Many in Vineland Lived Tragedies Brought by War," *TJ*, September 1, 1959.

26. Miles Lerman, interview by Joan Ringelheim, July 17, 2001, RG-50.030.0413, Jeff and Toby Herr Oral History Archive, U.S. Holocaust Memorial Museum, Washington, DC.

27. *TJ*, "Memorial Services Attended by 200," May 22, 1951.

28. *TJ*, "Chickens Have Long Ride," August 3, 1951.

29. *TJ*, "Poultrymen Hear Newcastle Review; Install Officers," February 6, 1953; latest incarnation: *TJ*, "New Organization Founded to Help Jewish Farmers," August 28, 1951.

30. David Bridger, ed., *The New Jewish Encyclopedia* (West Orange, NJ: Behrman House, 1976), 143.

31. David Slucki, "A Community of Suffering: Jewish Holocaust Survivor Networks in Postwar America," *Jewish Social Studies* 22, no. 2 (2017): 121.

32. *TJ*, "Tables Turned," May 14, 1956.

33. "Shmerke Kaczerginski and the Recordings for the Jewish Historical Commission," Yad Vashem, https://www.yadvashem.org/yv/en/exhibitions/music/postwar.asp.

34. *TJ*, "Former Resistance Fighter in Poland During Occupation of Nazis is Farband Speaker," February 20, 1953.

35. Michael Kirschenbaum, *Not to Believe: From Auschwitz to a New Jersey Chicken Farm* (United States: Gotham Street Books, 2014), 22–23.

36. David Nasaw, *The Last Million: Europe's Displaced Persons from World War to Cold War* (New York: Penguin, 2020), 415.

37. Harry Furman, interview by the author, March 14, 2015.

38. *TJ*, "Vineland to Be 'Bombed' on Feb. 26 in Test of City's Civil Defense Personnel," February 20, 1953.

39. Phillip R. Naftaly, "Jewish Chicken Farmers in the Egg Basket of the World: The Creation of Cultural Identity in Petaluma, California, 1904–1954" (PhD diss., New School for Social Research, 1999), 131.

40. *TJ*, "Howell Gets 236-Vote Plurality over Case in Vineland; Rest of GOP Ticket Supported," November 3, 1954.

41. Kenneth L. Kann, *Comrades and Chicken Ranchers: The Story of a California Jewish Community* (Ithaca, NY: Cornell University Press, 1993), 59.

42. Kann, *Comrades and Chicken Ranchers*, 202.

43. Dubrovsky, *Land Was Theirs*, 155.

44. Associated Press, "Rutgers Prof. Suspected of Red Ties May Resign," *TJ*, August 31, 1953.

45. *TJ*, "Farband Purim Fete Draws Large Audience at Center," March 3, 1953.

CHAPTER 12   NEW CONNECTIONS

1. *TJ*, "Over 300 Attend Farband Benefit," April 10, 1953.

2. Michael E. McCullough, "White Sparrow Inn Razed, But Memories Still Intact," *Press of Atlantic City*, October 2, 1988.

3. *TJ*, "Farband Passover Ball to Aid Israeli Agricultural School," April 3, 1953.

4. Miles Lerman, interview by Joan Ringelheim, July 17, 2001, RG-50.030.0413, Jeff and Toby Herr Oral History Archive, U.S. Holocaust Memorial Museum, Washington, DC (hereafter cited as Herr Archive, USHMM).

5. *TJ*, "43 Residents of Vineland Join U.S. Citizenship Ranks," April 30, 1953.

6. *TJ*, "Jewish Agricultural Society Opens South Jersey Office in Vineland with Liph as Head," July 25, 1952.

7. Minutes of the Board of Directors of the Jewish Agricultural Society Board Meeting, November 13, 1951, box 74, Records of the Baron de Hirsch Fund, Center for Jewish History, New York.

8. *Jewish Farmer*, "An Important Announcement," August 1953.

9. Samson Liph, "Jewish Agricultural Society Provides Aid to Settle Newcomers in Farm Community," *TJ*, February 26, 1954.

10. *Jewish Farmer*, "Jewish Poultry Farmers Association of S. Jersey," June 1953.

11. *TJ*, "Children Acquiring Gymnastic Skill Under Direction of Expert Teacher," August 27, 1953.

12. *Press of Atlantic City*, January 6, 1955, "Judge Awaits Europe Facts for Decision," 2. Farmers in Farmingdale, NJ, created a similar dispute resolution committee. Gertrude Wishnick Dubrovsky, *The Land Was Theirs: Jewish Farmers in the Garden State* (Tuscaloosa: University of Alabama Press, 1992), 149–150.

13. *TJ*, "Jewish Poultrymen's Mutual Aid Society Ready to Function," November 13, 1953.

14. *TJ*, "2 Vineland Groups Seek Hosts for City Children," June 2, 1954.

15. David Slucki, "A Community of Suffering: Jewish Holocaust Survivor Networks in Postwar America," *Jewish Social Studies* 22, no. 2 (2017): 116–145.

16. *TJ*, "Survivors of Prison Camp Now Enjoying Two Weeks of Fun as Guests in Vineland," July 20, 1953.

17. *Little Review* (Warsaw, Poland), "Musia the Dancer," October 21, 1927, https://labiennale.art.pl/wp-content/uploads/2017/02/4-MP-1308-1927-ENG.pdf.

18. *TJ*, "Former Ballerina Makes Children Happy" July 28, 1953, 4.

19. L. Korisky, "Musia (Miriaml) Dajches: A Short Biography," in *Miriam Dajches: 22.2.1921-27.8.1980* (Tel Aviv: Committee for the Perpetuation of the Memory of the Late Musia Dajches, 1983), 125–126, Center for Jewish History, New York.

20. Ely Swerdlin, interview by the author, July 21, 2020.

21. *TJ*, "Former Ballerina Makes Children Happy," July 28, 1953.

22. Swerdlin interview.

23. *TJ*, "Former Ballerina Makes Children Happy," July 28, 1953.

24. Ruth Deiches, interview by the author, August 14, 2015.

25. *TJ*, "New Poultryman Took to Vineland after Visit Here," July 24, 1953.

26. *TJ*, "Citizenship Papers Awarded to Five Vineland Residents," July 25, 1953.

27. *TJ*, "Survivors of Prison Camp Now Enjoying Two Weeks of Fun as Guests in Vineland," July 20, 1953.

28. *TJ*, "Cornerstone Laid for Synagogue in Dorothy," September 10, 1951.

29. *New York Times*, "Jewish Farmers Continue Upswing," June 26, 1953.

30. *NYT*, "Settlers on the Land," editorial, June 16, 1956, 18.

31. Sol Finkelstein, interview, July 17, 2003, transcript, Oral Histories: Egg Basket of the Nation, Jewish Federation of Cumberland County (NJ) (hereafter cited as Egg Basket oral histories, JFCC).

32. *TJ*, advertisement, October 10, 1958.

33. Arlene Stein, *Reluctant Witnesses: Survivors, Their Children and the Rise of Holocaust Consciousness* (New York: Oxford University Press, 2014), 34.

34. Nella Glick interview, July 16, 2003, transcript, Egg Basket oral histories, JFCC.

35. Saul Golubcow, email message to the author, July 22, 2016.

36. *TJ*, "Seven-Foot Cross Set Ablaze on Lawn in South Vineland," January 8, 1951.

37. Ben Leuchter, "Keeping Up with the Times," *TJ*, January 8, 1951.

38. Ben Leuchter, "Keeping Up with the Times," *TJ*, January 18, 1960.

39. *DJ*, "Magda Leuchter," October 15, 2014.

40. Janet Leuchter, interview by the author, July 16, 2015.

41. Miles Lerman, Eulogy for Ben Leuchter, January 21, 2001, Coconut Grove, FL (in the author's possession).

42. Janet Leuchter, interview by the author, July 16, 2015.

43. *Wisconsin State Journal* (Madison), "United Jewish Student Appeal Sets Its UW Goal at $10,000," April 3, 1949.

44. Rosalie L. Lerman, interview by Joan Ringelheim, December 1, 1998, RG-50.030.0396, Herr Archive, USHMM.

45. Joseph Brandes, *Immigrants to Freedom: Jewish Communities in Rural New Jersey since 1882* (Philadelphia: Jewish Publication Society of America, 1971), 338.

46. Arthur D. Goldhaft, *The Golden Egg* (New York: Horizon Press, 1957), 275.

47. *TJ*, "Gittone, Ritter, Stanger Hail New State of Israel at Public Celebration in Reber School," May 17, 1948.

48. *TJ*, "50,000 See Colorful Halloween Parade of Floats, Bands, Beauties," October 30, 1948.

49. *TJ*, "Israel's Land Settlement Plan Outlined by Agency Official," December 15, 1950.

50. *Jewish Farmer*, "Poultry Farmers Association Meeting in Vineland, N.J.," July 1954.

51. *TJ*, "Middle-Income Americans Training in Vineland for Farm Pioneering in Israel," December 1, 1949. The Halutzim movement had its origins in prewar Europe. The Hehalutz Organization of America operated training farms in Cream Ridge and Hightstown, NJ, and other sites in the United States and Canada in the late 1930s and 1940s. Isaac Landman, ed., *Universal Jewish Encyclopedia*, vol. 5 (New York: Universal Jewish Encyclopedia, 1941), 188–190; Jewish Telegraphic Agency, "Forty Members of American Hechalutz Sail for Palestine; Will Settle in Colonies," June 10, 1946.

52. *TJ*, "First Hechalutz Unit to Leave Vineland for Israel May 30," May 23, 1950.

53. *TJ*, "Hashavim Training Farm Dedicated to Father of Novelist," December 12, 1949; *Jewish Weekly Times* (Boston), "New Colony to Represent U.S. in Israel," May 25, 1950; *TJ*, "Hashavim Group to Sail, May 30 to Aid Israel," May 19, 1950.

54. Stan Slome, Israeli Farm Officials Visiting Here View War with Egypt as Unlikely," *TJ*, October 20, 1955; Jewish Telegraphic Agency, "All-American Cooperative Settlement to Be Established in Israel," September 5, 1951; Yaacov Morris, *On the Soil of Israel: The Story of Americans and Canadians in Agriculture* (Tel Aviv: Association of Americans and Canadians in Israel, 1965), 187.

55. Moshe Schwartz, "The Rise and Decline of the Israeli Moshav Cooperative: A Historical Overview," *Journal of Rural Cooperation* 27, no. 2 (1999): 133.

56. Schwartz, "Rise and Decline of the Israeli Moshav Cooperative," 136–137.

57. *Jewish Floridian*, "U.S. Farmers Nucleus for Start of Village, Orot, in Pioneers' Area," May 2, 1958.

58. Kenneth L. Kann, *Comrades and Chicken Ranchers: The Story of a California Jewish Community* (Ithaca, NY: Cornell University Press, 1993), 25.

59. Miles Lerman, July 17, 2001 interview, Herr Archive, USHMM.

60. Joyce Vanaman, "He Saved the Last Bullet for Himself," *Press of Atlantic City*, February 18, 1979.

61. Jonathan Dekel-Chen, interview by the author, September 1, 2021.

62. Rosalie L. Lerman, interview by William B. Helmreich, January 12, 1990, RG-50.165.0064, Herr Archive, USHMM.

63. *TJ*, "Hit Israeli Film to Be Shown at Grand Theatre," June 9, 1956.

64. *Jewish Farmer*, "Jewish Farmers Send Youth Representatives to Israel," July 1956.

65. *TJ*, "Crowd of 700 at Rally for Israel Asks U.S. State Dept. to Change Policies," February 23, 1956.

66. *TJ*, "Israel Honors Miles Lerman for Bond Sales Leadership," June 11, 1973.

67. Goldie Finkelstein, interview by Effie Mayerfeld, August 19, 1996, interview 18729, Visual History Archive, USC Shoah Foundation.

68. Chris Lerman, January 12, 1990 interview, Herr Archive, USHMM.

69. Lerman interview.

CHAPTER 13   FAMILY AND FRIENDS

1. Harriet Berneman, interview by the author, August 23, 2021.

2. Arlene Kurtis and Jona Lerman, *The Stone Pillow: The Life and Times of Jona Lerman* (West Palm Beach, FL: LDH Communications, 1999), 166.

3. Rosalie L. Lerman, interview by Joan Ringelheim, December 1, 1998, RG-50.030.0396, Jeff and Toby Herr Oral History Archive (hereafter cited as Herr Archive, USHMM), U.S. Holocaust Memorial Museum, Washington, DC.

4. Joe Finkelstein, interview by the author, March 15, 2015.

5. Ann Netzman, interview by Gertrude Kartzmer, March 4, 1996, interview 12839, Visual History Archive, USC Shoah Foundation (hereafter cited as VHA, USC Shoah).

6. Ann Netzman interview.

7. Tamara Netzman, interview by the author, June 6, 2006.

8. Tamara Netzman, interview by the author, January 26, 2005.

9. Tamara Netzman, email message to the author, March 14, 2007.

10. Toni Rinde, interview by Carolyn Ellis, October 7, 2010, University of South Florida Holocaust Survivors Oral History Project (hereafter cited as USF OHP), https:// digital.lib.usf.edu/SFS0022008/00001.

11. Stanley Igel interview by Alan Petigny, July 12, 1993, Samuel Proctor Oral History Program, University of Florida Digital Collections, http://ufdc.ufl.edu/UF00006677 /00001.

12. Rinde, October 7, 2010 interview, USF OHP.

13. Rinde interview.

14. Judy Garnatz, "Holocaust Survivor Recalls Life under Nazis' Jackboot," *Evening Independent* (St. Petersburg, FL), April 9, 1985.

15. "Agriculturalists," May 14, 1947, INS Ref. Number 52,219/71, *Subject Index to Correspondence and Case Files of the Immigration and Naturalization Service, 1903–1952*, NARA microfilm publication T458, 31 rolls, Records of the Immigration and Naturalization Service, Record Group 85. National Archives, Washington, DC.

16. Hasia Diner, interview by the author, September 14, 2021.

17. John M. Albora, "Former Polish Agriculturalist Now Poultry Producer Who Has Original Waterer for His Hens," *TJ*, September 5, 1952.

18. Stephen Igel, interview by the author, December 8, 2020.

19. Elizabeth Roth, interview, July 15, 2003, Oral Histories: Egg Basket of the Nation, Jewish Federation of Cumberland County (NJ).

20. Eva Neisser, "Chicken Farming: Not a Dream but a Nightmare," in *Between Sorrow and Strength: Women Refugees of the Nazi Period*, ed. Sibylle Quack (Cambridge: Cambridge University Press, 1995), 287.

21. Nathan Dunkelman, interview by the author, February 20, 2005.

22. Celina Rosenblum, interview by Joseph Preil, December 16, 1993, RG-50.002.0201, Herr Archive, USHMM.

23. Goldie Finkelstein, interview by Effie Mayerfeld, August 19, 1996, interview 18729, VHA, USC Shoah.

24. *TJ*, "Concentration Camp Survivor Addresses Newfield Kiwanis," October 24, 1951.

25. Shoshana Felman and Dori Laub, *Testimony: Crises of Witnessing in Literature, Psychoanalysis, and History* (New York: Routledge, 1992), 67.

26. Aaron Hass, *The Aftermath: Living with the Holocaust* (New York: Oxford University Press, 1995), 72.

27. Henry Greenspan, Sara R. Horowitz, et al., "Engaging Survivors: Assessing 'Testimony' and 'Trauma' as Foundational Concepts," *Dapim: Studies on the Holocaust* 28, no. 3 (2014): 218.

28. Greenspan et al., "Engaging Survivors," 219.

29. Richard L. Rashke, *Escape from Sobibor* (New York: Houghton Mifflin, 1982), 320.

30. Irving Raab, interview by Janie Brown, November 23, 1997, interview 35757, VHA, USC Shoah.

31. Associated Press, "Kills 1,000,000 Jews; Draws Death Penalty," *Dayton (OH) Daily News,* May 9, 1950.

32. *Kingsport (TN) News,* "'Gas Master' on Trial," May 15, 1950.

33. Bauer's death sentence was later commuted to life in prison.

34. Michael S. Bryant, *Eyewitness to Genocide: The Operation Reinhard Death Camp Trials, 1955–1966* (Knoxville: University of Tennessee Press, 2014), 179.

35. Bryant, *Eyewitness to Genocide,* 180.

36. Bryant, *Eyewitness to Genocide,* 178.

37. Dominick LaCapra, *History and Memory After Auschwitz* (Ithaca, NY: Cornell University Press, 1998), 11.

38. LaCapra, *History and Memory,* 182.

39. Associated Press, "Nazi Hunters Question Holocaust Survivor," *DJ,* August 25, 1993.

40. Robert D. McFadden, "John Demjanjuk, 91, Dogged by Charges of Atrocities as Nazi Camp Guard, Dies," *New York Times,* March 17, 2012.

41. Jewish Telegraphic Agency, "Wiesenthal Center Questions Statement by Survivor Placing Demjanjuk at Camp," August 26, 1993.

42. Associated Press, "Nazi Hunters Question Holocaust Survivor," *DJ,* August 25, 1993.

43. Maureen Fitzgerald, "Children Touched a Scarred Soul," *Philadelphia Inquirer,* March 10, 2000.

CHAPTER 14   DOWNTURN

1. *TJ,* "2,000 Enjoy Eggs for Breakfast as Visitors Jam City for Festival," June 19, 1954.

2. *TJ,* "Poultry & Egg Festival Highlights & Program," June 18, 1954; *TJ,* "20,000 Visitors Expected Here Tomorrow for First Annual Poultry, Egg Festival," June 18, 1954.

3. *TJ,* "Poultry Festival Attracts 15,000; Queen Is Chosen," June 21, 1954.

4. *TJ,* "Egg Prices Decline Sharply in March," April 9, 1954; *TJ,* "Cutback in Profit Seen for Poultry," April 9, 1954.

5. *Jewish Farmer,* "Poultry Farmers Association Meeting in Vineland, N. J.," July 1954.

6. *TJ,* "Poultryman Ends His Life, 3rd in 10 Days," July 19, 1954.

7. *TJ,* "Recent Purchaser of Poultry Farm Takes His Own Life," July 9, 1954.

8. *TJ,* "450 Egg Producers Meet to Seek Relief From Market Slump," July 9, 1954.

9. Ben Leuchter, "Keeping Up with the Times," *TJ,* July 16, 1954.

10. *TJ,* "Poultry Farmer Hanging Victim, Found by Agent," July 12, 1954; *TJ,* "Gun Blast Kills Poultryman; Brooded over Wife's Death," August 16, 1954, 1; *TJ,* "Poultryman's Wife Ends Life by Hanging," June 17, 1954.

11. *TJ,* "Jewish Poultrymen Stress Unity in Hard-Hit Industry," July 23, 1954.

12. Beth B. Cohen, *Case Closed: Holocaust Survivors in Postwar America* (New Brunswick, NJ: Rutgers University Press, 2007), 154.

13. Morris Freedman, "The New Farmers of Lakewood; A Jewish Community on the American Soil," *Commentary*, September 1950.

14. *TJ*, "Rabbi Douglas To Begin Series on Psychiatry," January 2, 1957.

15. Aaron Hass, *The Aftermath: Living with the Holocaust* (New York: Cambridge University Press, 1995), 80.

16. *TJ*, "Samson Liph Dies; Retired as JAS Official Last Year," April 30, 1956.

17. Samson Liph, *TJ*, "Jewish Agricultural Society Provides Aid to Settle Newcomers in Farm Community," February 26, 1954; *TJ*, "Jewish Agriculture Society Enlarges S. Jersey Service; Liph Is First Area Manager," January 23, 1953.

18. *TJ*, "Report of Committee Meeting of the Greater Vineland Poultry Council and Allied Industry," August 3, 1954.

19. *TJ*, "Poultrymen Unite in Drive to Relieve Price Squeeze," July 23, 1954.

20. *TJ*, "Jewish Poultrymen Stress Unity in Hard-Hit Industry," July 23, 1954.

CHAPTER 15   RURAL CHILDHOODS

1. Joseph Berger, *Displaced Persons: Growing Up in America After the Holocaust* (New York: Scribner, 2001), 92–93.

2. Cecily Sturges, "Freedom in Life on Poultry Farm Appreciated by Youthful Visitors," *TJ*, July 13, 1954, 5.

3. Ruby Trauner, "Working Class Words on Tenements and Gardens," *Bridges: A Journal for Jewish Feminists and Our Friends* 5, no. 2 (1995): 56–67.

4. Bernard Trossman, "Adolescent Children of Concentration Camp Survivors," *Canadian Psychiatric Association Journal* 13, no. 2 (1968): 121–123.

5. Helen Waiman Rasner, interview by the author, October 16, 2015.

6. *TJ*, "Aged Recluse Dies of Burns From Grass Fire," March 12, 1956.

7. Aron Swerdlin, interview by the author, July 19, 2020. Recollections of idyllic rural life by survivors' children in south Jersey echoes Michael Hoberman's description of an early account of small-town Jewish life by Joseph Leiser in his 1909 novel *Canaway and the Lustigs*. Michael Hoberman, *A Hundred Acres of America: The Geography of Jewish American Literary History* (New Brunswick, NJ: Rutgers University Press, 2019), 67.

8. Leah Lederman, interview by the author, May 4, 2014.

9. *Life*, advertisement, August 19, 1957.

10. Robert M. Prince, *The Legacy of the Holocaust: Psychohistorical Themes in the Second Generation* (New York: Other Press, 1999), 5. Fixation on food also manifested in the form of eating disorders. Aaron Hass, *In the Shadow of the Holocaust: The Second Generation* (New York: Cambridge University Press, 1996), 61.

11. Joe Finkelstein, interview by the author, March 15, 2015.

12. *TJ*, "Award Given for First Time Here," February 9, 1952.

13. Helen Epstein, *Children of the Holocaust: Conversations with Sons and Daughters of Survivors* (New York: G.P. Putnam's Sons, 1979), 51.

14. Saul Golubcow, interview by the author, September 1, 2016.

15. Zella Shabasson, interview by the author, December 16, 2013.

16. Helen Waiman Rasner, interview by the author, October 16, 2015.

17. Phyllis Fox, interview by the author, August 21, 2020.

18. *TJ*, "Drama Features Richland School Yule Program," December 28, 1953.

19. *TJ*, "Fifty Parents Attend Milmay School Program," December 30, 1958.

20. Dorothy Goldberg, interview by the author, March 1, 2020.

21. Lee Feinberg, interview by the author, October 28, 2013.

22. Sam Feigenbaum, interview by the author, May 3, 2014.

23. *TJ*, "Jewish School to Open September 8 at Almond Road," September 4, 1953.

24. Joe Finkelstein, interview by the author, March 15, 2015.

25. Finkelstein interview.

26. Saul Golubcow, interview by the author, September 1, 2016.

27. Epstein, *Children of the Holocaust*, 97.

28. Saul Golubcow, interview by the author, August 3, 2020.

29. David Lerman, interview by the author, March 15, 2015.

30. Ely Swerdlin, interview by the author, July 21, 2020.

31. Phyllis Dunkelman, interview by the author, September 1, 2020.

32. Holli Levitsky, "The Holocaust, the Catskills, and the Creative Power of Loss," in *Summer Haven: The Catskills, the Holocaust, and the Literary Imagination*, ed. Holli Levitsky and Phil Brown (Boston: Academic Studies Press, 2015), 55.

33. Jake Ehrenreich, "The Catskills (or What Was, Was and Is No More) from *A Jew Grows in Brooklyn*," in Levitsky and Brown, *Summer Haven*, 267, 269.

34. Louis Goldman, interview by the interview, May 18, 2006.

35. Eli Kuhnreich, interview by the author, May 22, 2020; Ruth Fajerman Hoffman, interview by the author, May 9, 2013.

36. Ruth Weinstein, *Back to the Land: Alliance Colony to the Ozarks in Four Generations* (Galloway, NJ: South Jersey Culture & History Center Regional Press, 2020), 155–156.

CHAPTER 16   HURRICANES

1. *TJ*, "Damage in Millions as Hazel Roars into Vineland; Roofs Off, Coops Demolished, Power Interrupted," October 16, 1954.

2. Helen Waiman Rasner, interview by the author, October 16, 2015.

3. Minutes of the Board of Directors of the Jewish Agricultural Society Board Meeting, October 26, 1954, box 75, Records of the Baron de Hirsch Fund, Center for Jewish History, New York.

4. *TJ*, "Four Fire Hydrants Opened by City to Provide Water for Parched Poultry Flocks," October 16, 1954.

5. *TJ*, "Over 60,000 Birds Housed in Area by Volunteer Crews," October 22, 1954.

6. *TJ*, "Over 60,000 Birds."

7. *Jewish Farmer*, "Vineland Farmers Celebrate Annual Get-Together," December 1954.

8. Burr Van Atta, "Harry Adler, 81, Retired County Judge in N.J.," *Philadelphia Inquirer*, May 30, 1986.

9. Miles Lerman and Milton Buki to Conference on Jewish Material Claims Against Germany, November 22, 1954, Records of the Geneva Office of the American Jewish Joint Distribution Committee, 1955–1964, Georgette Bennett and Leonard Polonsky Digitized JDC Text Archive (hereafter cited as Geneva Collection, JDC Digitized Archive), http://search.archives.jdc.org/multimedia/Documents/Geneva45-54/G45-54_ORG/G45-54_ORG_010/G45-54_ORG_010_0232.pdf#search=.

10. Saul Kagan to Moses W. Beckelman, January 11, 1955, Geneva Collection, JDC Digitized Archive, https://search.archives.jdc.org/multimedia/Documents/Geneva55-64/G55-64_ORG/G55-64_ORG_031/G55-64_ORG_031_1003.pdf#search=.

11. Saul Kagan to Charles Jordan, November 26, 1954, Geneva Collection, JDC Digitized Archive, http://search.archives.jdc.org/multimedia/Documents/Geneva45-54/G45-54_ORG/G45-54_ORG_010/G45-54_ORG_010_0227.pdf#search=.

12. Letter to Hexter, February 7, 1955, Geneva Collection, JDC Digitized Archive, http://search.archives.jdc.org/multimedia/Documents/NY_AR55-64/NY55-64_ORG_061/NY55-64_ORG_061_0396.pdf#search=.

13. William Bein to Moses W. Beckelman, April 25, 1955, Geneva Collection, JDC Digitized Archive, http://search.archives.jdc.org/multimedia/Documents/Geneva55-64/G55-64_ORG/G55-64_ORG_031/G55-64_ORG_031_1001.pdf#search=.

14. TJ, "Sheriff's Sale," January 12, 1956.

15. TJ, "Good Neighbor Policy," July 20, 1956.

16. TJ, "J.P.F.A. to Seek Funds to Assist Needy Member," August 10, 1956.

17. Marvin Smith, "Good Neighborliness Helps Couple to Continue Farming," TJ, April 26, 1957.

18. TJ, "Lerman Urges Start of Promotion Drive for Vineland Eggs," January 7, 1955.

19. TJ, advertisement, February 11, 1955.

20. Samson Liph, "JAS Activities Stepped Up to Assist Farmers Overcome Hardships of 1954," TJ, March 18, 1955.

21. Theodore Norman to Moses A. Leavitt, June 10, 1955, Geneva Collection, JDC Digitized Archive, http://search.archives.jdc.org/multimedia/Documents/NY_AR55-64/NY55-64_ORG_061/NY55-64_ORG_061_0374.pdf#search=; Theodore Norman to Moses A. Leavitt, February 17, 1956, Geneva Collection, JDC Digitized Archive, http://search.archives.jdc.org/multimedia/Documents/NY_AR55-64/NY55-64_ORG_061/NY55-64_ORG_061_0349.pdf#search=.

22. TJ, "1952 to 1962: Vineland's Multi-Million Dollar Growth Decade! A supplement to Today's Vineland Times Journal," July 20, 1962.

23. Del Brandt, "'Round Our Town," TJ, March 31, 1954.

24. TJ, "Mayor to Give City's Greetings to New Firm," February 2, 1955.

25. TJ, "Industrial Commission Starts Task of Expanding Employment in Vineland," February 26, 1955.

26. American Jewish Outlook (Pittsburgh), advertisement, March 16, 1956. The advertisement ran the same day in Jewish newspapers in Boston, Detroit, Indianapolis, and northern New Jersey.

27. Marvin Smith, "Roof Sprinklers, Aluminum Paint Provide Cooler Quarters for Flock on Igel Farm," *TJ*, June 15, 1956.

28. Toni Rinde, interview by Carolyn Ellis, October 7, 2010, University of South Florida Holocaust Survivors Oral History Project, https://digital.lib.usf.edu/SFS0022008/00001.

29. Rinde interview.

30. Corrine Olson, "VHS Sophomore Tells of 5 Days Battling Floods in Pocono Summer Camp," *TJ*, August 24, 1955.

CHAPTER 17   COPING

1. Helen Waiman Rasner, interview by the author, August 17, 2020.

2. Christopher Browning, *Remembering Survival: Inside a Nazi Slave-Labor Camp* (New York: Norton, 2010), 4.

3. Browning, *Remembering Survival*, 224.

4. Browning, *Remembering Survival*, 240.

5. Browning, *Remembering Survival*, 260.

6. Helen Waiman Rasner, interview by the author, August 17, 2020.

7. Ruth Deiches, interview by the author, August 14, 2015.

8. Aaron Hass, *In the Shadow of the Holocaust: The Second Generation* (New York: Cambridge University Press, 1996), 72.

9. Rosalie L. Lerman, interview by William B. Helmreich, January 12, 1990, RG-50.165.0064, Jeff and Toby Herr Oral History Archive (hereafter cited as Herr Archive, USHMM), U.S. Holocaust Memorial Museum, Washington, DC.

10. David Lerman, interview by the author, March 15, 2015.

11. Hasia R. Diner, *We Remember with Reverence and Love: American Jews and the Myth of Silence after the Holocaust, 1945–1962* (New York: New York University Press, 2009), 22.

12. Jacob M. Maze, "Farming by Jews in New Jersey: A Historical Review," in *Annual Report of the General Manager 1952* (New York: Jewish Agricultural Society, 1953), 26.

13. Arlene Stein, *Reluctant Witnesses: Survivors, Their Children, and the Rise of Holocaust Consciousness* (New York: Oxford University Press, 2014), 56.

14. Saul Golubcow, interview by the author, September 1, 2016.

15. David Lerman, interview by the author, January 6, 2015.

16. Sally Hyman Birnbaum, interview by the author, August 25, 2006.

17. Zella Shabasson, interview by the author, December 16, 2013.

18. Marjie Low Brown, interview by the author, August 16, 2020.

19. Thom Shanker, "Robert Kempner, 93: Prosecuted Nazis," *Chicago Tribune*, August 18, 1993.

20. Eric Pace, "Robert Kempner, 93, a Prosecutor at Nuremberg," *New York Times*, August 17, 1993.

21. *TJ*, "Poultry Club to Hear War Crimes Counsel," June 22, 1956.

22. *TJ*, "New German Law Hikes Benefits to Nazi Victims," July 2, 1956.

23. Martin S. Bergmann and Milton E. Jucovy, eds., *Generations of the Holocaust* (New York: Columbia University Press, 1990), 64.

24. Regina L. Gelb, interview by Susan Williams, July 7, 1992, RG-50.030.0078, Herr Archive, USHMM.

25. David Nasaw, *The Last Million: Europe's Displaced Persons from World War to Cold War* (New York: Penguin, 2020), 449.

26. Bergmann and Jacovy, *Generations of the Holocaust*, 70–71.

27. Marlene Cimons, "A Lie Haunts Holocaust Survivors," *Los Angeles Times*, June 15, 1980.

28. Ben Gallob, "Holocaust Survivors Who Lied about Their Age Can Now Get Federal Aid for Social Security," *JTA Daily News Bulletin*, August 20, 1981.

29. Joseph Berger, *Displaced Persons: Growing Up in America after the Holocaust* (New York: Scribner, 2001), 278–280. Berger similarly describes his mother's discomfort about revealing misstatements regarding their origins.

30. Sociologist Arlene Stein similarly describes how her father who fled to Soviet territory "fabricated" a story about surviving inside Poland in his reparations claim. Stein, *Reluctant Witnesses*, 71.

31. Stein, *Reluctant Witnesses*, 69.

32. Efrat Barel et al., "Surviving the Holocaust: A Meta-analysis of the Long-Term Sequelae of a Genocide," *Psychological Bulletin* 136, no. 5 (2010): 677–698.

33. Stein, *Reluctant Witnesses*, 6–7.

34. Cathy Caruth, ed., *Trauma: Explorations in Memory* (Baltimore: Johns Hopkins University Press, 1995), 3.

35. Judith Herman, *Trauma and Recovery: The Aftermath of Violence—From Domestic Abuse to Political Terror* (New York: Basic Books, 1992), 58.

36. Rosalie L. Lerman, interview by Joan Ringelheim, December 1, 1998, RG-50.030.0396, Herr Archive, USHMM.

37. James R. Hagerty, "Holocaust Survivor Rosalie Chris Lerman Sought neither Pity nor Revenge," *Wall Street Journal*, May 27, 2016.

38. Rosalie L. Lerman, January 12, 1990 interview, Herr Archive, USHMM.

39. Robert M. Prince, *The Legacy of the Holocaust: Psychohistorical Themes in the Second Generation* (New York: Other Press, 1999), 33.

40. Miles Lerman, interview by Joan Ringelheim, July 17, 2001, RG-50.030.0413, Herr Archive, USHMM.

41. Rosalie L. Lerman, interview by Joan Ringelheim, January 13, 1999, RG-50.030.0396, Herr Archive, USHMM.

42. Lerman interview.

CHAPTER 18   GRIEF AND FAITH

1. Andy Wallace, "Cowgirl Queen of the TV Screen for Countless Fans," *Philadelphia Inquirer*, January 28, 2013.

2. Israel W. Charny, *Holding on to Humanity: The Message of Holocaust Survivors: The Shamai Davidson Papers* (New York: New York University Press, 1992), 161.

3. David Slucki, "A Community of Suffering: Jewish Holocaust Survivor Networks in Postwar America," *Jewish Social Studies* 22, no. 2 (Winter 2017): 129; "immense impenetrable tragedy": Hasia R. Diner, *We Remember with Reverence and Love: American Jews and the Myth of Silence after the Holocaust, 1945–1962* (New York: New York University Press, 2009), 76.

4. Diner, *We Remember with Reverence and Love*, 12.

5. Janet Leuchter, interview by the author, July 26, 2015.

6. *TJ*, "Memorial Services Attended by 200," May 22, 1951; Diner, *We Remember with Reverence and Love*, 79–81.

7. *TJ*, "Large Crowd at Memorial Service for Jewish Martyrs; JNF Sponsors Tree-Planting," May 12, 1952.

8. *TJ*, "Farband Members Commemorate Warsaw Uprising," April 24, 1953; *TJ*, "Vineland JNF Plans Memorial for Martyrs," May 1, 1953.

9. Annette Greenblatt, interview by Shaun Illingworth and Stephanie Katz, October 6, 1999, Rutgers Oral History Archives,https://oralhistory.rutgers.edu/images/PDFs/greenblatt_annette.pdf.

10. *TJ*, "Jewish Memorial Meeting Attracts 650 Here Sunday," May 19, 1954.

11. *TJ*, "600 Attend Rites in Vineland for Jewish Martyrs," May 31, 1955; Diner, *We Remember with Reverence and Love*, 72.

12. *TJ*, "Memorial Forest to Be Completed in Coming Years," May 31, 1956.

13. Diner, *We Remember with Reverence and Love*, 69–70.

14. *TJ*, "Noted Jewish Poet, Dramatists Feature of Memorial Service," May 14, 1956.

15. *Forverts*, "Wandering Stars," November 28, 1948.

16. Henry Sapoznik, *Klezmer! Jewish Music from Old World to Our World* (New York: Schirmer Trade Books, 2011), 258.

17. Y. Shmulevitch, *Tenth Anniversary Journal of the Jewish Poultry Farmers' Association of South Jersey* (Vineland, NJ: Jewish Poultry Farmers Association, 1962), U.S. Holocaust Memorial Museum Library and Archives, Washington, DC, 32.

18. Miriam Isaacs, interview by the author, April 19, 2006.

19. Joseph Brandes, *Immigrants to Freedom: Jewish Communities in Rural New Jersey since 1882* (Philadelphia: Jewish Publication Society of America, 1971), 331.

20. *TJ*, "Jewish Library to Be Dedicated Thursday Night," December 7, 1954.

21. Stan Slome, "Saturday Night Concert at VHS Continues Strong, Varied Cultural Program at JPFA," *TJ*, December 16, 1955.

22. William B. Helmreich, *Against All Odds: Holocaust Survivors and the Successful Lives They Made in America* (New York: Simon & Schuster, 1992), 160; I. Harry Levin, "Vineland—A Haven for Refugees," *Tenth Anniversary Journal of the JPFA*, 4.

23. Memorial Day was observed on May 30, regardless of what day of the week on which it fell, until after a 1968 federal law established the three-day holiday weekend.

24. Helen Waiman Rasner, interview by the author, August 17, 2020.

25. Del Brandt, "Round Our Town," *TJ*, June 1, 1956.

26. Leah Lederman, interview by the author, May 4, 2014.

27. *San Francisco Examiner*, "'Depression Palace' Built from Odds and Ends," May 9, 1937.

28. Patricia A. Martinelli, *The Fantastic Castle of Vineland: George Daynor and the Palace Depression* (Charleston, SC: History Press, 2012), 46.

29. *TJ*, "Horse Show Headliners," May 25, 1956.

30. Joel C. Leuchter, "'Shooting Mansields' and Their Riding In-Laws Move to South Main Road Ranch," *TJ*, July 12, 1951.

31. *TJ*, "Starr Attraction," May 28, 1956.

32. Ely Swerdlin, interview by the author, July 21, 2020.

33. Del Brandt, "Round Our Town," *TJ*, May 31, 1956.

34. *TJ*, "Tasnady Wins as Track Opener Attracts 5,000," April 4, 1955.

35. Vineland's oldest congregation, Ahavas Achim, also still operated on Plum Street.

36. Nella Juffe and Maryann McLoughlin, *Flowers of Ice, Cobwebs of Lace* (Margate, NJ: Comteq, 2012), 105.

37. Juffe and McLoughlin, *Flowers of Ice*, 89.

38. Barbara Werner Schwarz, interview by the author, September 1, 2015.

39. Mark Werner, interview by the author, September 2, 2015.

40. Susan (Dover) Rosen, interview by the author, August 17, 2020.

41. Seymour Wasserstrum, interview by the author, July 28, 2015.

42. Françoise S. Ouzan, "New Roots for the Uprooted: Holocaust Survivors as Farmers in America," in *Holocaust Survivors: Resettlement, Memories, Identities*, ed. Dalia Ofer et al. (New York: Berghahn, 2012), 250.

43. Zeev W. Mankowitz, *Life Between Memory and Hope: The Survivors of the Holocaust in Occupied Germany* (New York: Cambridge University Press, 2002), 1; Angelika Königseder and Juliane Wetzel, *Waiting for Hope: Jewish Displaced Persons in Post–World War II Germany* (Evanston, IL: Northwestern University Press, 2001), 3–4.

44. Diner, *We Remember with Reverence and Love*, 150.

45. Jacob M. Maze, "Farming by Jews in New Jersey: A Historical Review," in *Annual Report of the General Manager 1952* (New York: Jewish Agricultural Society, 1953), 26.

46. Ruth Tauber Pomerantz, interview by the author, August 25, 2021.

47. *TJ*, "Dream to Materialize When Synagogue Opens," August 25, 1956.

48. Many of the biographical details about Schock come from the writings of his daughter. Annette Keen, "God of All Creatures," *Jewish Magazine*, June 2009, http://www.jewishmag.com/134mag/neshmat/neshmat.htm; Annette Keen, "For the Sin I have Sinned," *Jewish Magazine*, September 2011, http://www.jewishmag.com/158mag/yom_kippur_story/yom_kippur_story.htm.

49. Elizabeth Fisher, "Parts of Old Synagogue Installed in New Chapel," *Bucks County (PA) Courier Times*, October 10, 2006.

50. Aron Swerdlin, interview by the author, July 19, 2020.

51. Aaron Hass, *The Aftermath: Living with the Holocaust* (New York: Cambridge University Press, 1995), 157.

52. Helmreich, *Against All Odds*, 209.

53. Stan Slome, "Chaim Lindenblatt, Survivor of Nazi Terror, Looks to Landisville Synagogue as No. 1 Goal," *TJ*, November 22, 1954.

54. *TJ*, "Vineland Jewish Day School Dedicated as 700 Watch," January 29, 1957.

55. Rivka Sobel, "Yisro," *Torah MiTzion*, 2012, http://www.shemayisrael.com/parsha /sobel/archives/yisro71.htm.

56. Saul Golubcow, interview by the author, August 3, 2020; Saul Golubcow, "Betting on Belief," *Voices of Conservative Judaism*, Winter 2009/2010.

57. *Annual Report of the General Manager 1955* (New York: Jewish Agricultural Society, 1956), 13; *Jewish Farmer*, "Large Number of Jewish DP's Have Settled on Farms," July 1956.

58. *New York Times*, "Jewish Refugees Take Up Farming," June 17, 1956; JAS had referenced the 10 percent figure in its annual report a year earlier, but it didn't get attention beyond the Jewish press. *American Jewish World* (Minneapolis), "10% of Post-war Jewish Immigrants Turned to Farming," February 4, 1955.

59. *NYT*, "Settlers on the Land," June 16, 1956.

60. Stan Slome, "Saturday Night Concert at VHS Continues Strong, Varied Cultural Program of JPFA," *TJ*, December 16, 1955.

61. William Helmreich, "Don't Look Back: Holocaust Survivors in the U.S.," *Jerusalem Letter* 123 (October 1, 1991).

62. Barry R. Chiswick, "The Postwar Economy of American Jews," *Studies in Contemporary Jewry* 8 (1992), reprinted in Jeffrey S. Gurock, ed., *American Jewish History*, vol. 4, *American Jewish Life, 1920–1990* (New York: Routledge, 1998), 215–233.

63. Salomon J. Flink, *The Economy of New Jersey: A Report Prepared for the Department of Conservation and Economic Development of the State of New Jersey* (New Brunswick, NJ: Rutgers University Press, 1958), 517.

64. Joan Rubinstein Barch, "Jewish Egg Farmers in New Jersey" (master's thesis, Northeastern Illinois University, 1977), 27.

65. Flink, *Economy of New Jersey*, 518–519.

CHAPTER 19   FEED MEN AND A RECORD-BREAKING HEN

1. *TJ*, "Alampi Urges More Emphasis on Improving Egg Marketing," December 21, 1956.

2. *TJ*, "Alampi Urges More Emphasis on Improving Egg Marketing," December 21, 1956.

3. *TJ*, "Explosion, Fire at Rubinoff Feed Mill Burns Twenty-Three," January 2, 1951.

4. Genia Kuhnreich, interview by the author, May 21, 2020.

5. Samuel Brandsdorfer, interview, July 16, 2003, transcript, Oral Histories: Egg Basket of the Nation, Jewish Federation of Cumberland County (NJ).

6. Hasia R. Diner, *Roads Taken: The Great Jewish Migrations to the New World and the Peddlers Who Forged the Way* (New Haven, CT: Yale University Press, 2015), 6.

7. Irving Raab with Carol Cunningham Suplee, *99 Years: The Remarkable Story of Irving Raab* (Columbus, OH: Gatekeeper Press, 2018), 280.

8. Ryna Alexander, interview by the author, August 31, 2015.

9. William Kahane, interview by Sandra Stewart Holyoak, Shaun Illingworth, and Gino Namur, March 5, 2007, Rutgers Oral History Archives, https://oralhistory.rutgers.edu/images/PDFs/kahane_william.pdf.

10. Raab, *99 Years*, 280.

11. Morton L. Gordon, "The History of the Jewish Farmer in Eastern Connecticut" (DHL diss., Yeshiva University, 1974), 148.

12. Gordon, "History of the Jewish Farmer," 152.

13. Ben Leuchter, "Keeping Up with the Times," *TJ*, July 16, 1954.

14. Vineland Historical and Antiquarian Society, *Our First Fifty Years* (Vineland, NJ: Jacob Rubinoff, 1956).

15. *TJ*, advertisement, January 17, 1957.

16. "The Life of Tevis Goldhaft," in *Biographies of Professionals in Poultry Health* (American Association of Avian Pathologists, 1997), https://www.aaap.info/assets/documents/Bio%20-%20Goldhaft%20-%20Tevis.pdf.

17. *TJ*, advertisement, January 11, 1952.

18. *Courier-News* (Bridgewater, NJ), "Egged on by Scientists, Meg Busts Hens' Records," June 28, 1957.

19. *Central New Jersey Home News* (New Brunswick), "Meg's Daily Egg Record Now 256," July 17, 1957.

20. *New York Times*, "Hen Extends Egg Binge," May 30, 1957; *Central New Jersey Home News*, "Meg Lays Her Eggs at Record Rate, But She's No Comedienne," July 7, 1957.

21. Associated Press, "Champ Hen Egged On, Draws Goose Egg," *Courier-News*, August 15, 1957.

22. Associated Press, "Vineland Chick Still Clucking," *TJ*, September 23, 1957.

23. *Courier-News*, "Meg O'Day Still Scratches, This Time for Yearly Mark," September 18, 1957.

24. Lana Stern, interview by the author, August 12, 2020.

25. *TJ*, "Rubinoff Co. Launches Egg Promotion Campaign among N.Y. Foreign-Born," June 5, 1959.

26. Wayne Robinson, "Stuffed Chicken: The Hen Who Worked Her Tail Off Is Now in a Museum," *Philadelphia Evening Bulletin*, February 25, 1979.

CHAPTER 20   LABORERS

1. Idek Rosenblum, interview by Phyllis Stoleroff, December 18, 1997, interview code 37184, Visual History Archive, USC Shoah Foundation (hereafter cited as VHA, USC Shoah); Celina Rosenblum, interview by Phyllis Stoleroff, December 18, 1997, interview code 37191, VHA, USC Shoah.

2. *TJ*, "Poultryman Held in Murder of Roger Carletto," July 3, 1957.

3. Farmers used terms such as "bums" to describe the laborers. Leah Singer, interview, July 17, 2003, transcript, Oral Histories: Egg Basket of the Nation, Jewish Federation of Cumberland County (NJ) (hereafter cited as Egg Basket oral histories, JFCC).

4. Elizabeth Roth interview, July 15, 2003, transcript, Egg Basket oral histories, JFCC.

5. *TJ*, "Poultryman Attacked by Knife Wielding Laborer Loses Part of His Ear," July 17, 1954; Seymour Wasserstrum, interview by the author, July 28, 2015.

6. *TJ*, "Farmhand Arrested on Weapons Charge," September 9, 1955.

7. Diane Schilit, interview by the author, August 31, 2015.

8. Associated Press, "Agency Denies Hiring Criminals for Farms," *Trenton (NJ) Times*, August 25, 1960.

9. Leah Lederman, interview by the author, May 4, 2014.

10. *TJ*, "Farm Hand Held on Two Charges," August 18, 1955.

11. *TJ*, "Farm Worker Jailed on Disorderly Charge," November 17, 1954.

12. *TJ*, "Truck, Farm Hand Reported Missing," August 8, 1963.

13. *TJ*, "Poultryman Held in Murder of Roger Carletto," July 3, 1957.

14. *TJ*, "Poultryman Held in Murder."

15. Benjamin Kaplan, *The Eternal Stranger: A Study of Jewish Life in the Small Community* (New York: Bookman Associates, 1957), 158.

16. Ewa Morawska, *Insecure Prosperity: Small-Town Jews in Industrial America, 1890–1940* (Princeton, NJ: Princeton University Press, 1996), 216.

17. Aaron Hass, *The Aftermath: Living with the Holocaust* (New York: Cambridge University Press, 1996), 57.

18. Mark Werner, *Army Fatigues: Joining Israel's Army of International Volunteers* (Brooklyn, NY: Devora, 2008), xix.

19. Jan T. Gross, *Fear: Anti-Semitism in Poland after Auschwitz* (New York: Random House, 2006), 93.

20. Helen Waiman Rasner, interview by the author, October 16, 2015.

21. Celina Rosenblum, December 18, 1997, interview, VHA, USC Shoah.

22. Idek Rosenblum, December 18, 1997, interview, VHA, USC Shoah.

23. Idek Rosenblum interview.

24. Harry Rosenblum, interview by the author, August 30, 2015.

25. Tom Flynn, "Rosenblum Family Elated on Learning of His Release," *TJ*, July 8, 1957.

26. Flynn, "Rosenblum Family Elated."

27. *TJ*, "Joy Overcomes Rosenblums on His Release from Jail," July 9, 1957.

28. Ralph C. Squillace, "Aponte Confesses to Slaying of Roger Carletto," *TJ*, July 8, 1957.

29. *TJ*, "Joy Overcomes Rosenblums on His Release from Jail," July 9, 1957.

30. *TJ*, "Puerto Ricans in Area Express Horror at Slaying," July 9, 1957.

31. Isham B. Jones, *The Puerto Rican in New Jersey: His Present Status* (Newark, NJ: NJ State Department of Education, 1955), 9.

32. Joseph P. Fitzpatrick, *Puerto Rican Americans: The Meaning of Migration to the Mainland* (Englewood Cliffs, NJ: Prentice Hall, 1971), 17; Ismael García-Colón, *Colonial Migrants at the Heart of Empire: Puerto Rican Workers on U.S. Farms* (Oakland: University of California Press, 2020), 2.

33. García-Colón, *Colonial Migrants at the Heart of Empire*, 2.

34. Ismael García-Colón, interview by the author, June 21, 2021.

35. *TJ*, "First Puerto Rican Labor Arrives," April 14, 1962.

36. *TJ*, "Spanish Language A Must to Local Farmers Hiring Workers From Puerto Rico," October 13, 1951.

37. *TJ*, "Landis Ave. Merchant Sees Knowledge of Spanish as Way to Aid Puerto Ricans," September 20, 1952.

38. Jones, *Puerto Rican in New Jersey*, 39.

39. Jones, *Puerto Rican in New Jersey*, 18.

40. *TJ*, "Puerto Rican Club Offers Meeting Hall," July 17, 1958.

41. *TJ*, "Life of Poultry Laborer Called 'Slavery' by Judge," October 23, 1959.

42. Associated Press, "Agency Denies Hiring Criminals for Farms," *Trenton Times*, August 25, 1960.

43. Donald Janson, "State Sues Poultry Farmers on Migrant Labor Abuses," *New York Times*, August 24, 1976.

44. Cheryl Lynn Greenberg, *Troubling the Waters: Black-Jewish Relations in the American Century* (Princeton, NJ: Princeton University Press, 2006), 46–47.

45. Ben Leuchter, "Keeping up with the Times," *TJ*, December 5, 1959.

46. Murray and Fay Chamish interview, July 17, 2003, transcript, Egg Basket oral histories, JFCC.

47. Ismael García-Colón, interview by the author, June 21, 2021.

48. García-Colón, *Colonial Migrants at the Heart of Empire*, 116.

49. Jones, *Puerto Rican in New Jersey*, 19.

50. Celina Rosenblum, December 18, 1997 interview, VHA, USC Shoah.

CHAPTER 21   THE GOLDEN EGG

1. Arthur D. Goldhaft, *The Golden Egg* (New York: Horizon Press, 1957), 13.

2. Meyer Levin to Arthur D. Goldhaft, June 24, 1955, box 24, Meyer Levin Papers, Howard Gotlieb Archival Research Center, Boston University Libraries (hereafter cited as Levin Papers, Gotlieb ARC).

3. Goldhaft, *Golden Egg*, 263. The quotes from *The Golden Egg* that follow are from pages 229 to 268.

4. Janet Leuchter, interview by the author, July 26, 2015.

5. Yisroel Leifer, Esther T. Raab, and Izzy Raab, interview by William B. Helmreich, June 6, 1990, RG-50.165.0062, Jeff and Toby Herr Oral History Archive, U.S. Holocaust Memorial Museum, Washington, DC (hereafter cited as Herr Archive, USHMM).

6. Rosalie L. Lerman interview by William B. Helmreich, January 12, 1990, RG-50.165.0064, Herr Archive, USHMM.

7. Janet Leuchter, interview by the author, July 26, 2015.

8. Sol Finkelstein interview, July 17, 2003, transcript, Oral Histories: Egg Basket of the Nation, Jewish Federation of Cumberland County (NJ).

9. Rosalie L. Lerman, January 12, 1990 interview, Herr Archive, USHMM.

10. David Lerman, interview by the author, March 15, 2015.

11. *TJ*, advertisement, October 27, 1958.

12. David Lerman, interview by the author, March 15, 2015.

13. Joyce Vanaman, "He Saved the Last Bullet for Himself," *Press of Atlantic City*, February 18, 1979.

14. Yisroel Leifer, Esther T. Raab, and Izzy Raab, interview by William B. Helmreich, June 6, 1990, RG-50.165.0062, Herr Archive, USHMM.

15. David Lerman, interview by the author, March 15, 2015.

16. Selma Robinson, "New Seed on American Soil," *PM Daily*, May 23, 1948.

17. *TJ*, "Chaim Lindenblatt, Survivor of Nazi Terror, Looks to Landisville Synagogue as No. 1 Goal," November 22, 1954.

18. William Renzulli, interview by the author, November 15, 2021.

19. Associated Press, "City in N.J. Goes All Out for Italy Quake Aid," *Journal Times* (Racine, WI), December 10, 1980.

20. David Lerman, "A Son's Tribute," in *In Memoriam: Miles Lerman, 1920–2008* (United States: U.S. Holocaust Memorial Museum, 2008), 15.

21. Public remarks by Helen Dolotta, September 11, 1958, Levin Papers, Gotlieb ARC.

22. Meyer Levin to Arthur Goldhaft, October 17, 1958, Levin Papers, Gotlieb ARC.

23. A digitized copy of *The Golden Egg* housed in Cornell University's collection accessible via the Google Library Project does not include the offending passage and instead contains the more sympathetic language Levin suggested to Goldhaft.

24. *Jewish Farmer*, "Recent Controversy Settled," October 1958.

25. Kenneth Kann, *Comrades and Chicken Ranchers: The Story of a California Jewish Community* (Ithaca, NY: Cornell University Press, 1993), 186.

26. Kann, *Comrades and Chicken Ranchers*, 187.

27. Gertrude Wishnick Dubrovsky, *The Land Was Theirs: Jewish Farmers in the Garden State* (Tuscaloosa: University of Alabama Press, 1992), 86.

28. *Jewish Farmer*, "Society's Manager Addresses JPFA Meeting," July 1956.

29. Herman J. Levine, "A Salute to the Vineland Farmers," in *Tenth Anniversary Journal of the Jewish Poultry Farmers' Association of South Jersey* (Vineland, NJ: Jewish Poultry Farmers Association, 1962), U.S. Holocaust Memorial Museum Library and Archives, Washington, DC, 7.

30. Lou Joseph, "New Jewish Community Center in Dorothy Dedicated," *Press of Atlantic City*, October 22, 1956.

31. *TJ*, "Mrs. Roosevelt Criticizes Foreign Policy in Mideast at Israel Bond Rally Here," April 29, 1957.

32. Israel Goldman and Louis Goldman, interview by William B. Helmreich, June 12, 1990, RG-50.165.0033, Herr Archive, USHMM.

33. Meyer Levin, *In Search: An Autobiography* (New York: Horizon Books, 1950), 173.

34. Ralph Melnick, *The Stolen Legacy of Anne Frank: Meyer Levin, Lillian Helman, and the Staging of the Diary* (New Haven, CT: Yale University Press, 1997), 5–16; Lawrence Graver, *An Obsession with Anne Frank: Meyer Levin and the Diary* (Berkeley: University of California Press, 1995), 19–25.

35. Meyer Levin, "The Child Behind the Secret Door," *New York Times Book Review*, June 15, 1952.

36. Justin Worland, "Anne Frank's Diary Now Has a Co-author to Extend Copyright," *Time*, November 15, 2015.

37. Melnick, *Stolen Legacy of Anne Frank*, 151.

38. Melnick, *Stolen Legacy of Anne Frank*, 102.

39. Graver, *Obsession with Anne Frank*, 97.

40. Levin said he intended to donate any money he might receive over expenses to Jewish charities. Graver, *Obsession with Anne Frank*, 140.

41. Melnick, *Stolen Legacy of Anne Frank*, 169.

42. Graver, *Obsession with Anne Frank*, 146.

43. Ian Buruma, "The Afterlife of Anne Frank," *New York Review of Books*, February 19, 1998.

44. Graver, *Obsession with Anne Frank*, 170.

45. Levin to Goldhaft, October 17, 1958, Levin Papers, Gotlieb ARC.

46. *Jewish Farmer*, "Recent Controversy Settled," October 1958.

47. Hasia R. Diner, *We Remember with Reverence and Love: American Jews and the Myth of Silence after the Holocaust, 1945–1962* (New York: New York University Press, 2009), 96–109.

48. Jeffrey Shandler, *While America Watches: Televising the Holocaust* (New York: Oxford University Press, 1999), 27–40, 270; Elisabeth Bumiller, "The 'Miracle' Album of Auschwitz," *Washington Post*, August 25, 1980.

49. Shandler, *While America Watches*, 50.

50. *TJ*, "'Dr. Zhivago' Gaining in Popularity Locally," March 18, 1959.

51. *TJ*, advertisement, March 18, 1959.

52. *Philadelphia Inquirer*, "Arthur Goldhaft Dies; Leading Veterinarian," April 3, 1960.

53. *TJ*, "Dr. Arthur Goldhaft Dies Here at Age 74," April 2, 1960.

54. *TJ*, "Y's Men Told of Manufacture of Vaccines Here," November 19, 1965.

55. Victor S. Navasky, "The Ordeal of Meyer Levin," *New York Times Book Review*, February 3, 1974.

56. Philip Boroff, "Mandy Patinkin Shouts, Sings Yiddish in Anne Frank Play: Review," *Bloomberg News*, February 22, 2011.

57. Anne Frank House, "How Did Anne's Diary Become So Famous?," https://www.annefrank.org/en/anne-frank/diary/how-did-annes-diary-become-so-famous/.

CHAPTER 22   SEEKING HELP

1. Ben Leuchter, "Keeping Up with the Times," *Vineyard Times Journal*, April 10, 1959.

2. George Cable Wright, "Jersey Seeks Aid as Egg Tide Rises," *New York Times*, April 25, 1959.

3. Associated Press, "Disaster Stalks the Jersey Egg Farmer; Many Facing Ruin," *Central New Jersey Home News* (New Brunswick), June 19, 1959.

4. Subcommittee on Dairy and Poultry of the House Committee on Agriculture, "Poultry and Egg Prices," 86th Cong., 1st sess., 1959, 70.

5. George Cable Wright, "Jersey's Egg Producers Shaken by Price Slump," *NYT*, June 1, 1959.

6. Ben Leuchter, "Keeping Up with the Times," *TJ*, August 11, 1954.

7. William M. Blair, "Egg Farmers Ask Help by Congress," *NYT*, May 1, 1959.

8. Dan Brandenburg, interview by the author, June 5, 2020.

9. *Philadelphia Inquirer*, "Irving Schock," April 9, 1998.

10. Many of the biographical details about Schock come from the writings of his daughter. Annette Keen, "God of All Creatures," *Jewish Magazine*, June 2009, http:// www.jewishmag.com/134mag/neshmat/neshmat.htm; Annette Keen, "For the Sin I Have Sinned," *Jewish Magazine*, September 2011, http://www.jewishmag.com/158mag /yom_kippur_story/yom_kippur_story.htm.

11. Subcommittee on Dairy and Poultry of the House Committee on Agriculture, "Poultry and Egg Prices," 86th Cong., 1st sess., 1959, 67.

12. Richard Pearson, "Ezra Taft Benson, Mormon Chief, Dies," *Washington Post*, May 31, 1994.

13. Edward L. Schapsmeier and Frederick H. Schapsmeier, "Eisenhower and Agricultural Reform: Ike's Farm Policy Legacy Appraised," *American Journal of Economics and Sociology* 51. no. 2 (April 1992): 150.

14. *Argus-Leader* (Sioux Falls, SD), "Foss Promises Prosecution in Egg Throwing Incident," October 11, 1957.

15. *TJ*, "USDA Poultry Chief Sees Outlook for Producers Dim in Early 1957," October 19, 1956.

16. Subcommittee on Dairy and Poultry of the House Committee on Agriculture, "Poultry and Egg Prices," 86th Cong., 1st sess., 1959, 58.

17. "Marvin Smith, "Poultry Industry Leaders from South Want USDA to Extend No Further Help," *TJ*, June 18, 1959.

18. Associated Press, "Secretary Benson Accused of Bankrupting Farmers," *TJ*, May 1, 1959.

19. *TJ*, "JPFA Hears Reports on Poultry Hearings," May 8, 1959.

20. Subcommittee on Dairy and Poultry of the House Committee on Agriculture, "Poultry and Egg Prices, Pt. 2," 1959, 149.

21. *TJ*, "Hancock Raps Federal Aid for Poultrymen, But Board Votes to Ask for US Help," May 15, 1959.

22. *TJ*, "Hancock Says His Intent Misunderstood, Backs Aid," May 21, 1959.

23. Harry Rothman, "A Message from a Friend," in *Tenth Anniversary Journal of the Jewish Poultry Farmers' Association of South Jersey* (Vineland, NJ: Jewish Poultry Farmers Association, 1962), U.S. Holocaust Memorial Museum Library and Archives, Washington, DC, 8.

24. William B. Helmreich, *Against All Odds: Holocaust Survivors and the Successful Lives They Made in America* (New York: Simon & Schuster, 1992), 118.

25. Helmreich, *Against All Odds*, 118. The quote attributed to "one person familiar with the New Jersey farming community" matches the transcript of Helmreich's interview with Goldman. Israel Goldman and Louis Goldman interview by William B. Helmreich,

June 12, 1990, RG-50.165.0033, Jeff and Toby Herr Oral History Archive, U.S. Holocaust Memorial Museum, Washington, DC.

26. Helmreich, *Against All Odds,* 118.

27. *Jewish Farmer,* "Prominent N.J. Editor Warns of Danger Ahead," February 1959.

28. Cecilia Rasmussen, "Fire Writes the Final Chapter for the World's Largest Egg Ranch," *Los Angeles Times,* December 17, 2006.

29. John A. Osmundsen, "Heart Cases Wary of Egg Diet, But Medical Opinion Is Divided," *NYT,* June 1, 1959.

30. George Cable Wright, "Jersey's Egg Producers Shaken by Price Slump," NYT, June 1, 1959.

31. *TJ,* "A & P Opens New Supermarket Wednesday," August 4, 1959.

32. *Jewish Farmer,* "'Jewish Farmer' Says Farewell to Its Readers," December 1959.

33. *TJ,* "Jacob Rubinoff Co. Merges with Son-Mark Industries," March 7, 1960.

34. Nels Nelson, "'Human Touch' Brings $30 Million Business," *Philadelphia Daily News,* December 28, 1960.

35. Ben Leuchter, "Keeping Up with the Times," *TJ,* March 8, 1960.

36. Associated Press, "Disgruntled Egg Farmers Turn to Hoffa," *TJ,* April 20, 1960.

37. Sharon Katz Carestio, interview by the author, April 14, 2015; Ira Perry Katz, interview by the author, April 13, 2015.

38. Associated Press, "Egg Men, Sick of Life's Uncertainties, Accept James Hoffa as Union Leader," *Red Bank (NJ) Register,* April 14, 1960.

39. "Poultry Group Joins AFL-CIO; Meeting Slated," June 10, 1957.

40. Associated Press, "Disgruntled Egg Farmers Turn to Hoffa," *TJ,* April 20, 1960.

41. Associated Press, "Hoffa Promises SJ Poultrymen He'll Find Help," *TJ,* February, 20, 1960.

42. Jack Goldsmith, *In Hoffa's Shadow: A Stepfather, a Disappearance in Detroit, and My Search for the Truth* (New York: Farrar, Straus and Giroux, 2019), 52.

43. Larry Tye, *Bobby Kennedy: The Making of a Liberal Icon* (New York: Random House, 2016), 66–85.

44. Robert F. Kennedy, "Sifter Calls Hoffa Rule 'A Conspiracy of Evil,'" *Cincinnati Enquirer,* May 30, 1960.

45. Joseph A. Loftus, "Trial Set February 23 on Hoffa Ouster," *NYT,* January 21, 1960, 23; Associated Press, "Court Delays Hoffa's Trial," *NYT,* February 20, 1960.

46. Associated Press, "6 Teamster Aides Indicted on Funds," *NYT,* February 25, 1960.

47. Associated Press, "Deride Hoffa on Link with Egg Farmers," *Courier-Post* (Camden, NJ), March 31, 1960.

48. Associated Press, "Deride Hoffa on Link with Egg Farmers."

49. Associated Press, "Hoffa Meets NJ Poultrymen in Washington," *TJ,* March 4, 1960.

50. Marvin Smith, "1000 Poultrymen Ask Hoffa Affiliation," *TJ,* March 30, 1960.

51. Associated Press, "Probers Demand Ouster of Hoffa," *Fort Lauderdale (FL) News,* March 28, 1960.

52. Associated Press, "Poultry Farmers See Hoffa as Their Last Hope," *Central New Jersey Home News* (New Brunswick), April 14, 1960.

53. *TJ*, "Farm Chief Says Hoffa Can't Help," March 4, 1960.

54. Ben Leuchter, "Keeping Up with the Times," *TJ*, March 30, 1960.

55. Marvin Smith, "Teamsters Tell Poultrymen New Legislation Is Needed," *TJ*, May 13, 1960.

56. *TJ*, "On the Dotted Line," May 10, 1957.

57. Aaron Hass, *In the Shadow of the Holocaust: The Second Generation* (New York: Cambridge University Press, 1996), 57.

58. Norman H. Oshrin, "Hoffa Aide Calls Unionization 'Last Ditch Stand' for Poultrymen," *TJ*, July 1, 1960.

59. Michael V. Wrought, "Egg Farmers Regard Hoffa as Last Hope," *TJ*, March 31, 1960.

60. *International Teamster*, "IBT's Plans for Poultrymen," December 1960.

61. *Asbury Park (NJ) Press*, "Hoffa Won't Promise Farmers the 'Moon,'" June 23, 1960.

62. *Asbury Park (NJ) Press*, "Ocean County Poultry Union at Standstill," October 27, 1960.

63. Sharon Katz Carestio, interview by the author, April 14, 2015.

64. *TJ*, "Joins Parenti Staff," November 2, 1962.

65. Ira Perry Katz, interview by the author, April 13, 2015.

CHAPTER 23   ALTERNATIVE LIVELIHOODS

1. Interviews by the author with son of survivor who asked not to be identified, December 16, 2005 and July 2, 2020. Arnold Glanz is a pseudonym.

2. *TJ*, "Fire Destroys Coop, 6500 10-Week Birds," January 6, 1959.

3. For an account of Depression-era insurance fires in Petaluma, California, see Kenneth L. Kann, *Comrades and Chicken Ranchers: The Story of a California Jewish Community* (Ithaca, NY: Cornell University Press, 1993), 66.

4. *TJ*, "T-Men, Police Nab Illicit Still on Oak Road," May 3, 1958.

5. Dan Fagin, *Toms River: A Story of Science and Salvation* (New York: Bantam Books, 2013), 91–95.

6. *TJ*, "206 Poultry Farms in Vineland Empty," December 23, 1960.

7. *TJ*, "Demolition," January 8, 1960.

8. *TJ*, "Finkelstein Brothers Set Up 3 Allied Poultry Enterprises," January 23, 1959.

9. Murray Chamish and Fay Chamish interview, July 17, 2003, transcript, Oral Histories: Egg Basket of the Nation, Jewish Federation of Cumberland County (NJ) (hereafter cited as Egg Basket oral histories, JFCC).

10. George Cable Wright, "Jersey's Egg Producers Shaken by Price Slump," *New York Times*, June 1, 1959, 1.

11. Nathan Dunkelman, interview by the author, February 20, 2005.

12. Elizabeth Roth interview, July 15, 2003, transcript, Egg Basket oral histories, JFCC.

13. Ely Swerdlin, interview by the author, July 21, 2020.

14. Helen Waiman Rasner, interview by the author, October 16, 2015.

15. Martin Berwin, "Berwin Disputes Prophets of Poultry Industry Doom," *TJ*, March 29, 1963.

16. *TJ*, "Lerman Oil Co. Opens New Fuel Storage Plant," October 29, 1959.

17. *TJ*, "Lerman Family Nominated for SJ Home Show Title," August 3, 1961.

18. Ben Leuchter, "Keeping Up with the Times," *TJ*, April 11, 1961.

19. Deborah E. Lipstadt, *The Eichmann Trial* (New York: Schocken Books, 2011), 192–193.

20. Yad Vashem, "Eichmann's Trial in Jerusalem: Witnesses," https://www.yadvashem.org/yv/en/exhibitions/eichmann/witnesses.asp.

21. *TJ*, "Lerman to Head Israel Bond Drive in Vineland Area," March 29, 1962.

22. Associated Press, "Eichmann Tells Court He Only Took Orders, Had No Real Power," *Philadelphia Inquirer*, June 21, 1961.

23. *TJ*, "Eye Witnesses," May 12, 1961.

24. *TJ*, "Lerman Talks on Eichmann at Hadassah," May 17, 1961.

25. *Star-Gazette* (Elmira, NY), "Allow Furniture Stores Transfer," August 28, 1961; *Post-Standard* (Syracuse, NY), "Appeals Court Orders Firm to Explain Loss," March 15, 1963.

26. *Philadelphia Daily News*, "Jobs Shaky, 100 Become Own Bosses," January 25, 1962; *Courier-Post* (Camden, NJ), "Rubinoff Co. to Settle IRS Tax Claims," June 8, 1961.

27. *TJ*, "Rubinoff Workers Take Over Plant to Save 100 Jobs," January 24, 1962.

28. *Philadelphia Daily News*, "Jobs Shaky, 100 Become Own Bosses," January 25, 1962.

CHAPTER 24   TEENAGERS

1. Lee Feinberg, interview by the author, October 28, 2013.

2. Helen Waiman Rasner, interview by the author, August 17, 2020.

3. Marjie Low Brown, interview by the author, August 16, 2020.

4. Barry Kanner, interview by the author, September 2, 2015.

5. Ellen G. Friedman, *The Seven: A Family Holocaust Story* (Detroit: Wayne State University Press, 2017), 95.

6. Lee (Shabasson) Surwit, interview by the author, December 9, 2013.

7. Helen Waiman Rasner, interview by the author, August 17, 2020.

8. *TJ*, "Fumes Rout Patrons from Avenue Store," January 23, 1962.

9. Helen Waiman Rasner, interview by the author, August 17, 2020.

10. Aaron Hass, *In the Shadow of the Holocaust: The Second Generation* (New York: Cambridge University Press, 1996), 87.

11. Robert M. Prince, *The Legacy of the Holocaust: Psychohistorical Themes in the Second Generation* (New York: Other Press, 1999), 64.

12. Dorothy Goldberg, interview by the author, March 1, 2020.

13. Aaron Hass, *The Aftermath: Living with the Holocaust* (New York: Cambridge University Press, 1995), 133; Lucy Y. Steinitz with David M. Szonyi, eds., *Living after the Holocaust: Reflections by the Post-war Generation in America* (New York: Bloch, 1975), iii.

14. Sharyn C. Blumenthal, dir., *The Phoenix Effect*, DVD (Long Beach, CA, 2002), U.S. Holocaust Memorial Museum Library and Archives, Washington, DC.

15. Harry Furman, interview by the author, September 2004; Debra Stone, "A History Lesson to Remember," *TJ*, March 27, 1982.

16. *DJ*, "The Battle for Conscience," May 1, 2000.

17. Saul Golubcow, interview by the author, August 3, 2020.

CHAPTER 25   VALEDICTORY

1. *TJ*, "JPFA Achievements Cited at Tenth Annual Banquet," June 11, 1962.

2. Ben Leuchter, "A View from the Community," in *Tenth Anniversary Journal of the Jewish Poultry Farmers' Association of South Jersey* (Vineland, NJ: Jewish Poultry Farmers Association, 1962), U.S. Holocaust Memorial Museum Library and Archives, Washington, DC, 2.

3. *TJ*, "Vineland Labs to Manufacture Drugs in Israel," May 4, 1962.

4. Theodore Norman, "The Jewish Poultry Farmers Association Has Proven Its Stamina," *Tenth Anniversary Journal of the JPFA.*

5. Theodore Norman to the Board of Directors of the Jewish Agricultural Society, February 12, 1962, Records of the Baron de Hirsch Fund, I-80, box 69, Center for Jewish History, New York.

6. Subcommittee on Dairy and Poultry of the House Committee on Agriculture, "Problems of the Egg Industry," 87th Cong., 2nd sess., 1962, 4.

7. *TJ*, "Farmers Hopeful After Conferring with Schuman," November 9, 1962.

8. Arnold Hyman, interview by the author, December 22, 2013.

9. Sally Hyman Birnbaum, interview by the author, August 25, 2006.

10. Rosalie L. Lerman interview by William B. Helmreich, January 12, 1990, RG-50.165.0064, Jeff and Toby Herr Oral History Archive, U.S. Holocaust Memorial Museum, Washington, DC (hereafter cited as Herr Archive, USHMM).

11. James R. Hagerty, "Holocaust Survivor Rosalie Chris Lerman Sought Neither Pity Nor Revenge," *Wall Street Journal*, May 27, 2016.

12. *TJ*, "American Oil Co. Appoints Lerman as Area Distributor," February 16, 1963.

13. Associated Press, "This Refugee of 1947 Worth Fortune Today," *Charlotte Observer*, May 18, 1952; Louis James, "From Nazi Gas Chamber to Big U.S. Industrialist," *Times* (San Mateo, CA), May 26, 1959.

14. Harry Rosenblum, interview by the author, August 30, 2015.

15. Lee Feinberg, interview by the author, October 28, 2013.

16. David Lerman, interview by the author, March 15, 2015.

17. Rosalie L. Lerman, interview by Joan Ringelheim, December 1, 1998, RG-50.030.0396, Herr Archive, USHMM.

18. Julia Klein, "The Long Journey into the Light on Jersey Farmlands," *Philadelphia Inquirer*, August 12, 1979.

19. Hagerty, "Holocaust Survivor Rosalie Chris Lerman," May 27, 2016.

20. William B. Helmreich, *Against All Odds: Holocaust Survivors and the Successful Lives They Made in America* (New York: Simon & Schuster, 1992), 267–273.

21. Helmreich, *Against All Odds*, 117.

22. Helmreich, *Against All Odds*, 273.

23. *TJ*, "Mrs. Gertrude Field Dies at Age of 34," January 23, 1957.

24. *TJ*, "Final Rites for Chaim Gruenfeld," April 12, 1957.

25. Ben Leuchter, "Keeping Up with the Times," *TJ*, April 12, 1957.

26. *TJ*, "Isaac Mishnick, 52, Poultryman, Dies," April 29, 1959.

27. Sylvia Liebel Genoy, *The Black Unfolding: A Holocaust Memoir* (Margate, NJ: Comteq, 2015), 32.

28. *TJ*, "Poultryman and Millville Man Killed in Area Auto Accidents," February 4, 1963.

29. Harriet Berneman, interview by the author, August 23, 2021.

30. *TJ*, advertisement, February 21, 1963.

31. *TJ*, "Rubinoff Firm to Be Reorganized," April 7, 1964.

32. *TJ*, "Bankrupt Rubinoff Feed Mill Shuts Its Doors," April 13, 1964.

33. *TJ*, "Farm Worker Accused of Theft," September 7, 1967.

CHAPTER 26   AFTER FARMING

1. Herman J. Levine and Benjamin Miller, *The American Jewish Farmer in Changing Times* (New York: Jewish Agricultural Society, 1966), 46.

2. Levine and Miller, *American Jewish Farmer*, 98.

3. Ellen Eisenberg, *Jewish Agricultural Colonies in New Jersey, 1882–1920* (Syracuse, NY: Syracuse University Press, 1995), 174.

4. Jonathan Dekel-Chen, interview by the author, September 1, 2021.

5. Richard J. Whalen, *A City Destroying Itself: An Angry View of New York* (New York: William Morrow, 1965).

6. Michael W. Flamm, *In the Heat of the Summer: The New York Riots of 1964 and the War on Crime* (Philadelphia: University of Pennsylvania Press, 2017), 11–15.

7. Charles Hillinger, "Reserve Officer, Owner Slain in Holdup Gunfight at Store," *Los Angeles Times*, February 14, 1967.

8. *Miami Herald*, "Burned Out in Riot, He Returns and Dies," September 22, 1968.

9. Dorothy Goldberg, interview by the author, July 17, 2014.

10. Helen Epstein, *Children of the Holocaust: Conversations with Sons and Daughters of Survivors* (New York: G.P. Putnam's Sons, 1979), 196.

11. *TJ*, "Vineland Girl Shrinks the World at a Tender Age," December 21, 1964.

12. *Salute to Vineland*, VHS (1965; Philadelphia: WFIL-TV), Vineland Public Library.

13. *New York Times*, "Vineland Pins Hope on Industrial Park," November 30, 1975.

14. Jacqueline L. Urgo, "Vineland Businesses Enjoy a Renaissance," *Philadelphia Inquirer*, December 20, 1998.

15. Levine and Miller, *American Jewish Farmer*, 60.

16. Donald Janson, "State's Poultry Farms Are Rapidly Declining," *NYT*, December 29, 1975.

17. Ron Avery, "The Last Remnants of South Jersey's Alliance Colony of Jewish Farmers," *Courier-Post* (Camden, NJ), October 27, 1973.

18. Avery, "Last Remnants of South Jersey's Alliance Colony."

19. Janson, "State's Poultry Farms Are Rapidly Declining," December 29, 1975.

20. *Courier-Post* (Camden, NJ), "Vineland Lab Firm Enters Sales Pact," March 3, 1970; James P. Quaranta, "Landmark Lohmann Plant to Shut Down," *DJ*, October 18, 2006.

21. *TJ*, "Fire Set, Scrolls Destroyed in Vandalism at Synagogue," October 3, 1966.

22. *TJ*, "Jewish School Damage Traced to 5 Juveniles," October 8, 1975.

23. *TJ*, "Synagogue Ransacked by Vandals," July 28, 1980.

24. Eileen Bennett, "'Village' Plan Aims to Save Area's Historic Synagogues," *Press of Atlantic City*, June 22, 2003; Elizabeth Fisher, "Parts of Old Synagogue Installed in New Chapel," *Bucks County (Levittown, PA) Courier Times*, October 20, 2006.

25. *The Vineland, New Jersey Jewish Community: A Demographic Study* (Vineland, NJ: Alan Mallach/Associates, 1976), Rutgers University Libraries Special Collections & University Archives.

26. Eugen Schoenfeld, "Problems and Potentials," in *A Coat of Many Colors: Jewish Sub-communities in the United States*, ed. Abraham D. Lavender (Westport, CT: Greenwood, 1977), 71.

27. The decline of Vineland's Jewish community contrasts with the trajectory in another New Jersey poultry farming community: Lakewood. The growth of Beth Medrash Govoha, the largest yeshiva in the United States, has contributed to a surging Orthodox presence. David Landes, "How Lakewood, N.J. Is Redefining What It Means to Be Orthodox in America," *Tablet*, June 5, 2013, https://www.tabletmag.com/sections/community/articles/lakewood-redefining-orthodoxy.

28. Eileen Smith, "Rural Jewish Community Seeks Return to Vibrant Past," *Courier-Post* (Cherry Hill, NJ), September 26, 1999.

29. Joseph Berger, "Once Rarely Explored, the Holocaust Gains Momentum as a School Topic," *NYT*, October 3, 1988.

30. Associated Press, "Nation's First Jewish Agricultural Settlement Started in South Jersey," *Daily Register* (Red Bank, NJ), December 21, 1985.

31. Adrienne I. Possenti, "'Marrying Judge' Ends Career," *TJ*, February 8, 1982; *DJ*, "'Marrying' Judge Levin of Norma Is Dead at 83," December 17, 1988.

32. *TJ*, "Fire Destroys Stand at Beach," September 20, 1971.

33. *DJ*, "Maurice River Turned Into Trash Dump," letter to the editor, Buckley H. Modelle, September 22, 1992.

34. *DJ*, "A 'Norma Beach Reunion' Weekend Planned," June 17, 1986.

35. Deborah M. Marko, "Museum a 'Miracle' to Lerman," *DJ*, April 23, 1993.

36. *TJ*, "Lerman Flies to Israel on Study Mission," October 29, 1973.

37. Jim Perskie, "A Survivor's Search for Holocaust Memorial," *Courier-Post* (Cherry Hill, NJ), March 2, 1979.

38. David Enscoe, "Pact Signing Awed Vinelander," *TJ*, March 30, 1979.

39. *TJ*, "Former Israeli Leader Visiting Vineland Sunday," May 5, 1982.

40. *DJ*, "Miles Petroleum Sells 18 Area Gas Stations," November 1, 1984.

41. *TJ*, "T-J Sold to Detroit News," May 25, 1973; *Millville Daily*, "Gannett Buys ENA Properties," August 30, 1985.

42. Lisa Treister, interview by the author, July 30, 2015.

43. *DJ*, "Ben Leuchter, 74," January 16, 2001.

44. Richard Quinn, "Ben Zion Leuchter, 1926–2001," *DJ*, January 17, 2001.

45. *TJ*, "Memorial Set Up at Norma to 6 Million Jewish Martyrs," June 3, 1969.

46. Associated Press, "N.J. Remembers the Holocaust," *Trenton (NJ) Times*, April 27, 1979.

47. Jim Perskie, "A Survivor's Search for Holocaust Memorial," *Courier-Post* (Cherry Hill, NJ), March 2, 1979.

48. United Press International, "Commission Going on to Soviet Union," *Roswell (NM) Daily Record*, August 2, 1979.

49. *Jewish Exponent* (Philadelphia), "Miles Lerman, 88, Chair of U.S. Holocaust Council," April 17, 2013.

50. Lois Kaplan, "Holocaust Museum 'Not Just for Survivors,'" *Palm Beach (FL) Post*, March 20, 1989.

51. Dennis Hevesi, "Miles Lerman, a Leading Force Behind Holocaust Museum, Dies at 88," *NYT*, January 24, 2008.

52. Jeanette Lerman-Neubauer, "A Daughter's Tribute," in *In Memoriam: Miles Lerman, 1920–2008* (United States, 2008), 12.

53. Marko, "Museum a 'Miracle' to Lerman," April 23, 1993.

54. Jacqueline Trescott, "Holocaust Museum's Chairman Resigns," *Washington Post*, January 14, 2000.

55. Jeanette Lerman-Neubauer, *The Upside of Memory*, DVD (2005), U.S. Holocaust Memorial Museum Library and Archive, Washington, DC.

56. Ron Hayes, "Lessons of Holocaust Timeless, Expert Says," *Palm Beach (FL) Post*, February 5, 2005.

57. Joel Landau, "Loved Ones Remember Miles Lerman," *DJ*, January 25, 2008.

58. David Lerman, "A Son's Tribute," in *In Memoriam: Miles Lerman*, 14–15.

59. Jason Nark, "Auschwitz Survivor Kept Faith in Good," *Philadelphia Inquirer*, May 21, 2016.

POSTSCRIPT

1. Joseph P. Smith, "Economic Pillars," *DJ*, December 27, 1999.

2. Richard Quinn, "Dreams, Hope, Hard Work," *DJ*, March 9, 2001.

3. Deborah Marko, "State's Last Commercial Hatchery to Close," *DJ*, August 5, 1998.

4. JoNel Aleccia, "Backyard Chickens Dumped at Shelters When Hipsters Can't Cope, Critics Say," *NBC News*, July 7, 2013, https:// nbcnews.com/healthmain/backyard -chickens-dumped-shelters-when-hipsters-cant-cope-critics-say-6c10533508.

5. Robert Litt and Hannnah Litt, *A Chicken in Every Yard: The Urban Farm Store's Guide to Chicken Keeping* (Berkeley, CA: Ten Speed Press, 2011).

6. Joseph P. Smith, "Vineland Poultry Plant Halts Production," *DJ*, January 5, 2011.

7. Joseph P. Smith, "Manischewitz Plant Bites Dust," *DJ*, August 25, 2015; Daniel Kov, "Progresso Layoffs to Begin in March," *DJ*, February 3, 2017.

8. Barbara Kingsolver, *Unsheltered* (New York: HarperCollins, 2018), 7.

9. Kevin Riordan, "Movement Revives a Piece of History," *Philadelphia Inquirer*, July 25, 2017.

10. Riordan, "Movement Revives a Piece of History."

11. William Levin and Malya Levin, joint interview by the author, May 21, 2020.

12. Kevin Coyne, "Preserving the History of a Colony," *New York Times*, September 23, 2007.

13. Matt Silver, "Stockton Opens Center to Preserve Jewish Farming History," *Jewish Exponent* (Philadelphia), October 3, 2019.

14. Herb Bierig, interview by the author, May 19, 2020.

INDEX

ABOUT THE AUTHOR

SETH STERN is a legal journalist and editor at Bloomberg Industry Group. He previously reported for Bloomberg News, *Congressional Quarterly*, and the *Christian Science Monitor*. He coauthored *Justice Brennan: Liberal Champion*. He is a graduate of Harvard Law School, the Harvard Kennedy School, and Cornell University. His grandparents were Holocaust survivors who settled on a Vineland, New Jersey, chicken farm, which is where his mother grew up.

Printed in the United States
by Baker & Taylor Publisher Services